Food Tourism and Regional Development

T0383845

Food tourism is a topic of increasing importance for many destinations. Seen as a means to potentially attract tourists and differentiate destinations and attractions by means of the association with particular products and cuisines, food is also regarded as an opportunity to generate added value from tourism through local agricultural systems and supply chains and the local food system.

From a regional development perspective, this book goes beyond culinary tourism to also look at some of the ways in which the interrelationships between food and tourism contribute to the economic, environmental and social well-being of destinations, communities and producers. It examines the ways in which tourism and food can mutually add value for each other from the fork to the plate and beyond. Looking at products, e.g., cheese, craft beer, noodles, wine; attractions, restaurants and events; and diverse regional examples, e.g., Champagne, Hong Kong, Jamaica, Margaret River, southern Sweden, and Tuscany – the title highlights how clustering, networking and the cultural economy of food and tourism and foodscapes adds value for regions. Despite the attention given to food, wine and culinary tourism, no book has previously directly focussed on the contribution of food and tourism in regional development. This international collection has contributors and examples from almost every continent and provides a comprehensive account of the various intersections between food tourism and regional development.

This timely and significant volume will inform future food and tourism development as well as regional development more widely and will be a valuable reading for a range of disciplines including tourism, development studies, food and culinary studies, regional studies, geography and environmental studies.

C. Michael Hall is a Professor at the University of Canterbury, New Zealand; Docent, University of Oulu, Finland; and Visiting Professor, Linnaeus University, Kalmar, Sweden. Co-editor of *Current Issues in Tourism*, he has wide-ranging research interests in tourism, policy, food and environmental history.

Stefan Gössling is a Professor at the Department of Service Management, Lund University, and the School of Business and Economics, Linnaeus University, Kalmar, Sweden, and research coordinator at the Western Norway Research Institute's Research Centre for Sustainable Tourism. His research interests include tourism and climate change, tourism and development, mobility studies, renewable energy and low-carbon tourism, as well as climate policy and carbon trading.

Routledge Studies of Gastronomy, Food and Drink
Series Editor: C. Michael Hall, University of Canterbury, New Zealand

This ground-breaking series focusses on cutting-edge research on key topics and contemporary issues in the area of gastronomy, food and drink to reflect the growing interest in this as academic disciplines as well as food movements as part of economic and social development. The books in the series are interdisciplinary and international in scope, considering not only culture and history but also contemporary issues facing the food industry, such as security of supply chains. By doing so the series will appeal to researchers, academics and practitioners in the fields of Gastronomy and Food Studies, as well as related disciplines such as tourism, hospitality, leisure, hotel management, cultural studies, anthropology, geography and marketing.

The Business of Champagne: A Delicate Balance
Steven Charters

Alternative Food Networks
David Goodman, E. Melanie DuPuis and Michael K. Goodman

Sustainable Culinary Systems
C. Michael Hall and Stefan Gössling

Wine and Identity
Edited by Matt Harvey, Leanne White and Warwick Frost

Social, Cultural and Economic Impacts of Wine in New Zealand
Edited by Peter J. Howland

The Consuming Geographies of Food
Hillary J. Shaw

Heritage Cuisines: Traditions, Identities and Tourism
Edited by Dallen J. Timothy

Food Tourism and Regional Development
Edited by C. Michael Hall and Stefan Gössling

Food Tourism and Regional Development

Networks, products and trajectories

**Edited by C. Michael Hall
and Stefan Gössling**

LONDON AND NEW YORK

First published 2016
by Routledge

2 Park Square, Milton Park, Abingdon, Oxfordshire OX14 4RN
711 Third Avenue, New York, NY 10017

Routledge is an imprint of the Taylor & Francis Group, an informa business

First issued in paperback 2018

British Library Cataloguing in Publication Data
A catalogue record for this book is available from the British Library

Library of Congress Cataloging in Publication Data
Names: Hall, Colin Michael, 1961– editor. | Gèossling, Stefan, editor.
Title: Food tourism and regional development : networks, products and trajectories / edited by C. Michael Hall & Stefan Gèossling.
Description: New York, NY : Routledge, 2016. | Series: Routledge studies of gastronomy, food and drink | Includes bibliographical references and index.
Identifiers: LCCN 2015051203| ISBN 9781138912922 (hardback) | ISBN 9781315691695 (ebook)
Subjects: LCSH: Food tourism. | Food tourism—Economic aspects. | Economic development.
Classification: LCC TX631 .F66 2016 | DDC 641.01/3—dc23LC record available at http://lccn.loc.gov/2015051203

ISBN: 978-1-138-91292-2 (hbk)
ISBN: 978-1-138-59241-4 (pbk)

Typeset in Times New Roman
by Book Now Ltd, London

Contents

Figures

Tables

Contributors

Marisa Isabel Ramos Abascal, Facultad de Turismo y Gastronomía, Universidad Anáhuac, México Norte, Avenue Universidad Anáhuac 46, Lomas Anahuac, 52786 Naucalpan de Juárez, Huixquilucan, Estado de México, Mexico

Samuel Folorunso Adeyinka-Ojo, School of Hospitality, Tourism & Culinary Arts, Taylor's University, Lakeside Campus, Malaysia

Paul Ballantine, Department of Management, Marketing and Entrepreneurship, University of Canterbury, Christchurch, New Zealand

Deborah Che, School of Tourism and Hospitality Management, Southern Cross University, Gold Coast Campus, Locked Mail Bag #4, Coolangatta, Queensland 4225, Australia

Sidney C.H. Cheung, Institute of Future Cities, The Chinese University of Hong Kong, Hong Kong

Paul Cleave, Business School, University of Exeter, Exeter, Devon, UK

Francesc Fusté Forné, Universitat de Girona, Plaça Josep Ferrater i Móra 1, 17004, Girona, Catalonia, Spain & Lincoln University, Canterbury, New Zealand

Elsa Gatelier, Laboratoire REGARDS (EA 6292), UFR des Sciences Economiques, Sociales et de Gestion, Université de Reims Champagne-Ardenne, 57 bis, rue Pierre Taittinger, 51096 Reims CEDEX

Stefan Gössling, School of Business and Economics, Linnaeus University, Kalmar, Sweden and Research Centre for Sustainable Tourism, Western Norway Research Institute, Sogndal, Norway

C. Michael Hall, Department of Management, Marketing and Entrepreneurship, University of Canterbury, Christchurch, New Zealand; Department of Geography, University of Oulu, Finland; School of Business and Economics, Linnaeus University, Kalmar, Sweden

Cecilia Hegarty, PLATO Eastern and Border Region, Ireland. Regional Networks Executive (Cavan, Louth, Meath & Monaghan) HQ, Unit 4, M:tek 1 Building, Armagh Road, Monaghan, Ireland

Inger M. Jonsson, School of Hospitality, Culinary Arts and Meal Science, Örebro University, Sweden

Catheryn Khoo-Lattimore, Department of Tourism, Sport and Hotel Management, Griffith Business School, Nathan campus, Griffith University, 170 Kessels Road, Nathan QLD 4111, Australia

Sangkyun Kim, Department of Tourism, School of Humanities, Flinders University, GPO Box 2100, Adelaide SA 5001, Australia

Moya Kneafsey, Centre for Agroecology, Water and Resilience, Coventry University, Priory Street, Coventry, CV1 5FB, UK

Timothy J. Lee, Cluster of Tourism and Hospitality and Research Center of Asia Pacific Studies, Ritsumeikan Asia Pacific University, Beppu, Oita, 874-8577 Japan

Jiting Luo, Institute of Future Cities, The Chinese University of Hong Kong, Hong Kong

John Mulcahy, Food Tourism, Hospitality Education, and Tourist Accommodation Standards, Fáilte Ireland, Dublin, Ireland

Jang-Hyun Nam, Department of Food and Food Service Industry, Kyungpook National University, Gyeongsang-daero, Sangju-si, Gyeongsangbuk-do, 37224, South Korea

Jan-Henrik Nilsson, Department of Service Management, Lund University Helsingborg, Sweden

Bruce Prideaux, James Cook University, Cairns, Queensland, Australia

Christian M. Rogerson, School of Tourism & Hospitality, University of Johannesburg, South Africa

Hiran Roy, Department of Management, Marketing and Entrepreneurship, University of Canterbury, Christchurch, New Zealand

Ernest Taylor, Centre for Agroecology, Water and Resilience, Coventry University, Priory Street, Coventry, CV1 5FB, UK

Michelle Thompson, James Cook University, Cairns, Queensland, Australia

Ute Walter, School of Restaurant & Culinary Arts, Umeå University, Umeå, Sweden

Lotte Wellton, School of Hospitality, Culinary Arts & Meal Science, Örebro University, Sweden

Acknowledgements

The links between place, sustainability, food and tourism is both an academic as well as practical interest of the editors. Being both academics and owners of rural properties, we are deeply interested and involved in where our food comes from, how the food we and our neighbours produce fits into the food chain and with tourism and hospitality in particular, and the realities of trying to achieve low-carbon organic farming and lifestyles. These extremely personal and localised concerns are also intimately related to the "larger" issues that occupy much of our academic lives in relation to global environmental change, sustainable tourism development and consumption, the politics of mobility and tourism and the sheer environmental stupidity of much our fellow species members. When we are at Solberga Gård or Riverstones we know that we are able to walk outside and harvest our own meals, we are also very deeply aware that most people cannot, and that a large number of the world's population including those in the so-called developed countries in which we live do not have the luxury of regular nutritional meals.

The book arises from our ongoing project work on the interrelationships between food and tourism. Critical to its success has been a number of meetings and workshops, of which a conference on tourism, local foods and development held in Kalmar, Sweden, in September 2013 to which several of the authors in this volume contributed. The editors would like express their gratitude to Anneli Andersson for organising all practical details of the meeting.

Stefan would like to express his gratitude to the team at Linnaeus University, and in particular Ann-Christin Andersson and Martin Gren. He is also grateful to those trying to understand food structures and who work to prevent that we continue on the path of agriculture industrialisation. Lastly, I would like to sincerely thank Meike and Linnea – who have put up with my own farming ambitions for six years now.

Michael would like to thank a number of colleagues with whom he has undertaken food research or discussed food and tourism-related issues over the years. In particular, thanks to Tim Baird, Tim Coles, David Duval, Johan Hultman, John Jenkins, Ghazali Musa, Dieter Müller, Stephen Page, Girish Prayag, Yael Ram, Jarkko Saarinen, Anna Dóra Sæþórsdóttir, Liz Sharples, Brian and Delyse Springett, David Telfer, Sandra Wall and Allan Williams for their thoughts, as well as for the stimulation of *A Long Walk*, Beirut, Nick Cave, Bruce Cockburn, Elvis Costello, Stephen Cummings, Chris Difford and Glenn Tilbrook, Elvy, Ebba Fosberg, Hoodoo Gurus, Ivan and Alyosha, Ed Kuepper, Larkin Poe, Vinnie Reilly, David Sylvian, and *The Guardian*, KCRW, and BBC – without whom the four walls of a hotel room would be much more confining. Finally, Michael would like to thank the many people who have supported his work over the years, and especially to the J's and the C's who stay at home and mind the farm.

We would all like to extend our thanks to our editor Emma Travis at Routledge and to Pippa Mullins for her shepherding as well as to the rest of the Routledge team who have supported us over the project.

Part I
Introduction

1 From food tourism and regional development to food, tourism and regional development

Themes and issues in contemporary foodscapes

C. Michael Hall and Stefan Gössling

Introduction

Food is a major research focus in tourism and hospitality. This, of course, should not be surprising given that all tourists have to eat and that food service and provision is a core element of hospitality. However, since the 1980s, interest in the inter-relationships between food and tourism has grown from issues of provision and experience to the tourist to the wider contributions that tourist demand for food may play in the wider economy. These developments did not occur in isolation and can be understood in relation to two main reasons: first, concerns about the extent of economic and employment losses in many destinations, especially in developing countries, with respect to the impact of food importation for tourists (Telfer & Wall 1996); second, the restructuring of agricultural economies in developed countries as a result of globalisation, technological change and neoliberal governance (Whatmore, Lowe & Marsden 1991; Jenkins, Hall & Troughton 1998). The latter concerns became especially significant in Europe, where specific regional development programmes were established to encourage tourism in rural and peripheral areas, but significant government interventions were also undertaken in Australia, Canada, New Zealand and the United States (Hall & Jenkins 1998). The high level of national and regional government interest in tourism and its connections to stimulating the food and agricultural industries were also related to a number of perceived advantages of tourism as a means of economic diversification and development (Hall, Johnson & Mitchell 2000; Hall 2002; Richards 2002), including:

- the notion that gastronomic and cuisine-oriented tourists were high-yield markets (OECD 2012);
- the relative ease of linking food with other visitor products such as cultural and natural heritage attractions, and especially festivals and events, as part of providing a comprehensive offer (Bessière 1998; Bowen & De Master 2014);
- the labour-intensive nature of tourism and hospitality as a means of providing employment opportunities in rural areas with a limited employment base;

- the potential stimulation of specific agricultural products such as wine and artisan foods that were identified with locations and territories (Cavicchi & Santini 2011);
- the territorial nature of much agricultural productions, embodied in the notion of terroir and identity, was having a potentially strong relationship to the overall branding, imaging and positioning of a destination and/or region in a way that may enhance the image of all products and services available from that area (Ilbery et al. 2005; Everett & Aitchison 2008; Sims 2009, 2010; López-Guzmán & Sánchez-Cañizares 2012).

The above drivers of state intervention and activity in food and tourism were arguably also reflective of broader research interest of tourism in rural areas that over time focussed more explicitly on potential relationships with the agricultural sector, including such developments as farm stays, as mechanisms for farm and rural income diversification (Shucksmith et al. 1989; Ilbery 1991). Much of the discussion of the role of tourism in food systems and agriculture was also connected to debates on the "post-productivist" countryside (Shucksmith 1993; Ilbery & Bowler 1998) that saw the supposed decline of "productivism" in rural policy, which can be conceptualised as

> a commitment to an intensive, industrially driven and expansionist agriculture with state support based primarily on output and increased productivity. The concern [of productivism] was for 'modernization' of the 'national farm', as seen through the lens of increased production. By the 'productivist regime' we mean the network of institutions oriented to boosting food production from domestic sources which became the paramount aim of rural policy following World War II.
>
> (Lowe 1993: 221)

Tourism became incorporated into the post-productivist countryside because of the greater economic role given to non-agricultural actors in rural economies and policy making, as well as the growing importance of the environment and sustainability as policy goals. In addition, exurbanisation and rural–urban migration processes also led to the significance of lifestyle and amenity as a locational element. Halfacree and Boyle (1998: 9) even argued that 'migration of people to the more rural areas of the developed world ... forms perhaps the central dynamic in the creation of any post-productivist countryside'. Table 1.1 provides an illustration of some of the main themes in the productivist–post-productivist conceptualisation. However, as Wilson (2001) comments, so much of the post-productivist agricultural regime debate was UK-based. Furthermore, although influential in both rural studies and tourism and describing shifts in some, often economically marginal, locations for agriculture that also had high amenity values, the reality is that food producers are operating in a multifunctional agricultural regime in which global agri-business and corporations continue to dominate (Evans, Morris & Winter 2002; Mather, Hill & Nijnik 2006). At a global scale, post-productivist locations remain in the minority while shifts in the economics of agriculture and products and changes in technologies, that is, transportation and intensive irrigation, often mean that some areas, especially periurban locations, become highly contested spaces for productivist and post-productivist understandings of food production and the rural (Lawrence, Richards & Lyons 2013; Roche & Argent 2015).

Although the initial focus on food, tourism and regional development was primarily rural, tourism was also regarded as a response to urban economic restructuring. However, food was not a focus of urban tourism policy with the potential exception of urban neighbourhoods or quarters that could be marketed to visitors, particularly those that specialise in particular ethnic foods, because of the concentration of restaurants, cafés and markets that characterised the neighbourhood (Lin 1998).

This background is important because it emphasises that interest in the roles of food and tourism in regional development remains with us after over 30 years of

Table 1.1 Dimensions of productivism and post-productivism

Dimension	Productivism	Post-productivism
Ideology	Agriculture with central hegemonic position in society; agriculture as stewards of the countryside	Loss of central position of agriculture; changed notions of the countryside and the rural; agriculture perceived as a threat to the countryside
Policy	Strong state support and intervention; security of property rights	Reduced state support; increased regulation of agricultural practices through voluntary agreements and planning regulation; encouragement for better environmental practices
Policy actors	Agricultural policy actors extremely strong	Policy community widened; counter- and exurbanisation; sea change and tree change; increased demands on rural space
Food regime	Fordist; industrialised supply chains	Post-Fordist; alternative food networks
Agricultural production	Agri-business; highly commercialised, industrialised and corporatised; intensification; ongoing focus on increasing productivity levels	Diversification and pluriactivity; move from agricultural production to countryside consumption; critique of agri-business
Farming techniques	Increased mechanisation; decline in labour inputs; increased use of biochemical inputs	Sustainable agriculture; greater role for intellectual capital; organics
Environmental impacts	Growing incompatibility with environmental conservation objectives	Greater emphasis on farm-based environmental conservation practices

Source: Wilson (2001), Mather, Hill and Nijnik (2006), Lawrence, Richards and Lyons (2013), and Roche and Argent (2015).

study and that the subject is nothing new. In part this is because the processes of globalisation and economic change have continued over this time, to receive new impetus at times via neoliberal policies and financial crises. However, what has changed is a greater focus on sustainability, the environment and the relocalisation of food as a response to the perceived social, economic and dietary failings of the global food system that has developed over this period (Halweil 2002; DuPuis & Goodman 2005; Ostrom 2006; Marsden 2012). Therefore, the importance of the food, tourism and regional development inter-relationship requires new considerations that seek to understand not only the immediate contributions that tourism can make to the food economy, and vice versa, but also the broader context within which it is embedded.

This chapter provides a general introduction to the main themes of the volume by reviewing some of the key topics that emerge in the relevant literatures. It first seeks to briefly define the concept of food tourism before emphasising that the understanding of the food, tourism and regional development relationship needs to go beyond food tourism, which is where most research and state interventions are positioned, to embrace the various ways in which food and tourism are connected. Following a discussion of the local and regional development as more of a bottom-up approach to development, the introduction then discusses the characteristics of local food systems. However, it also notes that the local food system does not exist in isolation from the global food system and that the relationship between the two creates a number of paradoxes and issues within which tourism is implicated.

The chapter then briefly discusses some of the characteristics of the industrial food supply chain and its implications. This then creates a basis to examine how tourism is then utilised at the firm level to help in the capture of value that may otherwise be a loss to other actors in the supply chain to the end consumer. It highlights the emphasis on the creation of shorter supply chains, that is, direct sales to customers as well as business-to-business (B2B) sales. Important tourism-related initiatives in this area include farmers' markets, food events and festivals, and restaurants and their use of local food. The chapter then discusses more of the policy actor and producer-related collective efforts to enhance food and tourism relationships. This discussion focusses strongly on the role of clusters, networks and social capital as well as branding and the intellectual property of place, together with deliberative location-based development strategies to shape local foodscapes. These issues also highlight the multi-scaled nature of branding and development and the potential need for improved understanding of brand architecture. The chapter concludes with an overview of the book.

Food tourism

Food tourism is defined by Hall and Mitchell (2001: 308) as 'visitation to primary and secondary food producers, food festivals, restaurants and specific locations for which food tasting and/or experiencing the attributes of specialist food production region are the primary motivating factor for travel'. Wine tourism is a subset of food tourism, being defined as visitation to vineyards, wineries, wine festivals and wine shows in which grape wine tasting and/or experiencing the attributes of a grape wine region are the prime motivating factors for visitors (Hall 1996). Such definitions do not mean that any trip to an event is food tourism, rather the desire to experience a particular type of food or the produce of a specific region must be the major motivation for such travel. Indeed, food tourism may possibly be regarded as an example of "culinary", "gastronomic", "gourmet" or "cuisine" tourism that reflects consumers for whom interest in food and wine is a form of 'serious leisure' (Hall, Sharples et al. 2000; Hall & Mitchell 2001; Hjalager 2002; Boniface 2003; Hall, Sharples, Mitchell, et al. 2003; Mitchell & Hall 2003; Long 2004; Hall & Sharples 2008a; Henderson 2009; Horng & Tsai 2012; Hall & Gössling 2013a; Yeoman et al. 2015). Smith (2007: 100), for example, defined "culinary tourism" as 'any tourism trip during which the consumption, tasting, appreciation, or purchase of [local] food products is an important component [...] The central feature of culinary tourism is that it centers on local or regional foods/ beverages'.

Such definitional distinctions are significant because they also alert the reader to the potential dimensions of the food tourism market. However, for all these categories described as part of food tourism, food and wine rank as the main or major travel motivator. Such categories of tourism are therefore defined primarily by the consumer (Hall, Sharples & Smith 2003) by virtue of their tourist decision making being primarily determined by a cuisine or foodway or a specific food product, including beer, wine and spirits, or related elements such as food events, festivals, museums, restaurants or production (Sparks 2007; Kim, Eves & Scarles 2009).

Broadening the food tourism and regional development relationship

However, not everyone is interested in local foods at the destination (Cohen & Avieli 2004), and the range of culinary experiences and tastes is broad (Björk & Kauppinen-Räisänen 2014). For example, in a study of tourists in a restaurant in the city of Córdoba, Spain, only 10 per cent stated that cuisine was one of the main reasons for visiting the city, 68 per cent believed that the local cuisine is an important but not essential aspect of their trip, and the rest viewed it as being secondary (Sánchez-Cañizaresa & López-Guzmán 2012).

Therefore, although the image portrayed by many travel magazines and some researchers may suggest otherwise, many tourists are not foodies, defined as 'a person who devotes considerable time and energy to eating and learning about good food, however "good food" is defined' (Johnston & Baumann 2015: x). Although, as Johnston and Baumann note, many people dislike the term which often has pejorative overtones, they use the label 'because it captures the dominant role that food plays in many of our food-focused lives' and that if they 'could pinpoint the single greatest weakness within foodie discourse [they] would point to the lack of critical reflexivity about foodie privilege, especially in relation to the larger global food system' (Johnston & Baumann 2015: x). Indeed, much of their concerns over foodie culture, class and inequality could arguably be easily translated to discussions of food and tourism replete as it is with issues of access, democracy and distinction. It is partly for these sorts of reasons that Gössling and Hall (2013) suggested that tourism and hospitality, from both production and consumption perspectives, needed to be positioned in the context of a food system, what they referred to as a culinary system, in which food could be tracked from farm to plate (Figure 1.1) but which, from a sustainability perspective, has also been framed in a non-tourism fashion as a "local food system" (Feenstra 1997; Hinrichs 2000, 2003; Feagan 2007), "regional food system" (Food System Economic Partnership 2006; Clancy & Ruhf 2010; Donald et al. 2010) and "foodshed" (Kloppenburg, Hendrickson & Stevenson 1996; Feagan & Krug 2004; Kremer & Schreuder 2012; Ruhf 2015), as well as the embeddedness of local or regional spatialisations of food within national and global food systems (Hinrichs & Lyson 2007; Sage 2012).

The spatial frames within which food and tourism is placed are inherently important for regional development. This is in great part because, from a regulatory and institutional perspective, regions are the basis by which many policies and state interventions are made for development purposes, while different regional settings clearly have different environmental, cultural and economic attributes that also affect the capacity and trajectory of the food and tourism relationship. As Pike (2007) noted, despite globalisation and the so-called "placeless" or "virtual" economy, regions continue to provide a conceptual and analytical focus for often overlapping concerns with economic, social, political, cultural and environmental change. Although there is no single accepted definition of regional development, Pike et al. (2006) provide a good synthesis of the main approaches:

1   Promotion of development in all territories with the initiative often coming from below, similar to what in tourism would often be described as a community-based approach to planning or governance.
2   Decentralised, vertical cooperation between different tiers of government and horizontal cooperation between public and private bodies.
3   A territorial or locality-based approach to development. Territory refers to the delimited, bordered spatial units under the jurisdiction of an administrative and/or political authority.
4   Use of the development potential of each area in order to stimulate a progressive adjustment of the local economic system to the changing economic environment. This is in opposition to the large industrial project (e.g. infrastructure, events) approach that often characterises traditional top-down development policies.
5   Ensure provision of the key supply-side conditions for the development and attraction of economic activity as opposed to financial support, incentives and subsidies.

Economic concerns are undoubtedly significant. For example, for Beer et al. (2003: 5), the broad parameters of what is meant by local and regional development have been primarily interpreted in an economic sense since the 1980s and

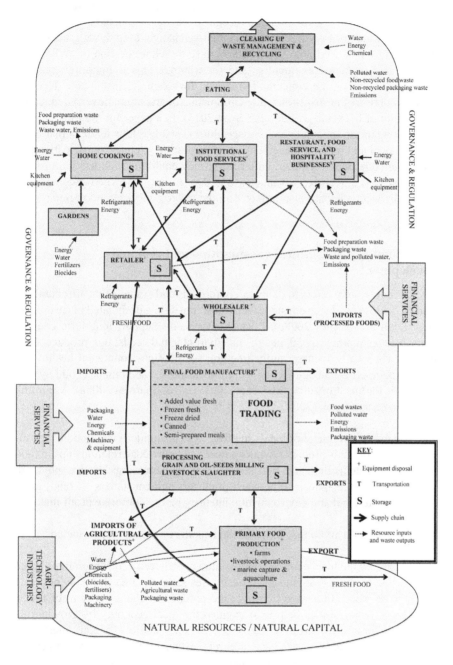

Figure 1.1 From farm to plate: the food consumption and production system
Source: Gössling and Hall (2013: 11).

refer 'to a set of activities aimed at improving the economic well-being of an area'. Nevertheless, it is important to recognise that development has a qualitative dimension whereas growth refers to quantitative change, even though the two are often confused! Indeed, Pike et al. (2007) raise the vital question of 'What kind of local and regional development and for whom?' This is important because it dovetails with similar concerns in tourism, for example, sustainable development, reduction of tourism-related environmental degradation, poverty reduction, and quality of life (Hall, Gössling & Scott 2015). In a paper for the International Labour Organisation, White and Gasser (2001) establish four features that characterise local and regional development strategies: they require participation and social dialogue; they are based on territory; they entail the mobilisation of local resources and competitive advantages; and they are locally owned and managed. These characteristics are also reflected in the interest in local and regional food systems.

Local food systems, ethical consumption and regional development

A local food system refers to deliberately formed food systems that are characterised by 'a close producer-consumer relationship within a designated place or local area' (Hall & Sharples 2008c). Local food systems support long-term connections; meet economic, social, health and environmental needs; link producers and markets via locally focussed infrastructure; promote environmental health; and provide competitive advantage to local food businesses and brands (Food System Economic Partnership 2006; Buck et al. 2007; Hall & Sharples 2008a). According to Anderson and Cook (2000, 237),

> The major advantage of localizing food systems, underlying all other advantages, is that this process reworks power and knowledge relationships in food supply systems that have become distorted by increasing distance (physical, social, and metaphorical) between producers and consumers ... [and] gives priority to local and environmental integrity before corporate profit-making.

Buck et al. (2007) argue that the potential benefits of such a system include

- Bolstering the local economy as less money is diverted to corporations based outside of the region and local businesses satisfy unmet demands or create new or more efficient systems for the production and movement of foods. 'These opportunities help to strengthen the local economy by growing the agricultural sector, creating jobs, providing more choices for consumers, contributing to the local tax base, and reinvesting local money exchanged for food back into local farms and businesses' (3);
- Producers and consumers are linked via efficient infrastructures, which can provide a competitive advantage for local farmers, processors, distributors, retailers and consumers alike, meaning that farmers receive a greater return

for their produce as there are fewer intermediaries. 'By sharing the risks and rewards of food production, processing, distribution, and retail with other local partners, farmers and businesses can explore opportunities to produce new varieties of foods or expand existing ventures to meet a local or regional need' (3);

- Positive effects on community development and revitalisation with consumers receiving fresher, healthier food and the opportunity to develop a relationship with the farmers;
- Supporting the viability of small and medium-sized family farms and fostering a sense of place, culture, history and ecology within a region as well as helping combat urban sprawl, obesity and hunger; and
- Generating environmental benefits particularly as a result of decreased energy and fuel consumption.

As noted above, the foodshed concept is closely related to the local food system idea with the difference being that it is more bioregionally oriented and is often directly concerned with food security (the capacity of a region to feed itself if external supplies were to be stopped) (Kloppenburg et al. 1996; Feagan & Krug 2004). Significantly, direct marketing via farmers' markets and food festivals along with other forms of tourism are often recognised as being integral components of a foodshed (Hall & Sharples 2008c) or local food system (Feagan, Morris & Krug 2004; Wittman, Beckie & Hergesheimer 2012). According to Feagan & Krug (2004) in order for a local foodshed to be established, several things need to happen:

- producers and consumers must be brought closer together to shorten food chains and to build 'community' and foster sustainability;
- there must be public awareness of the nature of the 'costs' associated with the industrial food system so that local consumers and producers will rethink their food production and purchasing decisions; and
- the means – mechanisms, places and opportunities – for meeting objectives must be made available.

The foodshed and local system concepts clearly show much commonality with local and regional development approaches. Furthermore, the community-based approach together with concerns over ethical and sustainable food consumption and production is also recognised at being at odds with some elements of the globalised and corporate food sector, especially because of the emphasis on local and place-based ownership. Ethical consumerism is generally associated with the consumption of goods and services, the production of which does not result in harm to people, animals or the environment (Thompson & Coskuner-Balli 2007; Dowd & Burke 2013; Niva et al. 2014), and covers a range of manifestations of new sustainable consumption and production practices often focussed on such concerns as fair trade, organic and free-range produce, Slow Food (and slow tourism), human rights, environmental sustainability and the production of consumer goods (Doane 2001; Pottinger 2013).

Another element of ethical consumerism is a strong stress on 'buying local' as a means not only of potentially reducing how far food has to travel and therefore impacts the environment but also of showing support for local producers (Hall & Gössling 2013b; Busa & Garder 2015; McCaffrey & Kurland 2015; Williams et al. 2015). The relationship between food tourism and local food systems has long been recognised as significant for regional development (Boyne, Hall & Williams 2003; Hall 2006), given that they help support food festivals and farmers' markets and also help provide a market for local produce. However, the role of tourism and especially international tourism in local food systems creates something of a paradox because it means that while the local food system is often regarded as a device to counter some of the negative elements of globalisation, tourism by its very nature is a potent force for encouraging globalisation. For example, in an examination of slow food and tourism and issues of sustainability, Hall (2012: 65) argued that even if one ignores the potential emissions of travel to consume artisan, local and slow food, 'there remains a significant issue in that in many cases the local food system still requires distant consumers to make artisan foods economic'. This argument also reflects Van der Meulen's (2008) observation that local food networks serve as an important signal and example to the mainstream, reflecting where society is going and where new opportunities for consumption and production lie. 'The actual practices do not represent a simple re-proposing of old traditional productions, rather they derive from a new reading of the internal and external environment based on the needs and characters of the modern consumer' (Nosi & Zanni 2004: 789). But this also means that probably some of the largest gains from the Slow Food movement and local food systems are likely to be realised by actors outside the initial Slow Food networks (Van der Meulen 2008) who are able to buy into such production for export purposes. For example, there is evidence that consumption of local food may be increased via availability in supermarkets (Penney & Prior 2014). Indeed, James (2015) suggests that the assumed alterity of many small-scale farmers from the so-called 'mainstream' food system has led to a focus on localised threats to farm well-being, such as urban development, and solutions, such as alternative food networks. However, she argues that this localised focus risks neglecting the way in which small-scale family farmers, such as those in her study on Sydney, Australia's, urban fringe, are directly connected to and reliant on the mainstream for their economic viability.

The situation by which local foods become desirable 'culture goods' (Bourdieu 1984) may well fulfil many of the Slow Food movement's goals (Petrini 2001, 2007). Yet in trying to conceive of a Slow Food-inspired practice of tourism, many issues remain. Most significantly is the extent to which Slow Food actually represents a move towards a more sustainable form of travel consumption. Unfortunately, this is probably not the case, as the movement appears unaware of the potential contradictions between mobility and sustainability, as Petrini (2007: 241) writes:

It is necessary to move, to meet people, to experience other territories and other tables. If we apply this conviction to the network it is vital to guarantee the circulation within it of people, from one side of the globe to the other,

without distinction and without restriction. The right to travel becomes fundamental, a premise on which to base cultural growth and the self-nourishment
of the network of gastronomes.

Some of these issues are illustrated in Figure 1.2, which shows some of the pathways by which local food systems are tied to national and global systems. In many
cases this is the result of direct exporting and importing of food to and from other
regions. However, tourism further promotes the potential of such linkages via the
role of tourists as sources of temporary local demand – which can lead to a growth
in production and search for further markets so as to pursue economies of scale,
while tourism itself provides business and consumer linkages to other locations,
whether by direct order or with respect to wholesale or retail relations.

The industrial and short food supply chains

The modern agrifood system, similar to the tourist system, has provided consumers with an unparalleled range of products, available virtually all year round, and
at prices that account for historically unprecedented minor shares of household
budgets (Sage 2012). However, this has come at significant environmental, economic and social cost (Lang 2010; Gössling & Hall 2013) with a loss of traditional
farming systems and products, food diversity and increasing food insecurity in many
locations as a result of lower local production and dependence on global food supply chains stretching thousands of kilometres. Importantly, this, together with the
supermarket dominance of the agri-food supply chain, which has altered relationships between farmers, processors, retailers and consumers, is regarded as a major
issue in both developed (Jackson 2008) and developing countries (Pant 2015). This
has meant increased dependence on the vagaries of global market forces/oligopo-
lies and fossil fuel at a time of growing concern over emissions from agricultural
production and supply as well as potential for interruption by pandemics (Gössling
& Hall 2013; Huff et al. 2015; McMichael, Butler & Dixon 2015). In addition, food
production in the modern agri-food system also affects environment and biodiversity as a result of changed farming methods and practices, such as the increased use
of biocides, chemical fertilisers, and deep ploughing and hedgerow and natural vegetation clearance. Sage (2012) also highlights that the superstructure of the global
food system is built upon rather limited genetic foundations and is 'narrowing
further as a result of agricultural modernisation and intensification' (2012: 100).

In the 1970s there was a widespread view that the full vertical integration of
agriculture was occurring, with food production, distribution and retailing coming
to be dominated on a global scale by major food conglomerates, such as Heinz,
Nestlé and Unilever (Burch, Dixon & Lawrence 2013). However, although the
global food system has been marked by increased horizontal and vertical integration, it has been the transnational supermarket chains, fast-food outlets and
other large food retailers rather than the food manufacturers that have ended up
exercising control over the agri-food supply chain (Lang & Heasman 2004), what
is sometimes referred to as "Big Food" (Coxall 2014; Booth & Coveney 2015).

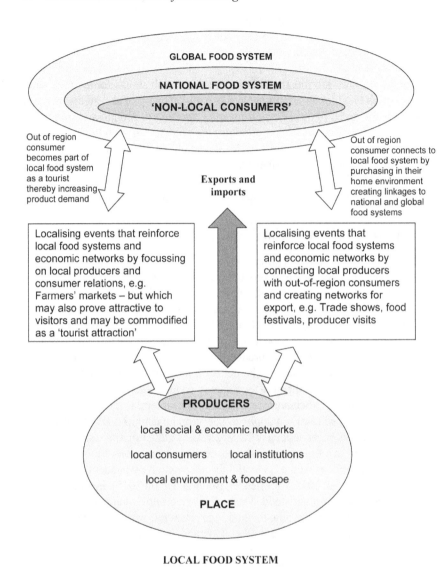

Figure 1.2 Place and producer connectivity to national and global food systems

As a result of their influence over distribution, consumption and production, the extreme dominance of food retailing in many countries by a limited number of companies has had enormous implications for traditional agricultural systems, family farms, rural communities and consumer sovereignty.

This restructuring of the agri-food supply chain has had far-reaching effects on all actors in the chain, from the input supplier who sells seeds, tractors, and fertilizers, to the farmer and food retailer, to the consumer ... These changes can be seen in: the development of flexible, 'just in time', modes of food production and distribution; the emergence of new health foods and functional foods associated with issues of nutrition and diet; the sale of convenience foods, reflecting social changes in work patterns and 'time-poor' lifestyles; the homogenization and standardization of tastes and diets; the emergence of new forms of regulation and quality management in response to food 'scares'; and growing consumer concerns about the safety of imported foods.

(Burch et al. 2013: 215)

It is to these concerns that much of the development of alternative food systems has been addressed (Kloppenburg et al. 2000; Allen et al. 2003; Follett 2009; Goodman, DuPuis & Goodman 2012; Hall & Gössling 2013a, 2013b). Nevertheless, it must be pointed out that although the usual conception of industrial food supply chains is that they are not engaged with "alternative" food production, such as organic foods, the modern reality is often quite different (Buck, Getz & Guthman 1997; DeLind 2000; Allen 2004; Fromartz 2006; Goodman et al. 2012). As Johnston, Biro and MacKendrick (2009: 510) observe, although the original organics movement

> emphasized the agrarian ideals of small-scale food production, community engagement, and ecological responsibility. While at least a rhetorical commitment to those goals is maintained, today's organic food sector has moved considerably beyond small-scale 'farm to table' distribution to a corporate model of large factory farms supplying distant supermarkets.

Indeed, the global distribution structure of exported organic foods has raised questions about the ecological and social impacts of organic food production; this is especially so in relation to the carbon footprint of organic food products transported within global commodity chains (Raynolds 2004). The corporatisation of organic foods has also meant that the intrinsic capacity of organic food production to enhance regional development objectives has been substantially questioned, especially given the extent to which small organic producers have been purchased by some of the world's largest food companies. However, not all intermediation runs in opposition to the development of local food systems. The spatial and temporal issues associated with food supply and demand, especially for urban centres and tourist destinations, means that intermediaries play a critical role in regional food systems and serve to integrate not only elements of the supply chain but also the actions of businesses with the innovation system (Frykors & Jonsson 2010). However, it should be noted that the critical role of intermediaries has been surprisingly little researched in food tourism and regional development, which is remarkable given their significance for the food service sector (Murphy & Smith 2009).

Food, tourism, regional development and shortening supply chains

The notion of alternative food supply chains is usually understood in the context of supply chain configurations that support organic farming, contextual quality production (e.g. health characteristics, environmental attributes, fair trade, local/ geographic designation, organic, slow) and/or direct selling practices (Renting, Marsden & Banks 2003). In contrast, an alternative food network, which includes the concept of a local food system, is a broader term that encompasses networks of producers, consumers and other actors that embody alternatives to the industrial mode of food supply (Sage 2003; Jarosz 2008; Goodman et al. 2012). The reconfiguration of supply chains is a core mechanism of the food – tourism and regional development relationship as it focussed on providing new ways to add value to producers and regions in response to long and complex industrial food chains. These configurations, discussed in a tourism context below, help create new linkages between consumers and producers as well as 'resocialise or respatialise food, thereby allowing the consumer to make new value judgments about the relative desirability of foods' (Renting et al. 2003: 398). A common denominator of alternative food supply chains is that they can be described as "short" for at least four reasons (Marsden, Banks & Bristow 2000; Renting et al. 2003; Ilbery & Maye 2005; Gössling et al. 2011; Kneafsey et al. 2013):

1   The physical distance that food travels between producer and end consumer may be shortened.
2   Consumer relations are "shortened" and redefined by providing transparent information on the provenance and quality attributes of food.
3   The chains "short-circuit" the long and often anonymous supply chains characteristic of the industrial mode of food production. This may include a reduction in the number of intermediaries but, at the very least, implies a change.
4   Short chains are potentially an important carrier for the "shortening" of relations between food production and locality, thereby encouraging a re-embedding of farming towards more environmentally sustainable modes of production as a result of greater consumer and fellow producer awareness and knowledge.

Some of the shifts and new ways of adding value for producers are illustrated in Figure 1.3 and will be discussed further below. One of the key dimensions of food and tourism, rather than food tourism, is the extent to which it highlights the capacity of tourism to influence local food production (Telfer & Wall 1996). Both tourism and food production (and adding value via manufacturing processes) are significant on their own for regional development. However, from a regional development perspective there is an understanding that deepening and strengthening the relationships between the two will allow for greater returns to both sectors as well as to regions as a whole (Everett & Slocum 2013; James & Halkier 2014).

Local economic development strategies that seek to encourage food and wine tourism tend to have a number of similar components (Centre for Environment and Society 1999; Hall 2005):

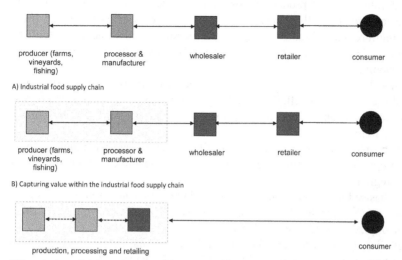

A) Industrial food supply chain

B) Capturing value within the industrial food supply chain

C) Shortening the supply chain, e.g. direct sales to the consumer from farm or cellar door sales or direct box sales. Retailing and processing incorporated into producer business activities

D) Producers' cooperate in production, running a market, sharing retail space and/or undertaking joint promotion campaigns

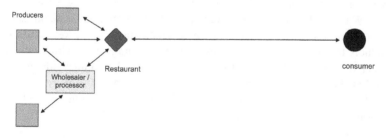

E) Local producer network supplying local restaurant

Figure 1.3 Industrial and alternative food supply chains

- reduce economic leakage by using local renewable resources rather than external sources, for example, use local materials for packaging, 'buy local' campaigns;
- recycle financial resources within the system by buying local goods and services, for example, hoteliers and restaurateurs need to purchase and promote local foods, produce wine or other beverages, use local banks and credit unions;

- add value to local produce before it is exported; for example, bottle and package food locally, consider using distinctive local packaging in order to reinforce local brand identity, use local food as an attraction to tourists, thereby increasing the circulation of tourist expenditure through the local economy;
- connect up local stakeholders, people and institutions to create trust, new linkages and more efficient exchanges, for example, local farmers and producers' cooperatives, develop local marketing networks, a "buy local" campaign;
- attract external resources, especially finance, skills and technology, where appropriate, for example, use the Internet to connect to customers outside of the region;
- emphasise local identity and authenticity in branding and promotional strategies, for example, list the place of origin on the label and encourage consistent use of place of origin by producers;
- sell directly to consumers via farm shops, direct mailing, farmers' and produce markets, local events and food and wine festivals; and
- create stronger and ongoing relationships between the consumer and the producer, for example, using cellar door or farm door sales, utilise newsletters, social media, websites and the Internet.

For example, the extremely influential and widely cited "Eat the View" project was set up by the UK Countryside Agency in 2001 to encourage tourism businesses to connect better with their local economy by using and selling locally produced food and drink products (e.g. Garrod, Wornell & Youell 2006; Jackson, Ward & Russell 2006; Everett 2008; Everett & Aitchison 2008). The long-term aim of the project was to 'create improved market conditions for products that originate from systems of land management which enhance or protect the countryside's landscape and character' (Countryside Agency 2001). "Eat the View" had a number of target outcomes that were expected to arise from improved local economic linkages between tourism and food production:

- to inform consumers about the impact of their decisions on the rural environment and economy and how they can take positive action to benefit the countryside;
- the development of systems for marketing/distributing/selling produce which will enable consumers to show support for local/sustainable production methods;
- the development of quality standards/accreditation systems to underpin markets for local/sustainable products;
- the development of local marketing/branding initiatives which will utilise unique features, for example, rare animal breeds, local customs;
- the development of new supply chain partnerships between retailers/producers which will increase the proportion of locally sourced/sustainable products;

- an increase in the proportion of produce sold through alternative markets to large retailers and bulk caterers, for example, local collaborative arrangements;
- an increase in the number of local/community-led food initiatives creating stronger local markets for produce and strengthening links between producers and consumers (adapted from Countryside Agency 2001).

Underlying the above strategy components is an awareness of the value for regional development of "short" economic and social practices of consumption and production in which new sets of relationships are being formed between and among producers and consumers at different scales. This can involve producers adding more value to their own product by engaging in processing and manufacturing themselves, that is, dairy farmers producing their own cheese (Figure 1.3B), and/or the development of new sets of direct relations between food producers and consumers that bypass wholesalers and retailers (Figure 1.3C and D). For the producer, such relationships can potentially lead to greater economic return. For the consumers it can potentially provide access to fresher and better quality foods and greater knowledge of the elements of the food chain as well as certain cultural capital. However, new relationships may also develop between producers in terms of supplying the various elements of the visitor experience as well as the exporting and promotion of local foodstuffs outside of the immediate region (Figure 1.3D and 1.3E).

Much of the research on short food supply chains in tourism and hospitality has focussed at the level of the firm. Initially, research was conducted in the area of wine tourism although studies were soon taken up in a range of different food and tourism relationships. However, although numerous advantages of such an approach have been noted at the level of the producer/firm, outlined below, it should be acknowledged that detailed studies of the flow on effects to the surrounding region and the distribution of benefits are limited. Furthermore, there is a major weakness with respect to understanding the strategies of firms that, in effect, are trying to manage consumers and business relationships in two different sectors, that is, food and tourism. For example, Hall and Baird (2014a) in studying the innovative practices of the New Zealand wine sector found that for many winegrowers the association with tourism also raises some fundamental issues about business strategy as it means their market orientation and consequent selection of business strategies may be split between wine tourists who visit the winery and consumers who purchase and drink wine. Although there is clearly overlap, the markets have distinct demands on firms with respect to product demand as well as the allocation of capital. Indeed, many studies of tourism innovation arguably fail to recognise the significance of the partial industrialisation of tourism systems whereby only a proportion of a firm's customer base and income is derived from tourism and, therefore, there is a need to distinguish the relative mix between tourism and non-tourism drivers in strategy. In fact, Hall and Baird (2014a) noted that those winegrowers with the highest level of innovation with respect to marketing were also the ones that were most engaged in wine tourism. This may reflect the insight that the more an environment presents opportunities including those to harness the role of competence utilisation in the context of innovation (Goh 2000), the more a firm will select the environmental change that improves its position in relation to its competitors, but it does not help with trying to develop a broader contribution to innovation and regional development outside of the immediate tourism networks and system. Overall the accrual of benefits from food and tourism has, therefore, been assumed rather than subject to micro-level empirical examination (Montanari & Staniscia 2009; Everett & Slocum 2013). Nevertheless, the advantages for the food producer in developing food tourism (Hall 2005a; Hall & Sharples 2008b; OECD 2012) are outlined in Table 1.2.

At the regional/destination level, a range of advantages to developing food-related tourist offers have been identified from the literature:

- High profile of some foods and cuisines can attract tourists and provide other regional business opportunities (Alonso & Liu 2012; Ron & Timothy 2013).
- Positive image of the region through association with a quality product (Hall & Mitchell 2008; Lin, Pearson & Cai 2011; Spilková & Fialová 2013).
- Food tourism can help differentiate a region's position in the tourism marketplace if connected with local foods (Lee & Arcodia 2011; Blichfeldt & Halkier 2014; Lee, Wall & Kovacs 2015).
- Food tourism is an attraction in its own right that can help extend the range of reasons for visiting a destination (Horng & Tsai 2012; Kirkman et al. 2013). Food tourism may, therefore, help extend length of stay and increase visitor expenditure on local product (Storchmann 2010).

Regional brand values of food (including wine, beer and spirits) can also be very good for destination and regional promotion. However, it is essential that they fit with the overall economic and brand strategy. For example, in 2002 New Zealand sought to reposition its national brand so that it was perceived internationally as innovative and creative in order to advantage non-tourism and agricultural enterprises. However, while the 'clean, green and smart' proposition had domestic appeal, it did not have broad international impact, particularly as the tourism sub-brand of "100% Pure" dominated the "New Zealand, New Thinking" trade brand. Therefore, while the food and tourism industries benefitted from being positioned as "clean and green", other industries such as ICT did not (Hall 2010). A possible negative aspect in some circumstances therefore may mean that if there is too much focus on the special interest food tourism market, other tourism and business opportunities may not be adequately explored and that potential tourists and investors may have a perception of a region that does not maximise broader regional development opportunities. Issues of brand architecture will be discussed further below.

As noted above, shortening the supply chain between producers and consumers as well as B2B relationships does not mean that a producer operates in isolation. Producers often cooperate in terms of sharing direct sales via a retail outlet as well

Table 1.2 Summary of advantages and disadvantages of tourism for producers

Advantages		Disadvantages	
Consumer exposure	Consumer exposure to products are increased, including opportunities for product sampling	Increased costs and management time	The operation of a tasting room or direct sales may be costly, particularly when it requires paid staff. While the profitability gap is higher on direct sales to the consumer, profit may be reduced if there is no charge for tastings
Brand awareness and potential loyalty	Via establishing relationships between branded products, brand values and the consumer	Inability to significantly increase sales	The number of visitors a business can attract is limited, and if a business cannot sell all of its stock, it will eventually need to use other distribution outlets
Customer relationships	Created by opportunities to meet staff and to see backstage "behind the scenes". Positive relations with consumers may lead to both direct sales and indirect sales through "word of mouth" advertising	Inappropriate market from the perspective of broader business products	The characteristics of the visitor market may differ significantly from other consumers that the business wishes to sell to
Better margins	Increased sales margins as a result of direct sale to consumer assuming that the absence of distributor costs is not carried over entirely to the consumer	Capital required	May be prohibitive, especially as some types of added value production for hosting visitors are capital-intensive, for example, viewing/tasting rooms

(Continued)

Table 1.2 (Continued)

Advantages		Disadvantages	
Additional sales outlet	And for smaller producers who cannot guarantee volume or constancy of supply, perhaps the only feasible sales outlet	Issues associated with seasonality	Seasonal demand periods may not be complimentary. Tourism, as with the production of food, is highly seasonal
Market intelligence on products and consumers	Derived from direct consumer feedback (both on existing products and the possibility to trial new additions to a product range) and via the use of a customer relationship database	Potential risks to production from biosecurity breaches	Food tourists on the property of primary producers can pose risks through the introduction of disease or weeds
Education of consumers	Can help generate awareness and appreciation of specific types of foods. The knowledge and interest generated by this may result in increased consumption	Additional health and safety requirements to be met	Visitors on a property require relevant health and safety legislation to be met. This may incur costs on the business, or regulations may restrict access to some food production areas, thus changing the nature of the visitor experience
New sales opportunities via direct sales and/or new B2B relationships, for example, to restaurants, retailers, wholesalers and vendors		Opportunity costs	Investments in tourist facilities mean that capital is not available for other investments

as through farmers' markets, and business associations as well as in cooperative branding exercises, some of which are undertaken in conjunction with the tourism industry. The next section briefly discusses farmers' markets which serve important tourism and recreation functions as well as community and food system functions, before also noting the significance of food events and festivals.

Farmers' markets

The definition of what constitutes a farmers' market has long been problematic (Brown 2002). As Pyle (1971: 167) recognised, 'everything that is called a farmers' market may not be one, and other names are given to meeting that have the form and function of a farmers market'. Other names for similar types of markets in North America include swap meets, flea markets, tailgate markets and farm stands (Brown 2001), although many of these are best understood as other forms of direct marketing from producer to consumer. Nevertheless, many markets will advertise that they are a farmers' market although they are technically not in the sense of all products available being a direct purchase from the grower of the produce. Furthermore, the different terms used for farmers' markets reflect retail change over time and different regional food supply and distribution channels (Hall 2013). Nevertheless, the core of "official" definitions of farmers' markets reflects the notion that farmers' markets are 'recurrent markets at fixed locations where farm products are sold by farmers themselves … at a true farmers' market some, if not all, of the vendors must be producers who sell their own products' (Brown 2001: 658).

The issue of how farmers' markets are defined is not just academic but, as Hall (2013: 101) observes, 'also reflects broader concerns of consumers and producers that the farmers' market and its produce be regarded as a space in which consumers can trust the "authentic" and "local" qualities of what is being offered'. The authentic and local dimension of farmers' markets remains a recurring theme in studies of farmers' markets (e.g. Payne 2002; Feagan et al. 2004; Selfa & Qazi 2005; Hall et al. 2008; Conner et al. 2009; Wittman et al. 2012). The issue of definition is also subject to the legal and regulatory environment that farmers' markets operate in. For example, in California the state's over 600 farmers' markets have been certified under state legislation since 1977, while the Province of Alberta in Canada has run an Approved Farmers' Market Program since 1973 (Hall 2013). Nevertheless, the importance of localism in defining farmers' markets is reflected in definitions of several national and regional farmers' market organisations (Table 1.3), where terms such as "local", "fresh" (which implies that food has only travelled a short distance from its origin) and "direct to consumer" or terms that imply that the goods are vendor-produced are frequently used (Hall 2013).

Farmers' markets have had substantial growth since they were (re)introduced in the United States, Canada, the UK, Australia and New Zealand (Brown 2001, 2002; Hall & Sharples 2008a; Basil 2012; Hall 2013). In the United States there were 1,755 farmers' markets operating nationwide in 1994, just under 4,500 by

2006 and 8,268 in 2014 (Hamilton 2002; USDA 2014). According to the USDA (2012), farmers' markets' sales in the United States are estimated at being slightly over $1 billion annually and more than 25 per cent of vendors at surveyed markets derived their sole source of farm income from farmers' markets. In roughly the same period in Canada, the number increased from 70 to over 260 (Hall 2013).

Table 1.3 Example definitions of farmers' markets

Country	Organisation	Definition
Australia	Australian Farmers' Market Association	'… a predominantly fresh food market that operates regularly within a community, at a focal public location that provides a suitable environment for farmers and food producers to sell farm-origin and associated value-added processed food products directly to customers'.
Australia – Victoria	Victorian Farmers' Market Association	'… a predominantly local fresh food and produce market that operates regularly at a public location which provides a suitable environment for farmers and food producers to sell their farm origin product and their associated value added primary products directly to customers'.
Canada – Alberta	Alberta Farmers' Market Association under the Alberta Approved Farmers' Market Program Guidelines	'Markets must maintain an annual average vendor split of 80/20 where 80% of the vendors are Albertans selling Alberta products which they, an immediate family member, a staff member or a member of a producer-owned cooperative or their staff have made, baked or grown. The remaining 20% of the vendors can be made up of out-of-province vendors, resellers or vendors selling commercially available products. Markets operating outside the 80/20 requirement will be granted conditional approval. Approval status will be revoked for any markets that have been conditional for two years without improvement … Preference must be granted to Alberta producers who make, bake, or grow their products'.
Canada – British Columbia	BC Association of Farmers' Markets	'Only the farmer and/or the family are permitted to sell at a member market. Re-sellers are not permitted. At member markets, our focus is on selling locally grown or processed farm-fresh foods, so only a limited number of crafters can be found at our markets. You won't find any imported products. Most of our foods travel from less than 300 kilometres away'.
Canada – Ontario	Farmers' Markets Ontario	'…is a seasonal, multi-vendor, community-driven (not private) organization selling agricultural, food, art and craft products including home-grown produce, home-made crafts and value-added products where the vendors are primary producers (including preserves, baked goods, meat, fish, dairy products, etc.)'.

New Zealand	New Zealand Farmers' Market Association	'…a food market where local growers, farmers and artisan food producers sell their wares directly to consumers. Vendors may only sell what they grow, farm, pickle, preserve, bake, smoke or catch themselves from within a defined local area. The market takes place at a public location on a regular basis'.
United Kingdom	National Farmers' Retail and Markets Association (FARMA)	'… a market in which farmers, growers or producers from a defined local area are present in person to sell their own produce, direct to the public. All products sold should have been grown, reared, caught, brewed, pickled, baked, smoked or processed by the stallholder'.
United States	Farmers' Market Coalition	'A farmers market operates multiple times per year and is organized for the purpose of facilitating personal connections that create mutual benefits for local farmers, shoppers and communities. To fulfill that objective farmers markets define the term local, regularly communicate that definition to the public, and implement rules/guidelines of operation that ensure that the farmers market consists principally of farms selling directly to the public products that the farms have produced'.
United States – California	California Farmers' Markets Association (CFMA)	'The Certified Farmers' Markets (CFM) are diversified markets offering both certifiable and non-certifiable goods for sale. The CFM provides producers with the opportunity to sell their fresh, local products directly to the consumers without the intervention of a middleman. Each CFM is operated in accordance with regulations established in the *California Administrative Code* (Title 3, Chapter 3, Group 4, Article 6.5, Section 1392) pertaining to Direct Marketing. Each market is certified by the County Agricultural Commissioner as a direct marketing outlet for producers to sell their crops directly to consumers without meeting the usual size, standard pack and container requirements for such products. However, all produce must meet minimum quality standards. The non-certifiable goods add variety and enhance the festive ambiance of the Farmers' Market. Although the State Direct Marketing regulations require the producers of fresh fruit, nuts, vegetables, flowers, honey, eggs, nursery stock, and plants be required to be certified, the same producer-to-consumer philosophy applies for all items sold at the Market. The resale of products is prohibited'.

Source: Alberta Agriculture and Forestry (2015), Australian Farmers' Market Association (2009), BC Association of Farmers' Markets (2011), California Farmers' Markets Association (2006: 1), Farmers' Market Coalition (2008), Farmers' Markets Ontario (2007), National Farmers' Retail and Markets Association (2009), New Zealand Farmers' Market Association (2007), Victorian Farmers' Market Association (2011), in Hall (2016: 90)

Farmers' markets may take a variety of forms in terms of space and time and vary according to the location of the market, whether there is a purpose-built building or not, and the period over which the market operates (Hall 2016). Many markets are seasonal because of supply and weather conditions, and in some regions there is a strong tradition of harvest and Christmas festivals. In some cases the markets may be associated with heritage buildings and precincts. For example, the Cambridge Farmers' Market in Canada has been operating for over 100 years and occupies a historic building and adjacent lot in the city core and enjoys the status of a designated heritage property (Smithers, Lamarche & Joseph 2008). However, the development of new market infrastructure and space in heritage precincts can be extremely controversial for both socioeconomic and architectural and aesthetic reasons (Tunbridge 2000, 2001). However, while markets can con-tribute to gentrification and local economies (Morales, Balkin & Persky 1995), urban redevelopment often places substantial pressures on market spaces as city governments and property owners seek higher returns, sometimes forcing them to move (Xu, Wan & Fan 2014). For example, the Maxwell Street Markets in Chicago have had to move several times. Its location 'remains impermanent, as new commercial development raises land values in the area' (Morales 2006: 1). Therefore, in assessing the role of markets in development processes, it becomes important not only to understand the economic linkages that markets provide to producers but also the site-specific development issues that may indicate issues of competing land uses and economic returns.

Farmers' markets, food producers and restaurant supply

Another significant local food system and tourism and hospitality function that farmers' markets provide is to act as a source of produce to restaurants (Figure 1.3E). As Roy, Hall and Ballantine (this volume) note, some of the perceived benefits of local food purchasing by restaurants include good public relations, supporting local producers, better quality, fresher and safer food, superior taste, supporting the local economy, ability to purchase small quantities and improved customer satisfaction (Inwood et al. 2009; Schmit & Hadcock 2012). Nevertheless, there are also a number of perceived barriers to restaurants purchasing include payment procedures, lack of knowledge about local sources, inconvenient order-ing and delivery times, limited availability and amounts, variable costs, packaging and handling, lack of authority to choose suppliers, inadequate distribution sys-tems, poor communication skills and additional time to process the food in the operation (Green & Dougherty 2008; Curtis & Cowee 2009; Inwood et al. 2009).

In Roy et al's study (this volume) of restaurants in Vancouver, Canada, only half of the respondent chefs sourced farmers' markets for produce (see also Duram & Cawley 2012), while almost two-thirds of the respondents sourced directly from producers. However, all of the respondents also sourced from a food service distributor. As noted earlier in this introduction, the role of interme-diaries remains important in local food systems and especially so for restaurants and cafés. Nevertheless, the role of distributors in accessing and aggregating local food produce and then supplying the restaurant and hospitality sector has received very little attention. This is surprising as often their capacities to enhance the local food system may be critical given that many hospitality businesses may not wish to deal with a larger number of farmers and vendors because of the time, quality and supply issues involved (Smith & Hall 2003; Nummedal & Hall 2006; Schmit & Hadcock 2012; Forbord 2015).

Food events

Events have assumed an important role in food tourism and marketing in recent years and have developed their own specialist professional organisations and niche area within tourism and visitor studies. At the same time the study of food and wine tourism has also grown in importance (Henderson 2009). Food events therefore lie at the intersection of these two fields. There also appears agreement that the number of food-related events being held around the developed world is growing rapidly although definitive figures are hard to determine (Griffin & Frongillo 2003; Chaney & Ryan 2012).

Public food events can be defined (after Ritchie 1984; Hall 1992) as one-time or recurring events of limited duration, developed primarily to enhance the awareness, sales, appeal and profitability of food and beverage products in the short and/or long term. Such events rely for their success on uniqueness, status, quality or timely significance to create interest and attract attention. A primary function of food events is to provide an opportunity for food products and related destinations an opportunity to secure a position of prominence in the market for a short, well-defined period of time in order to make sales. Significant secondary functions from the demand side include building and promoting product, firm and destination brand values, maintaining relationships with customers, encouraging new consumers, educating consumers and promoting visitation (Hall & Mitchell 2008). From the production side, secondary functions include promoting improved production methods and quality of product, reducing the length of supply chains and promoting sustainable agricultural development, particularly with respect to the development of farmers' markets. Nevertheless, food events are not just about external promotion to visitors and/or consumers outside of the host region, they also have substantial internal drivers for their hosting which relate to the consumption and production of food from particular locations and communities and to the maintenance of those communities. Food events are therefore strongly connected to senses of place and community pride in the products that they produce.

Festivals are a celebration of something the local community wishes to share and which involves the wider public as participants in the experience (Frost 2015). Festivals are 'an event, a social phenomenon, encountered in virtually all human cultures' (Falassi 1987: 1). Hu (2010: 8–9) defined a food festival as:

> A festival or public event that centers on specific food or food-related items or behaviors. Such a festival is usually a celebration of local food or food-related

pride, traditions, or specialties that the host community wishes to share, but can also be a tourist attraction that is created or rejuvenated particularly for 'outside visitors' in order to promote local tourism and/or culinary products.

Festivals are intimately related with the maintenance and celebration of community values and historically have had a strong relationship with food (Humphery & Humphery 1988). 'Both the social function and the symbolic meaning of the festival are closely related to a series of overt values that the community recognizes as essential to its ideology and worldview, to its social identity, its historical continuity, and to its physical survival, which is ultimately what festival celebrates' (Falassi 1987: 2). However, as a result of greater cultural and economic connectedness between places, community food festivals have increasingly taken on a role as a commoditised product that is externally promoted in order to attract visitors, promote the region or community or promote consumption of specific food products – all usually with an economic motive (Hall & Mitchell 2008). This is not to deny that events and festivals still have an important community-based social function but that such celebrations increasingly also have an economic and commercial dimension to them.

Many rural towns, especially in North America, often proclaim themselves as the "capital" of various food types as a way of celebrating their heritage and food production, while simultaneously using the food as a way of differentiating themselves as a place to visit. For example, in California, both Sacremento and Chico proclaim to be the almond capital of the world (Hallinan 1989), while Watsonville is the strawberry capital of the world. Similarly, Gilroy is the self-proclaimed garlic capital of the world and also hosts an annual garlic festival that usually attracts over 100,000 people each year (Hall & Sharples 2008b; Adema 2009). Events and festivals may also be duplicated from one location to another both as a means to attract visitors as well as to celebrate particular cultures. For example, Oktoberfest celebrations are now held throughout the world, often at locations with only a tenuous cultural link to Germany (Sharples & Lyons 2008). However, some locations, such as Kitchener-Waterloo in Ontario which hosts the largest Oktoberfest in North America, also use it to celebrate their strong German migrant heritage (Xiao & Smith 2004). Indeed, a significant longer-term issue in the sustainability of many rural food festivals is the extent to which their heritage dimensions are perceived as authentic by consumers (Lewis 1997; Bessiere 1998; Xie 2004; Picard & Robinson 2006), as well as the potential of the desire to commercialise food heritage for economic benefits from tourism affects heritage values.

The use of food events and festivals for tourism and economic development purposes has also allowed for renewed public and private investment in community-based food events because of the perceived direct benefits – that is, purchasing of local product and acquisition of product knowledge – and indirect benefits – that is, awareness of regional brand that they bring (Dodd et al. 2006; Hede 2008; Wood & Thomas 2008; Blichfeldt & Halkier 2014). Importantly, sampling of product at an event may also encourage return visitation (Houghton 2001). Çela et al. (2007) assessed the economic impact of 11 community-based food festivals in Northeast Iowa (from May to October 2005). The total economic impact of visitors (n = 22,806) in local food festivals was estimated to be almost $2.6 million in terms of sales; $1.4 million in terms of personal income; and generated 51 jobs. However, local food events are rarely held in isolation from producers and other significant actors in the local food system. Therefore, a major theme in examining tourism in local food systems is the way in which the food network operates, particularly with respect to the interrelationships between the different sectors.

Intangible capital, clusters and networks

In terms of production, Hall (2002) argued that critical to the success of regional food tourism business strategies is characterised by the development of one or more forms of intangible capital: intellectual property, networks, brand and talent. Intellectual property and brand are closely entwined, for example, because of the extent to which food and tourism are products which can be differentiated on the basis of regional identity (Feagan 2007; Goodman et al. 2012). For example, wine is often identified by its geographical origin, for example, Burgundy, Champagne, Rioja; similarly, cheese, for example, parmesan, camembert, which in many cases have been formalised through a series of appellation controls founded on certain geographical characteristics of a place that also serve as protectable intellectual property (Bowen & Zapata 2009; Bowen 2010; Blakeney et al. 2012). It should therefore be of little surprise that the relationship between wine, food and tourism is extremely significant at a regional level through the contribution that regionality provides for product branding, place promotion and, through these mechanisms, economic development (Ilbery & Kneafsey 2000a, 2000b; Hall 2002; Marcotte, Bourdeau & Leroux 2012; West & Domingos 2012; Peris-Ortiz, Rama & Rueda-Armengot 2016). As Moran (1993: 266) observed:

> Burgundy gives its name to one of the best known wines in the world but at the same time the region of Burgundy becomes known because of its wine. Moreover, the little bits of it, often only a few hectares, also derive their prestige from the wines that are produced there. In Burgundy, the process has developed to the extent that in order to capitalize on the reputation of their most famous wines many of the communes … have taken the name of their most famous vineyard. Corton was added to make Aloxe-Corton, Montrachet to make both Puligny-Montrachet and Chassagne-Montrachet, Romanee to make Vosne-Romanee, St Georges to make Nuits-St Georges and so on.

Appellation controls and geographically designated origins have long served to act as a form of intellectual property in terms of rural space as well as product (Moran 1993; Skilton & Wu 2013). Regional speciality food and drink products have also come to be registered as intellectual property as designated quality labels within EU and national law (Ilbery & Kneafsey 2000a; Newman et al. 2014). A process which Ilbery and Kneafsey (2000b) appropriately described within the context of globalisation as "cultural relocalisation" and which is having substantial ramifications for international trade agreements.

Networks and clusters

Networks and cluster relationships are a significant part of the development of intangible capital of food and tourism-related regional development and are arguably the area of research that has most drawn on relevant regional development and regional studies theory (Hall 2004; Bertella 2011; OECD 2012; Eriksen & Sundbo 2015; Kim & Jamal 2015). Networking refers to a wide range of cooperative behaviour between otherwise competing organisations and between organisations linked through economic and social relationships and transactions. Often the term is synonymous with inter-firm cooperation. Industry clusters exist where there is loose geographical concentration or association of firms and organisations involved in a value chain producing goods and services and which is relatively innovative. The suggestion that business clusters add value to a region implies a new set of public policies, one that shifts the focus of attention from an individual place or individual firm to a region and clusters of businesses and the interaction between them (Rosenfeld 1997; Nordin 2003). A cluster may be defined as a concentration of companies and industries in a geographic region that are interconnected by the markets they serve and the products they produce, as well as by the suppliers, trade associations and educational institutions with which they interact (Porter 1990). Many commentators argue that such chains of firms are the primary "drivers" of a region's economy, on whose success other businesses and sectors, such as the construction industry, depend on in terms of their own financial viability. They are also regarded as extremely significant for innovation practices and for knowledge circulation (Hall & Baird 2014a). However, objective criteria for clusters are exceedingly difficult to isolate, and there are arguably as many definitions as there are types of organisations using the term (Rosenfeld 1997: 8). For example, Rosenfeld (1997: 9) argues that, to all intents and purposes, networks are a result of mature and animated clusters, not the source of a local production system, whereas clusters are systems in which membership is simply based on interdependence and making a contribution to the functioning of the system. In attempting to clarify the differences between clusters and networks, Nordin (2003), in her examination of the cluster concept in tourism, quotes from the OECD (1999: 12):

> Clusters differ from other forms of co-operation and networks in that the actors involved in a cluster are linked in a value chain. The cluster concept goes beyond 'simple' horizontal networks in which firms, operating on the same end-product market and belonging to the same industry group, co-operate on aspect such as R&D, demonstration programmes, collective marketing or purchasing policy. Clusters are often cross-sectoral (vertical and/or lateral) networks, made up of dissimilar and complementary firms specialising around a specific link or knowledge base in the value chain.

However, in trying to operationalise this approach, three substantial problems occur. First, how does one measure the density of networks so that the shift from a network to a cluster can be observed. Second, and perhaps more significantly, for food and tourism-related development, how might the value chain of tourism be described? From the perspective of the producers or, perhaps more importantly, given the destination-bound nature of most tourism activity, from the perspective of the consumer, who consumes tourism products from different firms across time and space during a trip? Third, what role does the geography of a place or destination play in clustering? Indeed, an outcome of asking these questions is that it provides insights into the key role of positionality in understanding the actions of actors within local food and tourism systems. For example, in examining innovation in New Zealand wine tourism, Hall and Baird (2014a) found that reasons why wineries innovated were related to increasing productivity, reducing energy consumption and reducing environmental impact. Indeed, the environmental and energy efforts of the winegrowers engaged in wine tourism were larger than those of other sectors of the New Zealand tourism industry. However, this was because of the institutional requirements of the New Zealand wine industry not because of any direct influence from tourism consumers or tourism agencies. Some of these elements are included in Figure 1.4 which presents some of the local food chains discussed above in the context of the region.

An industry cluster includes firms that sell inside as well as outside the region and also supports firms that supply raw materials, components and business services to them. Clusters in a region form over time and stem from the region's economic,

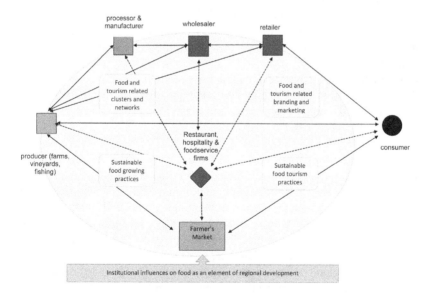

Figure 1.4 Local food chains in the context of food, tourism and regional development

political and cultural foundations, its existing companies and local demand for products and services (Waits 2000). Firms and organisations involved in clusters are able to achieve synergies and leverage economic advantage from shared access to information and knowledge networks, supplier and distribution chains, markets and marketing intelligence, competencies and resources in a specific locality. The cluster concept therefore focusses on the linkages and interdependencies among actors in value chains (Enright & Roberts 2001; Hall 2004; OECD 2012).

Wine has been recognised as one industry in which clustering may be a significant competitive factor (Porter 1990; Blandy 2000; Nordin 2003; Deery, O'Mahony & Moors 2012; Boatto et al. 2013; Peris-Ortiz et al. 2016). Cluster formation is regarded as a significant component in the formation of positive external economies for firms, including those of the wine and food industry, with tourism being recognised as an important component (Porter 1990). Telfer (2001a, 2001b) argued that cluster development and strategic alliances have been a significant component of the contribution of wine and food tourism to regional development in the Niagara region of Canada (see also Plummer, Telfer & Hashimoto 2006; Jones, Singh & Hsiung 2015). Although one of the lessons of cluster development programmes is that there is no precise "one size fits all" formula (Blandy 2000; Rodríguez, Williams & Hall 2014), a number of factors have been recognised as significant in the development of food and wine clusters and the associated external economy which serves to reinforce the clustering process (Hall 2005; Boatto et al. 2013; Jones et al. 2015). These include:

- the life cycle stage of innovative clusters;
- government financing and policies;
- the skills of the region's human resources;
- the technological capabilities of the region's research and development activities;
- the quality of the region's physical, transport, information and communication infrastructure;
- the availability and expertise of capital financing in the region;
- the cost and quality of the region's tax and regulatory environment; and
- the appeal of the region's amenities and lifestyle to people that can provide intellectual and economic capital.

However, scale is only part of reason that clusters and their regions prosper. Equally important to the circuitry of the system is the "current", or the flow of information, knowledge, technological advances, innovations, skills, people and capital into, out of and within the cluster, from point to point (Hall 2004; Doloreux & Lord-Tarte 2012; James & Halkier 2014; Hjalager, Johansen & Rasmussen 2015). Conventional data often cannot distinguish between a simple industry concentration and a working cluster. However, in a cluster, the social ecology is as important as the agglomeration economies. As Rosenfeld (1997: 10) comments, 'The "current" of a working production system is even less easily detected, often embedded in professional, trade and civic associations, and in informal socialisation patterns ... The "current" depends on norms of reciprocity and sufficient levels of trust to encourage professional interaction and collaborative behaviour'. To which, of course, we can also provide the current of information that is also provided by service encounters with tourists (Hall & Baird 2014a; Hjalager & Wahlberg 2014; Eriksen & Sundbo 2015).

For Rosenfeld (1997: 10) clusters are 'a geographically bounded concentration of interdependent businesses with active channels for business transactions, dialogue, and communications ... that collectively shares common opportunities and threats'. Importantly, this definition asserts that "active channels" are as important as "concentration", and without active channels even a critical mass of related firms is not a local production or social system and therefore does not operate as a cluster. Therefore, in seeking to understand the processes of cluster development, recognition of social capital and the relative efficiency of channels of social exchange becomes vital (Hall 2004). Indeed, the co-location of firms can sometimes lead as much to a lack of social exchange as it does to a positive sharing of knowledge and ideas (Hall 2004).

Such a situation may well be critical with respect to maximising the contribution of clusters to regional development. In the case of Porter's (1990) example of a Californian wine cluster, and Blandy's (2000) reference to the South Australian wine industry cluster, both authors failed to recognise that the wine industry had been in those locations for well over a hundred years with the economic and social relationships of wine firms reinforced by the family networks established over that period, with tourism being a late arrival in both cases as a component of the cluster (Hall 2004, 2005). Furthermore, given that the areas had been wine regions for such a long period and that wine is an environmentally dependent resource, it should therefore be unsurprising that certain elements of a cluster formation had developed in this time. Moreover, certain "traditional" economic location factors that relate to accessibility and closeness to market are still extremely important. Perhaps a more significant question is, what understanding does existing work on clusters provide us for identifying the factors in developing new clusters, particularly in regions which have undergone fundamental economic restructuring and that seek to utilise tourism to revitalise their food economy and food system. Unfortunately, unless research indicates how firms interact and clusters work at the micro scale, the answer is likely to be very little. It is also critical to recognise that networks undergo path-dependent evolutionary change, that is, 'the degree to which networks constructed in particular contexts for particular purposes are consolidated over time' (Amin & Thrift 1997: 153), paying attention to:

- the thickness and degree of openness or closure of networks;
- the asymmetry of power between networks of interdependencies;
- the learning abilities of networks;
- the role of information in networks; and
- the set of institutionalised obligations that exist in networks.

For example, in a study of local food networks in rural Denmark, Eriksen and Sundbo (2015) found that the main drivers of the development of local food

networks are the pursuance of transparency and knowledge of origin, the existence of entrepreneurship potential, the coordination of networks by means of
joint strategies and the overcoming of conflict patterns. However, they also
noted that these factors can also be barriers to further development of local
food networks. Several other barriers to creating effective links between food
producers and the tourism industry have also been identified (Hall 2004):

- the often perceived secondary or tertiary nature of tourism as an activity in
  the food or wine industry, accompanied by a perception that there is an imbal-
  ance of benefits from business and sectoral relationships with the greater
  advantage accruing to tourism firms;
- a dominant product focus of some food producers and marketers that neglects
  the benefit and service dimensions of their product;
- a relative lack of experience and understanding by food producers of the tourism industry, and a subsequent lack of capacity with respect to marketing and
  service product development; and
- the relative absence of effective intersectoral economic and social linkages,
  including appropriate institutional structures, which leads to a lack of inter-
  and intra-organisational cohesion within the wine industry, and between the
  wine industry and the tourism industry.

Hall (2001, 2005) identified several other factors which may also affect cluster
and network success:

- spatial separation – the extent of spatial separation between producers within
  a region due to physical resource factors;
- administrative separation – the existence of multiple public administrative
  agencies and units within a region;
- the existence of a "champion" to promote the development of a network; and
- the hosting of meetings to develop relationships.

Of these, the role of champions as well as the involvement of local government
was regarded as especially important in the creation of wine and food tourism
networks and associated new product development in the New Zealand situation (Hall 2004; Baird & Hall 2014; see also Coles, Dinan & Hutchison 2014).
Such an observation is significant as Audretsch and Feldman (1997) noted that
the generation of new economic knowledge tends to result in a greater propensity
for innovative activity to cluster during the early stages of the industry life cycle,
and to be more highly dispersed during the mature and declining stages of the life
cycle. Arguably, a further factor may well be a relative lack of social innovation
capital in certain regions possibly related to difficulties in attracting or retaining
intellectual capital, external network knowledge and entrepreneurial skills that
influence path dependency (Hall 2005; Deery, O'Mahony & Moors 2012).

   Figure 1.5 draws some of these threads together to indicate how a tourism-
involved local food system can develop over time. The literature suggests that

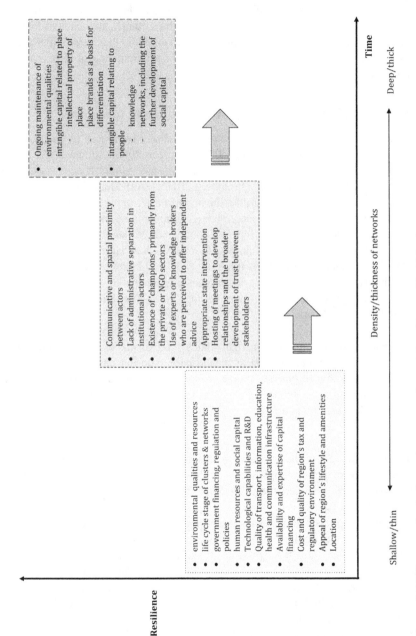

- environmental qualities and resources
- life cycle stage of clusters & networks
- government financing, regulation and policies
- human resources and social capital
- Technological capabilities and R&D
- Quality of transport, information, education, health and communication infrastructure
- Availability and expertise of capital financing
- Cost and quality of region's tax and regulatory environment
- Appeal of region's lifestyle and amenities
- Location

- Communicative and spatial proximity between actors
- Lack of administrative separation in institutional actors
- Existence of 'champions', primarily from the private or NGO sectors
- Use of experts or knowledge brokers who are perceived to offer independent advice
- Appropriate state intervention
- Hosting of meetings to develop relationships and the broader development of trust between stakeholders

- Ongoing maintenance of environmental qualities
- intangible capital related to place
  - intellectual property of place
  - place brands as a basis for differentiation
- intangible capital relating to people
  - knowledge
  - networks, including the further development of social capital

Resilience

Shallow/thin

Density/thickness of networks

Deep/thick

Time

Figure 1.5 Life course for the increasing connectedness and resilience of local food systems

the resilience of a local food system, that is, the capacity to withstand change and still maintain its primary characteristics, is related to the density of the networks within the system. These networks, as discussed above, are themselves a function of the encouragement and use of various forms of capital over time, as well as the maintenance of the resource base of the system. Importantly, the value of tourism in the local food system in such an approach is to maintain the desired qualities of the system itself and its contribution to regional development, not the expansion of tourism per se.

From the intangible to the tangible: tourism and foodscapes

One food concept which has been gaining increased awareness in recent years is that of the "foodscape" (Dolphijn 2004; Yasmeen 2006; Adema 2007; Sobal & Wansink 2007). A simple definition of a foodscape is that it consists of 'the actual sites where we find food' (Freidberg 2010: 1869). Burgoine et al. (2009) takes a similar approach and examines the opportunities to purchase food in a specific local environment. Such research being significant, of course, in identifying "food deserts" in which certain types of foods and retailers may be unavailable or limited (Whitehead 1998; Raja, Ma & Yadav 2008; Horner & Wood 2014; Widener & Shannon 2014). Johnston et al. (2009: 512) stress the importance of the built environment in defining foodscapes as 'the spatial distribution of food across urban spaces and institutional settings' (see also Parham 2012, 2015). Importantly, a foodscape is a

> dynamic social construction that relates food to places, people, meanings *and* material processes. Just as a landscape painting has a mediated, indirect relationship to place, a foodscape may variously capture or obscure the ecological origins, economic relationships, and social implications of food production and consumption.
>
> (Johnston & Baumann 2015: 3)

Importantly though, while we agree with Johnston and Baumann (2015: 3) that the term "foodscape" highlights how 'cultural understandings of food and the food system are mediated through social mores and cultural institutions like the mass media [and that the concept] implies a dynamic relationship between food culture (e.g. taste and meaning), and food materiality (e.g. social structure, physical landscape, ecology)', our focus is not just the foodscape occupied by foodies, what they term the "gourmet foodscape". Instead, as stressed early in this chapter, while food tourism is a significant element of the food, tourism and regional relationship, and sometimes has somewhat of a "flagship" element to it for many destinations, the number of food tourists or foodies who engage in tourism, as some authors are now to want (Yeoman et al. 2015), is small as a proportion of overall tourist demand.

The notion of a foodscape has been applied in a number of different areas but reinforces the 'idea that food environments can be a powerful and independent determinant of food behaviour' (Mikkelsen 2011: 210). Drawing on environ-mental psychology, design and servicescape research, the concept emphasises that what people eat, together with how it is produced, is embedded in a physical landscape and surrounds as well as its associated social and cultural context. The foodscape also serves as an attractor to people as well as a factor in food choice, consumption and behaviour and is therefore significant for tourism (Adema 2009; Long 2010; Lindenfeld & Silka 2011; Ron & Timothy 2013; Heatherington 2014; Fusté Forné 2015). Indeed, in externally oriented food sys-tems it is likely that there is a degree of co-evolution between the foodscape and tourism development.

A number of studies have noted the health dimensions of foodscapes, particu-larly with respect to issues of obesity, with Mikkelsen (2011: 211) commenting 'that the notion of foodscapes is well suited to capture the different change agendas related to healthier and more sustainable production and consumption'. Indeed, several authors note the importance of "ethical" foodscapes (Goodman, Maye & Holloway 2010). As Morgan (2010: 1854) notes, 'the ethical foodscape actually consists of a wide spectrum of products, each of which espouses a set of values that claims to make a positive contribution to one or more of the following causes: human health, the environment, the local economy, poor primary produc-ers in the global south, animal welfare and bio-diversity'. The foodscape is, as Morgan (2010) observes, not a homogenous entity, although it is apparent that the notion connects with a range of ethical consumption and alternative food sup-ply chain issues. Yet, it is also important to emphasise that the food consumption and production and the political-economic processes within which it is embedded does have a real effect on landscapes.

In addition to their direct role in linking farmers and producers to consumers, farmers' markets also have a significant role of enlivening public space. As a result the hosting of farmers' markets and food events has therefore become an important urban regeneration tool and are often proposed as part of economic revitalisation and urban redevelopment projects (Hall 2016). The concept of regeneration includes both physical – that is, concerned with material architec-ture and image, physical plant and infrastructure, urban design and form – and social/immaterial dimensions – that is, concerned with improving the quality of life of those who already live in areas targeted for regeneration; attracting new permanent and temporary migrants; and rebranding a location as more hospitable (Hollows et al. 2014). Hall (2016) argues that these concerns have been particu-larly applied to regeneration of heritage precincts and cultural quarters. A cultural quarter is defined by as:

> a geographical area of a large town or city which acts as a focus for cultural and artistic activities through the presence of a group of buildings devoted to housing a range of such activities, and purpose designed or adapted spaces to create a sense of identity, providing an environment to facilitate and encour-age the provision of cultural and artistic services and activities.
>
> (Roadhouse 2010: 24)

From an urban and regional policy perspective, cultural quarters are regarded by governments as serving several significant roles as development catalysts within the broader field of "culture-led" regenerations (Evans 2005). The social and environmental aspects of quartering are also regarded as having benefits such as providing a sense of collective belonging or enhanced local social identity and sense of social inclusion (Bell & Jayne 2004), which may provide a basis for more sustainable urban development (Darlow 1996). Interestingly, these are some of the very same social benefits that are also ascribed to the development of farmers' markets in the context of local food systems. Nevertheless, the use of farmers' markets in urban redevelopment projects potentially amplifies the paradoxical relationships between the local and the global food and economic systems; as McCarthy (2005: 298) stresses, 'perhaps of greater urgency', cultural quarters are regarded as 'a means to enhance image via branding or re-branding in order to attract mobile capital and visitor income in the context of globalising forces and city competition'. As Hall (2016) suggests, from this perspective, farmers' markets not only serve to enliven space and create "atmosphere" for both local and visitor alike, but also by emphasising local food systems and community relations they serve as attractions for tourists who wish to experience the local, as well as creating lifestyle consumptionscapes. In a study of the Greater Toronto area, Donald and Blay-Palmer (2006) suggest that contrary to widely held views, the creative food industry (specialty, ethnic and organic SMEs) is not just about promoting exclusive foods for the pleasure of urban elite and instead offers an opportunity for a more socially inclusive and sustainable urban development model.

In contrast, Eaton (2008) questions whether the focus on farmers' markets and local food in the Niagara region of Canada has shifted from a focus on retaining and conserving heritage and encouraging sustainable food to being more concerned with attracting tourists and consequently leading to the commodification of place. Kohn (2009) is even harsher in his criticism and writes of 'dreamworlds of deindustrialization' with reference to the Distillery District, a 13-acre industrial heritage site located on the edge of downtown Toronto, Canada. He argues that the Distillery District's combination of industrial ruin with 'Retail shops selling handmade contemporary furniture, Swedish beds, Italian kitchen fixtures, wearable art, artisanal cheese, and gold jewellery', as well as a Summer Sunday market, illustrates many of the forces that are reconfiguring cities: commodification, gentrification, the city as theme park and spectacle, post-industrialism and the consumer preferences of the so-called "creative class". Indeed, Kohn (2009: ii) suggests 'the Distillery District makes the economic transformation from Fordism to post-Fordism visible. It brazenly exposes dynamics of gentrification and commodification of culture'. Similarly, with reference to the provision of "local" food and drink in the same location, Mathews and Picton (2014: 337) argue that 'craft beer works as a vehicle in the manufacture of new spaces of cultural consumption. Specifically, craft beer production and consumption are used to aestheticize the industrial past and pacify resistance to central-city gentrification'.

Parham takes the notion of foodscapes and urban quarters even further by introducing the notion of "food quarters" what she defined as 'a "fuzzy edged" food-centred area of an urban settlement, predicated on human scales, highly mixed, walkable and fine grained urbanism' (2012: 3). Markets are at the centre of the food quarter, although they are not necessarily a farmers' market, while they also service elite and non-elite consumption needs. Importantly, they are 'likely to be supported by a diverse range of food related land uses including cafes and restaurants and its users may be visiting its market and food businesses as part of a mix of food consumption techniques including online methods' (Parham 2012: 3). However, as discussed above, such food quarters not only support economic and environmental renewal but are also marked by food-led gentrification. Nevertheless, despite the underpinning gentrifying tendencies that may also contribute to social exclusivity, she concluded that in the three London food quarters she studied (Borough Market, Broadway Market and Exmouth Market), 'these spaces also suggest consciously designing for food is broadly a good thing for sustainable cities, producing authentic places important for experiencing food led conviviality in everyday life' (Parham 2012: 4).

Multiscale development strategies

Arguably one of the biggest problems facing effective regional development utilising food and tourism is that of scale (Born & Purcell 2006). Although this chapter has emphasised the local nature of regional development strategies (Pike et al. 2006), what may benefit one level of jurisdiction or governance may not be appropriate at another either economic development or branding. Maximising the benefits of cuisine, food and tourism requires different levels of governance and economic activity working together (Figure 1.6). Yet this is extremely difficult. What may be good for an individual business or producer may not be good for the region. For example, while a region may promote itself as a source of high-quality certified local products, an individual producer could create greater value by producing a relatively low-value mass product with no need to define where it was produced.

The wine, food and tourism industries often rely on regional and national branding for market leverage and promotion. The accompanying set of economic and social linkages through brand use becomes an important source of differentiation and added value for regions. Yet the branding at one level may not be appropriate for another. Destinations therefore need to consider how different layers of branding fit together to provide a coherent image in different markets. However, there is limited research on the implications of this for food, tourism and regional development (Hall & Baird 2014b). Nevertheless, the notion of "brand architecture" – how brands are organised, managed and marketed – has become an increasingly important consideration for how places can improve their own branding (Dooley & Bowie 2005), especially via greater coordination of different brand elements, stakeholders and actors (Figure 1.7). In wine marketing, wine brands have a number of different overlapping components. These can be broadly categorised as place brand elements, product elements and corporate brands, with the corporate and product elements usually having

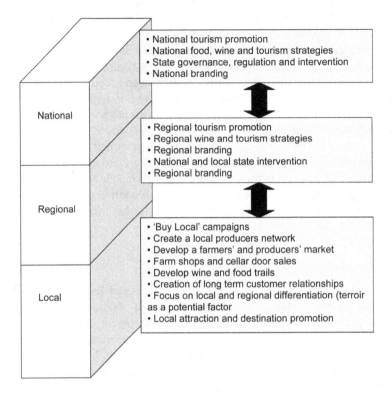

National

Regional

Local

- National tourism promotion
- National food, wine and tourism strategies
- State governance, regulation and intervention
- National branding

- Regional tourism promotion
- Regional wine and tourism strategies
- Regional branding
- National and local state intervention
- Regional branding

- 'Buy Local' campaigns
- Create a local producers network
- Develop a farmers' and producers' market
- Farm shops and cellar door sales
- Develop wine and food trails
- Creation of long term customer relationships
- Focus on local and regional differentiation (terroir as a potential factor
- Local attraction and destination promotion

Figure 1.6 Relationships between national, regional and local strategies

a strong commercial element to them (Figure 1.8). Within the development of place brand architecture, two broad strategies can be identified (Muzellec & Lambkin 2009):

> an integration strategy which seeks to achieve image alignment between formal and informal national, corporate and product brands; and a separation strategy which seeks to shape different images for different stakeholders.

Moreover, from a broader perspective of economic development and brand strategy, there needs to be an understanding about how food and tourism fit in with the general image of a location and what value, if any, do they provide for non-food production and the region as a whole, are they complimentary or in conflict? It is therefore likely that, as with any form of economic development, significant tensions may develop between stakeholders and different levels of public authority as they strive to maximise economic benefits for their constituency (Hall 2010). Given the increasing demands on food-related spatial and intangible resources, the implications of the relationships between not only food

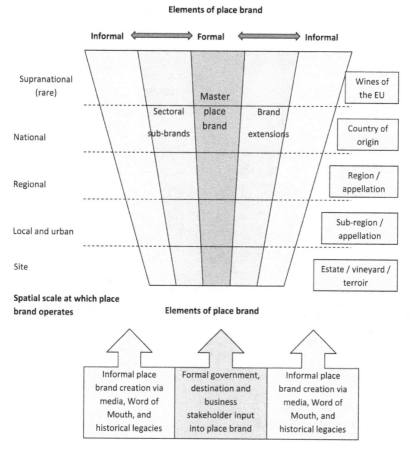

Elements of place brand

Informal ⟺ Formal ⟺ Informal

Supranational (rare)

Wines of the EU

Master place brand

Sectoral sub-brands

Brand extensions

National

Country of origin

Regional

Region / appellation

Local and urban

Sub-region / appellation

Site

Estate / vineyard / terroir

Spatial scale at which place brand operates

Elements of place brand

Informal place brand creation via media, Word of Mouth, and historical legacies	Formal government, destination and business stakeholder input into place brand	Informal place brand creation via media, Word of Mouth, and historical legacies

Figure 1.7 Brand architecture structure of food place brands with wine examples
Source: Modified from Hall and Baird (2014b).

and tourism, but also food, tourism and other actors in regions, should become a significant research agenda for the future.

Overview and conclusions: food, tourism and regional developments

The various chapters in this book tackle a range of different elements of the relationships between food, tourism and regional development that figure in the literature discussed above (Figure 1.9). Chapters 2 to 6 all have a strong focus on network formation. The issue of value creation in sustainable food networks is examined in Chapter 2, while network relations in a specific Swedish regional context are also a focus of Chapter 3. The broad drivers of tourism development

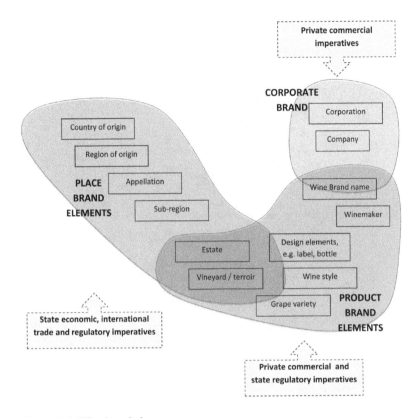

Figure 1.8 Wine brand elements
Source: Adapted from Hall and Baird (2014b).

in agricultural regions is the subject of a West Australian case study in Chapter 4, while, in contrast, Chapter 5 discusses a specific driver of rural destination development in Sarawak in the form of food events. Chapter 6 provides a comparative study of network development in Ireland and the United States.

Chapters 7 to 11 have a substantial cultural economy focus. In Chapter 7, Kim examines the Udon Noodle, while in Chapter 8 the significance of the food heritage of Hong Kong for local visitors is discussed. Chapter 9 examines the role of events in positioning the food culture of Namyangju City in Korea for economic development purposes, while a more historical approach to issues of commodification and change is taken in Chapter 10, which provides an account of Devon in the UK. Chapter 11 by Taylor and Kneafsey provides a Jamaican case study of the cultural economy of food and tourism. The final chapter in this section by Ramos Abascal (Chapter 12) stresses the capacities of gastronomy to cross political and regulatory barriers as a part of the increased mobility of populations over time, with consequence implications for future food-related travel.

Chapters 13 to 16 provide different perspectives on the role of the region in food and tourism. Chapter 13 by Gatalier compares wine tourism development in two different European regions, while Mulcahy questions the very value of a regional approach for food tourism in Chapter 14 using Ireland as an example. Chapter 15 by Rogerson examines the significance of craft beer and tourism-related local development in South Africa. Specific regional issues are also taken up in Chapter 16 which discusses the tourism value of protected designation of origin of cheese in Spain.

The final section highlights some of the barriers that exist to the utilisation of local food by restaurants and some of the difficulties in enabling local food systems. Chapter 17 discusses the Vancouver case, while Chapter 18 is an example from Sweden. The final chapter provides an overview of the main themes of the book and highlights some future research issues.

The potential of tourism to contribute to regional economic development via food and cuisine depends on a range of economic, environmental, social and political factors, including the degree of inter-sectoral linkage, the pattern of visitor expenditure and leakage. Where substantial imports of goods and services are necessary to maintain tourism, the importance of local food supply chain networks and

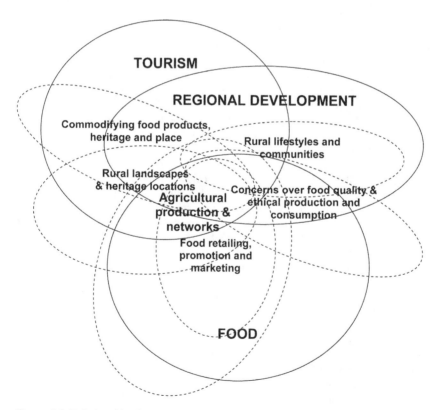

Figure 1.9 Relationships between food, tourism and regional development

relationships need to be examined in relation to tourism and the potential provision of local food. Most importantly, the question of "who benefits?'" should be fundamental to assessing regional economic development policies and strategies when considering the role of food and tourism. For both large- and small-scale food and wine businesses, tourism can be very important in terms of brand development. However, tourism needs to be seen as part of the overall development of a food or wine business rather than necessarily an end in itself. The manner in which food and wine tourism is used as a component of the business mix will therefore depend on the stage of business development, overall business and community goals, location and target markets. In other words, for it to be viable in the long term and contribute to local economic well-being, food and tourism needs to be seen and understood within the context of regional planning, sustainable food production, desired lifestyles, and participant values as well as business decision making.

References

Adema, P. (2007) 'Foodscape: an emulsion of food and landscape', *Gastronomica*, 7(1): 3.

Adema, P. (2009) *Garlic Capital of the World: Gilroy, Garlic, and the Making of a Festive Foodscape*, Jackson: University Press of Mississippi.

Alberta Agriculture and Forestry (2015) *Alberta Approved Farmers' Market Program Guidelines*. Available online: <http://www1.agric.gov.ab.ca/$Department/deptdocs.nsf/all/apa2577> (accessed 1 April 2015).

Allen, P. (2004) *Together at the Table: Sustainability and Sustenance in the American Agrifood System*, Pennsylvania: University of Pennsylvania Press.

Allen, P., FitzSimmons, M., Goodman, M. and Warner, K. (2003) 'Shifting plates in the agrifood landscape: the tectonics of alternative agrifood initiatives in California', *Journal of Rural Studies*, 19(1): 61–75.

Alonso, A.D. and Liu, Y. (2012) 'Visitor centers, collaboration, and the role of local food and beverage as regional tourism development tools: the case of the Blackwood River Valley in Western Australia', *Journal of Hospitality & Tourism Research*, 36(4): 517–536.

Amin, A. and Thrift, N. (1997) 'Globalization, socio-economics, territoriality', in R. Lee and J. Wills (eds) *Geographies of Economies*, London: Arnold, pp. 147–157.

Anderson, M.D. and Cook, J.T. (2000) 'Does food security require local food systems?' in J.M. Harris (ed.) *Rethinking Sustainability: Power, Knowledge and Institutions*, Ann Arbor: University of Michigan Press, pp. 228–248.

Audretsch, D.B. and Feldman, M.P. (1997) *Innovative Clusters and the Industry Life Cycle*, Discussion Paper 1161. London: Centre for Economic Policy Research.

Australian Farmers' Market Association (2009) *About*. Available online: <http://www.farmersmarkets.org.au/> (accessed 1 October 2009).

Baird, T. and Hall, C.M. (2014) 'Between the vines: wine tourism in New Zealand', in P. Howland (ed.) *Social, Cultural and Economic Impacts of Wine in New Zealand*, Abingdon: Routledge, pp. 191–207.

Basil, M. (2012) 'A history of farmers' markets in Canada', *Journal of Historical Research in Marketing*, 4(3): 387–407.

BC Association of Farmers' Markets (2011) *About the BCAFM*. Available online: <http://www.bcfarmersmarket.org/about-bcafm> (accessed 26 March 2012).

Beer, A., Haughton, G. and Maude, A. (2003) *Developing Locally: An International Comparison of Local and Regional Economic Development*, Bristol: Policy Press.

Bell, D. and Jayne, M. (2004) *City of Quarters: Urban Villages in the Contemporary City*, Aldershot: Ashgate.

Bertella, G. (2011) 'Knowledge in food tourism: the case of Lofoten and Maremma Toscana', *Current Issues in Tourism*, 14(4): 355–371.

Bessiere, J. (1998) 'Local development and heritage: traditional food and cuisine as tourist attractions in rural areas', *Sociologia Ruralis*, 38(1): 21–34.

Björk, P. and Kauppinen-Räisänen, H. (2014) 'Exploring the multi-dimensionality of travellers' culinary-gastronomic experiences', *Current Issues in Tourism*, doi:10.10 80/13683500.2013.868412

Blakeney, M., Coulet, T., Mengistie, G. and Mahop, M.T. (eds) (2012) *Extending the Protection of Geographical Indications: Case Studies of Agricultural Products in Africa*, Abingdon: Earthscan by Routledge.

Blandy, R. (2000) *Industry Clusters Program: A Review, South Australian Business Vision 2010*, Adelaide: Government of South Australia.

Blichfeldt, B.S. and Halkier, H. (2014) 'Mussels, tourism and community development: a case study of place branding through food festivals in rural North Jutland, Denmark', *European Planning Studies*, 22(8): 1587–1603.

Boatto, V., Galletto, L., Barisan, L. and Bianchin, F. (2013) 'The development of wine tourism in the Conegliano Valdobbiadene area', *Wine Economics and Policy*, 2(2): 93–101.

Boniface, P. (2003) *Tasting Tourism: Travelling for Food and Drink*, Burlington: Ashgate.

Booth, S. and Coveney, J. (2015) *Food Democracy: From Consumer to Food Citizen*, Springer Singapore: Springer.

Born, B. and Purcell, M. (2006) 'Avoiding the local trap: scale and food systems in planning research', *Journal of Planning Education and Research*, 26: 195–207.

Bourdieu, P. (1984) *Distinction*, London: Routledge.

Bowen, S. (2010) 'Embedding local places in global spaces: geographical indications as a territorial development strategy', *Rural Sociology*, 75(2): 209–243.

Bowen, S. and De Master, K. (2014) 'Wisconsin's "Happy Cows?" Articulating heritage and territory as new dimensions of locality', *Agriculture and Human Values*, 31(4): 549–562.

Bowen, S. and Zapata, A. (2009) 'Geographical indications, terroir, and socioeconomic and ecological sustainability: the case of tequila', *Journal of Rural Studies*, 25(1): 108–119.

Boyne, S., Hall, D. and Williams, F. (2003) 'Policy, support and promotion for food-related tourism initiatives: a marketing approach to regional development', *Journal of Travel & Tourism Marketing*, 14(3–4): 131–154.

Brown, A. (2001) 'Counting farmers markets', *Geographical Review*, 91: 655–674.

Brown, A. (2002) 'Farmers' market research 1940–2000: an inventory and review', *American Journal of Alternative Agriculture*, 17(4): 167–176.

Buck, D., Getz, C. and Guthman, J. (1997) 'From farm to table: the organic vegetable commodity chain of northern California', *Sociologia Ruralis*, 37(1): 3–20.

Buck, K., Kaminski, L.E., Stockmann, D.P. and Vail, A.J. (2007) *Investigating Opportunities to Strengthen the Local Food System in Southeastern Michigan, Executive Summary*, Ann Arbor: University of Michigan – School of Natural Resources and Environment.

Burch, D., Dixon, J. and Lawrence, G. (2013) 'Introduction to symposium on the changing role of supermarkets in global supply chains: from seedling to supermarket: agri-food supply chains in transition', *Agriculture and Human Values*, 30(2): 215–224.

Burgoine, T., Lake, A., Stamp, E., Alvanides, S., Mathers, J. and Adamson, A. (2009) 'Changing foodscapes 1980–2000, using the ASH30 Study', *Appetite*, 53(2): 157–165.

Busa, J.H. and Garder, R. (2015) 'Champions of the movement or fair-weather heroes? Individualization and the (A)politics of local food', *Antipode*, 47(2): 323–341.

California Farmers' Markets Association (2006) *California Farmers' Markets Association Rules and Regulations for Certified Farmers' Markets*, Walnut Creek: California Farmers' Markets Association.

Cavicchi, A. and Santini, C. (2011) 'Brunellopoli: a wine scandal under the Tuscan sun', *Tourism Review International*, 15(3): 253–267.

Çela, A., Knowles-Lankford, J. and Lankford, S. (2007) 'Local food festivals in Northeast Iowa communities: a visitor and economic impact study', *Managing Leisure*, 12(2/3): 171–186.

Centre for Environment and Society (1999) *Local Food Systems: Lessons for Local Economies Conference Proceedings*, Colchester: University of Essex.

Chaney, S. and Ryan, C. (2012) 'Analyzing the evolution of Singapore's World Gourmet Summit: an example of gastronomic tourism', *International Journal of Hospitality Management*, 31(2): 309–318.

Clancy, K. and Ruhf, K. (2010) 'Is local enough? Some arguments for regional food systems', *Choices*, 25(1): 123–135.

Cohen, E. and Avieli, N. (2004) 'Food in tourism: attraction and impediment', *Annals of Tourism Research*, 31(4): 755–778.

Coles, T., Dinan, C. and Hutchison, F. (2014) 'Tourism and the public sector in England since 2010: a disorderly transition?' *Current Issues in Tourism*, 17(3): 247–279.

Conner, D.S., Montria, A.D., Montria, D.N. and Hamm, M.W. (2009) 'Consumer demand for local produce at extended season farmers' markets: guiding farmer marketing strategies', *Renewable Agriculture and Food Systems*, 24: 251–259.

Countryside Agency (2001) *Eat the View – Promoting Sustainable, Local Products*, Cheltenham: The Countryside Agency.

Coxall, M. (2014) *Ethical Eating: A Complete Guide to Sustainable Food*, UK & Spain: Cornelio Books.

Curtis, K.R. and Cowee, M.W. (2009) 'Direct marketing local food to chefs: chef preferences and perceived obstacles', *Journal of Food Distribution Research*, 40(2): 26–36.

Darlow, A. (1996) 'Cultural policy and urban sustainability: making a missing link?' *Planning Practice and Research*, 11: 291–301.

Deery, M., O'Mahony, G. and Moors, R. (2012) 'Employing a lifecycle typology to generate a unified and strategic approach to regional wine tourism development', *Tourism Planning & Development*, 9(3), 291–307.

DeLind, L. (2000) 'Transforming organic agriculture into industrial organic products: reconsidering national organic standards', *Human Organization*, 59(2): 198–208.

Doane, D. (2001) *Taking Flight: The Rapid Growth of Ethical Consumerism*, London: New Economics Foundation.

Dodd, T., Yuan, J., Adams, C. and Kolyesnikova, N. (2006) 'Motivations of young people for visiting wine festivals', *Event Management*, 10: 23–33.

Doloreux, D. and Lord-Tarte, E. (2012) 'Context and differentiation: development of the wine industry in three Canadian regions', *The Social Science Journal*, 49(4): 519–527.

Dolphijn, R. (2004) *Foodscapes: Towards a Deleuzian Ethics of Consumption*, Delft: Eburon.

Donald, B. and Blay-Palmer, A. (2006) 'The urban creative-food economy: producing food for the urban elite or social inclusion opportunity?' *Environment and Planning A*, 38(10): 1901–1920.

Donald, B., Gertler, M., Gray, M. and Lobao, L. (2010) 'Re-regionalizing the food system?' *Cambridge Journal of Regions, Economy and Society*, 3: 1–5.

Dooley, G. and Bowie, D. (2005) 'Place brand architecture: strategic management of the brand portfolio', *Place Branding and Public Diplomacy*, 1(4): 402–419.

Dowd, K. and Burke, K.J. (2013) 'The influence of ethical values and food choice motivations on intentions to purchase sustainably sourced foods', *Appetite*, 69: 137–144.

DuPuis, E.M. and Goodman, D. (2005) 'Should we go "home" to eat? Toward a reflexive politics of localism', *Journal of Rural Studies*, 21(3): 359–371.

Duram, L. and Cawley, M. (2012) 'Irish chefs and restaurants in the geography of "local" food value chains', *The Open Geography Journal*, 5: 16–25.

Eaton, E. (2008) 'From feeding the locals to selling the locale: adapting local sustainable food projects in Niagara to neocommunitarianism and neoliberalism', *Geoforum*, 39(2), 994–1006.

Enright, M. and Roberts, B. (2001) 'Regional clustering in Australia', *Australian Journal of Management*, 26: 65–86.

Eriksen, S.N. and Sundbo, J. (2015) 'Drivers and barriers to the development of local food networks in rural Denmark', *European Urban and Regional Studies*, doi:10.1177/0969776414567971

Evans, G. (2005) 'Measure for measure: evaluating the evidence of culture's contribution to regeneration', *Urban Studies*, 42(5/6): 959–983.

Evans, N., Morris, C. and Winter, M. (2002) 'Conceptualizing agriculture: a critique of post-productivism as the new orthodoxy', *Progress in Human Geography*, 26(3): 313–332.

Everett, S. (2008) 'Beyond the visual gaze? The pursuit of an embodied experience through food tourism', *Tourist Studies*, 8(3): 337–358.

Everett, S. and Aitchison, C. (2008) 'The role of food tourism in sustaining regional identity: a case study of Cornwall, South West England', *Journal of Sustainable Tourism*, 16(2): 150–167.

Everett, S. and Slocum, S.L. (2013) 'Food and tourism: an effective partnership? A UK-based review', *Journal of Sustainable Tourism*, 21(6): 789–809.

Falassi, A. (ed.) (1987) *Time Out of Time: Essays on the Festival*, Albuquerque: University of New Mexico Press.

Farmers' Market Coalition (2008) *Welcome to the FMC*. Available online: <http://farmers-marketcoalition.org/> (accessed 26 March 2012).

Farmers' Markets Ontario (FMO) (2007) *Membership Information*. Available online: <http://www.farmersmarketsontario.com/MembershipInfo.cfm> (accessed 1 October 2007).

Feagan, R. (2007) 'The place of food: mapping out the "local" in local food systems', *Progress in Human Geography*, 31(1): 23–42.

Feagan, R. and Krug, K. (2004) 'Towards a sustainable Niagara foodshed: learning from experience', in *Leading Edge 2004 The Working Biosphere*, 3–5 March. Georgetown: Niagara Escarpment Commission.

Feagan, R., Morris, D. and Krug, K. (2004) 'Niagara region farmers' markets: local food systems and sustainability considerations', *Local Environment*, 9(3): 235–254.

Feenstra, G.W. (1997) 'Local food systems and sustainable communities', *American Journal of Alternative Agriculture*, 12(1): 28–36.

Follett, J. (2009) 'Choosing a food future: differentiating among alternative food options', *Journal of Agricultural and Environmental Ethics*, 22(1): 31–51.

Food System Economic Partnership (2006) *Alternative Regional Food System Models: Successes and Lessons Learned: A Preliminary Literature Review*, Michigan: Food System Economic Partnership.

Forbord, M. (2015) 'Food as attraction: connections between a hotel and suppliers of specialty food', *Scandinavian Journal of Hospitality and Tourism*, doi:10.1080/1502225 0.2015.1108860

Freidberg, S. (2010) 'Perspective and power in the ethical foodscape', *Environment and Planning A*, 42(8): 1868–1874.

Fromartz, S. (2006) *Organic Inc. Natural Foods and How They Grew*, Toronto: Harcourt.

Frost, N. (2015) 'Anthropology and festivals: festival ecologies', *Ethnos: Journal of Anthropology*, doi:10.1080/00141844.2014.989875

Frykors, C.T. and Jonsson, H. (2010) 'Reframing the multilevel triple helix in a regional innovation system: a case of systemic foresight and regimes in renewal of Skåne's food industry', *Technology Analysis & Strategic Management*, 22(7): 819–829.

Fusté Forné, F. (2015) 'Cheese tourism in a World Heritage site: Vall de Boí (Catalan Pyrenees)', *European Journal of Tourism Research*, 11: 87–101.

Garrod, B., Wornell, R. and Youell, R. (2006) 'Re-conceptualising rural resources as countryside capital: the case of rural tourism', *Journal of Rural Studies*, 22(1): 117–128.

Goh, A.L.S. (2000) 'A correlation-based impact analysis of competence utilization on innovation performance', *International Journal of Applied Entrepreneurship*, 1(3): 1–19.

Goodman, D., DuPuis, E.M. and Goodman, M.K. (2012) *Alternative Food Networks: Knowledge, Practice, and Politics*, Abingdon: Routledge.

Goodman, M.K., Maye D. and Holloway L. (2010) 'Ethical foodscapes: premises, promises and possibilities', *Environment and Planning A*, 42: 1782–1796.

Gössling, S., Garrod, B., Aall, C., Hille, J. and Peeters, P. (2011) 'Food management in tourism: reducing tourism's carbon "foodprint"', *Tourism Management*, 32(3): 534–543.

Gössling, S. and Hall, C.M. (2013) 'Sustainable culinary systems: an introduction', in C.M. Hall and S. Gössling (eds) *Sustainable Culinary Systems: Local Foods, Innovation, Tourism and Hospitality*, Abingdon: Routledge, pp. 3–44.

Green, G.P. and Dougherty, M.L. (2008) 'Localizing linkages for food and tourism: culinary tourism as a community development strategy', *Community Development*, 39(3): 148–158.

Griffin, M.R. and Frongillo, E.A. (2003) 'Experiences and perspectives of farmers from upstate New York farmers' markets', *Agriculture and Human Values*, 20: 189–203.

Halfacree, K. and Boyle, P. (1998) 'Migration, rurality and the post-productivist countryside', in P. Boyle and K. Halfacree (eds) *Migration into Rural Areas: Theories and Issues*, Chichester: Wiley, pp. 1–20.

Hall, C.M. (1992) *Hallmark Tourist Events*, London: Belhaven Press.

Hall, C.M. (1996) 'Wine tourism in New Zealand', in G. Kearsley (ed.) *Tourism Down Under II, Conference Proceedings*, Dunedin: Centre for Tourism, University of Otago, pp. 109–119.

Hall, C.M. (2001) 'The development of rural wine and food tourism networks: factors and issues', in M. Mitchell and I. Kirkpatrick (eds) *New Directions in Managing Rural Tourism and Leisure: Local Impacts, Global Trends*, Ayr: Scottish Agricultural College, Auchincruive.

Hall, C.M. (2002) 'Local initiatives for local regional development: the role of food, wine and tourism', in E. Arola, J. Kärkkäinen, and M. Siitari (eds) *The 2nd Tourism Industry*

& *Education Symposium, Tourism and Well-Being*, Jyväskylä: Jyväskylä Polytechnic, pp. 47–63.

Hall, C.M. (2004) 'Small firms and wine and food tourism in New Zealand: issues of collaboration, clusters and lifestyles', in R. Thomas (ed.) *Small Firms in Tourism: International Perspectives*, Oxford: Elsevier, pp. 167–181.

Hall, C.M. (2005) 'Rural wine and food tourism cluster and network development', in D. Hall, I. Kirkpatrick, and M. Mitchell (eds) *Rural Tourism and Sustainable Business*, Clevedon: Channelview, pp. 149–164.

Hall, C.M. (2006) 'Introduction: culinary tourism and regional development: from Slow Food to slow tourism?' *Tourism Review International*, 9(4), 303–305.

Hall, C.M. (2010) 'Tourism destination branding and its affects on national branding strategies: Brand New Zealand, clean and green but is it smart?' *European Journal of Tourism and Hospitality Research*, 1(1): 68–89.

Hall, C.M. (2012) 'The contradictions and paradoxes of Slow Food: environmental change, sustainability and the conservation of taste', in S. Fullagar, K. Markwell, and E. Wilson (eds) *Slow Tourism: Experiences and Mobilities*, Bristol: Channel View, pp. 53–68.

Hall, C.M. (2013) 'The local in farmers markets in New Zealand', in C.M. Hall and S. Gössling (eds) *Sustainable Culinary Systems: Local Foods, Innovation, Tourism and Hospitality*, Abingdon: Routledge.

Hall, C.M. (2016) 'Heirloom products in heritage places: farmers markets, local food, and food diversity', in D. Timothy (ed.) *Heritage Cuisines: Traditions, Identities and Tourism*, Abingdon: Routledge, pp. 88–103.

Hall, C.M. and Baird, T. (2014a) 'Innovation in New Zealand wine tourism businesses', in G.A. Alsos, D. Eide, and E. Madsen (eds) *Handbook of Research on Innovation in Tourism Industries*, Cheltenham: Edward Elgar, pp. 249–274.

Hall, C.M. and Baird, T. (2014b) 'Brand New Zealand wine: architecture, positioning and vulnerability in the global marketplace', in P. Howland (ed.) *Social, Cultural and Economic Impacts of Wine in New Zealand*, Abingdon: Routledge, pp. 105–119.

Hall, C.M. and Gössling, S. (eds) (2013a) *Sustainable Culinary Systems: Local Foods, Innovation, Tourism and Hospitality*, Abingdon: Routledge.

Hall, C.M. and Gössling, S. (2013b) 'Conclusion: re-imagining sustainable culinary systems', in C.M. Hall and S. Gössling (eds) *Sustainable Culinary Systems: Local Foods, Innovation, Tourism and Hospitality*, Abingdon: Routledge, pp. 293–304.

Hall, C.M., Gössling, S. and Scott, D. (eds) (2015) *The Routledge Handbook of Tourism and Sustainability*, Abingdon: Routledge.

Hall, C.M. and Jenkins, J. (1998) 'Rural tourism and recreation policy dimensions', in R. Butler, C.M. Hall, and J. Jenkins (eds) *Tourism and Recreation in Rural Areas*, Chichester: John Wiley, pp. 19–42.

Hall, C.M., Johnson, G. and Mitchell, R. (2000) 'Wine tourism and regional development', in C.M. Hall, L. Sharples, N. Macionis, and B. Cambourne (eds) *Wine Tourism around the World*, Oxford: Butterworth-Heinemann, pp. 196–225.

Hall, C.M. and Mitchell, R. (2001) 'Wine and food tourism', in N. Douglas, N. Douglas, and R. Derrett (eds) *Special Interest Tourism: Context and Cases*, Brisbane: John Wiley & Sons Australia, pp. 307–329.

Hall, C.M. and Mitchell, R. (2008) *Wine Marketing: A Practical Approach*, Oxford: Butterworth-Heinemann.

Hall, C.M., Mitchell, R., Scott, D. and Sharples, L. (2008) 'The authentic market experiences of farmers' markets', in C.M. Hall and L. Sharples (eds) *Food and Wine Festivals and Events around the World: Development, Management and Markets*, Oxford: Butterworth-Heinemann, pp. 197–231.

Hall, C.M. and Sharples, L. (eds) (2008a) *Food and Wine Festivals and Events around the World: Development, Management and Markets*, Oxford: Butterworth-Heinemann.

Hall, C.M. and Sharples, L. (eds) (2008b) 'Food events, festivals and farmers' markets: an introduction', in C.M. Hall and L. Sharples (eds) *Food and Wine Festivals and Events around the World: Development, Management and Markets*, Oxford: Butterworth-Heinemann, pp. 3–22.

Hall, C.M. and Sharples, L. (eds) (2008c) 'Food events and the local food system: marketing, management and planning issues', in C.M. Hall and L. Sharples (eds) *Food and Wine Festivals and Events around the World: Development, Management and Markets*, Oxford: Butterworth-Heinemann, pp. 23–46.

Hall, C.M., Sharples, E., Cambourne, B. and Macionis, N. (eds) (2000) *Wine Tourism around the World: Development, Management and Markets*, Oxford: Butterworth-Heinemann.

Hall, C.M., Sharples, E., Mitchell, R., Cambourne, B. and Macionis N. (eds) (2003) *Food Tourism around the World: Development, Management and Markets*, Oxford: Butterworth-Heinemann.

Hall, C.M., Sharples, E. and Smith, A. (2003) 'The experience of consumption or the consumption of experiences? Challenges and issues in food tourism', in C.M. Hall, E. Sharples, R. Mitchell, B. Cambourne, and N. Macionis (eds) *Food Tourism around the World: Development, Management and Markets*, Oxford: Butterworth-Heinemann, pp. 314–336.

Hallinan, T.S. (1989) 'River City: right here in California?' *Yearbook of the Association of Pacific Coast Geographers*, 51: 49–64.

Halweil, B. (2002) *Home Grown: The Case for Local Food in a Global Market*, Washington, DC: WorldWatch Institute.

Hamilton, L.M. (2002) 'The American farmers market', *Gastronomica*, 2(3): 73–77.

Heatherington, T. (2014) 'Tasting cultural ecology: foodscapes of sustainability in the Mediterranean', *Gastronomica*, 14(2): 16–26.

Hede, A. (2008) 'Food and wine festivals: stakeholders, long-term outcomes and strategies for success', in C.M. Hall and L. Sharples (eds) *Food and Wine Festivals and Events around the World*, Oxford: Elsevier, pp. 85–101.

Henderson, J.C. (2009) 'Food tourism reviewed', *British Food Journal*, 111(4): 317–326.

Hinrichs, C.C. (2000) 'Embeddedness and local food systems: notes on two types of direct agricultural market', *Journal of Rural Studies*, 16(3): 295–303.

Hinrichs, C.C. (2003) 'The practice and politics of food system localization', *Journal of Rural Studies*, 19(1): 33–45.

Hinrichs, C.C. and Lyson, T.A. (eds) (2007) *Remaking the North American Food System: Strategies for Sustainability*, Lincoln: University of Nebraska Press.

Hjalager, A.M. (2002) 'A typology of gastronomy tourism', in A.M. Hjalager and G. Richards (eds) *Tourism and Gastronomy*, London: Routledge, pp. 21–36.

Hjalager, A.M., Johansen, P.H. and Rasmussen, B. (2015) 'Informing regional food innovation through lead user experiments: the case of blue mussels', *British Food Journal*, 117(11): 2706–2723.

Hjalager, A.M. and Wahlberg, M. (2014) 'Museum guests as contributors to regional food innovation', *Museum Management and Curatorship*, 29(1): 50–65.

Hollows, J., Jones, S., Taylor, B. and Dowthwaite, K. (2014) 'Making sense of urban food festivals: cultural regeneration, disorder and hospitable cities', *Journal of Policy Research in Tourism, Leisure and Events*, 6(1): 1–14.

Horner, M. and Wood, B. (2014) 'Capturing individuals' food environments using flexible space-time accessibility measures', *Applied Geography*, 51: 99–107.

Horng, J.S. and Tsai, C.T.S. (2012) 'Culinary tourism strategic development: an Asia-Pacific perspective', *International Journal of Tourism Research*, 14(1): 40–55.

Houghton, M. (2001) 'The propensity of wine festival to encourage subsequent winery visitation', *International Journal of Wine Marketing*, 13(3): 32–41.

Hu, Y. (2010) 'An exploration of the relationships between festival expenditures, motivations, and food involvement among food festival visitors', PhD thesis, University of Waterloo, Canada.

Huff, A.G., Beyeler, W.E., Kelley, N.S. and McNitt, J.A. (2015) 'How resilient is the United States' food system to pandemics?' *Journal of Environmental Studies and Sciences*, 5(3): 337–347.

Humphery, T.C. and Humphery, L.T. (eds) (1988) *'We Gather Together': Food and Festival in American Life*, Ann Arbor: UMI Research Press.

Ilbery, B. (1991) 'Farm diversification as an adjustment strategy on the urban fringe of the West Midlands', *Journal of Rural Studies*, 7(3): 207–218.

Ilbery, B. and Bowler, I. (1998) 'From agricultural productivism to post-productivism', in B. Ilbery (ed.) *The Geography of Rural Change*, London: Longman, pp. 57–84.

Ilbery, B. and Kneafsey, M. (2000a) 'Registering regional specialty food and drink products in the United Kingdom: the case of PDOs and PGIs', *Area*, 32(3): 317–325.

Ilbery, B. and Kneafsey, M. (2000b) 'Producer constructions of quality in regional speciality food production: a case study from south west England', *Journal of Rural Studies*, 16: 217–230.

Ilbery, B. and Maye, D. (2005) 'Food supply chains and sustainability: evidence from specialist food producers in the Scottish/English borders', *Land Use Policy*, 22(4): 331–344.

Ilbery, B., Morris, C., Buller, H., Maye, D. and Kneafsey, M. (2005) 'Product, process and place an examination of food marketing and labelling schemes in Europe and North America', *European Urban and Regional Studies*, 12(2): 116–132.

Inwood, S.M., Sharp, J.S., Moore, R.H. and Stinner, D.H. (2009) 'Restaurants, chefs and local foods: insights drawn from application of a diffusion of innovation framework', *Agriculture and Human Values*, 26(3): 177–191.

Jackson, L.L. (2008) 'Who "designs" the agricultural landscape?' *Landscape Journal*, 27(1): 23–40.

Jackson, P., Ward, N. and Russell, P. (2006) 'Mobilising the commodity chain concept in the politics of food and farming', *Journal of Rural Studies*, 22(2): 129–141.

James, L. and Halkier, H. (2014) 'Regional development platforms and related variety: exploring the changing practices of food tourism in North Jutland, Denmark', *European Urban and Regional Studies*, doi:10.1177/0969776414557293

James, S.W. (2015) 'Beyond "local" food: how supermarkets and consumer choice affect the economic viability of small-scale family farms in Sydney, Australia', *Area*, doi:10.1111/area.12243

Jarosz, L. (2008) 'The city in the country: growing alternative food networks in metropolitan areas', *Journal of Rural Studies*, 24(3): 231–244.

Jenkins, J., Hall, C.M. and Troughton, M. (1998) 'The restructuring of rural economies: rural tourism and recreation as a government response', in R. Butler, C.M. Hall, and J. Jenkins (eds) *Tourism and Recreation in Rural Areas*, Chichester: John Wiley, pp. 43–68.

Johnston, J. and Baumann, S. (2015) *Foodies: Democracy and Distinction in the Gourmet Foodscape*, 2nd edn, London: Routledge.

Johnston, J., Biro, J. and MacKendrick, N. (2009) 'Lost in the supermarket: the corporate-organic foodscape and the struggle for food democracy', *Antipode*, 41: 509–532.

Jones, M.F., Singh, N. and Hsiung, Y. (2015) 'Determining the critical success factors of the wine tourism region of Napa from a supply perspective', *International Journal of Tourism Research*, 17(3): 261–271.

Kim, S. and Jamal, T. (2015) 'The co-evolution of rural tourism and sustainable rural development in Hongdong, Korea: complexity, conflict and local response', *Journal of Sustainable Tourism*, 23(8–9): 1363–1385.

Kim, Y.G., Eves, A. and Scarles, C. (2009) 'Building a model of local food consumption on trips and holidays: a grounded theory approach', *International Journal of Hospitality Management*, 28: 423–432.

Kirkman, A., Strydom, J.W. and Van Zyl, C. (2013) 'Stellenbosch Wine Route wineries: management's perspective on the advantages and key success factors of wine tourism', *Southern African Business Review*, 17(2): 93–112.

Kloppenburg, J., Hendrickson, J. and Stevenson, G.W. (1996) 'Coming in to the food-shed', *Agriculture and Human Values*, 13: 33–42.

Kloppenburg, Jr. J., Lezberg, S., De Master, K., Stevenson, G. and Hendrickson, J. (2000) 'Tasting food, tasting sustainability: defining the attributes of an alternative food system with competent, ordinary people', *Human Organization*, 59(2): 177–186.

Kneafsey, M., Venn, L., Schmutz, U., Balázs, B., Trenchard, L. Eyden-Wood, T., Bos, E., Sutton, G. and Blackett, M. (2013) *Short Food Supply Chains and Local Food Systems in the EU. A State of Play of their Socio-Economic Characteristics*, Luxembourg: Publications Office of the European Union.

Kohn, M. (2009) 'Dreamworlds of deindustrialization', *Theory & Event*, 12(4): doi:10.1353/tae.0.0096

Kremer, P. and Schreuder, Y. (2012) 'The feasibility of regional food systems in metropolitan areas: an investigation of Philadelphia's foodshed', *Journal of Agriculture, Food Systems, and Community Development*, 2(2): 171–191.

Lang, T. (2010) 'From "value-for-money" to "values-for-money?" Ethical food and policy in Europe', *Environment and Planning A*, 42: 1814–1832.

Lang, T. and Heasman, M. (2004) *Food Wars: The Global Battle for Mouths, Minds and Markets*, London: Earthscan.

Lawrence, G., Richards, C. and Lyons, K. (2013) 'Food security in Australia in an era of neoliberalism, productivism and climate change', *Journal of Rural Studies*, 29: 30–39.

Lee, A.H., Wall, G. and Kovacs, J. (2015) 'Creative food clusters and rural development through place branding: culinary tourism initiatives in Stratford and Muskoka, Ontario, Canada', *Journal of Rural Studies*, 39: 133–144.

Lee, I. and Arcodia, C. (2011) 'The role of regional food festivals for destination branding', *International Journal of Tourism Research*, 13(4): 355–367.

Lewis, G.H. (1997) 'Celebrating asparagus: community and the rationally constructed food festival', *Journal of American Culture*, 20(4): 73–78.

Lin, J. (1998) *Reconstructing Chinatown: Ethnic Enclaves and Global Change*, Minneapolis: University of Minnesota Press.

Lin, Y.C., Pearson, T.E. and Cai, L.A. (2011) 'Food as a form of destination identity: a tourism destination brand perspective', *Tourism and Hospitality Research*, 11(1): 30–48.

Lindenfeld, L. and Silka, L. (2011) 'Growing Maine's foodscape, growing Maine's future', *Maine Policy Review*, 20(1), 48–52.

Long, L. (ed.) (2004) *Culinary Tourism: Exploring the Other through Food*, Lexington: University of Kentucky Press.

Long, L. (ed.) (2010) 'Culinary tourism and the emergence of an Appalachian cuisine: exploring the foodscape of Asheville, NC', *North Carolina Folklore Journal*, 57(1): 4–19.

López-Guzmán, T. and Sánchez-Cañizares, S. (2012) 'Gastronomy, tourism and destination differentiation: a case study in Spain', *Review of Economics and Finance*, 1: 63–72.

Lowe, P., Murdoch, J., Marsden, T., Munton, R. and Flynn. A. (1993) 'Regulating the new rural spaces: the uneven development of land', *Journal of Rural Studies*, 9: 205–222.

Marcotte, P., Bourdeau, L. and Leroux, E. (2012) 'Branding et labels en tourisme: réticences et défis', *Management & Avenir*, 47(7): 205–222.

Marsden, T. (2012) 'Third natures? Reconstituting space through place-making strategies for sustainability', *International Journal of Sociology of Agriculture and Food*, 19(2): 257–274.

Marsden, T., Banks, J. and Bristow, G. (2000) 'Food supply chain approaches: exploring their role in rural development', *Sociologia Ruralis*, 40(4): 424–438.

Mather, A., Hill, G. and Nijnik, M. (2006) 'Post-productivism and rural land use: cul de sac or challenge for theorization?' *Journal of Rural Studies*, 22(4): 441–455.

Mathews, V. and Picton, R.M. (2014) 'Intoxifying gentrification: brew pubs and the geography of post-industrial heritage', *Urban Geography*, 35(3): 337–356.

McCaffrey, S.J. and Kurland, N.B. (2015) 'Does "local" mean ethical? The US "buy local" movement and CSR in SMEs', *Organization & Environment*, 28(3): 286–306.

McCarthy, J. (2005) 'Cultural quarters and regeneration: the case of Wolverhampton', *Planning, Practice & Research*, 20(3): 297–311.

McMichael, A.J., Butler, C.D. and Dixon, J. (2015) 'Climate change, food systems and population health risks in their eco-social context', *Public Health*, 129(10): 1361–1368.

Mikkelsen, B. E. (2011) 'Images of foodscapes: Introduction to foodscape studies and their application in the study of healthy eating out-of-home environments', *Perspectives in Public Health*, 131(5): 209–216.

Mitchell, R. and Hall, C.M. (2003) 'Consuming tourists: food tourism consumer behaviour', in C.M. Hall, E. Sharples, R. Mitchell, B. Cambourne, and N. Macionis (eds) *Food Tourism around the World: Development, Management and Markets*, Oxford: Butterworth-Heinemann, pp. 60–81.

Montanari, A. and Staniscia, B. (2009) 'Culinary tourism as a tool for regional re-equilibrium', *European Planning Studies*, 17(10): 1463–1483.

Morales, A. (2006) *New Maxwell Street Market Its Present and Future*, Evanston, IL: Maxwell Street Foundation.

Morales, A., Balkin, S. and Persky, J. (1995) 'The value of benefits of a public street market: the case of Maxwell Street', *Economic Development Quarterly*, 9(4): 304–320.

Moran, W. (1993) 'Rural space as intellectual property', *Political Geography*, 12(3): 263–277.

Morgan, K. (2010) 'Local and green, global and fair: the ethical foodscape and the politics of care', *Environment and Planning A*, 42: 1852–1867.

Murphy, J. and Smith, S. (2009) 'Chefs and suppliers: an exploratory look at supply chain issues in an upscale restaurant alliance', *International Journal of Hospitality Management*, 28(2): 212–220.

Muzellec, L. and Lambkin, M.C. (2009) 'Corporate branding and brand architecture: a conceptual framework', *Marketing Theory*, 9(1): 39–54.

National Farmers' Retail and Markets Association (FARMA) (2009) *Certified Farmers' Markets. Find a Farmers' Market*. Available online: <http://www.farmersmarkets.org.uk/findafmkt.htm> (accessed 1 April 2012).

Newman, C.L., Turri, A., Howlett, E. and Stokes, A. (2014) 'Twenty years of country-of-origin food labeling research: a review of the literature and implications for food marketing systems', *Journal of Macromarketing*, 34(4): 505–519.

New Zealand Farmers' Market Association (2007) *Fresh Market Locations*. Available online: <http://www.farmersmarket.org.nz/locations.htm> (accessed 1 October 2007).

Niva, M., Mäkelä, J., Kahma, N. and Kjærnes, U. (2014) 'Eating sustainably? Practices and background factors of ecological food consumption in four Nordic countries', *Journal of Consumer Policy*, 37(4): 465–484.

Nordin, S. (2003) *Tourism Clustering and Innovation: Paths to Economic Growth and Development*, ETOUR Utredningsserien Analys och Statistik 2003: 14, Östersund: European Tourism Research Institute, Mid-Sweden University.

Nosi, C. and Zanni, L. (2004) 'Moving from "typical products" to "food-related services": the Slow Food case as a new business paradigm', *British Food Journal*, 106(10/11): 779–792.

Nummedal, M. and Hall, C.M. (2006) 'Local food in tourism: an investigation of the New Zealand South Island's bed and breakfast sector's use and perception of local food', *Tourism Review International*, 9(4): 365–378.

OECD (Organisation for Economic Co-operation and Development) (1999) *Proceedings, Boosting Innovation: The Cluster Approach*, Paris: OECD Publishing.

OECD (Organisation for Economic Co-operation and Development) (2012) *Food and the Tourism Experience: The OECD-Korea Workshop*, OECD Studies on Tourism, Paris: OECD Publishing.

Ostrom, M. (2006) 'Everyday meanings of "local food": views from home and field', *Community Development*, 37(1): 65–78.

Pant, G. (2015) 'Globalising Asia and the politics of food security', *World Affairs: The Journal of International Issues*, 19(2): 24–43.

Parham, S. (2012) *Market Place: Food Quarters, Design and Urban Renewal in London*, Newcastle upon Tyne: Cambridge Scholars.

Parham, S. (2015) *Food and Urbanism: The Convivial City and a Sustainable Future*, London: Bloomsbury Publishing.

Payne, T. (2002) *U.S. Farmers Markets – 2000: A Study of Emerging Trends*, Washington, DC: Agricultural Marketing Service, USDA.

Penney, U. and Prior, C. (2014) 'Exploring the urban consumer's perception of local food', *International Journal of Retail & Distribution Management*, 42(7): 580–594.

Peris-Ortiz, M., Rama, M. and Rueda-Armengot, C. (eds) (2016) *Wine and Tourism. A Strategic Segment for Sustainable Economic Development*, Dortrecht: Springer.

Petrini, C. (2001) *Slow Food: Collected thoughts on Taste, Tradition, and the Honest Pleasures of Food*, White River Junction: Chelsea Green.

Petrini, C. (2007) *Slow Food Nation. Why our Food Should Be Good, Clean, and Fair*, New York: Rizzoli International.

Picard, D. and Robinson, M. (eds) (2006) *Festivals, Tourism and Social Change*, Clevedon: Channel View.

Pike, A. (2007) 'Editorial: whither regional studies?' *Regional Studies*, 41(9): 1143–1148.

Pike A., Rodríguez-Pose A. and Tomaney J. (2006) *Local and Regional Development*, London: Routledge.

Pike A., Rodríguez-Pose A. and Tomaney J. (2007) 'What kind of local and regional development and for whom?' *Regional Studies*, 41(9): 1253–1269.

Plummer, R., Telfer, D. and Hashimoto, A. (2006) 'The rise and fall of the Waterloo-Wellington Ale Trail: a study of collaboration within the tourism industry', *Current Issues in Tourism*, 9(3): 191–205.

Porter, M. (1990) *The Competitive Advantage of Nations*, London: Macmillan.

Pottinger, L. (2013) 'Ethical food consumption and the city', *Geography Compass*, 7(9): 659–668.

Pyle, J. (1971) 'Farmers' markets in United States: functional anachronisms?' *Geographical Review*, 61: 167–197.

Raja, S., Ma, C. and Yadav, P. (2008) 'Beyond food deserts measuring and mapping racial disparities in neighborhood food environments', *Journal of Planning Education and Research*, 27(4): 469–482.

Raynolds, L.T. (2004) 'The globalization of organic agro-food networks', *World Development*, 32(5): 725–743.

Renting, H., Marsden, T. and Banks, J. (2003) 'Understanding alternative food networks: exploring the role of short food supply chains in rural development', *Environment and Planning A*, 35(3): 393–412.

Richards, G. (2002) 'Gastronomy: an essential ingredient in tourism production and consumption?' in A.M. Hjalager and G. Richards (eds) *Tourism and Gastronomy*, London: Routledge, pp. 3–20.

Ritchie, J. B. (1984) 'Assessing the impact of hallmark events: conceptual and research issues', *Journal of Travel Research*, 23(1): 2–11.

Roadhouse, S. (ed.) (2010) *Cultural Qu4rters: Principles and Practice*, 2nd edn, Bristol: Intellect.

Roche, M. and Argent, N. (2015) 'The fall and rise of agricultural productivism? An Antipodean viewpoint', *Progress in Human Geography*, 39(5): 621–635.

Rodríguez, I., Williams, A. and Hall, C.M. (2014) 'Tourism innovation policy: implementation and outcomes', *Annals of Tourism Research*, 49: 76–93.

Ron, A. and Timothy, D.J. (2013) 'The land of milk and honey: Biblical foods, heritage and Holy Land tourism', *Journal of Heritage Tourism*, 8(2–3): 234–247.

Rosenfeld, S.A. (1997) 'Bringing business clusters into the mainstream of economic development', *European Planning Studies*, 5(1): 3–23.

Ruhf, K.Z. (2015) 'Regionalism: a New England recipe for a resilient food system', *Journal of Environmental Studies and Sciences*, 5(4): 650–660.

Sage, C. (2003) 'Social embeddedness and relations of regard: alternative "good food" networks in south-west Ireland', *Journal of Rural Studies*, 19(1): 47–60.

Sage, C. (2012) *Environment and Food*, London: Routledge.

Sánchez-Cañizaresa, S.M. and López-Guzmán, T. (2012) 'Gastronomy as a tourism resource: profile of the culinary tourist', *Current Issues in Tourism*, 15(3): 229–245.

Schmit, T.M. and Hadcock, S.E. (2012) 'Assessing barriers to expansion of farm-to-chef sales: a case study from upstate New York', *Journal of Food Research*, 1(1): 117–125.

Selfa, T. and Qazi, J. (2005) 'Place, taste, or face-to-face? Understanding producer–consumer networks in "local" food systems in Washington State', *Agriculture and Human Values*, 22: 451–464.

Sharples, L. and Lyons, H. (2008) 'Beer festivals: a case study approach', in C.M. Hall and L. Sharples (eds) *Food and Wine Festivals and Events around the World*, Oxford: Elsevier, pp. 166–177.

Shucksmith, D.M., Bryden, J., Rosenthall, P., Short, C. and Winter, D. (1989) 'Pluriactivity, farm structures and rural change', *Journal of Agricultural Economics*, 40(3): 345–360.

Shucksmith, M. (1993) 'Farm household behaviour and the transition to post-productivism', *Journal of Agricultural Economics*, 44: 466–478.

Sims, R. (2009) 'Food, place and authenticity: local food and the sustainable tourism experience', *Journal of Sustainable Tourism*, 17(3): 321–336.

Sims, R. (2010) 'Putting place on the menu: the negotiation of locality in UK food tourism, from production to consumption', *Journal of Rural Studies*, 26: 105–115.

Skilton, P.F. and Wu, Z. (2013) 'Governance regimes for protected geographic indicators impacts on food marketing systems', *Journal of Macromarketing*, 33(2): 144–159.

Smith, A. and Hall, C.M. (2003) 'Restaurants and local food in New Zealand', in C.M. Hall, L. Sharples, R. Mitchell, N. Macionis, and B. Cambourne (eds) *Food Tourism around the World: Development, Management, and Markets*, Oxford: Elsevier, pp. 249–267.

Smith, S.J. (2007) 'Leisure travel', in R. McCarville and K. Mackay (eds) *Leisure for Canadians*, State College: Venture Publishing, pp. 93–102.

Smithers, J., Lamarche, J. and Joseph, A. (2008) 'Unpacking the terms of engagement with local food at the farmers' market: insights from Ontario', *Journal of Rural Studies*, 24(3): 337–350.

Sobal, J. and Wansink, B. (2007) 'Kitchenscapes, tablescapes, platescapes, and food-scapes', *Environment & Behavior*, 39(1): 124–142.

Sparks, B. (2007) 'Planning a wine tourism vacation? Factors that help to predict tourist behavioral intentions', *Tourism Management*, 28: 1180–1192.

Spilková, J. and Fialová, D. (2013) 'Culinary tourism packages and regional brands in Czechia', *Tourism Geographies*, 15(2): 177–197.

Storchmann, K. (2010) 'The economic impact of the wine industry on hotels and restaurants: evidence from Washington State', *Journal of Wine Economics*, 5(1): 164–183.

Telfer, D. (2001a) 'Strategic alliances along the Niagara Wine Route', *Tourism Management*, 22: 21–30.

Telfer, D. (2001b) 'From a wine tourism village to a regional wine route: an investigation of the competitive advantage of embedded clusters in Niagara, Canada', *Tourism Recreation Research*, 26: 23–33.

Telfer, D. and Wall, G. (1996) 'Linkages between tourism and food production', *Annals of Tourism Research*, 23: 635–653.

Thompson, C.J. and Coskuner-Balli, G. (2007) 'Enchanting ethical consumerism the case of community supported agriculture', *Journal of Consumer Culture*, 7(3): 275–303.

Tunbridge, J. (2000) 'Heritage momentum or maelstrom? The case of Ottawa's Byward Market', *International Journal of Heritage Studies*, 6(3): 269–291.

Tunbridge, J. (2001) 'Ottawa's Byward Market: a festive bone of contention?' *The Canadian Geographer/Le Géographe Canadien*, 45(3): 356–370.

United States Department of Agriculture (USDA), Agricultural Marketing Service (2012) *Farmers Market Services*, Washington, DC: Marketing Services Division, USDA Agricultural Marketing Service.

United States Department of Agriculture (USDA), Agricultural Marketing Service (2014) *National Count of Farmers Market Directory Listing Graph: 1994–2014*, Washington, DC: Marketing Services Division, USDA Agricultural Marketing Service.

Van der Meulen, H.S. (2008) 'The emergence of Slow Food', in W. Hulsink and H. Dons (eds) *Pathways to High-tech Valleys and Research Triangles: Innovative Entrepreneurship, Knowledge Transfer and Cluster Formation in Europe and the United States*, Dortrecht: Springer, pp. 245–247.

Victorian Farmers' Market Association (2011) *About the VFMA*. Available online: <http://www.vicfarmersmarkets.org.au/content/about-vfma> (accessed 25 March 2012).

Waits, M.J. (2000) 'The added value of the industry cluster approach to economic analysis, strategy development, and service delivery', *Economic Development Quarterly*, 14: 35–50.

West, H.G. and Domingos, N. (2012) 'Gourmandizing poverty food: the Serpa Cheese Slow Food Presidium', *Journal of Agrarian Change*, 12(1), 120–143.

Whatmore, S., Lowe, P. and Marsden, T. (eds) (1991) *Rural Enterprise: Shifting Perspectives on Small-Scale Production*, London: David Fulton Publishers.

White, S. and Gasser, M. (2001) *Local Economic Development: A Tool for Supporting Locally Owned and Managed Development Processes that Foster the Global Promotion of Decent Work*, Geneva: Job Creation and Enterprise Development Department, ILO.

Whitehead, M. (1998) 'Food deserts: what's in name?' *Health Education Journal*, 57: 189–190.

Widener, M. and Shannon, J. (2014) 'When are food deserts? Integrating time into research on food accessibility', *Health & Place*, 30: 1–3.

Williams, L.T., Germov, J., Fuller, S. and Freij, M. (2015) 'A taste of ethical consumption at a slow food festival', *Appetite*, 91: 321–328.

Wilson, G. (2001) 'From productivism to post-productivism ... and back again? Exploring the (un) changed natural and mental landscapes of European agriculture', *Transactions of the Institute of British Geographers*, 26(1): 77–102.

Wittman, H., Beckie, M. and Hergesheimer, C. (2012) 'Linking local food systems and the social economy? Future roles for farmers' markets in Alberta and British Columbia', *Rural Sociology*, 77(1): 36–61.

Wood, E. and Thomas, R. (2008) 'Festivals and tourism in rural economies', in J. Ali-Knight, M. Robertson, A. Fyall, and A. Ladkin (eds) *International Perspectives of Festivals and Events: Paradigms of Analysis*, Oxford: Butterworth-Heinemann, pp. 149–158.

Xiao, H. and Smith, S.L.J. (2004) 'Residents' perceptions of Kitchener-Waterloo Oktoberfest: an inductive analysis', *Event Management*, 8(3): 161–175.

Xie, P.E. (2004) 'Visitors' perceptions of authenticity at a rural heritage festival: a case study', *Event Management*, 8: 151–160.

Xu, H., Wan, X. and Fan, X. (2014) 'Rethinking authenticity in the implementation of China's heritage conservation: the case of Hongcun Village', *Tourism Geographies*, 16(5): 799–811.

Yasmeen, G. (2006) *Bangkok's Foodscape: Public Eating, Gender Relations and Urban Change*, Bangkok: White Lotus.

Yeoman, I., McMahon-Beattie, U., Fields, K., Albrecht, J. and Meethan, K. (eds) (2015) *The Future of Food Tourism: Foodies, Experiences, Exclusivity, Visions and Political Capital*, Bristol: Channel View.

Part II

Local food systems, tourism and trajectories of regional development

2 Value creation in sustainable food networks

The role of tourism

Jan-Henrik Nilsson

Introduction

For decades, most parts of Europe have been facing large-scale restructuring in agriculture, leading to decrease in employment opportunities and population decline in rural areas. Larger production units, specialisation and increasing use of technology have improved productivity. Only a small portion of the continent's population are now capable of feeding us all. In the post-war period, this progress was supported by national governments and the European Union as a means to improve food security (Emanuelsson 2009; Johansson 2011). It took decades for the downsides for rural regions to become visible. Since 2000, the common agricultural policy has focussed on rural development. Issues related to sustainability and preservation of small-scale farming have become prioritised in national and European policies (European Union 2012; Regeringskansliet 2015). In many parts of Europe, tourism is now increasingly viewed as one possible strategy to improve social and economic sustainability in rural areas. Tourism represents a new way of viewing the countryside, from being areas for primary production to becoming "landscapes of experience". Despite this shift in orientation, food production is still very much in focus. However, recent developments in food tourism open up for new form of value creation in the relationship between agriculture and tourism (Hjalager & Richards 2002; Croce & Perri 2010; Hall & Gössling 2013).

The combination of food production and tourism experiences create special possibilities for rural areas for developing food tourism. The efforts to promote food tourism as part of wider rural development strategies are very diverse and complex processes and involve actors on many geographical levels, from the European Union down to local communities (Eriksson 2013). The European Union emphasise tourism as one of its prioritised strategies to encourage rural restructuring; food tourism is an important part of this. Food tourism projects may also be a part of wider strategies aimed at region building or cross-border cooperation, for instance, as a part of Inter-reg projects (Nilsson, Eskilsson & Ek 2010). However, most of the projects encouraged and sponsored by the European Union take place within national and regional structures.

In Sweden, the Ministry of Rural Development (Regeringskansliet) has put considerable resources into a strategy called *Sverige – det nya matlandet* ("Sweden – the new country of food"), which started in 2007. It communicates the 'government's vision to create growth and employment' (Regeringskansliet 2012: 2) through ventures related to food, often in combination with tourism. The strategy focusses on five main fields of action: primary production, public sector food, food processing, food tourism and the restaurant business. The efforts are parts of the general rural development programme, co-financed by the national government and the European Union. In the period between January 2007 and June 2012, 2000 projects received financial support in the order of SEK 870 million, approx. €95 million (Regeringskansliet 2012). Although it is unclear how much of the support was targeted to tourism, the strategy can be said to represent a higher level of ambition in relation to food tourism than previously. Under the strategy, a number of regional projects aiming at developing regional food culture and food-related experiences are supported in cooperation with regional actors and regional government bodies. One such project is called "Food and experiences in the South East", covering the provinces of Småland and Öland in southern Sweden. This is the same area where the study presented in this chapter takes place (see also Chapter 3, this volume). There is thus an increasing political engagement in promoting food tourism as a means to strengthening small-scale rural development at the same time as economic, social and environmental sustainability is taken into consideration.

Food tourism takes place; local and regional networks create arenas where new forms of value creation are created. The importance of network building in food tourism is exemplified in Hjalager (2002) who analysed commercial relationships from a value chain perspective, which describes the 'development logic of gastronomy tourism' (2002: 32). She describes four different value orders, on different levels of complexity, in the relationship between food production, gastronomy and tourism. Three main aspects of tourism development play an important part in the value-creating processes described in all four value orders: network building, marketing and quality management (Bessière 1998). It is evident that food tourism is built up in relations between food producers, restaurants, tourists and a number of other local actors. Such relations are especially important for sustainable food systems, since ecological gastronomy to a large degree depends on deliveries of high-quality local products. Value creation in food tourism thus builds on relations in local networks (Hall 2004; see also Chapter 18, this volume).

Based on a study of ecological food tourism in south-east Sweden, the aim of this chapter is to describe and analyse how economic, social and ecological value is created in relations between food producers, restaurants and consumers, with a special emphasis on the role of tourism in value creation. The outline of this chapter will be as follows: First the study itself is presented along with the methods used. Thereafter the results are presented following four themes: market access, managing capacity and demand, environmental issues, and development strategies. In the conclusions, the various forms of value creation found in the study are summarised.

Methodology

The study includes producers (farms), restaurant owners and restaurant customers in south-eastern Sweden, in the provinces of Småland and Öland. This area has a size of about 30,700 km² with a population of a little under 800,000 inhabitants and is predominantly rural with a few small towns. There is only one city (Jönköping) with more than 100,000 inhabitants. The conditions for production, distribution and sales in restaurants are thus different from those in other parts of Europe. Conditions for agriculture also differ substantially within the region itself. The province of Småland consists to a large extent of uplands with poor soils and short growing seasons, whereas the island of Öland has a milder, maritime climate.

In total, 24 producers representing 20 businesses and 20 chefs representing as many restaurants were interviewed. Producers were identified with the help of the regional branches of LRF (Swedish Farmers Association) and KRAV, the national certification agency for ecological (equivalent to organic) producers, trade and restaurants. KRAV is a member of the International Federation of Organic Agriculture Movements (IFOAM). However, in addition to organic production, KRAV's vision is that food production should also be economically and socially sustainable. The criteria for the choice of producers were that they should graft their own produce and/or have direct – often farm – sales to individual consumers. Most of the producers included in the sample are consequently farmers, with one exception, a firm selling and processing game bought from hunters. Fourteen of the farms focus on meat production, mainly cattle and sheep, but also pigs, game and goats. Five farms focus on vegetable production, including niche products such as herbs or hawthorn. There are also three farms with dairy production, and six producing sausage, smoked ham or jams. The scale of production ranges from very small, generating part incomes, to large, involving 550 ha of arable land.

With regard to restaurants, public sector restaurants, that is, schools and day-care centres, were excluded; from the remaining ones, every third was chosen from a list provided by KRAV using a random selection approach, representing a broad variety of categories. There are six hotel restaurants, three of them belonging to large hotel chains. Eight of the restaurants have rural locations, the rest are situated in small or middle-sized towns. Out of the interviewed chefs, six were also the owners, and another nine had managerial positions. Finally, ten "ethical consumers" of ecologic food were identified based on snowball sampling. The consumers all have an active interest in food and gastronomy. They represent members of Slow Food and environmental organisations, participants in cooking classes and events, writers of food-related issues and teachers of home economics.

Out of 50 interviews, 25 were conducted face-to-face, whenever this was feasible (travel distances) or accepted by the respondents, and the remaining (25) interviews were carried out by phone. Interviews were semi-structured and conducted from April to June 2013. Interviews lasted between 30 and 90 minutes, and all were recorded and transcribed. There is an almost even gender distribution in the sample (30 men and 24 women), and the sample includes respondents aged 20 to 70. Responses were anonymous and using random Christian names in the presentation, respondents' identities were protected.

In the analysis, the interview material was organised according to four categories, as seen in the outline of the following section. The categories were developed inductively from the content (Spiggle 1994; Kvale 1997; Silverman 2010). Thus, the following section does not report the answers by the groups of interviewees separately. Instead different aspects of the value-creating process are reported, focussing on the relations between the three groups of interviewees. Thereby, the systemic approach of the study is emphasised.

Results

Market access

The producers examined in this project are either reprocessing their products or selling directly to consumers. This way they follow a strategy that differs from the conventional way that Swedish farmers have organised their market relations. Agriculture in Sweden has for a century been organised in a number of large-scale cooperatives owned by the farmers, in businesses like dairies, mills, slaughterhouses and saw mills (Alvstam & Törnqvist 1986). The farmers' produce is still mostly sold through these businesses, basically disconnecting farmers from consumers. Following the deregulation of agriculture around 1990 (Rabinowicz 2006), opening up Sweden for large-scale imports, the cooperatives have become more commercialised, often merged with international businesses. This tendency has further strengthened their emphasis on large-scale production.

Some of the producers in this study sell parts of their produce through the cooperatives or similar large-scale businesses. For others, their volumes are too small to justify a detour by lorry and the price offered too low to make it worthwhile. The opposite is true for some large producers: 'We have negotiated such a good price with Scan (the national meat cooperative) that it is not profitable to sell locally' (Karin). The quasi monopoly situation is to the advantage of large-scale producers and large-scale retail. Many farmers state that 'logistics is the worst problem' (Erik); the main logistics companies are reluctant to carry small batches. Those producers who make deliveries to retailers have similar problems; the larger chains do not want to go outside their conventional distributers. Instead, other solutions have to be sought.

Although the picture is very diverse and the individual producers are very versatile, two distribution strategies dominate among respondents. They either organise distribution on their own or they try to sell as much as possible on the farms. There are also signs that new forms of cooperation are developing. Some of the mid-scale producers in Småland have organised a common distribution system through a haulage contractor (Anders). Other networks are based on personal relations; producers bring deliveries for one another when possible. Distance and irregularity are however large problems, forcing most of them to do their own deliveries.

One of the strategies that have been emphasised in recent policy work (Regeringskansliet 2012) is to build closer networks between producers and restaurants, thereby increasing profitability for producers, highlight local products and dishes, and raise the level of local innovation. For the producers, the advantage of selling to restaurants compared to direct sales to consumers lies in the volumes (Gunilla). It is also possible to get a higher price than through conventional sales channels.

When speaking with chefs and restaurant managers, they are all in favour of serving ecological food, but there are a series of obstacles. The main obstacle for mainstream restaurants is price, 'It's a very tough business, margins are very tight' (Charlie). These restaurants say they can't push price levels enough to support higher prices on, for instance, vegetables and meat. For some of them (even though they are certified), the value added is unclear, 'why would I pay 20 kronor more for pork?' (Lars). Upmarket restaurants are different is this respect. They have generally a higher level of knowledge and are able to present the advantages with ecologic food to their guests. This makes it possible to charge a higher price. Otherwise, the economic advantages of locally produced food as recorded by restaurant managers were mainly connected to market relations. It was seen as a means to improve the restaurants' image and as something on which to build the restaurants' storytelling (Edvard). For those restaurants which profile themselves as local and innovative, the ecological aspects become parts of their story.

There are a number of factors encouraging consumers to buy ecological food directly from local producers. Most answers highlight a wish to trace the origins of the food people are eating, to know where it comes from. The acts of buying directly from farmers and visiting farms give consumers both actual knowledge about the food and a sense of authenticity. The superior taste of ecological products is also frequently mentioned; ecology and taste are closely connected. In this context, taste is influenced by the experience of being in place and by relations to producers (Doris). Consumers were also emphasising reduced impacts on the environment, food security and their concern for the small farmers and the local community (even when it is not their own local community).

A couple of the interviewed consumers state that there is a problem finding regionally produced food in cities. The availability of regional ecologic food in conventional shops and supermarkets is limited (Gustav); and as some producers mentioned, there is a problem with visibility (Leif). Large producers and distributers often get advantageous display since they often are allowed to unpack their goods on the shelves. Minor products are squeezed to less visible sites. Most of the ecologically certified food sold in conventional shops are not regionally produced; with the exception of root vegetables and meat, it is mostly imported (observations in Lund and Helsingborg).

In the south of Sweden, there are irregular farmers' markets in summer and autumn; and in the larger towns, there are a few shops specialised in ecological food. The marketing channels of regional ecological food thus seem to target a specific "conscious" segment. Young city people, without access to a car, have few opportunities to buy regional ecological food (Ellen). Distribution of regional ecological food to cities is, therefore, an urgent issue if markets are to increase. Not the least because city people, for various reasons, are likely to be willing to choose ecological food if it is available locally. Solving that problem would also reduce unnecessary driving to the countryside to purchase food.

Managing capacity and demand

Agriculture is a highly seasonal business, especially in high latitudes where the growing and grazing seasons are limited. This makes it difficult for small producers to manage continuous deliveries because the supply requirements can differ too much. Unpredictable deliveries make planning difficult for some restaurant managers; others are more flexible and manage to adjust their menus to supplies. To some producers, restaurant managers appear to have a double-sided attitude towards local food. They speak highly of it but have difficulties with day-to-day management, for instance, to handle a large number of suppliers (Britta, Quintus). Another important issue is simply related to the constitution of animal bodies, in particular beef. Restaurants tend to have high demand on the "better" parts of the animal, parts that only make up a small portion of the body: 'Restaurants are tricky customers. They want 20 kilos of fillet of beef, and that's not available on a cattle. Yes, they are a bit inflexible, only wanting some pieces like fillet, entrecote or sirloin' (Fredrik). The producer, on the other hand, needs to sell all of it; otherwise, it becomes impossible to manage (Nils). One reason for this mismatch, according to some producers, is a lack of skills in many kitchens. Some chefs confirm that they are accustomed to use ready-mades and other industrial products; many seldom work from basic ingredients (Anna). Thus, the semi-industrial restaurant system, together with all the year-round availability of food products through large-scale distribution systems, seems to work against innovation based on local deliveries.

The interviewed "conscious" consumers act very differently from restaurant chefs in this respect. One common denominator among them is the fact that they all cook their meals from basic ingredients and never use pre-fabricated food. Most interviewees also displayed a high level of knowledge about food and cooking. They also mentioned seasonality as a quality, 'it is a good thing that Swedish strawberries are only available in the summer' (Carina). This means that this is a group of people which is potentially very interesting for producers; dealing with them makes it easier to match supply and demand. Many of them use a broad spectrum of ingredients when cooking – a large variety of roots and vegetables, as well as different parts of the animal.

The most prominent values of the relationship between restaurants and producers are tied to the human sides of their relations, and to the concern of the local community, of the social economy (see Pietrykowski 2004). These aspects are expressed in terms of personal relations, friendship, loyalty, trust and security. Producers are trusted to deliver as promised. The chefs can be sure that the quality is as expected. It seems like the producers cannot afford to let their regular customers down. Personal relations are particularly important in relation to food security; 'It is important to me [as chef] how the animal lives, and that the transports are not too long. That's why it is important to me to have personal contact with the people I am dealing with. I trust them to do a good job' (Petter). Trust is closely related to personal knowledge; people simply trust people they know.

The producers perceive the same kind of values when making direct contact with consumers at farmers' market, at festivals and when people are visiting farms and farm shops. Interestingly, these kinds of contacts are also highly valued by consumers. It is an experience in itself to visit the place where the animals are reared whose meat you are purchasing. Producers also have the possibility to improve their margins by circumventing middle men and selling directly to consumers. Out of the 20 producers in the study, 12 have shops on their farms. A couple of meat producers sold directly to consumers with the means of meat boxes, ready-made 20–50-kg packages of meat sold at a reasonable price. One obvious problem with delivery directly to consumers through these channels is the time consumption for farmers. There is therefore a difficult balance between managing production and marketing.

Environmental issues

The production of food is a major contributor of greenhouse gas (GHG) emissions. From a Nordic perspective, the largest contributors are related to meat production and transportation (Björklund, Holmgren & Johansson 2009). Despite the fact that this relationship has been known for quite a long time, the awareness was limited among all three categories of respondents. The main attitude was to place environmental problems outside their own realm. Many producers seem to think that nature-based production per se is environmentally friendly. Some even denounce the fact that cattle contribute to GHG emissions: 'it is all seen from the authorities perspective, they have got it into their minds that cow shit comes with gases and stuff; but we don't see any environmental problems. We don't have any heavy emissions … we heat the smoke [for smokers] with coal, and coal is not poisonous' (Pamela). The interviews with restaurant managers and chefs show a great variation in their level of knowledge and reflection of environmental issues. The relation between food consumption, mainly in relation to meat, and climate change was not mentioned at all. However, chefs took a broader perspective on the relationship between their businesses and the environment. They were raising issues like cleaning procedures, use of detergents, transports and waste management. The interviewed consumers were more aware of the relation between food and the environments than the other two categories, but still only a few spoke directly about the impact of their own consumption. The only problems all three groups brought forward are the roles of transportation and waste.

When consumers were asked about their thoughts on ecology and food quality, the answers differed. Most of them related food quality with health, both in relation to their own choice of what to buy and in relation to the choice between ecological products and conventional ones. Ecological food is considered healthier; there are fewer additives and less remnants of polluting substances. When buying meat, ethical considerations concerning animal welfare, transports and its possible impact on health and quality dominated the responses. In relation to vegetables, the impact of artificial fertilisers and pesticides was in focus. However, the main division in these consumers' minds was not between ecological and conventional alternatives but between what they considered good or bad food. Most of them think of good food as something made properly at home, based on basic ingredients such as vegetables, roots, fish and good meat. Bad food, on the other hand, is fast food, ready-made dishes, sweets, cookies, crisps and soft drinks.

Some of the respondents preferred ecological food because of its superior quality, 'an ecological carrot tastes completely different' (Ivar), or 'I have sometimes bought cheap [imported] fillet of pork, but it was impossible to cook' (Hugo). The main arguments for choosing ecological food, which many of the consumers did when possible, are more altruistic. Consumers pointed at their general concern for the environment, at animal rights issues such as the issues around transports, and at their wishes to support small ecological farmers and producers. In these discussions, it became obvious that most of them make strong connections between ecological food and locally produced food, even if the latter is conventionally produced. The consumers' views on ecological and organic foods are thus fairly complex; some of them are speaking about making compromises between various factors in their purchase. Apart from availability, price is mentioned by many, especially young people, as an obstacle to buying ecologic food, 'I prefer buying certified food, but it is sometimes too expensive' (Ellen).

Besides the fact that local food is considered qualitatively better, the interviewees favour it in support of local, regional or even national farmers. Some, especially those who had close ties to the countryside, emphasised the role of food production for protecting the traditional rural landscape. From these interviews, it is evident that food quality, and even more food safety, is closely connected to territoriality. With few exceptions, respondents always tried to buy Swedish food when available. There was a similar attachment to regional brands, 'I always buy milk from the regional dairy' (Carina). Distances and transportation were only discussed by two of the consumers; the rest spoke in terms of territorial units, using traditional regional brand names. Only one consumer was discussing distances at any depth, questioning the relevance of national borders in connection with regional food, 'Italian apples are often better to buy, they come by train, not by lorry as the Swedish ones' (Ivar). Objectively speaking, this is highly relevant since distances from the respondents' places of residence to Denmark and northern Germany are shorter than to the north of Sweden.

Although the guests seldom specifically ask about the food, they appreciate when the origin of the ingredients is mentioned in conversation with the staff or on the menus; they also appreciate when the restaurant is certified. They like going to places that are favouring ecologic food, but it is seldom their main reason for choosing a particular restaurant. Instead other qualities are mentioned by the consumers. They are generally very critical to the standard of average Swedish restaurants. They are looking for restaurants which display high-quality food and service, but without being luxurious: 'It is some sort of craftsmanship I am looking for when I eat other people's food [...] the ability to mix and bring forward flavours that I can't manage myself' (Adam). 'They don't want to pay for food they would have cooked better themselves' (Gustav). Other issues like style, location and image are of course also important for the guests. None of the guests mentioned price as an important factor other than in relation to the extremes; they avoid both luxury and cheap places: 'I would never pay 99 crowns for a piece of pork in one of those cheap places' (Filippa).

Interestingly, most of the respondents from the restaurant sector did not distinguish between ecological food and local food when environmental issues were discussed. This is contrary to the Swedish certification system, KRAV, which is mainly concerned with environmental aspects. According to the restaurant managers, their guests have a higher interest in local than in ecological food. Only one group of consumers ask specifically for ecological certification – the corporate customers (Fritjof). A number of companies and organisations have policies favouring purchasing certified goods and services, making them important ethical consumers. This is particularly interesting for hotels and restaurants with meeting facilities.

From the interviews with producers, it became evident that certification is a very controversial issue. The producers' views on KRAV, the dominant Swedish actor, were very much divided. All agree that KRAV's position in the Swedish market is so strong that you cannot ignore it. However, the certification process is criticised by the producers on three different points. The first has to do with the rigidity of regulations. Many farmers feel that they cannot act properly in case something unexpected occurs: 'I am not allowed to buy ensilage from my [conventional] neighbour when I ran out of fodder; instead I have to transport it from far away' (Camilla). The general opinion points in the direction that KRAV sometimes makes it difficult to be ecological; they should look at practicalities instead of being too strict on rules. Some of these complaints have to do with the fact that the transformation from conventional to ecologic farming makes you more vulnerable. As a result, some producers are sceptical. Two producers and one restaurant have left the organisation, and another producer has plans to do the same. A large degree of producers reported to have an ambition to be as ecological as possible, but without following all rules set by KRAV. Another line of criticism concerns the costs, paper work and control. KRAV is seen as a costly and bureaucratic organisation that goes too far in their ambition to control. On the other hand, there was one group of producers that criticised KRAV from the opposite direction. They urged them to be stricter and not allow any compromise. Interestingly, one ecologic producer made an advertisement just before Christmas 2013 where their stricter rules were compared with KRAV rules (Sydsvenskan 2013). To chefs KRAV is much less controversial; in general they perceive the system as trustworthy, but also as a bit too bureaucratic. There are a lot of forms to fill in, and some rules are considered unnecessary. Some of them complain about how KRAV supervisors constantly question everything; some even compare it to trespassing (Niklas). Most consumers think quite highly of the KRAV system; many of them use the term KRAV more or less as a synonym for "ecological". Of course, they seldom see the downsides.

Development strategies

'It is impossible to make money on production [of vegetables]' (Johan). This statement from one of the interviewed farmers exemplifies a fundamental concern for most producers. In general, prices on agricultural products have gone down relatively following improved productivity, increased economies of scale and price pressure due to international competition. With contemporary low prices, small producers have difficulties in surviving on production alone: 'If I would sell my 33 tons [of vegetables] directly to corporate buyers, I would not make ends meet' (Brita). There are two basic ways to solve this problem. The first is by moving up the value chain by re-processing the products or developing a service out of the product. The second way is to get in direct contact with the consumers and thereby avoid costly middle men. Of course, these two approaches may be combined.

Having moved up the value chain, it is essential to target the right customers. According to most of the respondents, the main part of people buying directly from producers, in farm shops, at festivals and farmers market come from outside the region and are middle-class. 'Most of our customers are middle aged city people, and Danes with summer houses' (Camilla). 'The customers are educated people, many with high incomes [...] 80 per cent academics. They belong to a category who can afford to eat well' (David). On the other hand, many producers complain that it is very difficult to get local people interested in local and especially in ecologic food. For some it is probably a matter of price, but it is also a cultural thing. 'Here in Vimmerby, people don't seem to be keen on paying for what they eat. They only care about the price' (Karin).

According to the producers, local people are not very interested in novelties, 'there is no tradition of eating vegetables in Småland' (Quintus). Beef and pork is easier to sell locally, but people are sceptical of lamb and wild boar (Nils, Pamela). This makes niche products, and particularly ecologic food, very dependent on outsiders. 'Now [in June], tourists from big cities have arrived and all the ecologic food is gone immediately' (Johan). The supply of high-quality food outside of large towns seems to be very dependent on tourism and the seasonal patterns of tourism. There is also a close connection between tourism and the supply of up-market restaurants in Sweden. Outside the three metropolitan regions (Stockholm, Gothenburg and Malmö) a very high percentage of restaurants listed in the national guide of prominent restaurants (the "White Guide") are located in tourist regions on the coast or in the mountain chain (Nilsson 2013). There are thus good reasons for producers and restaurants to target outsiders first if they want to work with niche products.

One way of adding value to food products is to relate to older and 'purer' ways of cooking and processing. In line with this, we can see a re-emergence of traditional dishes and products. Traditional cheese, the regional cheesecake, products made from brown beans and the local fermented sausage (*isterband*) are some examples of this kind of innovation by heritage revival. Interestingly, there is only one product seen in the material that is alien to local tradition, hawthorn. Despite that, marmalades, syrups and juices from these little sour berries seem to be rather successful products.

Development is also seen in diversification; it is only very large farms that can survive as conventional producers in the old way. Farmers rebuild parts of their buildings into accommodation for visitors in agro-tourism; they develop new forms of market channels such as farm shops and new experiences on the farms and various kinds of events. A majority of producers emphasised the importance of food festivals at Easter, at harvest time in September and at Christmas. Especially in connection with the harvest festival in Öland, there were a lot of events held on the farms in cooperation between various kinds of producers. Apart from these common events, many farms have their own ways of attracting visitors with the help of minor events. Most of these relate to simple things like showing animals to children. For many children in cities, it is exciting with lamb, pigs and chicken.

The consumers display different patterns of consumption depending of where they are consuming 'local' food. When they visit farms and producers in their own region, their shopping is guided by their needs for foods, that is, they are buying vegetables and meat for their own consumption. But, when visiting other regions and countries, they start to behave like tourists. They buy local specialities at markets or at farms: 'buying wine directly from a cellar in France – that's heaven!' (Ivar). They are also actively looking for regional food at restaurants; they want to try something special when they are away from home. In this respect, their views of farmers and consumers confirm one another; tourists are vital for sales.

Public authorities are in various ways trying to promote innovation in local food production, not the least through network building and product development. Most respondents are generally positive to these initiatives; especially the initiatives taken by the provincial governments (länsstyrelse) were praised for their endurance. One critical point was that there were too many projects around. Although, for instance, EU projects might be reasonable as such, they are too often short-lived (Anders, Leif). Some respondents express a certain fatigue with projects after having "wasted" a lot of time on short-lived projects.

Although public authorities, at all geographic levels, aim at promoting innovation in rural sustainable food systems, there are still a series of institutional obstacles raised by the authorities which may have serious impacts on small businesses. For example, health inspectors try to enforce very costly regulations in cafés and shops; and cash registers are going to be compulsory, which is quite costly for a small farm shop. One of the farmers organised a "pig safari" in the summer, as a family event. This raised the attention of someone at the provincial government, who demanded the farmer to pay a 6000 Sek (€700) fee for "public display of animals" (Rosemarie). Restrictions on sale of alcohol are also a problem for many small cafes and restaurants. Sweden has a restrictive system controlling sales of alcoholic beverages, which involves a state monopoly on retail sales and strict control of licensing. Licenses are normally quite costly (fees differ between municipalities) and there is a series of regulations to follow. The most bizarre outcome of the alcohol regulations is that wine farmers are not allowed to sell their own wine on the farms or in their restaurants (Malm 2010; Malm, Gössling & Hall 2013). This way, producers are deprived of a potentially very valuable source of income from their own production.

Conclusions

The purpose of this chapter was to analyse value creation in sustainable food systems and especially the impact of tourism on such systems. Based on the study in southern Sweden, we will first draw some general conclusions about how value is created in these systems. Thereafter, the role of tourism in these value-creating processes will be explained and discussed. Conceptually, sustainable food networks would consist of systems of actors such as producers, processers, retailers, restaurants and consumers who develop and share commercial and non-commercial relations in the context of food. In this case, we are discussing networks that lack single dominant actors, even if distributers and retail chains are able to set agendas that have large indirect effects on the actions of producers and restaurants. Both the public sector and non-governmental organisations, such as Länsstyrelsen and LRF, are also important players in the networks, acting as cohesive factors and resource bases for innovation and development. The networks are at the same time initiated from political actors and spontaneous.

This study shows that a considerable level of value creation takes place in these relations; and even if these relations are multi-facetted, it is possible to establish a few categories. There is obviously a great deal of *economic* value to be gained through cooperation. For producers and restaurants there are advantages in coordinating distribution, marketing and activities like events. Furthermore, margins can be increased if producers are able to take control over distribution. This is also important in order to reduce the kind of vulnerability caused by being dependent on large distributers and chain stores. To consumers, local food systems often give opportunities to buy in bulk, for instance, large bags of potatoes or boxes of meat; this way they are able to buy high-quality goods at a reasonable price.

Social and *relational* forms of value were put forward by many respondents as very valuable outcomes of sustainable food systems. This is, however, a highly complex category, articulated in terms of authenticity, personal knowledge, friendship, kinship and a sense of common responsibility for the region. To a large part, the value of these kinds of relations could be explained in terms of social capital; trust was a term mentioned by many chefs when explaining the advantages of working with local producers. Cooperation in the networks examined in this study is also important for creating arenas for learning and exchange of knowledge.

It is a very complex and contradictory matter to discuss value creation in *ecological* terms; impressions point in different directions. For consumers, the ecologic value is obvious. Through local food systems, they gain better access to tasty, healthy and secure products. This can by no means be taken for granted in peripheral parts of Sweden, regions which are very dependent on large-scale distribution systems. Another positive effect of ecological food production lies in its contribution to biodiversity and the maintenance of the cultural landscape. Aesthetic elements could thus be added to the ecological values. There are numerous pieces of evidence in the study of how cultural heritage practices promote diversity in production and supply. These kinds of relations may thus act as counterforces against centralised simplification. There are, on the other hand, aspects of these systems that are more problematic from an ecologic perspective. The worst problems are related to meat production and transportation. Even ecological meat production, especially beef and lamb, contribute to climate change at the same time as there are many advantages compared to conventional meat production, that is, in animal welfare and landscape protection. The distribution systems are rather inefficient, to a large extent depending on the peripheral character of the region. Another problem, which is seen in central regions as well, is that consumers are dependent on cars to access producers (Andersson & Johnsson 2013). Unfortunately, the system is thus based on highly unsustainable forms of transport (Hall & Gössling 2013).

In this study, a pattern has become visible, showing that local ecological food is produced, sometimes processed and sold locally but, to a large extent, consumed by tourists. *The impact of tourism* on food systems is thus very significant. Most importantly, tourism increases the demand on sustainable food products, especially on high-value goods and niche products. The study has shown that a considerable part of the market consists of urban people who are prepared to pay a premium for high quality and, for various reasons, find it important to support small-scale production. These groups of people are also essential for the development of events such as food festivals and farmers' markets. Interestingly, the nature of the local changes here. Tourists buy food at farm sales where it is local to the producers, but not for the tourists. Long-distance transport is still part of the transaction; the difference is that the tourists, instead of the food, are doing the transportation to their homes.

This study has also identified tourism as an important driver of *innovation* in the food systems. Tourists are prepared to try new and other things than most locals. Without tourism it would be difficult to find a market for things like lamb, wild boar, a wide range of ecologic vegetables, farm-made cheese or products made from hawthorn. Tourists also seem to be more influenced by recent trends in gastronomy, such as the growing interest in heritage ingredients and dishes influenced by the new Nordic cuisine. The new Nordic cuisine emphasised purity and freshness, seasonality, health concerns, use of regional ingredients, innovative use of traditions, and ecological awareness (Det nye nordiske køkken 2004). This interest in the genuinely Nordic follows a streak of Romanticism about wilderness, remoteness and rurality (cf. Dahlgren 2010; Redzhepi 2010). Contrary to these tendencies, the study has found the locals to be much less interested in local and sustainable food. They could to a large extent be viewed as an unused resource. Involving the locals in regional food projects and trying to enhance their level of interest seems to be a major challenge for the future. To summarise: tourism could be thought of as a necessary prerequisite for the existence of

74   *Jan-Henrik Nilsson*

sustainable food networks in peripheral regions. However, in order to make these systems prosperous and sustainable in the long run, it seems necessary to develop the home market.

References

Alvstam, C.-G. and Törnqvist, G. (eds) (1986) *Svenskt näringsliv i geografiskt perspektiv*, Malmö: Liber.
Andersson, R. and Johnsson, E. (2013) 'Gastronomiska nätverk – en fallstudie på Kullahalvön', Bachelor's thesis, Department of Service Management and Service Studies, Lund University, Sweden.
Bessière, J. (1998) 'Local development and heritage: traditional food and cuisine as tourist attractions in rural areas', *Sociologia Ruralis*, 38(1): 21–34.
Björklund, J., Holmgren, P. and Johansson, S. (2009) *Mat & klimat*, Stockholm: Medströms förlag.
Croce, E. and Perri, G. (2010) *Food and Wine Tourism: Integrating Food, Travel and Territory*, Wallingford: CABI.
Dahlgren, M. (2010) *Det naturliga köket*, Stockholm: Norstedts.
Det nye nordiske køkken (2004) *Nynordiskmad*. Available online: <www.nynordiskmad. org> (accessed 11 July 2015).
Emanuelsson, U. (2009) *The Rural Landscapes of Europe: How Man Has Shaped European Nature*, Stockholm: Formas.
Eriksson, B.E. (2013) 'Aktörer i samverkan: ett matturistiskt fält växer fram', in J. Syssner and L. Kvarnström (eds) *Det turistiska fältet och dess aktörer*, Lund: Studentlitteratur.
European Union (2012) *The Common Agricultural Policy – A Story to be Continued*. Available online: <ec.europa.eu> (accessed 11 July 2015).
Hall, C.M. (2004) 'Small firms and wine and food tourism in New Zealand: issues of collaboration, clusters and lifestyles', in R. Thomas (ed.) *Small Firms in Tourism: International Perspectives*, Oxford: Elsevier, pp. 167–181.
Hall, C.M. and Gössling, S. (eds) (2013) *Sustainable Culinary Systems. Local Foods, Innovation, Tourism and Hospitality*, London: Routledge.
Hjalager, A.-M. (2002) 'A typology of gastronomy tourism', in A.-M. Hjalager and G. Richards (eds) *Tourism and Gastronomy*, London: Routledge, pp. 21–36.
Hjalager, A.-M. and Richards, G. (eds) (2002) *Tourism and Gastronomy*, London: Routledge.
Johansson, K. (2011) *Sveriges första femton år som medlem i EU. Jordbrukets utveckling*. Jordbruksverket, Rapport 2011:33.
Kvale, S. (1997) *Den kvalitativa forskningsintervjun*, Lund: Studentlitteratur.
Malm, K. (2010) 'Vinturism i Sverige. Hinder och möjligheter för svenska vinodlare,' Bachelor thesis, Linneus University, Sweden.
Malm, K., Gössling, S. and Hall, C.M. (2013) 'Regulatory and institutional barriers to new business development: the case of Swedish wine tourism', in C.M. Hall and S. Gössling (eds) *Sustainable Culinary Systems: Local Foods, Innovation, Tourism and Hospitality*, Abingdon: Routledge, pp. 241–255.
Nilsson, J.H. (2013) 'Nordic eco-gastronomy', in C.M. Hall and S. Gössling (eds) *Sustainable Culinary Systems: Local Foods, Innovation, Tourism and Hospitality*, Abingdon: Routledge, pp. 189–204.

Nilsson, J.H., Eskilsson, L. and Ek, R. (2010) 'Creating cross-border destinations: inter-reg programmes and regionalisation in the Baltic Sea area', *Scandinavian Journal of Hospitality and Tourism*, 10(2): 153–172.

Pietrykowski, B. (2004) 'You are what you eat: the social economy of the Slow Food Movement', *Review of Social Economy*, 62(3): 307–321.

Rabinowicz, E. (2006) 'The Swedish agricultural policy reform of 1990', in D. Blandford and B. Hill (eds) *Policy Reform and Adjustment in the Agricultural Sectors of Developed Countries*, Wallingford: CABI, pp. 105–122.

Redzhepi, R. (2010) *NOMA. Tid och plats i det nordiska köket*, Göteborg: Tukan förlag.

Regeringskansliet (2012) *Sverige – det nya matlandet. Nya jobb genom god mat och upplevelser*, Stockholm: Regeringskansliet.

Regeringskansliet (2015) *Sweden – Rural Development Programme*. Available online: <www.jordbruksverket.se> (accessed 11 July 2015).

Silverman, D. (2010) *Doing Qualitative Research*, 3rd edn, London: Sage.

Spiggle, S. (1994) 'Analysis and interpretation of qualitative data in consumer research', *Journal of Consumer Research*, 21(3): 491–503.

Sydsvenskan (2013) 'Ängavallen farm shop (Advertisement)', *Sydsvenskan*, 8 December.

3 Developing regional food systems

A case study of restaurant–customer relationships in Sweden

Stefan Gössling and C. Michael Hall

Introduction

The interest in interrelationships between regional development, tourism and food has grown rapidly in recent years, as national and regional governments, destinations and agricultural organisations have started to see a potential in food products as a means to foster regional economic development. In the context of tourism, expectations have been voiced that local and regional foodstuffs can have more important roles in the marketing of destinations, add value to guest experiences and lead to self-reinforcing cycles of economic development, from which farmers and restaurants can profit. However, while there are various initiatives by regional government bodies to further develop links between tourism, farming and restaurants, only limited attention has been paid to potential barriers: Are there reasons why chefs or restaurant owners would rather not use local or organic produce? And, with regard to consumers, are tourists interested in local foodstuffs and would they be willing to pay premiums for local food products? This chapter addresses these interlinkages with a focus on restaurants and customers (tourists) in south-eastern Sweden.

Regional development, food and tourism

Destinations and regional organisations are increasingly seeking to develop local food products and culinary experiences, also with the objective to enhance the viability of local food production (Boyne, Hall & Williams 2003; Hall & Gössling 2013; see also Chapter 1, this volume). As outlined by Everett and Aitchison (2008), such local food products may incur a potentially higher willingness to pay (WTP) by tourists, attract wealthier tourist segments and hence allow lengthening of the season, as greater profit margins make operations more viable. Telfer and Wall (1996) add that employment of local staff can further increase food linkages, underlining the potential advantage of employment generation and local food expertise development. A number of publications has also emphasised the potential of local food experiences to contribute to sustainable development, to help maintain regional identities and to support agricultural diversification (Hall, Johnson & Mitchell 2000; Hall 2004; Knowd 2006; Clark & Chabrel 2007; Sims 2009). Everett and Slocum (2013) conclude that in light of these perceived benefits, there is a great potential to develop food tourism, which is now generally seen as a vehicle for regional development, strengthening local production through backward linkages in tourism supply chain partnerships (Telfer & Wall 1996; Montanari 2009; Renko, Renko & Polonijo 2010). In rural areas where food production constitutes a large percentage of the economic output, food tourism is considered to offer new opportunities to promote and distribute local produce while enhancing visitor experiences through the expression of community identity and cultural distinctiveness (Rusher 2003). Taken together, these benefits represent a strong argument to develop food–tourism relationships.

From the tourists' viewpoint, food is now widely recognised as an essential part of the tourism experience (Hjalager & Richards 2002; Boniface 2003; Hall et al. 2003; Hall & Sharples 2008). Locally distinctive food can be important both as a tourist attraction in itself and in helping to establish and shape the image of a destination (Hall et al. 2003; Cohen & Avieli 2004; du Rand & Heath 2006; Hall & Mitchell 2008). The market potential for gastronomic tourism has been outlined in various publications (Hjalager & Richards 2002; Hall 2003; Hall et al. 2003; du Rand & Heath 2006), and a wide range of food tourism typologies and food tourism phenomena have been discussed and studied (Everett & Slocum 2013): Agritourism (also farm tourism) focuses on farm visits for food purchases, as well as stimulation/experience and education/knowledge (Busby & Rendle 2000; Veeck, Chee & Veeck 2006). Culinary tourism includes upscale food experiences, but also exploratory eating of unknown foods as a way of encountering or consuming other places (Gyimóthy & Mykletun 2009). Food-based attractions include special events, such as food festivals or cooking holidays (Hall & Sharples 2008; Di Domenico & Miller 2012). Farmers' markets, local (regional) menus, as well as locally grown foods and beverages have become important attractions (Telfer & Wall 2000; Torres 2002; Hall 2013; Malm, Gössling & Hall 2013). These examples of food-related events suggest that the interest in food has grown and that efforts to more strategically develop food products as an important part of the destination image would tap into this trend and have considerable appeal for tourists.

In some destinations, initiatives have been successful in creating culinary profiles (Marsden, Banks & Bristow 2000; Venn et al. 2006), while also contributing to regional development. For example, in Norway, regional food producers have been financially supported by the government to develop new and marketable food products from locally produced raw materials. In investigating one such local food brand, Rørosmat ("Food from Røros"), Lange-Vik and Idsø (2013) found that 90 per cent of the production was exported out of the region, a sign of the considerable success of the food network, which had become known and appreciated even outside the region itself. Success factors for this network were low debt levels, cooperation between different producers in a food cluster, high levels of re-investment in the brand and the interest among hotels and restaurants to offer local foods and to emphasise local and traditional food experiences in their marketing and storytelling. Notably, proudness over local foods communicated by chefs apparently had an important role in creating an interest of visitors in these food products and to increase WTP. These findings indicate the complexity in developing food networks and achieving regional development benefits through food in tourism, given that successful initiatives demand cooperation between food producers and restaurants, while also requiring a considerable interest in food on the side of tourists. These interrelationships are the focus of this chapter.

Tourism development and food in Sweden

Tourism's economic importance in Sweden is comparably small, given the sector's contribution of about 2.6–2.8 per cent to GDP (Tillväxtverket 2015). In absolute terms, tourism accounted for SEK 286.5 billion in trade volume (€31 billion, exchange value July 1, 2014), a volume that has increased by 78.9 per cent since 2000 in nominal prices. Yet, the sector's export value is, at SEK 96.5 billion (€10.5 billion), higher than the value of iron and steel exports (SEK 50.1 billion; €5.4 billion) or food exports (SEK58.9 billion; €6.4 billion). In terms of employment, tourism generated 159,200 jobs in 2014, an increase of almost 22 per cent over 2000. Most of this growth is a result of employment in hotels and restaurants, where more than 25,000 new jobs were created since 2000, also reflecting a higher household expenditure on tourism consumption, with Swedish households' tourism spending increasing by 75 per cent in the period 2000–2014 (Tillväxtverket 2015).

The observed growth trend in tourism is in line with industry and government ambitions to significantly develop the sector. Tourism actors in Sweden expect tourism to increasingly contribute to GDP and job creation (Tillväxtverket 2012), and in 2010, Svensk Turism AB, an organisation representing 10,000 Swedish tourist companies and owning 50 per cent of Sweden's marketing organisation Visit Sweden, presented a vision and strategy to double Swedish tourism within 10 years. The National Strategy for Swedish Tourism is now widely accepted as an important instrument for national, regional and local development, with a vision to '… with a focus on sustainability double Swedish tourism within ten years to become the country's most important economic sector and to turn Sweden into a self-evident choice for global travellers' (Svensk Turism AB 2010). Svensk Turism AB's (2010) stated goal is for the sector to reach a turnover of SEK 500 billion (€54 billion) and an additional 100,000 men-years of employment by 2020, compared to 2010 (Svensk Turism AB 2010). To achieve this, the focus is on the development of destinations.

Even though the government's food strategy is not directly linked to tourism, it is a potentially important aspect of Sweden's tourism development strategy. The government's strategy to turn Sweden into a recognised food country has been presented under the motto "Sweden, the new food country" (Sverige det nya matlandet) (Regeringskansliet 2010). The vision is to increase profitability for farmers and producers, to positively contribute to rural development, to double food exports and to increase the number of tourists visiting Sweden for reasons related to food. In order to achieve this, the strategy has included marketing efforts in important tourist markets by VisitSweden, Business Sweden, Ministry of Agriculture and other actors to create a new image of Sweden as the new food country (Regeringskansliet 2010). As outlined in various documents, initiators of the strategy see important connections between food production and tourism, even though it is unclear how much of the programme (an estimated SEK 1034 million or €112 million over the period 2007–2013; Regeringskansliet 2010) is directly linked to tourism.

As pointed out by Marsden, Murdoch and Morgan (1999), consumer concern over food has grown over decades, as the globalisation of national economies and the structures of global supply chains have raised concerns over safety, health and the environment. Consumers are increasingly concerned about the origins of the food they are eating, as well as conditions of production and supply. In Sweden, food awareness has grown and food interest is now considerable. This can largely be seen as a result of various interlinked initiatives. One important actor, The Swedish Environmental Protection Agency, has published various reports on food waste (e.g. Naturvårdsverket 2015), in an effort to create greater awareness of food-related issues in environmental contexts. Reports by the government on consumption impacts have also been discussed widely in the media (e.g. SOU 2005), all helping to raise awareness of the importance of food in sustainable development. At the same time, a wide range of initiatives made food more interesting for consumers, including the launch of a national "White Guide", introducing Sweden's best restaurants (www.whiteguide.se); a Swedish food product championship (www.eldrimner.se); Sweden's national chef team (www.kocklandslaget.se); or regional initiatives such as "young organic chefs" (www.ungaekokockar.se) (see also Chapter 2, this volume). Against this background, the following sections present the results from two research projects, focussed on perspectives of chefs and domestic/international tourists in terms of their interest in local and/or organic foods and the opportunities and barriers for the development of regional food tourism.

Method

Two surveys sought to understand the perspectives of chefs and tourists with regard to food. Chefs were identified on an ad hoc basis, that is, a list of restaurants in the counties Skåne, Kalmar and Småland was used to pick restaurants at random and to subsequently call these to discuss interview opportunities. None was declined, and a total of 20 chefs in 20 restaurants of different sizes and with different food choices were identified. Nine interviews were conducted face-to-face, and 11 by telephone, as personal meetings could not be arranged or because the remote location of the restaurant made a visit difficult. All interviews were conducted in March–May 2013 and lasted between 30 and 60 minutes. Introductory questions focussed on the choice of job (Why did you become a chef? What do you appreciate in your job? Which views do you have on food?) and were followed by more specific enquiries regarding the choice of foodstuffs, definitions and importance of local produce, perspectives on tourists/guests, the role of local and organic food in preparing menus and perspectives on food production.

International and domestic tourists were interviewed in the tourist offices in Kalmar and Växjö, that is, representing visitors to the counties of Kalmar and Småland. The sample comprised about equal shares of Swedish tourists (51.6 per cent) and international tourists (48.4 per cent), the latter including 22 nationalities, and in particular German (22.4 per cent of total sample), Danish (12.7 per cent), Dutch (7.4 per cent) and Norwegian (4.4 per cent) visitors. Interviews were carried out on a daily basis throughout July. Questionnaire-based personally administered questionnaires were used during interviews, and data was collected online with the help of tablets. To be eligible for inclusion, respondents had to be at least 18 years old and to qualify as leisure tourists. A total of 715 valid responses were recorded in Kalmar, and 485 in Växjö, comprising 1,200 answers, with a 55 per cent female to 45 per cent male distribution. Questions addressed the importance of food in the destination choice and destination experience, the importance of local food and purchasing behaviour at home, and WTP for regional and organic foodstuffs in restaurants.

Results – restaurants

The introductory questions focussed on chefs' perceptions of food and the most important aspects of their work, which chefs associate with satisfied customers. Chefs usually work without direct customer contacts, and many emphasised that they were always interested in feedback, irrespective of positive or negative customer attitudes. Creativity in composing new dishes and commendations for food creations were commonly identified as drivers in the profession. Chefs also outlined that their job presupposes an interest in life-long learning. The importance of food for humans, including its psychological significance, was another aspect mentioned, along with notions that food is something that brings people together over cultures. Chefs also stated that they have, in very general terms, a positive attitude towards both organic and/or locally produced foodstuffs.

Asked about the choice of foodstuffs, chefs identified six aspects that steer purchasing behaviour: price, origin, quality, organic, availability and wholesalers' bonus systems. Not all of these are equally relevant, and the cost of foodstuffs is the single most important variable for purchases. Quality and origin, the latter referring to either Swedish or local produce, were also important and often mentioned as mutually interdependent aspects of food purchases. Most chefs relied on large wholesalers for the majority of their foodstuffs and a number of smaller suppliers to obtain local and/or organic foods, seasonal and niche products. An important exception may be hotels, which are guided by principles of efficiency and which more often appeared to have agreements with wholesalers for all of their food requirements. Where these agreements are linked to bonus systems or discounts based on purchase volumes, interest in small-scale organic/local/niche supplies is low. Likewise, where availability of products or the reliability of deliveries is uncertain, as may be the case with small-scale providers, this reduces the interest of chefs in such products: closeness to a producer, several chefs emphasised, does not mean it is convenient to buy supplies from them. Overall, the cost of foodstuffs is the major barrier to more local and/or sustainable purchases, with chefs indicating that there are small margins to be spent. For some chefs, price is the only important variable, while others saw economic advantages in local food purchases, including opportunities for marketing and storytelling. A benefit of local foodstuffs was also their higher quality, which reduces the share of food that has to be thrown away. These advantages may in many cases make up for higher supply prices. Local foods are also seen to involve guests to a greater degree and to ideally create an interest in food, while providing unique selling points. Specifically chefs in a-la-carte restaurants mentioned these benefits.

With regard to awareness, there was a general uncertainty as to how to define "local" or "regional" food. Often, "local" was seen as within a 10-km radius of the restaurant, while others measured "local" in terms of community boundaries or in terms of specific landscapes. Notions of "organic" food were even more unspecified, and one in two chefs freely admitted that s/he was unable to define "organic food". Where attempts at definitions were made, they often had a generic character, such as "not sprayed", "good for the environment", "natural", "no additives". Only a few chefs raised specific issues, such as transport-related problems (climate change), or outlined that food waste constitutes a problem. Organic and local foods were often seen as interconnected issues, and one in four chefs suggested that food production implies environmental problems. Yet, one of the most notable findings of the interviews was that chefs had a very limited understanding of sustainability and concepts of "local" and "organic" food. This also needs to be seen in light of the fact that one in two chefs stated that "the environment" is not relevant for food-related decisions, neither professionally nor at home. The last question addressed future food production and use. When asked about preferable changes, one in two chefs stated that they would like consumers to become more interested in food and to ask more critical questions about food production. Chefs also pointed at the need for producers to become better organised logistically, which would make it easier for restaurants to purchase locally produced foodstuffs. As outlined, these perspectives need to be seen in comparison to environmental knowledge, which is limited among chefs.

Results – tourists

Results indicate complex relationships with food among visitors. Even though 44.2 per cent stated that food had no importance for the choice of holiday destinations, 21.6 per cent suggested that food was important or very important (n = 1198). Food has thus only secondary importance in motivating tourists to visit south-eastern Sweden, and though 49.2 per cent of the tourists stated that they are fairly interested in food, and another 25.8 per cent very interested, there is a clear case to be made for food offers to play a greater role for destination choices in the future. Notably, only a quarter of all respondents, 24.0 per cent, stated that their interested in food was limited or that they had no interest in food whatsoever (n = 1192).

To better understand how tourism–food relationships could be developed, respondents were also asked how often they bought foodstuffs directly from farmers, fishermen or other producers. Some 10.7 per cent responded that they did so regularly, that is, at least once a week, and another 28.5 per cent stated that they buy directly from producers several times per year (n = 1200). On the other side of the spectrum, 33.9 per cent of respondents stated that they never buy food outside department stores, and another 27.0 per cent reported that they do this very rarely (n = 1196). This indicates that almost two-thirds of respondents do not engage in direct food purchases, which are an important mechanism of reconnecting with food production. A more detailed picture emerges when comparing respondents' consideration of various related factors in the context of food purchases, including price, quality, local products, health and organic certification. Quality is clearly the most important aspect of food purchases, rated very high by 61.4 per cent, followed by the food's healthiness at 40.6 per cent (Table 3.1). Notably, both aspects are largely a matter of perception, as it is often difficult to objectively judge quality and health aspects of specific foods. As organic foodstuffs have the lowest purchasing priority at 20.9 per cent, this also indicates that the quality of a food is not measured in terms of organic production. Another important finding is that price is prioritised by only 22.5 per cent of respondents when making food purchases, though it is an important variable for most (44.7 per cent; n = 1,197). Overall, this would suggest that if a foodstuff is perceived to be qualitatively superior, and perhaps also healthy, the cost of the product is less relevant. Finally, with regard to local products, only a quarter of respondents value these highly when making purchasing decisions. One reason for this low share may be that tourists are not informed enough about specific local products and that marketing efforts to present local foods as high-quality foods could have benefits for food producers.

To understand relationships between tourism and restaurants, and the potential to strengthen linkages between regional production and restaurant attractiveness, respondents were asked about the importance of food for holiday experiences, as well as their eating-out habits. With regard to holiday experiences, more than half (52.8 per cent) stated that food has some importance, and another 21.7 per cent stated that it is of great importance. Only a quarter of respondents, 25.5 per cent, suggested that food had little or no importance at all for their holiday experiences. In line with these results, the analysis shows that a considerable share of respondents eat only occasionally in restaurants, though only small differences between fastfood, pizza/Asian, lunch and a-la-carte restaurant choices are visible (Table 3.2).

Table 3.1 Priorities for food purchases

	Very high	*High*	*Low*	*No importance*
Price	22.5%	44.7%	23.5%	9.3%
Quality	61.4%	37.7%	0.9%	0.0%
Local products	26.4%	41.6%	22.7%	9.3%
Health	40.6%	49.3%	8.7%	1.4%
Organic	20.9%	31.7%	27.6%	19.9%

n = 1197

Table 3.2 Eating preferences and frequencies by restaurant type

	Every week	Every month	A few times a year	More rarely
Fast food	7.4%	29.4%	35.0%	28.2%
Pizza, Asian	5.4%	42.9%	32.5%	19.3%
Lunch restaurant	20.6%	27.3%	30.1%	22.0%
A la carte	6.4%	25.3%	37.1%	31.1%

n = 1197

Lunch restaurants are now a standard for many, and this is reflected in the comparatively high share of respondents stating to eat in lunch restaurants at least once a week (20.6 per cent). Cheap restaurant choices, including fast-food, pizza and Asian food, are not very different from a-la-carte choices. In all cases, about an equal share of respondents stated that they eat at least once a month (25.3–42.9 per cent), a few times per year (30.1–37.1 per cent) or "more rarely" (19.3–28.2 per cent) in restaurants.

Factors of relevance for restaurant choices (n = 1192) include, in particular, eating habits (55.2 per cent), followed by specific restaurant types offering a particular style of food (44.0 per cent), price (42.5 per cent), the desire to be inspired (30.5 per cent) and "high class" (21.9 per cent). Local produce (15.6 per cent) or organic food choices (9.7 per cent) have a very limited relevance in restaurant choices. Price is thus not the most important factor steering demand, and even though local and organic foods are not highly prioritised, a considerable share of respondents, 36.0 per cent, suggests a positive WTP of up to 10 per cent premiums for local/organic foods, with another 31.3 per cent indicating a WTP premiums of 11–25 per cent (n = 1196). A quarter of respondents, 25.8 per cent, stated that they would be unwilling to pay more for organic food, while on the other side of the spectrum, 7.0 per cent reported to be willing to pay more than 26 per cent on top of standard prices in order to be served local or organic food. These results confirm that there is a substantial share of customers who are willing to pay more for organic or regional food, if a clear case for such choices is made. Notably, even a 10 per cent premium paid on the end price should cover the cost of additional organic foodstuff purchases.

Discussion

This chapter has investigated perspectives of chefs and tourists with regard to local and organic foods, as favourable opinions of local and organic foodstuffs among chefs as well as WTP for such foods by tourists would represent important preconditions for the expansion of local and organic food production. A key finding in this regard is that chefs have a generally very limited understanding of environmental issues, with half of those interviewed stating that they are able to neither define the term 'organic' nor assign any importance to pro-environmental choices either at home or work. Even those chefs with an interest in organic and local foodstuffs had a very limited understanding of aspects related to food sustainability, including, for instance, biodiversity loss (Sage 2012); freshwater consumption (Hoekstra & Chapagain 2007); use of pesticides, herbicides and fungicides (Koutros et al. 2008; Bhalli et al. 2009); or greenhouse gas emissions in food processing, storage, transport and cooking (Gössling et al. 2011). The absence of a more profound understanding of these interrelationships may consequently be seen as the single most important reason for the limited interest in additional purchases of local or organic foodstuffs. Currently, the most important reasons for buying local produce are their potential marketability, opportunities for storytelling and quality differences. Notably, there are no incentives at all to buy organic foodstuffs, as customer demand for such foods is understood to be very limited.

Results thus suggest that improving knowledge and awareness of food sustainability among chefs represents a key challenge for systemic change in restaurants, as attitudes to sustainable foods depend on knowledge: this would include an understanding of the differences between globally sourced and local foods, and the implications of such food supply choices for global food security (Khoury et al. 2014), but also embrace other aspects of the food system such as the benefits of vegetarian food choices (Tilman & Clark 2015) in an increasingly stressed global food production system (Sakschewski et al. 2014). An alternative approach that could work in the shorter term, and which does not presuppose additional training of chefs, is to highlight the benefits of local products in terms of marketing and storytelling opportunities, as a way to find unique selling points by increasing the share of local products, and in particular niche products. This approach may also work for organic foodstuffs, which may be used more frequently to address and confirm customer quality expectations – factors that could potentially increase guest loyalty. Quality characteristics of local foodstuffs could also be emphasised by food producers to address food pride and creativity of chefs. Other barriers to local food purchases outlined by chefs, including, in particular, the variability in production, the additional effort of dealing with various suppliers and unreliability in deliveries, need to be addressed as well, but they are less likely to negatively influence interest in local foods than, for instance, issues of higher costs.

With regard to food consumers, results indicate that only a share of tourists purchase foods directly from producers. This would indicate that linkages between producers and consumers are not well developed: direct purchases create closer relationships with food producers and often a better understanding of food production processes; they reflect greater interest in food origins and potentially increase willingness to accept higher food prices. This, in turn, would be an important precondition for restaurants to successfully integrate local food products in their menus, given cost considerations of chefs. The situation is even more difficult for organic foods. Even though not the focus of this project, research indicates that perspectives of consumers as to what is 'organic' food are heterogeneous and that motives to purchase organic foods are guided by aspects of health, taste, environmental concern, food safety, animal welfare, local economy support and trends (Hughner et al. 2007). The successful inclusion of organic foods in restaurants will consequently depend on the efforts made to present these foods in terms of being healthier, for instance, by outlining that these are pesticide-free as well as other quality aspects such as their taste. As with local foodstuffs, these aspects could be easily linked with marketing efforts and storytelling. Yet, as three-quarters of the tourists are generally interested in food, and given that there is positive WTP of at least 10 per cent premiums for local and/or organic food choices among 38 per cent of the tourists, there is considerable potential to use synergies between local/organic food preferences and opportunities for restaurants to increasingly use these on the basis of adjusted marketing efforts, confirming research in other cultural contexts (Loureiro & Hine 2002; Batte et al. 2007; Janssen & Hamm 2012).

Conclusion

There is widespread consensus in Sweden that the use of regional foods in restaurants is important to stimulate regional development, to foster interest in more sustainable foods in the population, and to support sustainable food production systems more generally. In this chapter, interlinkages between restaurants and tourists were investigated in order to better understand barriers to and opportunities for sustainable food use policies. For this purpose, the perceptions of chefs and tourists were investigated. The most important finding is that chefs appear to have a very limited understanding of environmental issues and that these are no professional drivers of the foodstuff purchasing behaviour of chefs. Moreover, perceptions of high costs and unreliable supplies of locally sourced foodstuffs, along with greater administrative burdens to specific food purchases, are reasons for chefs to largely rely on conventional foods delivered by wholesale suppliers. Yet, chefs take pride in their work and seek to present customers with food that is creative and attractive. In this regard, they see a considerable benefit in the potential of local foodstuffs to be used for marketing and storytelling purposes. This potential is matched by the tourists' interest in sustainable foods, provided that these are marketed on the basis of health benefits and taste. As more than a third of all tourists state that they are willing to pay premiums of at least 10 per cent for food that is local, this can help to overcome cost-perception barriers among chefs.

In terms of a broader perspective on food systems, it should be of interest that there is a rapidly growing number of tourists eating in restaurants – a development that is in conflict with the observation that chefs may have a very limited understanding of sustainability issues related to food production. To change culinary systems towards greater sustainability (Gössling & Hall 2013), it would thus seem highly relevant to increase levels of environmental awareness and knowledge of chefs. Notably, this will not only include changes from purchases of globally sourced to local foodstuffs, or from conventional to organic production: given world population growth and changing diets in favour of higher-order foods, it will also be necessary to discuss how vegetarian choices can be increasingly supported by restaurants as well as retailers (Tjärnemo & Södahl 2015). Future research should address these issues, as there appears to be a huge potential for restaurants to contribute to healthier and more sustainable food systems, with benefits for food producers and customers.

References

Batte, M.T., Hooker, N.H., Haab, T.C. and Beaverson, J. (2007) 'Putting their money where their mouths are: consumer willingness to pay for multi-ingredient, processed organic food products', *Food Policy*, 32(2): 145–159.

Bhalli, J.A., Ali, T., Asi, M.R., Khalid, Z.M., Ceppi, M. and Khan, Q.M. (2009) 'DNA damage in Pakistani agricultural workers exposed to mixture of pesticides', *Environmental and Molecular Mutagenesis*, 50(1): 37–45.

Boniface, P. (2003) *Tasting Tourism: Travelling for Food and Drink*, Burlington: Ashgate.

Boyne, S., Hall, D. and Williams, F. (2003) 'Policy, support and promotion for food-related tourism initiatives: a marketing approach to regional development', *Journal of Travel & Tourism Marketing*, 14(3–4): 131–154.

Busby, G. and Rendle, S. (2000) 'The transition from tourism on farms to farm tourism', *Tourism Management*, 21(6): 635–642.

Clark, G. and Chabrel, M. (2007) 'Measuring integrated rural tourism', *Tourism Geographies*, 9(4): 371–386.

Cohen, E. and Avieli, N. (2004) 'Food in tourism: attraction and impediment', *Annals of Tourism Research*, 31: 755–778.

Di Domenico, M. and Miller, G. (2012) 'Farming and tourism enterprise: experiential authenticity in the diversification of independent small-scale family farming', *Tourism Management*, 33(2): 285–294.

du Rand, G.E. and Heath, E. (2006) 'Towards a framework for food tourism as an element of destination marketing', *Current Issues in Tourism*, 9(3): 206–234.

Everett, S. and Aitchison, C. (2008) 'The role of food tourism in sustaining regional identity: a case study of Cornwall, South West England', *Journal of Sustainable Tourism*, 16(2): 150–167.

Everett, S. and Slocum, S.L. (2013) 'Food and tourism: an effective partnership? A UK-based review', *Journal of Sustainable Tourism*, 21(6): 789–809.

Gössling, S., Garrod, B., Aall, C., Hille, J. and Peeters, P. (2011) 'Food management in tourism: reducing tourism's carbon "foodprint"', *Tourism Management*, 32: 534–543.

Gössling, S. and Hall, C.M. (2013) 'Sustainable culinary systems: an introduction', in C.M. Hall and S. Gössling (eds) *Sustainable Culinary Systems: Local Foods, Innovation, Tourism and Hospitality*, Abingdon: Routledge, pp. 3–44.

Gyimóthy, S. and Mykletun, R.J. (2009) 'Scary food: commodifying culinary heritage as meal adventures in tourism', *Journal of Vacation Marketing*, 15(3): 259–273.

Hall, C.M. (ed.) (2003) *Wine, Food and Tourism Marketing*, Binghampton: Haworth.

Hall, C.M. (ed.) (2004) 'Small firms and wine and food tourism in New Zealand: issues of collaboration, clusters and lifestyles', in R. Thomas (ed.) *Small Firms in Tourism: International Perspectives*, Oxford: Elsevier, pp. 167–181.

Hall, C.M. (ed.) (2013) 'The local in farmers' markets in New Zealand', in C.M. Hall and S. Gössling (eds) *Sustainable Culinary Systems: Local Foods, Innovation, Tourism and Hospitality*, London: Routledge, pp. 241–255.

Hall, C.M. and Gössling, S. (eds) (2013) *Sustainable Culinary Systems: Local Foods, Innovation, Tourism and Hospitality*, London: Routledge.

Hall, C.M., Johnson, G. and Mitchell, R. (2000) 'Wine tourism and regional development', in C.M. Hall, L. Sharples, N. Macionis, and B. Cambourne (eds) *Wine Tourism around the World*, Oxford: Butterworth Heinemann, pp. 196–225.

Hall, C.M. and Mitchell, R. (2008) *Wine Marketing*, Oxford: Elsevier.

Hall, C.M. and Sharples, E. (eds) (2008) *Food and Wine Festivals and Events around the World: Development, Management and Markets*, Oxford: Butterworth Heinemann.

Hall, C.M., Sharples, L., Mitchell, R., Macionis, N. and Cambourne, B. (eds) (2003) *Food Tourism around the World: Development, Management and Markets*, Oxford: Butterworth-Heinemann.

Hjalager, A.-M. and Richards, G. (eds) (2002) *Tourism and Gastronomy*, London: Routledge.

Hoekstra, A.Y. and Chapagain, A.K. (2007) 'Water footprints of nations: water use by people as a function of their consumption pattern', *Water Resources Management*, 21: 35–48.

Hughner, R.S., McDonagh, P., Prothero, A., Shultz, C.J. and Stanton, J. (2007) 'Who are organic food consumers? A compilation and review of why people purchase organic food', *Journal of Consumer Behaviour*, 6(2–3): 94.

Janssen, M. and Hamm, U. (2012) 'Product labelling in the market for organic food: consumer preferences and willingness-to-pay for different organic certification logos', *Food Quality and Preference*, 25(1): 9–22.

Khoury, C.K., Bjorkman, A.D., Dempewolf, H., Ramirez-Villegas, J., Guarino, L., Jarvis, A., Rieseberg, L.H. and Struik, P.C. (2014) 'Increasing homogeneity in global food supplies and the implications for food security', *Proceedings of the National Academy of Sciences*, 111(11): 4001–4006.

Knowd, I. (2006) 'Tourism as a mechanism for farm survival', *Journal of Sustainable Tourism*, 14: 24–42.

Koutros, S., Lynch, C.F., Ma, X., Lee, W.J., Hoppin, J.A., Christensen, C.H., Andreotti, G., Freeman, L.B., Rusiecki, J.A., Hou, L., Sandler, D.P. and Alavanja, M.C.R. (2008) 'Heterocyclic aromatic amine pesticide use and human cancer risk: results from the US Agricultural Health Study', *International Journal of Cancer*, 124(5): 1206–1212.

Lange-Vik, M. and Idsø, J. (2013) 'Rørosmat: the development and success of a local food brand in Norway', in C.M. Hall and S. Gössling (eds) *Sustainable Culinary Systems: Local Foods, Innovation, Tourism and Hospitality*, London: Routledge, pp. 85–94.

Loureiro, M.L. and Hine, S. (2002) 'Discovering niche markets: a comparison of consumer willingness to pay for local (Colorado grown), organic, and GMO-free products', *Journal of Agricultural and Applied Economics*, 34(3): 477–488.

Malm, K., Gössling, S. and Hall, C.M. (2013) 'Regulatory and institutional barriers to new business development: the case of Swedish wine tourism', in C.M. Hall and S. Gössling (eds) *Sustainable Culinary Systems: Local Foods, Innovation, Tourism and Hospitality*, London: Routledge, pp. 241–255.

Marsden, T., Banks, J. and Bristow, G. (2000) 'Food supply chain approaches: exploring their role in rural development', *Sociologia Ruralis*, 40(4): 424–438.

Marsden, T., Murdoch, J. and Morgan, K. (1999) 'Sustainable agriculture, food supply chains and regional development: editorial introduction', *International Planning Studies*, 4(3): 295–301.

Montanari, A. (2009) 'Culinary tourism as a tool for regional re-equilibrium', *European Planning Studies*, 17(10): 1463–1483.

Naturvårdsverket (2015) *Matavfallsmängder i Sverige*. Available online: <http://www.naturvardsverket.se/Documents/publikationer6400/978-91-620-8694-7.pdf?pid=11891> (accessed 13 October 2015).

Regeringskansliet (2010) *Sverige – det nya matlandet. Uppdaterad handlingsplan. Nya job genom god mat och upplevelser.* Available online: <http://www.swedenabroad.com/ SelectImageX/251302/Sverige.det.nya.matlandet.pdf> (accessed 14 October 2015).

Renko, S., Renko, N. and Polonijo, T. (2010) 'Understanding the role of food in rural tourism development in a recovering economy', *Journal of Food Products Marketing*, 16(3): 309–324.

Rusher, K. (2003) 'The Bluff Oyster festival and regional economic development: festivals as culture', in C.M. Hall, E. Sharples, R. Mitchell, N. Macionis, and B. Cambourne (eds) *Food Tourism around the World: Development, Management and Markets*, Oxford: Butterworth Heinemann, pp. 192–205.

Sage, C. (2012) *Environment and Food*, London: Routledge.

Sakschewski, B., von Bloh, W., Huber, V., Müller, C. and Bondeau, A. (2014) 'Feeding 10 billion people under climate change: how large is the production gap of current agricultural systems?' *Ecological Modelling*, 288: 103–111.

Sims, R. (2009) 'Food, place and authenticity: local food and the sustainable tourism experience', *Journal of Sustainable Tourism*, 17: 321–336.

SOU (2005) *Bilen, biffen, bostaden. Hållbara laster – smartare konsumtion.* SOU 2005:51. Available online: <http://www.regeringen.se/contentassets/b45b24cd21144e3193749b 9b278d661c/bilen-biffen-bostaden-hallbara-laster-smartare-konsumtion> (accessed 13 October 2015).

Svensk Turism AB (2010) *Nationell strategi för svensk besöksnäring.* Available online: <http://www.svenskturism.com/nationell-strategi> (accessed 14 October 2015).

Telfer, D. and Wall, G. (1996) 'Linkages between tourism and food production', *Annals of Tourism Research*, 23(3): 635–653.

Telfer, D. and Wall, G. (2000) 'Strengthening backward economic linkages: local food purchasing by three Indonesian hotels', *Tourism Geographies*, 2(4): 421–447.

Tillväxtverket (2012) *Årsbokslut för svensk Turism* 2011. Available online: <www.till växtverket.se> (accessed 14 October 2015).

Tillväxtverket (2015) *Growth in Tourism Creating Employment and Export Value for Sweden.* Available online: <http://www.tillvaxtverket.se/sidhuvud/englishpages/tour-ismindustryissuesandstatistics/tourismsannualaccounts2014.4.6b18fb3e14790c1c68e6 02fc.html> (accessed 13 October 2015).

Tilman, D. and Clark, M. (2015) 'Food, agriculture & the environment: can we feed the world & save the earth?' *Daedalus*, 144(4): 8–23.

Tjärnemo, H. and Södahl, L. (2015) 'Swedish food retailers promoting climate smarter food choices – Trapped between visions and reality?' *Journal of Retailing and Consumer Services*, 24: 130–139.

Torres, R. (2002) 'Toward a better understanding of tourism and agriculture linkages in the Yucatan: tourist food consumption and preferences', *Tourism Geographies*, 4(3): 282–306.

Veeck, G., Che, D. and Veeck, J. (2006) 'America's changing farmscape: a study of agricultural tourism in Michigan', *The Professional Geographer*, 58(3): 235–248.

Venn, L., Kneafsey, M., Holloway, L., Cox, R., Dowler, E. and Tuomainen, H. (2006) 'Researching European "alternative" food networks: some methodological considerations', *Area*, 38(3): 248–258.

4 Growing tourism from the ground up

Drivers of tourism development in agricultural regions

Michelle Thompson and Bruce Prideaux

Introduction

The transformation of farming in many developed economies – from a traditional family farm model to one based on large-scale, highly mechanised company-owned agricultural enterprises – has severely affected many small rural communities leading to significant reductions in farm work forces and loss of essential services (Marsden & Sonnino 2008; Renting et al. 2009; Kneafsey 2010). In circumstances of this nature, affected communities can either search for alternative economic sectors or face the prospect of further decline and in some cases abandonment. Tourism is one sector that has shown some potential to revitalise rural economies, provided the community is able to develop a suite of experiences that can be profitably marketed. However, this is not always the case; despite considerable injections of public funding, some agricultural communities have been unsuccessful in generating tourism demand. A growing body of research has focussed on this issue, and while broadly concluding that agricultural areas may be able to offer a range of experiences that may be attractive to tourists, they also suggest that tourism should not be seen as a panacea for the regeneration of declining regional communities (Sharpley & Telfer 2002; Giaoutzi & Nijkamp 2006; Hall & Page 2006; Sznajder, Przezbórska & Scrimgeour 2009; Torres & Momsen 2011).

Much of the research that has been undertaken into the development of tourism in agricultural areas has focussed on agri-tourism, but ignored the broader issues associated with the steps required for agricultural regions to effect the transition from an agriculture-based economy to a mixed agriculture/tourism economy. This chapter aims to assist in addressing this gap by examining the role of drivers in the transformation process from an agricultural region that typically focusses on the production and sale of agricultural products to external markets to an agricultural region that also promotes the consumption of agricultural products within the region by tourists.

Agri-tourism and agricultural regions

In response to calls for greater understanding of specific areas of tourism demand, researchers have developed an expanding list of special interest tourism (SIT) or niche sectors. These include eco-tourism, heritage tourism, cultural tourism, food tourism, cruise tourism, wildlife tourism, agri-tourism and so on. In the sense that the division of tourism into special interests or niches offers the opportunity for greater understanding of corresponding target market interests, this trend has some merit. However, the shift in focus from the broad to the narrow has led to problems such as double counting where a tourist may be classed as belonging to a specific niche one day based on the activity they participated in and a member of a different niche the following day because they participated in a different activity. For example, a tourist who drives to a heritage site could be counted as both a drive tourist and a heritage tourist. As McKercher, Okumus and Okumus (2008) observed, the tendency to divide tourism activity into ever smaller categories has seen the emergence of a myopic perspective of the overall tourism phenomenon with specific activities viewed in isolation of the bundle of tourist attributes that constitute a tourist destination. This myopic perspective also contributes to inaccuracies when determining the size of target markets for specific SIT sectors, often resulting in over-estimating demand (McKercher, Okumus & Okumus 2008). From a supply-side perspective, many niche classifications become redundant when there is no clear definition of a specific type of SIT or there is an inability to accurately represent the evolutionary nature of the tourist activity to which it refers.

Tourism that incorporates elements of agriculture, such as farm tours, agricultural festivals and museums, farmers' markets and food tastings, is often referred to as agri-tourism. However, there is ongoing academic debate about the definition of agri-tourism. Some researchers define it as a specific form of activity that occurs on-farm (Ilbery et al. 1998; McGehee 2007; McGehee, Kim & Jennings 2007; Barbieri & Mshenga 2008), whereas others argue for the inclusion of activities that occur within a broader agricultural setting (Sonnino 2004; Che, Veeck & Veeck 2005; Philip, Hunter & Blackstock 2010; Tew & Barbieri 2012). More recently, Gil Arroyo, Barbieri and Rozier Rich (2013) recommended a much broader systems-based perspective of agri-tourism that includes elements of entertainment, education, farm and agricultural settings, as well as staged or authentic activities conducted on working agricultural facilities. In terms of the current understanding of agri-tourism, Sznajder, Przezbórska and Scrimgeour (2009) observed that the supply side is undergoing constant transformation with the introduction of new experiences requiring an ongoing re-evaluation of the activities that may be defined and classified as agri-tourism.

The problems encountered in defining agri-tourism stem from the perspectives taken by different researchers. At an attraction level, a specific farm-based tourism experience for example, the SIT approach that yielded the term "agri-tourism" has some merit. However, on a larger scale, where the farm-based activity is considered in conjunction with other attractions and tourism-related infrastructure from a destination perspective, the SIT approach poses considerable problems as highlighted by some researchers (Philip, Hunter & Blackstock 2010; Gil Arroyo, Barbieri & Rozier Rich 2013). The debate about definition and description highlights broader deficiencies that exist within SIT classifications, particularly limitations in accurately reflecting the evolution of this concept in practice. Few researchers specialising in tourism in agricultural regions (TAR) have adopted a holistic approach that recognises agri-tourism as one of a possible number of tourism activities that may operate in agricultural regions. One consequence has been a failure to achieve a more comprehensive understanding of the range of often complementary tourism activities that may occur in regions of this nature. The confusion surrounding the term agri-tourism, and the myopic view often associated with SIT research (McKercher, Okumus & Okumus 2008), highlights the need to consider a more inclusive understanding. This commences with the adoption of a more inclusive terminology that overcomes existing limitations and extends understanding.

Building on previous research (Thompson 2013; Thompson & Prideaux 2014), this chapter has adopted a holistic approach for understanding the structure and operation of the tourism phenomenon in agricultural regions. Recognising that tourism is a system comprised of many niche experiences as well as supporting infrastructure, Thompson and Prideaux (2014) introduced the term *tourism in agricultural regions* (TAR). Compared to traditional classifications of tourism, which adopt an activity-based approach, TAR enables researchers to adopt a whole-of-system approach that encompasses a broad range of tourism activities, some of which may not be based on agriculture. Examples include nature-based activities, heritage, events, cycling, accommodation and regional culture.

Central to the successful development of a tourism sector in an agricultural region is the process of transforming existing resources, including the agricultural landscape and its products, the natural environment, history, cultural heritage and infrastructure, to create an economically sustainable tourism sector. In terms of Crouch and Ritchie's (1999) model of destination competitiveness, this process is one where a region's comparative advantages, described as factor endowments, are converted into a competitive advantage, described as a destination's ability to effectively utilise all its resources in the long term.

Recognition of an agricultural region's comparative advantages enables an assessment to be made about its potential pull factors and, based on an understanding of potential tourist markets, identify tourist push factors that it may target. Push factors are defined as factors that encourage travel such as the need for rest and relaxation, ability to pay, adventure, prestige and social interaction (Dann 1977). Pull factors are the attributes of a destination that are attractive to visitors such as landscapes, novelty, heritage, culture, nature, value and activities (Klenosky 2002). The conversion of comparative advantages into a competitive advantage is described as the process of transformation, the end result of which confers on a region the opportunity to develop a suite of pull factors that match the push factors of its potential market sectors. However, as Prideaux (2009: 264) cautioned, the operation of push-and-pull factors is often affected by a range of inhibiting factors defined as 'a general term that describes factors of any type (including trends, drivers, random events, policy) and from any source that places restrictions on growth and also on change'.

Previous research has identified a range of drivers and barriers that may affect the transformation of comparative advantages into a competitive advantage.

Drivers are defined as 'factors that influence the future course of events' (Prideaux 2009: 67). Drivers may include internal forces, such as support for development within the community and pre-existing skills, and external forces, such as a favourable political climate, access to investment funds in the public and private sectors, technological advances and changes in demand. In relation to agricultural regions, drivers identified in the literature include entrepreneurship and innovation (Barbieri & Mshenga 2008; Haugen & Vik 2008; Park, Doh & Kim 2014); networking (Hall, Johnson & Mitchell 2000; Hall 2004; Che, Veeck & Veeck 2005; Knowd 2006; Schmitt 2010; Bertella 2011); farmer skills and attributes (Sidali, Schulze & Spiller 2007; Alonso 2010); and agency support (Ilbery et al. 1998; Schmitt 2010).

Barriers can be described as factors that inhibit development and may be internal, including a lack of community support, or external, including institutional inertia, geographical (peripheral location), inappropriate technology, skill deficiencies, lack of demand and lack of investment capital. The literature (Weaver & Fennell 1997; Ecker et al. 2010; Jensen et al. 2014) has identified numerous barriers that may inhibit the process of transformation, which include: the regulatory framework; financial constraints; lack of infrastructure; government inefficiencies; non-supportive tourism industry; lack of regional collaboration at business level; crises such as swine flu or bushfires; and changes in demand. Issues such as geographic isolation and marketing (Che, Veeck & Veeck 2005), the efficiency of distribution networks (Hjalager 1996), industry engagement (Hall 2005) and lack of interpersonal skills (Busby & Rendle 2000) demonstrate that the absence of essential drivers can also be regarded as barriers.

Other aspects of tourism development in agricultural regions have been addressed in the literature. These include regional development (Sonnino 2004; Schmitt 2010), motivations of entrepreneurs (Getz & Carlsen 2000; Ollenburg & Buckley 2007) and linkages between agriculture and tourism (Telfer & Wall 2000; Torres 2003). However, their role as key drivers in the transformation process is not as well understood. While acknowledging the need to develop a more comprehensive understanding of the potential for barriers to inhibit the transformation of comparative advantages to a competitive advantage, the focus of this research is principally on the role of drivers.

As an aid to understanding the complex relationships that occur within destinations and how destinations evolve over time, a number of models have been suggested, the best known of which is Butler's (1980) Tourism Area Life Cycle. As Getz (1986) observed, models are valuable tools that provide a visual representation of a research phenomenon and can be particularly useful in enhancing our understanding of new concepts such as TAR. Getz (1986) proposed two main classes of models: theoretical models which provide a conceptual understanding, and process models which focus on planning and have the capacity to be operationalised. Theoretical models can be grouped further into descriptive, explanatory and predictive. In relation to the role of models within the tourism literature, Getz (1986: 23) stated that 'Models – first descriptive, then explanatory and finally predictive in nature – are the building blocks of theory'. Both approaches serve different purposes. Given that the aim of this chapter is to investigate the process of transformation, an explanatory model was developed to identify the range of processes that influence the development of TAR. Previous research has focussed either on modelling specific aspects of agri-tourism (Evans & Ilbery 1989; Morley, Sparkes & Thomas 2000) or developing a more holistic understanding (McGehee 2007; Porcaro 2010). However, there remains a paucity of models that have considered the complex range of factors that underpin tourism development, hence the need for a new model that illustrates the process of transformation.

Methodology

The aim of this chapter is to develop a more detailed understanding of the drivers that assist the processes of transformation of an agriculture-based economy to a mixed agriculture/tourism economy. A case study methodology was adopted based on the ability of this approach to identify underlying relationships and provide insights that can be used to build theoretical models (Yin 2009). A preliminary assessment of agricultural regions that have successfully transitioned from agriculture to a mixed agriculture/tourism economy generated several potential sites including the Hunter Valley north of Sydney and the Margaret River region of Western Australia. Margaret River was selected as it is an internationally renowned food and wine region, with a variety of tourism experiences development from its diverse resource base, which includes agriculture.

Semi-structured interviews were conducted with 25 representatives from the agriculture, food, wine and tourism sectors, as well as regional support agencies and government representatives. Yin (2009) regards interviews as one of the most important sources for case studies, allowing for probing and clarification of issues to explore underlying themes (Veal 2005). Participants were identified using a snowball technique to gain a richness of information (Miles & Huberman 1994), with interviews continuing until no new information was offered (Creswell 2013). The interviews were audiotaped to enable accurate transcription of the qualitative findings, which were thematically coded using N-Vivo software. Triangulation of the interview themes with content and historical analysis of secondary sources was used to establish converging lines of enquiry, with an emphasis on the corroboration of findings (Yin 2009).

Secondary data were sourced from both grey (industry reports and statistics, oral histories and books) and academic literature where available. The grey literature was an invaluable aid in the search for understanding the role of many of the factors that impacted on the development of Margaret River. The so-called grey literature, described as authoritative reports that have not been subject to academic peer review, often provide information not available in the academic literature. Considerable gaps in understanding could result without referring to the knowledge provided by sources of this nature. As Jeffery (2000: 64) observed, 'The importance of grey literature is becoming increasingly recognised. For many organisations it encapsulates the knowledge and know-how and thus is a vital business asset … (and) in a research and development environment represents the cutting edge of this knowledge and so its management is of uttermost importance'.

Study site

Margaret River is located on Australia's south-western coastline, approximately three-hour drive by car south of Perth (Figure 4.1). The region has a growing reputation both domestically and internationally as a producer of premium wine. Tourists first began visiting the region in the 1920s, but it did not rise to national prominence until the region's wine industry began to attract tourism interest in

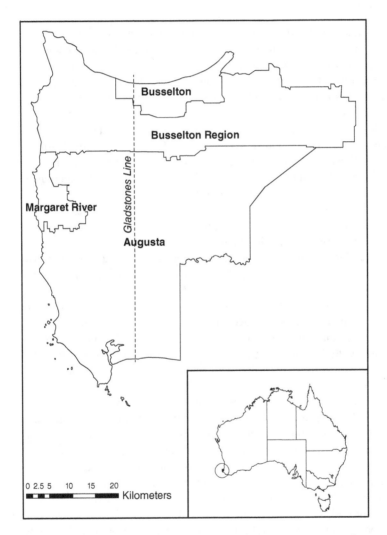

Figure 4.1 Location of the study site, Margaret River, Western Australia created by Diane
Jarvis, James Cook University

the 1980s. Aside from wine, the region offers a range of nature-based experiences centred on limestone caves and forests as well as surfing, beaches and events. More recently, there has been growing interest in the region's agricultural outputs other than wine, such as cheese, olives and value-added products.

Agriculture has a long history in the region but, for most of the period prior to the establishment of viticulture, its dairy and beef sectors struggled to make a return on investment (Andrijich, Forrestal & Jordan 2003). Gladstones (1965) identified parts of the region as being suitable for viticulture, prompting three Perth-based medical practitioners to pioneer commercial viticulture, with the first commercial vine plantings in 1967. Growth in the region's reputation as a wine producer stimulated investment in its tourism sector. For the purposes of this chapter, the case study site covers the Council boundaries of Augusta-Margaret River and Busselton (Figure 4.1). The Augusta Margaret River Tourism Association and Geographe Bay Tourism Association promote each Council area respectively, as well as across the Margaret River wine region, which is designated by the Gladstone Line (west of 115°W 18′E).

Results

Results from the analysis of the semi-structured interviews identified a range of drivers and barriers that have affected the development of tourism in the Margaret River region. To develop a comprehensive understanding of the roles of drivers in a specific setting, the barriers which the drivers must overcome first need to be identified.

Barriers

The analysis of the interviews identified a number of barriers to tourism development, which can be grouped into six main categories: economic, environmental, sociocultural, regulatory (legislative), administrative and product-based. These barriers are outlined in Table 4.1. The categories of barriers are not mutually exclusive. Thus, a lack of natural and agricultural resources, for example, can be categorised as environmental, but may also create barriers in terms of limiting product development, changing sociocultural structures within a region and

Table 4.1 Barriers to tourism development

Barriers	*Supporting quotes*
Economic: • Economic climate • High cost of living • Viability of agriculture • Insurance premiums	'Up until the 1960s and 1970s it was very reasonable to buy land down here, now it is some of the most expensive agricultural land in the country' (Participant 20). 'Well in the end it's the economic thing. There won't be any growth in it [agriculture industry] until people can make a living ... And there is no agriculture in Australia that is a guaranteed living' (Participant 7).

(Continued)

Table 4.1 (Continued)

Barriers	Supporting quotes
Environmental: • Balanced approach to development • Mining industry • Lack of natural resources	'You've got this great conflicting challenge between development and over development and effectively the very thing that people come to see which is a nature-based experience. That's probably one of the biggest challenges that this destination has going forward, it's trying to balance those two things' (Participant 5). 'Big issue for everyone but also for food producers. This is huge, this should be a food producing area – you don't bring oil and gas into this' (Participant 8).
Sociocultural: • Changes in demand • Attract/maintain workforce • Adopt technology	'The biggest challenge is getting enough people to come through the region to make the businesses viable' (Participant 10). 'But seasonal workers getting help – to hand pick, etc has always been a challenge for the grape growers' (Participant 5).
Regulatory/legislative: • Legislation • Lack of government support • Planning regulations	'It's all the food standards seem to be getting more and more complicated and harder and harder. They really are. And they are off-putting for people' (Participant 8). 'The other challenge in setting this up, in agri tourism on farms, is getting local government approval to do the things' (Participant 10).
Administrative: • Boundary lines • Lack of (tourism) statistics • Lack of government support	'So whilst the Gladstone Line defines the wine region, the fact that everyone's leveraging off the two names means that the region's blurred' (Participant 5). 'There is nothing done on any level and it needs to come from government to attract investment. It would be great to have government support' (Participant 8).
Product: • Packaging • Brand integrity • Competitive market environment • Distribution channels • Match supply and demand	'... the myth of MR food runs ahead of reality. Because in reality there is not a lot of food producers down here' (Participant 7). 'Making sure that the quality is available – that we don't have to wait a week for something that's already been sitting there for a week' (Participant 25).

reducing regional economic viability. Once identified, barriers can be overcome or reduced through policy initiatives and appropriate investments at the government level and targeted investment at the private sector level.

Drivers

Drivers, previously defined as factors that facilitate development, can only be identified in a specific region when they are able to mitigate the effects of barriers. Analysis of the interview transcripts and secondary data sources revealed a number of drivers, six of which were identified as core drivers (see Table 4.2). The results identified innovation, networks and collaboration, and people (farmer skills and attributes) as important drivers, confirming findings from previous studies (see above the literature

Table 4.2 Drivers of tourism development

Drivers	Supporting quotes
Geography: • Location • Landscape	'What else would be the drivers for tourism? It's mainly just the environment I suppose the greatest driver' (Participant 12). 'We are very lucky because of our geographic location – the coastline – and because of that we have a unique Mediterranean climate, which lends itself it olive- and oil- also linking back to our heritage in dairy with chocolate experience – building on those ideas to create tourism adventures' (Participant 3).
Innovation: • People • Products • Processes • Promotion	'Leeuwin Estate I suppose was the first big winery that really focused on a visitor, rather than just making wine and part of that was also kicking off the Leeuwin Estate concerts' (Participant 1). 'As far as an innovative design – that [one property] would be the best I've seen around here. Incorporating all the different elements. It's almost got every single land use on that property and that's why it works I guess. A lot of it is the way it's marketed as well. It's got an innovative marketing strategy put in place' (Participant 16).
Networks/ collaboration: • Informal and formal • Within and across sectors	'… we got the [food producer's] association going and the main things were marketing, [and to] act as a vehicle, a voice for the producers. Look when you have an issue in the region and someone wants to talk to food producers, who do they go to?' (Participant 8). 'People don't have a problem with putting their hand up and offering their properties to assist with events for a combination to have the performers stay there' (Participant 12).
People: • Innovative • Collaborative • Leadership • Visionary • Willing to invest	'We've been very fortunate that we've had some individuals that came to the district that had a vision and obviously they had wealth – to create a brand' (Participant 22). 'There is certainly some extremely high profile people dotted around the region that all do their bit' (Participant 5).
Culture: • Internal – adds to sense of place • External – match changes in demand	'[much of the early development] … comes back to that surfing culture and that lifestyle element' (Participant 20). 'To me – it's always been thought that the wine brought everyone down here. I don't think that's true – obviously the surfing was one of the main activities and attractions down here for people – young guys, people, anybody' (Participant 15).
Branding: • Well known for premium wine – leveraged food/tourism	'Definitely the name [MR brand] is big. And the name has come from the wine industry but now it's being filtered on. It's a real thing, people associate MR with quality' (Participant 8). '… anything (food) with MR on it sells. It's actually very easy because all of the ground work for MR brand is already in there. People associate it with good quality and want to buy it' (Participant 18).

review section). However, the remaining drivers – geography, branding and culture – are not as widely recognised. According to participant responses, these drivers were central to the development of tourism in the Margaret River region.

Interviewees also discussed a number of additional drivers, such as the diversity of the tourism product, success of the wine industry, financial capacity and distribution channels, which provided a more comprehensive understanding of the six core drivers. For example, geography was discussed with reference to landscape and location, as highlighted in the following:

> It's [Margaret River is] the holiday region for Perth. So it's the closest place to Perth where it starts to get a bit greener, a bit nicer, it's 200 km from Perth … You didn't have to go far from Perth before you are in the South West … but this has always been the most desirable location close to Perth.
>
> (Participant 23)

Similarly, when interviewees referred to culture as a driver, they often commented on the region's internal culture (described in Table 4.1). However, some also commented on the external culture, recognising that 'there was also a change in the [sic] drinking habits of Australians … there was a shift in that from just beer to beer and wine' (Participant 1). Hence, cultural changes in demand (external culture) were considered an additional aspect of culture.

Explanatory model

The explanatory model (Figure 4.2) illustrates how comparative advantages, in this case agricultural resources, provide the foundation on which tourism experiences may be developed. Over time, these resources undergo a process of transformation stimulated by a range of drivers that overcome or mitigate barriers that may be present. The process of transformation may include external sponsored change (generated by a range of actors in the private and public sectors), a response to events (such as natural disasters or crop disease), as well as the interactions of complex drivers and barriers. Collectively, these factors exercise a cumulative influence over the transformation process, enabling a region to harness its potential (comparative advantage) and create tourism experiences (competitive advantage) to produce a situation where its pull factors broadly align with the push factors of its target markets.

In Figure 4.2, the existing agricultural sector is shown in the lower part of the diagram, while the factors that collectively constitute tourism are shown in the top part of the diagram. If potential comparative advantages (including landscapes, agricultural outputs and heritage) can be transformed into tourism products and experiences, the region has some scope for attracting tourists. To develop a tourism sector, barriers need to be identified and strategies developed to overcome or mitigate these. For example, in the case of Margaret River its distance from Perth remained a major barrier until the highway network was upgraded and the region began attracting upmarket accommodation. The actual level of attraction will depend on the ability of a region's tourism experiences

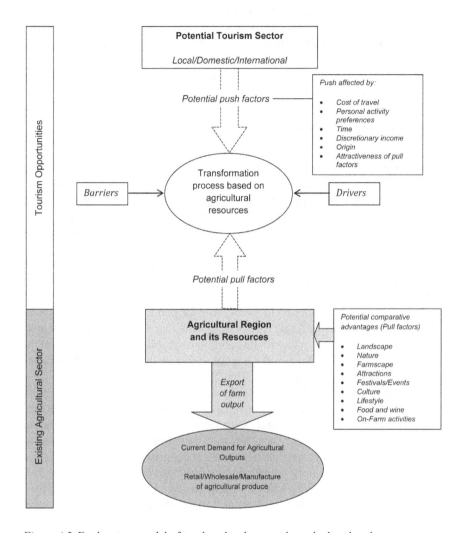

Figure 4.2 Explanatory model of tourism development in agricultural regions

and products to attract tourists. This relationship is shown as the region's pull factors and consumer push factors.

Figure 4.2 illustrates a number of dimensions that operate within an agricultural region, where it is solely structured for export of agricultural output or has developed a more complex economy that includes both product exports as well as produce consumed by tourists within the region. The model assists in the development of a more comprehensive understanding of various forces that affect opportunities for tourism development in agricultural regions. Given the chaotic nature and complexity of many of the factors involved, it can be expected that the outcomes will differ between regions both spatially and temporally. The model also explains why it is sometimes difficult to convert apparent comparative advantages into a competitive advantage. For example, where a region possesses considerable comparative advantages but lacks the capacity to transform these into a competitive advantage, perhaps because of institutional barriers, the strength of inhibiting factors will be greater than the factors pushing transformation.

Discussion and conclusion

Prior to the introduction of viticulture, a range of barriers had inhibited the development of the Margaret River's tourism industry. These barriers included distance, regulations, financial constraints and boundary issues. Viticulture became the catalyst that enabled Margaret River to emerge as a major regional tourist destination and enhanced its capacity to overcome existing barriers with drivers.

This chapter has challenged the existing understanding of agri-tourism as a form of SIT by adopting an alternative, more holistic approach. The TAR approach recognises that apart from agriculture, other resources such as nature and cultural assets may be important in attracting tourists to agricultural regions. This approach does not mean that the contemporary understanding of agri-tourism is redundant. Rather, it implies a continuing role for understanding agri-tourism as a form of SIT that operates at an enterprise level within a larger agricultural area. This approach overcomes many of the definitional problems discussed within the literature (McKercher, Okumus & Okumus 2008; Philip, Hunter & Blackstock 2010; Gil Arroyo, Barbieri & Rozier Rich 2013).

The chapter also identified the role that drivers play in overcoming the inhibiting effects that barriers have on a region's growth potential. In Margaret River, viticulture was identified as a catalyst that initiated the transformation process. The relationships between the various factors that affect the capacity of a region to build on its agricultural resources to support a tourism industry are shown in Figure 4.2. These factors are not exhaustive and it can be expected that the role that barriers and drivers play will vary between regions based on factor endowment, location, public policy settings and the push factors of various tourist sectors.

References

Alonso, A.D. (2010) 'Olives, hospitality and tourism: a Western Australian perspective', *British Food Journal*, 112(1): 55–68.

Andrijich, F., Forrestal, P. and Jordan, R. (2003) *Margaret River*, Fremantle, Australia: Fremantle Arts Centre Press.

Barbieri, C. and Mshenga, P.M. (2008) 'The role of firm and owner characteristics on the performance of agritourism farms', *Sociologia Ruralis*, 48(2): 166–183.

Bertella, G. (2011) 'Knowledge and food tourism: the case of Lofoten & Maremma Toscana', *Current Issues in Tourism*, 14(4): 355–371.

Busby, G. and Rendle, S. (2000) 'The transition from tourism on farms to farm tourism', *Tourism Management*, 21(6): 635–642.

Butler, R. (1980) 'The concept of tourist area resort cycle of evolution: implications for management of resources', *Canadian Geographer*, 14(1): 5–12.

Che, D., Veeck, A. and Veeck, G. (2005) 'Sustaining production and strengthening the agritourism product: linkages among Michigan agritourism destinations', *Agriculture and Human Values*, 22: 225–234.

Creswell, J.W. (2013) *Qualitative Inquiry and Research Design: Choosing among Five Approaches*, 3rd edn, London: Sage.

Crouch, G.I. and Ritchie, J.R. (1999) 'Tourism, competitiveness, and societal prosperity', *Journal of Business Research*, 44(3): 137–152.

Dann, G. (1977) 'Anomie, ego-enhancement and tourism', *Annals of Tourism Research*, 4(4): 184–194.

Ecker, S., Clarke, R., Cartwright, S., Kancans, R., Please, P. and Binks, B. (2010) *Drivers of Regional Agritourism and Food Tourism in Australia*. Available online: <http://data.daff.gov.au/brs/data/warehouse/pe_abarebrs99001744/Agritourism_2010_REPORT_11a.pdf>_(accessed 10 April 2015).

Evans, N.J. and Ilbery, B.W. (1989) 'A conceptual framework for investigating farm-based accommodation and tourism in Britain', *Journal of Rural Studies*, 5(3): 257–266.

Getz, D. (1986) 'Models in tourism planning: towards integration of theory and practice', *Tourism Management*, 7(1): 21–32.

Getz, D. and Carlsen, J. (2000) 'Characteristics and goals of family and owner-operated businesses in the rural tourism and hospitality sectors', *Tourism Management*, 21: 547–560.

Giaoutzi, M. and Nijkamp, P. (eds) (2006) *Tourism and Regional Development*, Cheltenham: Ashgate.

Gil Arroyo, C., Barbieri, C. and Rozier Rich, S. (2013) 'Defining agritourism: a comparative study of stakeholders' perceptions in Missouri and North Carolina', *Tourism Management*, 37: 39–47.

Gladstones, J.S. (1965) 'The climate and soils of South Western Australia in relation to vine growing', *The Journal of the Australian Institute of Agricultural Science*, December: 275–288.

Hall, C.M. (2004) 'Small firms and wine and food tourism in New Zealand: issues of collaboration, clusters and lifestyles', in R. Thomas (ed.) *Small Firms in Tourism: International Perspectives*, Oxford: Elsevier, pp. 167–181.

Hall, C.M. (2005) 'Rural wine and food tourism cluster and network development', in D. Hall, I. Kirkpatrick, and M. Mitchell (eds) *Rural Tourism and Sustainable Business*, Clevedon: Channel View Publications, pp. 149–164.

Hall, C.M., Johnson, G. and Mitchell, R. (2000) 'Wine tourism and regional development', in C.M. Hall, L. Sharples, N. Macionis, and B. Cambourne (eds) *Wine Tourism around the World*, Oxford: Butterworth Heinemann, pp. 196–225.

Hall, C.M. and Page, S. (2006) *Geography of Tourism and Recreation: Environment, Place and Space*, 3rd edn, Abingdon: Routledge.

Haugen, M.S. and Vik, J. (2008) 'Farmers as entrepreneurs: the case of farm-based tourism', *International Journal of Entrepreneurship and Small Business*, 6(3): 321–336.

Hjalager, A.M. (1996) 'Agricultural diversification into tourism: evidence of a European community development programme', *Tourism Management*, 17(2): 103–111.

Ilbery, B., Bowler, I., Clark, G., Crockett, A. and Shaw, A. (1998) 'Farm-based tourism as an alternative farm', *Regional Studies*, 32(4): 355–364.

Jeffery, K. (2000) 'An architecture for grey literature in a R&D context', *International Journal on Grey Literature*, 1(2): 64–72.

Jensen, K.L., Bruch, M., Jamey Menard, R. and English, B.C. (2014) 'Analysis of factors influencing agritourism business in expansion', Paper presented at the *2014 Southern Agricultural Economics Association Meetings*, Dallas, Texas, 1–4 February 2014. Available online: <http://ageconsearch.umn.edu/bitstream/161401/2/Agritourism%20 SAEA%20Paper.pdf> (accessed 5 May 2015).

Klenosky, D. (2002) 'The "pull" of tourism destinations: a means-end investigation', *Journal of Travel Research*, 40: 385–395.

Kneafsey, M. (2010) 'The region in food – important or irrelevant?' *Cambridge Journal of Regions, Economy and Society*, 3(2): 177–190.

Knowd, I. (2006) 'Tourism as a mechanism for farm survival', *Journal of Sustainable Tourism*, 14(1): 24–42.

Marsden, T. and Sonnino, R. (2008) 'Rural development and the regional state: denying multifunctional agriculture in the UK', *Journal of Rural Studies*, 24(4): 422–431.

McGehee, N.G. (2007) 'An agritourism systems model: a Weberian perspective', *Journal of Sustainable Tourism*, 15(2): 111–124.

McGehee, N.G., Kim, K. and Jennings, G.R. (2007) 'Gender and motivation for agri-tourism entrepreneurship', *Tourism Management*, 2: 280–289.

McKercher, B., Okumus, F. and Okumus, B. (2008) 'Food tourism as a viable market segment: it's all how you cook the numbers!' *Journal of Travel and Tourism Marketing*, 25(2): 137–148.

Miles, M.B. and Huberman, A.M. (1994) *Qualitative Data Analysis: An Expanded Sourcebook*, 2nd edn, London: Sage.

Morley, A., Sparkes, A. and Thomas, B. (2000) 'Strategic and regional initiatives in the agri-food industry in Wales', *British Food Journal*, 102(4): 274–289.

Ollenburg, C. and Buckley, R. (2007) 'Stated economic and social motivations of farm tourism operators', *Journal of Travel Research*, 45(4): 444–452.

Park, D.-B., Doh, K.-R. and Kim K.-H. (2014) 'Successful managerial behaviour for farm-based tourism: a functional approach', *Tourism Management*, 45: 201–210.

Philip, S., Hunter, C. and Blackstock, K. (2010) 'A typology of for defining agritourism', *Tourism Management*, 31: 754–758.

Porcaro, P. (2010) 'The Italian agritourism model – 3Ps – policy, product and promotion: recommendations for developing agritourism in Australia', in *CAUTHE Conference 2010: Tourism and Hospitality: Challenge the Limits*, School of Management, University of Tasmania, Hobart, Tasmania.

Prideaux, B. (2009) *Resort Destinations: Evolution, Management and Development*, Oxford: Butterworth Heinemann.

Renting, H., Rossing, W., Groot, J., Van der Ploeg, J., Laurent, C., Perraud, D., Stobbelaar, D.J. and Van Ittersum, M. (2009) 'Exploring multifunctional agriculture. A review of conceptual approaches and prospects for an integrative transitional framework', *Journal of Environmental Management*, 90(2): S112–S123.

Schmitt, M. (2010) 'Agritourism – From additional income to livelihood strategy and rural development', *The Open Social Science Journal*, 3: 41–50.

Sharpley, R. and Telfer, D.J. (eds) (2002) *Tourism and Development: Concepts and Issues*, Clevedon: Channel View Publications.

Sidali, K.L., Schulze, H. and Spiller, A. (2007) 'Success factors in the development of farm vacation tourism', Poster session presented at the *105th EAAE Seminar: International Marketing and International Trade of Quality Food Products*, Bologna, Italy, 8–10 March. Available online: <http://ageconsearch.umn.edu/bitstream/7887/1/pp07si01. pdf> (accessed 5 June 2011).

Sonnino, R. (2004) 'For a piece of bread? Interpreting sustainable development through agritourism in Southern Tuscany', *Sociologia Ruralis*, 4(3): 285–300.

Sznajder, M., Przezbórska, L. and Scrimgeour, F. (2009) *Agritourism*, Oxfordshire: CABI.

Telfer, D.J. and Wall, G. (2000) 'Strengthening backward economic linkages: local food purchasing by three Indonesian hotels', *Tourism Geographies*, 2(4): 421–427.

Tew, C. and Barbieri, C. (2012) 'The perceived benefits of agritourism: the provider's perspective', *Tourism Management*, 33(1): 215–224.

Thompson, M. (2013) 'Drivers of agri-tourism development: the case of Margaret River', in the *19th Asia Pacific Tourism Association (APTA) Conference: Integrated Tourism and Hospitality Management: Innovative Development for Asia and Pacific*, Bangkok.

Thompson, M. and Prideaux, B. (2014) 'The significance of cultural heritage in food and wine regions: stories from the Barossa, Australia', in *Charting the New Path: Innovations in Tourism and Hospitality – Innovations, Research and Education*, The Global Tourism and Hospitality Conference and 11th Asia Tourism Forum, Hong Kong.

Torres, R. (2003) 'Linkages between tourism and agriculture in Mexico', *Annals of Tourism Research*, 30(3): 546–566.

Torres, R. and Momsen, J. (eds) (2011) *Tourism and Agriculture: New Geographies of Consumption, Production and Rural Restructuring*, Abingdon: Routledge.

Veal, A.J. (2005) *Business Research Methods: A Managerial Approach*, 2nd edn, Frenchs Forest: Pearson Education Australia.

Weaver, D.B. and Fennell D.A. (1997) 'The vacation farm sector in Saskatchewan: a profile of operations', *Tourism Management*, 18(6): 357–365.

Yin, R.K. (2009) *Case Study Research: Design and Methods*, 4th edn, California: Sage.

5 The role of regional foods and food events in rural destination development

The case of Bario, Sarawak

Samuel Folorunso Adeyinka-Ojo
and Catheryn Khoo-Lattimore

Introduction

For many years, tourism has been used as a tool to develop economies of rural areas (Sharpley 2002, 2007). However, current research shows that rural tourist destinations struggle to market themselves, mainly because they lack distinguishable characteristics (Haven-Tang & Sedgley 2014). Rural destinations tend to sell common tourism attributes which include nature, landscape, cultural heritage, behaviour of the host community and local gastronomy. In this regard, Bario is no exception. Bario is a local village in east Malaysia located in the north-east of Sarawak, very close to the international border with Indonesian Kalimantan. It has an approximate population of 1,200 residents, of which a majority are indigenous Kelabits (Malaysian Government 2011). Given that Bario sits between 3,200 and 6,000 feet above the sea level, it is only accessible via a Twin-Otter small aircraft twice a day. Land accessibility takes between 12 and 14 hours from the nearest city of Miri. Alternatively, one can hike or trek for two days from Ba'kelalan to reach Bario. These difficulties with physical access for both local residents and visitors add to the complexities that rural tourist destinations are already facing in terms of marketing. In order to help promote their village, local tourism entrepreneurs in Bario organised its first Pesta Nukenen – Bario Slow Food and Cultural Festival – in 2006. Now in its tenth year, the event has attracted an increasing number of attendees and is included in the official Sarawak Tourism Board's (STB) calendar of events. Prior to the commencement of Pesta Nukenen, the village has been promoted through its Bario rice products. In this chapter, we explore the viability of villages such as Bario in using regional foods and food events as determinants for rural destination development.

Literature review

Regional foods

The terms "regional food", "local food" or even "ethnic food" have been used interchangeably (Montanari & Staniscia 2009) to describe food that is produced locally and does not require imported raw material (Nummendal & Hall 2006).

Regional food is linked to tradition and heritage inheritance, and these are divided into local, socioeconomic and customs (Tregear et al. 1998). This also means regional food typically has historical associations with individuals or groups of people from lower socioeconomic backgrounds (Tregear et al. 1998). In our study, we adopted the definition of regional food in its simplest form, that is, food produced from a specific local or geographical area or from a particular region. Regional food has been used as a political strategy to boost economic and rural development in regions that suffer economic recession and lack modern development in all social and economic ramifications (OECD 1995; Kneafsey 2000; Hall 2004, 2005). Subsequently, destination marketing organisations are beginning to realise the significance of local food and drink as important attributes of rural destination development (Hall, Johnson & Mitchell 2000; Haven-Tang & Jones 2005; Tregear et al. 1998). Furthermore, consumers, retailers as well as producers often distinguish agricultural products on the basis of origins (Hall & Mitchell 2005). This emphasises the notion of perceived authenticity as an important factor for the acceptability of a regional food as being truly "regional". Therefore, tourists see the appeal of tasting and experiencing regional food in the destinations where such foods are produced (Tregear et al. 1998).

Regional food events for rural destination development

Regional food events are increasingly viewed as a very important element of the travel experience for actual and potential visitors to the different places they plan to visit (Stille 2001). In fact, 'visitation to primary and secondary food producers, food festivals, restaurants and specific locations from which food tasting and/or experiencing the attributes of specialist food production regions are the primary factor for travel' (Hall & Mitchell 2001: 308). Many regional food events are also Slow Food events, a term used to describe events associated with an international movement promoting 'locally sourced ingredients, traditional recipes and taking time to source, prepare and enjoy food' (Dickinson & Lumsdon 2010: 80). The notion of "slow food" is promoted by the Slow Food movement to enhance eating habits and lifestyle of the people in contrast to the unhealthy and fast-paced modern lifestyle (Tam 2008) and to encourage the involvement of more people in artisanal and small-scale food production (Hall 2012). The underlying concept of Slow Food is often presumed to complement the ideals of rural destination offerings (Nilsson et al. 2011; Hall 2012). Studies have also shown that Slow Food festivals are important factors in rural development, because they create social economies based on the conscious ideas of individual's choice, consumption, social life and heritage (Pietrykowski 2004; see also Chapter 9, this volume).

Two theoretical approaches which actors or those involved in the production of regional foods may adopt have been suggested. The first is the supply chain strategy (Pacciani et al. 2001). This strategy includes the integration of local network of actors in the production, processing and marketing of regional foods in order to bring about socioeconomic well-being, employment opportunities for the community and high revenue yield for the local producers through efficient and effective management of regional foods supply chain (Pacciani et al. 2001). The second approach is built on the conceptualisation of regional foods as formidable developmental resources for rural destination. Both approaches suggest that in a rural context, food events and tourism are seen as ways of promoting small producers to be more economically and socially sustainable through increase in visitor's spending, extension of tourist seasons (Chiffoleau 2009), encouraging local and regional food entrepreneurship and networking (Hall 2004, 2005; Mykletun & Gyimothy 2010), and building local identity (Hall 2005; Sims 2009). Studies have shown that regional food events have the capacity to actually transform a rural destination for developmental purposes (Brunori & Rossi 2000). It has also been argued that regional food and its related events are local resources that are indispensable for the social and economic development of rural areas (Terluin 2003). In other words, rural development will be accelerated as a result of economic empowerment of the local community members through increasing demand for regional food production.

Thus far, existing literature and empirical studies seem predominantly concentrated on the role of regional foods and food events as vehicles for social development and community empowerment rather than as promotional tools for marketing a rural destination and developing a destination identity. There is however an implication in recent work that suggests that when a destination is tagged rural and "slow", it may attract tourists who are looking forward to enjoying memorable authentic experiences (Dickinson & Lumsdon 2010; Fullagar, Markwell & Wilson 2012). Therefore, this study aims to fill this gap by exploring how Slow Food events featuring regional foods can be used to market a rural destination such as Bario, our study context. We were particularly interested in understanding if Slow Food festivals can create rural destination awareness; form identity for the destinations they are held in; and generate tourist activities and loyalty. We also note that regional foods and food tourism has been used to enhance destination development mostly in developed countries such as Germany, Spain, the United States (Montanari & Staniscia 2009), Italy (Nilsson et al. 2011), Poland (Borowska 2010) and England (Everett & Aitchison 2008). This is, therefore, one of the first studies to investigate the role of regional foods and food events in a developing country. Consequently, this study is positioned to contribute to the existing knowledge in this field from the context of a developing country.

Methodology

Data collection

Given the aims and exploratory nature of the study, a qualitative approach was adopted. In particular, we conducted participant observation by visiting the annual Pesta Nukenen in Bario every year over a period of three years from 2012 to 2014. In total, we conducted a total of 15 days of participant observation before, during and after the three events, which generated 35 pages of research or field notes in bulleted points. While attending the Slow Food festival, we also conducted in-depth interviews with 35 stakeholders who were present at the Slow Food events as needed until the point of data saturation (Jennings 2010). A combination of convenience and purposive sampling techniques was used in recruiting respondents. In line with our research questions, we constructed a semi-structured protocol that covers questions on how respondents found out about the Slow Food festival and/ or Bario; what they thought about the festival in Bario; and if they were likely to return. Each of the in-depth interviews lasted an average of 45 minutes and was digitally recorded. In most cases, transcription was undertaken on the same day as the in-depth interview was completed so that the collected data would still be fresh in the researchers' minds (Prayag & Ryan 2011).

Thematic data analysis was adopted because it is a qualitative analytic method that involves identifying themes by systematically reading the data very carefully and then re-reading the data several times (Fereday & Muir-Cochrane 2006). This study also adopted the six stages of thematic analysis as recommended by Braun and Clarke (2006) which calls for researchers to familiarise themselves with the data, develop initial codes, search for relevant themes, review emerging themes, define and label codes, and finally produce a report of the findings. The thematic analysis, however, took a more focussed approach as the authors specifically looked out for codes and themes that will answer the three research questions. Notes from the participant observation were used as supplementary data and content analysed for the themes developed from the in-depth interviews.

Findings and discussion

The reporting of the findings is aligned with the research questions posed earlier. First, data is presented on the role of regional foods and food festivals in creating rural destination awareness. The findings are then outlines of the role of regional foods and food festivals in forming identity for the destinations they are held in, which is Bario. In this respect, findings point to the potential of food events in generating tourist activities and destination attractions. This is followed by findings on local food experience and satisfaction for repeat visit and tourist loyalty. Finally, regional foods and food events are indicated as determinants in rural destination development.

Respondent profile

Table 5.1 summarises the 35 respondents who participated in in-depth interviews. The 35 respondents consist of 15 tourists, 15 local residents, 1 agricultural investor, 1 marketing and branding expert for Bario, and 3 key informants from government agencies (immigration, STB and Ministry of Tourism Sarawak). Most of these visitors had stayed between three and seven nights in Bario at the time of their interviews, with one to four more days to spend after the respective food festivals.

Table 5.1 Summary of the respondents

Year	Tourists	Local residents	Government agencies	Bario rice investor	Marketing and branding expert	Total
2012	5	5	1	–	–	11
2013	3	4	–	–	–	7
2014	7	6	2	1	1	17
Total	15	15	3	1	1	35

The role of regional foods and food festivals in creating rural destination awareness

As highlighted above, although destination awareness is important in generating tourist arrivals and activities, it is a main issue for many rural destinations due to their remoteness, lack of infrastructure and limited marketing resources. This could be because the core tourist attractions in rural areas often lack the iconic backdrops of infrastructure, superstructure and historical sites available in popular tourist destinations to create awareness (Haven-Tang & Jones 2005; Harmaakorpi, Kari & Parjanen 2008); therefore, regional foods can be used to create a unique selling proposition for rural destinations. However, can regional foods and food events be utilised as a tool to generate awareness for Bario as a holiday destination? This was not the case with Pesta Nukenen for Bario, as a 27-year-old Australian commented:

> I got to know Bario through Lonely Planet website and Internet. I came to Bario with my two friends for jungle trekking and to experience the place. But we were told about the slow food festivals on arrival at Bario airport.

Findings show that very few of the foreign tourists were in Bario for the Pesta Nukenen. In fact, most of the tourists knew Bario because of the recreational forest that is positively mentioned on the Internet. This confirms previous studies of Bario as being a favourite eco-tourist destination (Jiwan, Alan & Lepun 2007; Adeyinka-Ojo & Khoo-Lattimore 2013). Visitors from Malaysia who attended the food events in Bario were invited by word-of-mouth through friends and relatives. Word-of-mouth is viewed as an important information source in influencing a consumer's (tourist) choice of destination (Reisinger & Turner 2002), particularly for a small-scale food festival in a rural setting.

The role of regional foods and festivals in forming destination identity

Destination identity relates to the promotion of a tourist destination by the local, regional or national tourism organisations and deals with how these agencies want the destination to be perceived or seen (Kaplanidou & Vogt 2003). The following participant statement by a resident and shop owner shows that, at least for the residents, Bario's regional crop has been a significant determinant in forming Bario's identity as a destination:

Here in Bario, the whole foods are produced locally for the benefits of our people and to sell our Bario rice in the city, which has placed Bario on the world map. For me, Bario rice is a local and regional identity in Malaysia.

A key informant from the Ministry of Tourism, Sarawak seemed to understand the significance of Bario's crops:

The most important point is that local and regional food should be original not the one from outside but foods that are produced and identify with the local people. In Bario, they have pineapple and Bario rice these have received global recognition in Italy ... So the community in Bario has been staging slow food events for years to promote the local food as a mark of regional identity.

Findings such as these are consistent with those of Jiwan et al. (2007) who postulated that Bario's pineapple and rice had promoted the name of Bario to the outside world long before the introduction of tourism. Although pineapples and rice identify "Asianness" in general, Bario did indeed receive an international award and recognition in Italy in 2002 for producing them (Bulan & Bulan-Dorai 2004). This finding is consistent with the work of Lin, Pearson and Cai (2009) who argued that food can be used as a form of destination identity, and regional food generally involves different features associated with a particular destination. Everett and Aitchison (2008) and Fox (2007) also suggest that regional food can play an important role in achieving a consistent identity. Unfortunately, however, even though its local rice and culture may have inadvertently sold the word "Bario", people who have heard of Bario may associate the name with a product brand and not necessarily a tourist destination that they are going to visit in the near future.

Food events as generators of tourist activities and destination attractions

Food is regarded as one of the tourist destination attractions especially where such destinations are well established and known for different food offerings. The participants were asked why they chose to attend food event in Bario. This was important in order to explore the participants' responses if food event and regional food was the motivating factor for their visit to Bario. A 72-year-old Australian tourist admitted:

To experience something different like the food, the food here is different I don't get rice cooked like this in other destinations, ... it is really exotic, it's something I really like to try ... something you don't get anywhere ... it is something that attracts more visitors to Bario.

An informant from the STB echoed:

Ok, for me it is ... very nice to see all the villages coming together and bringing crops and foods, I think it is an exciting event to see the diverse cultures and food to attract more tourists to Bario and to promote tourism.

These findings are corroborated by past studies that illustrate how tourist destination attractions have been supported through food as an important factor in tourism marketing (Lin et al. 2009). Although we cannot be sure that food was the main attraction for the tourists in Bario, Pesta Nukanen did add value for visitors. In developed economies, regional food has been used both in urban and rural destinations to attract tourists (Jones & Jenkins 2002; Cambourne & Macionis 2003; Henderson 2004). In developing a strong destination tourist attraction, there is a need for 'a clear and desirable identity' (Lin et al. 2009: 32). Notably, previous studies indicate that tourists were attracted to destinations with unique regional and ethnic foods identity to have a memorable food consumption experience (Reynolds 1993; Cohen & Avieli 2004), and this seems to also be the case for a rural destination in a developing country.

Local food experience and satisfaction for tourist loyalty

Local food experience and satisfaction are key attributes of the determinants of rural destination development. Local food satisfaction can not only improve the profile of the rural destination as a regional food basket but also build rural destination loyalty and subsequently increase tourist arrivals and receipts. Pesta Nukenen seems to be a promising vehicle for encouraging tourist satisfaction and loyalty as evidenced in this confession by a 54-year-old American tourist:

> This local food event in Bario is pleasant, exciting, nice and fulfilling. Honestly, I cannot believe what I'm seeing in terms of the varieties of local foods, lots of people, … in fact this food event is like a family thing … a great experience, great event. We all queued, both tourists and locals, to collect our food, sit at the same table and eat together. It is a unique experience and satisfaction … it shows Bario is good place to spend a holiday.

These findings confirm that regional foods play an important role in terms of contribution to tourists' experiences, enjoyment and satisfaction (Yuksel & Yuksel 2002) and the decision to revisit (Yoon & Uysal 2005). In fact, two of the 15 tourists interviewed were visiting Bario for the second time, while one was visiting for the fourth time.

Regional foods and food events as determinants in rural destination development

In achieving rural development using food production and staging of food event, there is a need to engage multiple destination stakeholders especially the local community, government agencies and tourists. This is because the primary responsibility of producing the local food lies with the local residents. On the part of the respective government agencies such as the Ministry of Agriculture and Tourism, they must encourage local food production. Comments include that of a key informant from Ceria Group rice factory in Bario:

So in year 2011, we came to Bario and saw that the land was suitable for planting paddy rice and most of the lands were lying idle and wasted due to lack of good irrigation system ... we got approval from PEMANDU a unit in the Prime Minister's Department of Malaysia ... so we built seven dams and connected them with pipes for the irrigation system.

To illustrate the importance of food as a determinant of rural development, a key informant at the Department of Immigration in Kuching, Sarawak, Malaysia, commented:

Well the Bario rice, pineapple and Bario salt are important tourist attractions in Bario. We think there should be better services to complement the food production and food event ... so we are building the biggest project in Bario, the new immigration office at about RM20 million (or US$5.5 million) in order to improve the quality of tourism services to the visitors through infrastructures development.

Interestingly, a previous study conducted in Bario shows that 'the most significant economic development to date is an initiative to network with local agriculture authorities to boost outside sales of Bario's special form of rice, which is renowned throughout the country (Malaysia) for its sweet fragrance' (Bulan & Bulan-Dorai 2004: 207–208). Indeed, the authors' observations over the three years of the Bario food festival from 2012 to 2014 confirm that the developmental projects in Bario were connected to Bario as a regional food producer.

The study was interested to see if and how Slow Food events featuring regional foods can help market a rural destination such as Bario, and four themes were identified that point to the potential of regional food and food events to be conceptualised as a marketing arm for Bario. Specially, regional foods and food events have the capacity to create destination awareness, form destination identity, generate tourist activities and contribute to tourist satisfaction. In Bario, the potential of regional foods also functions as a catalyst for rural development. These findings are illustrated in a framework in Figure 5.1.

Implications

In the case of Bario, the roles of regional food and food event in rural destination development are important to a certain extent. Notably, the ongoing agricultural activities in Bario indicate that regional food produced in Bario has been able to attract investment in agriculture. For example, in July 2014, the Ceria Group rice mill factory was commissioned to help develop Bario. The company built seven dams to sustain the irrigation for rice farming in Bario. Paddy rice is currently the mainstay of Bario economy, which has been perceived by stakeholders as promoting Bario to the outside world (Jiwan et al. 2007). In this regard, Bario has the potential to be developed as a "food basket" for the region. Furthermore, the investment in rice farming has created employment opportunities for the locals,

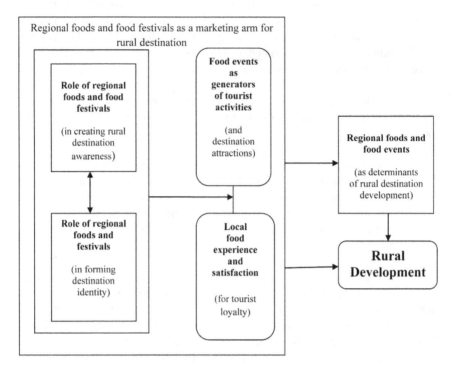

Figure 5.1 Framework for the role of regional foods and food events in rural destination
marketing and development

increase in rice production output, and revenue for the local rice distributors and
retailers to sell the surplus rice outside Bario. This study did not explore in detail
the role forestry plays, but Bario prides itself in forest, farming and food (also
referred to as FFFs by the locals) as its major tourist attractions.

Due to limited available seats in the small aircraft, many potential visitors could not attend the Slow Food event in Bario. As a result, a concrete road
was built between Bario and its nearest village, Pa 'Umor, to link with the log-
ging road. In addition, an ultra-modern immigration office has been developed.
Accessibility to Bario has also been improved with the increase in the number of
daily flights from two to three with effect from July 2014. Similarly, the number
of flights per day increased from two to six during the 2014 Pesta Nukenen to
cater to the tourists who attended the Slow Food event. Relevant government
agencies, corporate organisations and individuals are making efforts to provide
the basic amenities that are lacking in Bario, such as electricity. So far, they have
collaboratively developed solar panels and constructed a community clinic and a
staff residential apartment. The developmental project and improved air services
in Bario are directly linked to the regional food production and the staging of the
annual Slow Food event in Bario. These changes in Bario point to the potential

roles of regional foods and food festivals in rural destinations in a developing country and correspond with the findings made by scholars on rural tourist destinations in developed countries (Kalkstein-Silkes 2007; Lee & Arcodia 2011; Nilsson et al. 2011).

On the other hand, the numbers of foreign tourists at the Slow Food events in Bario over 2012–2014 were not encouraging due to a lack of awareness. Those who attended the events did so because they were already there for reasons other than Pesta Nukenen. There is therefore a need that those with the responsibilities to develop Bario and its local events focus on the marketing and communication of Pesta Nukenen as well as its rice and pineapple to attract some more active participation in Bario as a viable tourist eco-destination.

Conclusion

From a theoretical perspective, this study has extended past studies which mainly verified the role of regional foods and food events in developing the social, economic and political welfare of rural communities. This study explored the functions of regional foods in developing a rural destination from a marketing perspective. The findings confirm that although regional food events can generate tourist satisfaction and loyalty, they may not yet be able to fully create rural destination awareness or form identity for the destinations they are held in. However, it confirms previous work that regional foods and food festivals do indeed bring about positive developments into a rural destination, even in a developing country where resources can be restricted. As a remote destination, Bario has been able to attract paddy rice investment, donors, government sponsored projects and support from the Malaysian federal marketing authority to improve its local food production and marketing. In view of this evidence, it is concluded that regional foods and food events can be conceptualised as determinants for rural destination development.

Acknowledgements

The funding for this project has been made possible through the research grant obtained from the Malaysian Ministry of Education Long Term Research Grant Scheme Programme (Reference No. JPT.S(BPKI)2000/09/01/015Jld.4(67)).

References

Adeyinka-Ojo, S.F. and Khoo-Lattimore, C. (2013) 'Slow Food events as a high yield strategy for rural tourism destinations – the case of Bario, Sarawak', *Worldwide Hospitality and Tourism Themes*, 5(4): 353–364.

Borowska, A. (2010) 'The role of traditional and regional food products in rural development in Poland', *Socialiniai Tyrimai/Social Research*, 18(1): 50–52.

Braun, V. and Clarke, V. (2006) 'Using thematic analysis in psychology', *Qualitative Research in Psychology*, 3: 77–101.

Brunori, G. and Rossi, A. (2000) 'Synergy and coherence through collective action: some insights from wine routes in Tuscany', *Sociologia Ruralis*, 40(4): 409–423.

Bulan, S. and Bulan-Dorai, L. (2004) *The Bario Revival*, Kuala Lumpur: Home Matters Network.

Cambourne, B. and Macionis, N. (2003) 'Linking food, wine and tourism: the case of the Australian Capital Region', in C.M. Hall, L. Sharples, B. Cambourne, N. Macionis, and R. Mitchell (eds) *Food Tourism around the World: Development, Management and Markets*, Oxford: Butterworth-Heinemann, pp. 268–284.

Chiffoleau, Y. (2009) 'From politics to co-operation: the dynamics of embeddedness in alternative food supply chains', *Sociologia Ruralis*, 49(3): 218–235.

Cohen, E. and Avieli, N. (2004) 'Food in tourism: attraction and impediment', *Annals of Tourism Research*, 31(4): 755–778.

Dickinson, J. and Lumsdon, L. (2010) *Slow Travel and Tourism*, London: Earthscan.

Everett, S. and Aitchison, C. (2008) 'The role of food tourism in sustaining regional identity: a case study of Cornwall, South West England', *Journal of Sustainable Tourism*, 16(2): 150–167.

Fereday, J. and Muir-Cochrane, E. (2006) 'Demonstrating rigor using thematic analysis: a hybrid approach of inductive and deductive coding and theme development', *International Journal of Qualitative Methods*, 5(1): 1–11.

Fox, R. (2007) 'Reinventing the gastronomic identity of Croatian tourist destinations', *International Journal of Hospitality Management*, 26(3): 546–559.

Fullagar, S., Markwell, K. and Wilson, E. (eds) (2012) *Slow Tourism: Experiences and Mobilities*, Bristol: Channel View.

Hall, C.M. (2004) 'Small firms and wine and food tourism in New Zealand: issues of collaboration, clusters and lifestyles', in R. Thomas (ed.) *Small Firms in Tourism: International Perspectives*, Oxford: Elsevier, pp. 167–181.

Hall, C.M. (2005) 'Rural wine and food tourism cluster and network development', in D. Hall, I. Kirkpatrick, and M. Mitchell (eds) *Rural Tourism and Sustainable Business*, Clevedon: Channel View, pp. 149–164.

Hall, C.M. (2012) 'The contradictions and paradoxes of Slow Food: environmental change, sustainability and the conservation of taste', in S. Fullagar, K. Markwell, and E. Wilson (eds) *Slow Tourism: Experiences and Mobilities*, Bristol: Channel View, pp. 53–68.

Hall, C.M., Johnson, G. and Mitchell, R. (2000) 'Wine tourism and regional development', in C.M. Hall, L. Sharples, N. Macionis, and B. Cambourne (eds) *Wine Tourism around the World*, Oxford: Butterworth Heinemann, pp. 196–225.

Hall, C.M. and Mitchell, R. (2001) 'Wine and food tourism', in N. Douglas and R. Derrett (eds) *Special Interest Tourism*, Brisbane: Wiley, pp. 307–329.

Hall, C.M. and Mitchell, R. (2005) 'Gastronomic tourism – comparing food wine experiences', in B. Novelli (ed.) *Niche Tourism: Contemporary Issues, Trends and Cases*, Oxford: Butterworth Heinemann, pp. 73–88.

Harmaakorpi, V., Kari, K. and Parjanen, S. (2008) 'City design management as a local competitiveness factor', *Place Branding and Public Diplomacy*, 4: 169–181.

Haven-Tang, C. and Jones, E. (2005) 'Using local food and drink to differentiate tourism destinations through a sense of place: a story from Wales-Dinning at Monmouthshire's Great Table', *Journal of Culinary Science and Technology*, 4(4): 69–85.

Haven-Tang, C. and Sedgley, D. (2014) 'Partnership working in enhancing the destination brand of rural areas: a case study of made in Monmouthshire, Wales, UK', *Journal of Destination Marketing and Management*, 3: 59–67.

Henderson, J.C. (2004) 'Food as a tourism resource: a view from Singapore', *Tourism Recreation Research*, 29(3): 69–74.

Jennings, G. (2010) *Tourism Research*, 2nd edn, Milton: Wiley.

Jiwan, M., Alan, R. and Lepun, P. (2007) *Agro-eco-tourism Potential and Benefits for Sustaining Kelabit Community in Bario*, Department of Agriculture Sciences, Faculty of Agriculture and Food Sciences, Universiti Putra Malaysia Bintulu Campus, Sarawak.

Jones, A. and Jenkins, I. (2002) 'A Taste of Wales – Blas ArGymur: institutional malaise in promoting Welsh food tourism products', in A.-M. Hjalager and G. Richards (eds) *Tourism and Gastronomy*, London: Routledge, pp. 115–131.

Kalkstein-Silkes, C.A. (2007) 'Food and food related festivals in rural destination branding', PhD thesis, Purdue University, Indiana.

Kaplanidou, K. and Vogt, C. (2003) *Destination Branding: Concept and Measurement*, Department of Park, Recreation and Tourism Resources, Michigan State University.

Kneafsey, M. (2000) 'Tourism, place identities and social relations in the European rural periphery', *European Urban and Regional Studies*, 25(1): 157–176.

Lee, I. and Arcodia, C. (2011) 'The role of regional food festivals for destination branding', *International Journal of Tourism Research*, 13(4): 355–367.

Lin, Y.-C., Pearson, T.E. and Cai, L.A. (2009) 'Food as a form of destination identity: a tourism destination brand perspective', *Tourism and Hospitality Research*, 11(1): 30–48.

Malaysian Government (2011) *Population and Housing Census of Malaysia: Preliminary Count Report 2010*, Malaysia.

Montanari, A. and Staniscia, B. (2009) 'Culinary tourism as a tool for regional re-equilibrium', *European Planning Studies*, 17(10): 1463–1483.

Mykletun, R., and Gyimothy, S. (2010) 'Beyond the renaissance of the traditional Voss sheep's-head meal: tradition, culinary art, scariness and entrepreneurship', *Tourism Management*, 31(3): 434–446.

Nilsson, J.H., Svard, A.C., Widarsson, A. and Wirell, T. (2011) 'Cittaslow' eco-gastronomic heritage as a tool for destination development', *Current Issues in Tourism*, 14(4): 373–386.

Nummendal, M. and Hall, C.M. (2006) 'Local food in tourism: an investigation of the New Zealand South Island's bed and breakfast sector's use and perception of local food', *Tourism Review International*, 9(4): 365–378.

OECD (1995) *Niche Markets as a Rural Development Strategy*, Paris: OECD.

Pacciani, A., Belletti, G., Marescotti, A. and Scaramizzi, S. (2001) 'The role of typical products in fostering rural development and the effects of regulation (EEC) 2081/92', Paper presented at *Policy Experiences with Rural Development in Diversified Europe, 73rd EAAE Seminar*, Ancona, Italy, 28–30 June 2001.

Pietrykowski, B. (2004) 'You are what you eat: the social economy of the Slow Food movement', *Review of Social Economy*, 62(3): 307–321.

Prayag, G. and Ryan, C. (2011) 'The relationship between the "push" and "pull" factors of a tourist destination: the role of nationality – an analytical qualitative research approach', *Current Issues in Tourism*, 14(2): 121–143.

Reisinger, Y. and Turner, L.W. (2002) 'Cultural differences between Asian tourist markets and Australian Hosts, Part 1', *Journal of Tourism Research*, 40(3): 295–315.

Reynolds, P.C. (1993) 'Food and tourism: towards an understanding of sustainable culture', *Journal of Sustainable Tourism*, 1(1): 18–54.

Sharpley, R. (2002) 'The challenges of economic diversification through tourism: the case of Abu Dhabi', *International Journal of Tourism Research*, 4: 221–235.

Sharpley, R. (2007) 'Flagship attractions and sustainable rural tourism development: the case of the Alnwick Garden, England', *Journal of Sustainable Tourism*, 5(6): 527–537.

Sims, R. (2009) 'Food, place and authenticity: local food and the sustainable tourism experience', *Journal of Sustainable Tourism*, 17(3): 321–336.

Stille, A. (2001) 'Slow Food- an Italian answer to globalisation', *The Nation*, 9 August. Available online: <www.thenation.com≥ (accessed 20 June 2015).

Tam, D. (2008) 'Slow journeys: what does it mean to go slow?' *Food Culture and Society*, 11(2): 207–218.

Terluin, I. (2003) 'Differences in economic development in rural regions of advanced countries: an overview and critical analysis of theories', *Journal of Rural Studies*, 19: 327–344.

Tregear, A., Kuznesof, S. and Moxey, A. (1998) 'Policy initiatives for regional foods: some insights from consumer research', *Food Policy*, 23(5): 383–394.

Yoon, Y. and Uysal, M. (2005) 'An examination of the effects of motivation and satisfaction on destination loyalty: a structural model', *Tourism Management*, 26(1): 45–56.

Yuksel, A. and Yuksel, F. (2002) 'Measurement of tourist satisfaction with restaurant service: a segment-based approach', *Journal of Vacation Marketing*, 9(1): 52–68.

6 Local foods, rural networks and tourism development

A comparative study between Michigan, United States, and the North Midlands, Ireland

Cecilia Hegarty and Deborah Che

Introduction

Structural changes have reshaped the "farmscape". Fundamental changes include ever-increasing farm sizes, technology-intensive production and commodity-driven conditions such as genetically modified crops and cloning (*The Economist* 2011). However, with falling commodity prices, global competition and global shifts in consumer tastes, farmers must diversify. The rural tourism diversification strategy can bring greater variation in work tasks, reduce seasonality and prevent social isolation that comes with traditional farming (*Irish Times* 2010). Rural tourism can also allow visitors to 'go back to their roots' and educate their children about the 'farm to fork' experience.

Tourism plays an important role in diversifying rural economies, preserving rural space and maintaining rural lifestyles. This chapter investigates issues facing entrepreneurs in order to identify ways of strengthening tourism and product development. A combination of focus groups, surveys and interview techniques were conducted in the United States and Ireland. The American case study focusses on the state of Michigan, which is the second most agriculturally diverse state, producing more than 200 commodities (Meyer 2011). The Irish case study concentrates on the North Midlands, where tourism has regenerated the area and preserved rural landscapes and heritage. The chapter explores entrepreneurial views towards product quality, development potential and market orientation with two aspects of business survival and growing the industry being identified: working cooperatively and using the available local resources to produce, market and sell products. Finally, the article reflects upon supporting change in rural areas that is reflected in tourism development.

This chapter firstly describes the context and challenges for local foods and rural tourism development. The Methods section then explains how the cases of Michigan and North Midland counties (NMCs) were derived and documents the case history. By comparing the cases, evidence is produced from both countries showing how rural networks operate to form clusters and illustrate the value of local resources that can make these businesses more successful and competitive. These entrepreneurs illustrate how engagement with tourism can be rewarding.

Study background

Local foods and tourism development in rural areas

A decline in the agricultural sector in developed countries has prompted rural tourism development. In 1990, agriculture employed more than 25 per cent of the labour force in predominantly rural regions of only three OECD countries, while services accounted for more than 25 per cent of employment in predominantly rural regions of all OECD countries (Bryden & Bollman 2000). Moreover, intensive farming on larger holdings has allayed shortages in home-grown food products. While agricultural production has remained high in the United States, the number of farms, particularly mid-sized ones, has declined. In the US Midwestern state of Michigan, farmland has decreased from about 11 million acres (4,428,140 hectares) in 1982 to under 10 million acres (4,026,041 hectares) in 2012 (US Department of Agriculture 2012). Farmland conversions for quasi-rural housing developments has seriously affected agriculture's long-term viability since farmland as a resource works best when kept in large, landscape-sized blocks (*The Fruit Growers News* 2004). As an alternative to selling land for development, to address higher operating costs, increased global competition, relatively low commodity prices and changing consumer tastes, Michigan farmers have shifted from strictly wholesale operations and diversified into agri-tourism comprising retail businesses featuring gift shops with local, niche products and attractions such as corn mazes and kids' play areas (Youssef 2009).

Likewise, the Irish agricultural industry showed a continued decline during the 1990s. The 1991 agricultural census indicated a decrease of 57,500 farms within 16 years, resulting in a 24 per cent reduction in the aging, primary industry workforce (Teagasc 2001). Only 13 per cent of Irish farm holders were under the age of 35 years. The most recent national farm survey has shown through an analysis of the demographic data by region that the highest incidence of off-farm employment occurred on farms in the West and Midlands regions (under study in this investigation) where the incidence of off-farm employment for the farmer and/or the spouse was 60 and 57 per cent respectively, compared to the national average of 51 per cent (Hennessy et al. 2011).

While agricultural bodies and advocates are enthusiastic about retaining agricultural traditions, they recognise that they alone cannot sustain viable rural populations. The main sources of concern for rural Ireland include its declining population, the disadvantages in attracting new jobs and retaining existing employment, persistent relative poverty and the decreasing number of farm and farm-related jobs (Hynes, Morrissey & O'Donoghue 2005). The rural population as a whole is dependent on a wider spectrum of activities, which includes tourism (Department of Agriculture and Rural Development for Northern Ireland 2000). Rural tourism can help maintain the landscape, arts and crafts population and thus rural services (e.g. public transport, emergency services). It can also increase appreciation of the natural resource base, which is important when considering the alternative uses of the rural landscape.

Global trends have spurred rural tourism development. Positive perceptions of the idyllic rural lifestyle present rural entrepreneurs with market opportunities for establishing and diversifying rural enterprises for tourism. The rural area also has drawing power for urbanites who are attracted by the availability of land and lifestyle (Keeble & Tyler 1995; Carter & Rosa 1998; Parker 2009; Nelson, Oberg, & Nelson 2010; Gosnell & Abrams 2011). Their in-migration can lead to new product innovations, niche markets and changes in destination life cycles (Storey et al. 1987; Hegarty & McDonagh 2003; Stockdale 2006). Government intervention has been significant in encouraging farmers to become involved in rural tourism as a means of generating income and maintaining a living countryside (European Commission 2003; Daugstad, Rønningen & Skar 2006).

While the bulk of US government agricultural support involves commodity price support payments going mainly to large-scale soybean, corn, wheat and soybean farmers (McFerson 2014), the US Department of Agriculture's long-standing but relatively modestly funded Federal-State Marketing Improvement Program (FSMIP) supports specialty crops and alternative farm marketing, including tourism. FSMIP has funded projects that would further specialty agricultural production, agriculture-based education and entertainment. Small- to mid-sized diversified farms in Michigan and around the United States are ideally suited to providing these products and services.

The University of California Small Farm Program (2011) defines agri-tourism as 'a commercial enterprise at a working farm, ranch, or agricultural plant conducted for the enjoyment of visitors that generates supplemental income for the owner'. In the United States, the core product of agri-tourism is agri-entertainment (Bagi & Reeder 2012). Specific agri-tourism products include educational tours (e.g. school group farm tours, nature walks, workshops), special events (e.g. public annual/holiday festivals and private birthdays, weddings, corporate picnics), children/family amusements (e.g. playgrounds, horseback riding, crop art/mazes, farm animal petting zoos, hayrides) and Pick-Your-Own (U-Pick) fruits and vegetables.

European Union (EU) funding programmes such as the European Regional Development Fund, EU Rural Development Fund, International Fund for Ireland and the Operational Programme for Rural Development and the Interreg I and II Programmes and LEADER I, II and + programmes have invested heavily in Irish rural tourism (Department of Agriculture, Food and Rural Development 1994; Government Information Services 1999; Fitzpatrick Associates Economic Consultants 2000). Prior to diverse EU programmes to support tourism (e.g. LEADER (an acronym in French referring to an EU series of programmes meaning Links between actions for the development of the rural economy)), rural development schemes in Ireland focussed on compensatory allowances to support farming incomes in less favoured areas that compose 74.8 per cent of the country and which support many of Ireland's honey-pot destinations today.

The foundation attractions in Irish rural tourism (Ó Cinnéide & Walsh 1990) supply a range of products appealing to both active and passive tourists. These rural tourists generally are in search of subliminal experiences and desire to be removed from daily experiences. The product range includes farm activities (e.g. turf cutting, farmhouse cooking and animal feeding), off-farm activities (e.g. fishing, rock climbing, bird/dolphin watching, hill/forest walks, canoeing, golf, orienteering, shooting and cycling), general (e.g. health farms, heritage or nature trails, art, crafts and Gaelic language), entertainment (e.g. music or dance in traditional pubs, barns or community centres) and heritage attractions (e.g. abbeys, museums, gardens, caves, churches and castles).

Challenges to rural development

Rural regions face many challenges in developing tourism. Traditional farmers have been resistant to change. Among the most common reasons why farm tourism projects fail are poor marketing, failure to understand the tourism business, inadequate planning, lack of people skills and failure to maintain standards (Knowd 2006). The absence of complimentary tourism ventures can be another challenge to developing a rural tourism destination (Weaver & Fennell 1997). Rural tourism operators need to link with each other in order to identify weaknesses in product development that prevent the locality from reaching its tourism potential. Rural cooperatives have been advocated as early as the 1970s (see Faber 1976). Working cooperatively and symbiotically can strengthen indigenous entrepreneurship (Holmlund & Fulton 1999). The extent of local interaction with rural tourism entrepreneurs, the local business community and local residents is important. Embedded business networks are key to the success of new small-scale artisanal or organic producers and quality local food systems (Che, Veeck & Veeck 2005; Selfa & Qazi 2005; Stræte 2008; McCarthy 2014).

The lack of available labour and appropriate infrastructure can act as a growth inhibitor for rural tourism enterprises that rely upon voluntary labour (e.g. family or neighbours). Sourcing staff to work in seasonal tourism enterprises is difficult. Hiring college students seeking full-time summer employment, particularly those with backgrounds in agriculture and returning to the area over the extended school break, may be one way of dealing with seasonality (Black & Nickerson 1997). Transportation into, out of and around rural regions is of concern not only to business operations (e.g. transporting goods, staff mobility) but also to attracting customers.

Competition from the larger urban environment is another factor challenging rural tourism development. Rural businesses can succeed by offering a certain product range or unique, authentic experiences that cannot be found outside of the region. While national retail chains and Internet vendors can offer lower prices and convenience, rural retailers can successfully draw customers by emphasising personalised service, cultivating community goodwill and adapting service strategies to meet local consumer needs (Hurst, Niehm & Littrell 2009; Jackson & Stoel 2011; Hurst & Niehm 2012).

Methods

The methods used in this study to develop the cases independently were a combination of focus groups, surveys and interviews. The three sub-regions under study in the American case were chosen because of their location and the type of tourist they attracted, while in the Irish case the seven sub-regions were devised according to the natural resources present which steered the type of enterprise innovation. Both cases therefore had broad representation of the enterprise diversity within Michigan and the North Midlands.

In the Michigan case, focus groups of agri-tourism producers were convened during 2002 to determine the impact of agriculture-based destinations on Michigan's tourism economy. A range of individual agri-tourism producers were invited to participate in focus groups in order to identify the diversity of Michigan's agricultural products. These included apples/cider, wine, peaches, cherries, asparagus, pumpkins and squash. Farmers selling fruits and vegetables and resulting value-added products were selected as these small- to medium-sized producers were heavily represented in Michigan agri-tourism relative to larger commodity-oriented corn, soybean and dairy farmers. The focus groups also ensured the geographical diversity of producers, customer bases, marketing techniques and the residential and commercial pressures facing farmers. Focus groups were convened in south-west Michigan, northern Michigan's Traverse City area, and rapidly suburbanising central and south-east Michigan (Figure 6.1). The focus groups centred around key issues in marketing and developing Michigan agri-tourism, experiences with agri-tourism, the potential and impact of agri-tourism and what constituted successful and unsuccessful agri-tourism operations.

Utilising the focus group material, a comprehensive survey was developed at Western Michigan University and by the Michigan Department of Agriculture and Rural Development (formerly Michigan Department of Agriculture) to assess the impact of agri-tourism on Michigan's economy. The survey contained questions about location, products and services, visitation, income, employees, wages, revenues and advertising. Several sets of Likert-type questions were designed to identify opinions related to the benefits of these businesses. The survey also incorporated open-ended questions related to current and future concerns. Surveys were delivered to approximately 1,500 operations. Additional surveys were distributed at various industry meetings and conventions during late 2002 and early 2003. Approximately 20 per cent, or 311 surveys (301 usable), were returned by June 2003 and are included in this analysis.

In the Irish case, the first author conducted a nationwide entrepreneurial census through non-random postal questionnaires in order to generate a descriptive profile of rural entrepreneurs. Mail surveys for this research were facilitated by collaboration with LEADER II Local Action Groups (LAGs), since the Irish small-medium enterprises had no official statistics, County Enterprise Boards did not have a central database, and the tourism boards did not have annual reports specific to the rural environment. In total there are 48 LAGs, 15 of which are located in Northern Ireland. LEADER has a number of operational programmes. The LEADER II programme, operational during 1994–1999, was selected. Survey administration was timed to coincide with the 2001 national census and was presented in English with Gaelic additions for Gaeltacht areas. The survey

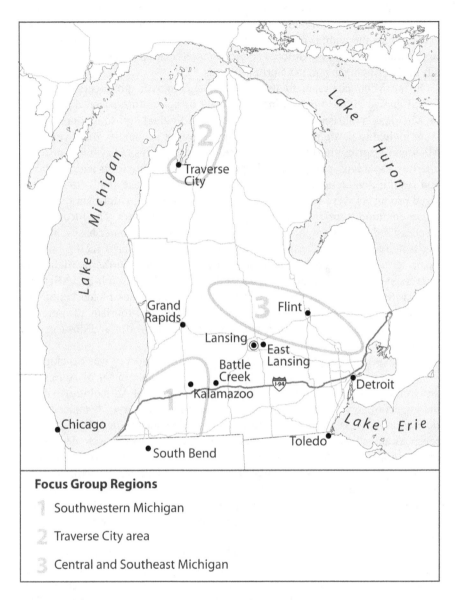

Figure 6.1 Map of Michigan featuring study areas
Source: Deborah Che.

focussed on aspects of business setup, operation, support and entrepreneurial background. From a sample population of 2,697 entrepreneurs, there were 506 usable responses (18.7 per cent). These surveys highlighted the diverse nature of rural tourism providers in Ireland. Their innovativeness and unique variations provided evidence of tourism themed to specific regions. Secondly, they gave some indication of the value of social networks and the dominance of family enterprise within the industry.

Out of the nationwide survey, interviews were conducted with entrepreneurs within the North Midlands study region that has a developing tourism destination status. Interviews were set up to assess the impact of rural tourism on the local economy. This involved collaboration on the EU Fifth Framework programme. The Irish study region included the five NMCs of Westmeath, Longford, Roscommon, Cavan and Leitrim. This region, which is located in the centre of the Republic of Ireland, is at its southerly point approximately a 1.5-hour drive from Dublin. The route partly follows the main inland estuary, the Shannon-Erne waterway. A popular tourist trail which heads south-west from Dublin to the more established, urbanised destinations of Galway, Mayo and the Ring of Kerry bypasses the North Midlands region. The NMCs at best act as a traffic corridor for both domestic and international tourists following their individual trails towards Donegal and Northern Ireland. Residents, business owners and would-be entrepreneurs are beginning to realise they must give visitors more reasons to make the North Midlands their final destination or to get them to stop off en route to their final destinations.

An audit of the enterprises in the North Midlands region showed a possible sample population of 164 enterprises offering a range of products and services. Sixty-seven entrepreneurs were approached for the interviewing process, of which 64 participated. Interviews, which followed a semi-structured approach, concentrated on the following themes: background information on how the business developed and how resources were used to support business operations; experiences of rural tourism development; key issues in marketing and developing rural tourism such as business linkages and local networks; and the impact of rural tourism in the North Midlands region.

In summary, both cases incorporated widespread mail surveys and more in-depth qualitative analysis. Entrepreneurs in both cases were questioned on similar aspects about the tourism markets, visitor expectations and the future of their industry.

Results

Developing tourism products and services

In rural Michigan, agri-tourism primarily consisted of day activities such as U-pick, animal petting zoos and educational tours. In south-west Michigan, farms attracted visitors from Chicagoland (the Chicago metropolitan area), often for an extended weekend since the region supported B&Bs, hotels and motels. In addition, some visitors owned a holiday/second home in the region. The Traverse City region in the northern part of the study region, in particular, accommodated second home owners during the summer months where product development has evolved to satisfy a high-end market with a lot of disposable income.

An educational product has been developed throughout Michigan where mid-sized farms provide pre-industrial farm experiences. One northern Michigan entrepreneur described his working farm as a place where 'people can come out and see animals, chickens, sheep, goats, cows. People can come out and interact with the animals, which they like ... it's not your average farmer's "going to have them out in the barnyard"'. These agri-tourism enterprises also developed farm-themed special events such as festivals orientated around blossoms, cherries, apples/cider and the fall harvest in addition to holidays such as Valentine's Day, Mother's Day, Fourth of July and Halloween.

At the Michigan agri-tourism destinations, value-added products were available for purchase – key to profitability in an era of declining prices for commodities. Adding value to apples included the sale of caramel apples, apple pies/dumplings, cider and doughnuts. A Michigan winery, which was one of the few in the United States and worldwide that did not use any chemicals (i.e. sulfites) in its processes, attracted long-distance customers with its niche, non-chemical wine. According to this operator, a group came from St. Louis (over 400 miles or 644 kilometres away) and 'got three or four cases of wine and went back home. I mean, they made a trip out of it. They stayed overnight, but when something like that happens, then you know you're doing good'. By drawing people who stay overnight, these businesses provided the products and attractions that increase tourist expenditures and thus benefits to rural areas.

Tourism products in rural Ireland have developed from basic accommodation enterprises to ventures offering more activities that have a distinctly unique or local character. For instance, farmhouse accommodation allowed visitors to spend the night and become actively involved with farm life. Land-based enterprises had an organic element. In one case, mostly domestic tourists learned about how to become more organic in growing crops/fruit or about waste disposal. Arts and crafts were made from naturally occurring materials such as bog oak, inspired by the surrounding landscape. Historic houses in the region dating back to the famine times provided genealogical interest and attracted historians and international visitors interested in tracing their ancestry. Entrepreneurs have begun to realise that it is important that the products or services they offer give tourists a good reason to stop off and spend time and money in the area, tie in thematically with other products or services in the region, and that support services such as cash-dispensing machines, restaurants and shops are available. Increasing tourist spending and revenue is hard work in a developing tourism destination. One entrepreneur tried out new business components (a number of cycle routes) that gave tourists a reason to stay 4–5 hours or an extra night: 'it's a filtering process to build up local interest'. The North Midlands region also has a developing tourism sector based on its inland water resources, chiefly the Shannon-Erne waterway and its outlets on which many of the smaller villages are situated. The cruising industry supported the passing tourist trade and supplemented the number of services in these local villages. Mythology associated with the lakes added to the quality of fishing experiences. Interpretative centres helped demystify unexpected landscape changes such as mounds and historic forts.

There is a growing consensus, however, that the region, which lives up to visitors' expectations, 'could be better promoted'.

Cooperative marketing and promotion with regional businesses owners

Working cooperatively with other entrepreneurs to share visitors and promote tourism can strengthen its development. In Michigan, cooperation included referrals and joint marketing efforts. One south-west Michigan farmer who did not have an orchard sent Chicago visitors seeking a U-pick experience to other tourist farms in the region. Without this cross-referencing, he did not feel that agri-tourism businesses had a chance to survive. According to another entrepreneur, such cross-referencing was the:

> best thing you could do for your customer, because you made a happy customer, whether they spent the money with you or not ... and they won't forget that. And you have to remember that you're not giving your business away because they will tell somebody, or they will be back. What goes around comes around.

The same was true even in the smaller Traverse City area as one individual explained: '... I don't think most farms are competing unless you're right next door to each other. You know, people aren't going to drive 45 minutes to go get something somewhere else'.

With regard to promotion, the agri-tourism entrepreneurs surveyed highlighted cooperative marketing efforts with other operators (Table 6.1). Few entrepreneurs worked with the tour companies due to the long time it took to establish relationships and tours.

Similarly in the North Midlands region, a level of goodwill and cooperation existed among operators. For instance, as one entrepreneur in an angling enterprise phrased it: 'I would recommend bed and breakfast places to people if they wanted to stay for a while ... [we] need more links between businesses'. Besides making a profit, Irish entrepreneurs are enthusiastic about promoting the region as a stop-off destination, 'what is important is that the customer gets what they are coming for'. While the landscape within the region is not like the popular west coastal areas of Ireland, 'the location is good, it's not too far from Dublin, Galway, Belfast, Limerick' which are the main cities or towns in both Northern Ireland and the Republic of Ireland. Entrepreneurs operating similar businesses tended to cooperate with each other, but were as likely to cooperate with

Table 6.1 Cooperative marketing efforts in Michigan and North Midlands

Cooperative marketing	Michigan	North Midlands
With accommodation owners	17.2%	55%
With caterers	6.2%	55%
With tour companies	3.5%	23%

non-similar ventures to satisfy their business needs. As one small hotel owner described: 'We do a lot of linking with [similar-sized enterprise in area] and we use local painters, publishers and it's the same for our food sources, they are locally derived too'. As seen in Table 6.1 for both promotion and catering purposes, 55 per cent of entrepreneurs said they worked with others locally, while only 23 per cent worked with local transport companies including tour companies to bring tourists into, around, and out of the rural destination. Hence, it is evident in both cases that busloads of tourists might not be the best form of revenue for rural entrepreneurs in micro and small-scale enterprises. Even in instances where the business can adequately provide for the high volume of customers, tensions can be created among local community residents when the masses descend from buses. In summary, working with other entrepreneurs helped the tourists as much as the businesses: 'It helps the tourist because [name of study region] is not strong on tourism, the idea is to combine resources, training, and marketing ... and share visitors when there are so many small attractions'.

Marketing and promotion clusters

In addition to businesses working with other regional businesses for marketing purposes, cooperative marketing links with government agencies were important in tourism promotion. In both cases government assisted in tourism promotion through free distribution of printed directories at tourist information centres, visitor centres and rest stops. A winery entrepreneur in Michigan distributed 8,000 brochures via the state tourism information centre and commented on its effectiveness:

> I was amazed at how well organized our state tourist information centres are. I never realized how much there was to see in this state until I went into a couple of them ... the wineries are all together. There's different attractions and they're all together, so when people come in, they're not having to shuffle through or sort through all these thousands of information pieces to get kind of what they're looking for. And that person at the counter knows exactly where every piece is in that place, too.

Also in Michigan, one tourist farm was able to set up a display in the tourist centre during its key fall harvest season that included brochures, some of the products they were selling and photos of activities such as hayrides.

Similarly in the North Midlands region, government-supported visitor centres showcased local arts and crafts and rural paintings to 'give people an opportunity to see what talents lie in the area and what the area has to offer'. In the North Midlands where the national body for promoting tourism, Bord Fáilte (now Fáilte Ireland), faced a lot of criticism over their treatment of rural businesses and developing destinations, entrepreneurs turned towards local bodies and created new clusters, which entrepreneurs found more beneficial in marketing the region. Clustering provided an authenticity stamp for newly diversified tourism businesses as 'The name was chosen because it is a landmark spot for the town so it was appropriate to call it this, considering locals all know where we are'. Clustering was also perceived to be important in making tourists aware of the range of activities offered. While there were not yet many good examples in the North Midlands region of the cooperation between entrepreneurs and government, when entrepreneurs were asked about promoting the North Midlands region in the future, they generally agreed that government had to become a more prominent marketing force. Entrepreneurs suggested regional festivals and trade shows, something which had been tried out in the Michigan case. On a positive note, government assistance at the North Midlands regional level was perceived to be more useful in terms of funding and training as it was locally adapted.

Importance of transportation networks and local resources

Rural tourism in Michigan and the North Midlands depended on natural, built and human resources. In the Michigan case, the natural resources were mainly the farm landscapes set amidst encroaching urban sprawl. Highways and state roads in Michigan, which were prevalent in a state oriented around the automobile, provided a major infrastructural resource for rural tourism in this region. In southern Michigan, I-94 is the main route between Detroit and Chicago. In the south-western part of the state, approximately 50,000 people a day drive on I-94. The agri-tourism enterprises wanted to draw a percentage of those people off the highway. To do so, the Southwest Michigan Tourist Council, in conjunction with the Michigan Department of Agriculture and Rural Development (formerly Michigan Department of Agriculture), developed a 'Drive Among the Blossoms' tourist route linking all the businesses in south-west Michigan that were agriculture-related. In terms of human resources, the entrepreneurs were providers of agricultural education and good old-fashioned service. As one agri-tourism entrepreneur on the growing edge of the Detroit metro area explained: 'we are giving people an experience, it's a family experience, and it goes on for generations'. Thus customers came in part for a sense of rural hospitality and service that has seemingly been lost in big cities. When customers visited the farm, they met the owners and the frontline staff who were most important in the agri-tourism experience: 'If they [customers] don't see a smiley face ... it's really easy for them to walk right back out'.

In terms of setting the North Midlands region apart from other rural areas across Ireland, the enterprises in the region aimed to incorporate natural, physical and sociocultural resources in their product and service offerings. Entrepreneurs noted that natural resources such as the landscape, waterways, hills, mountains or scenery and built resources of interpretative centres, museums, architectural or industrial heritage were critical to developing North Midlands tourism. Road or rail infrastructure provided important access to the region. Rail infrastructure existed, but the services were 'few and far between'. Rail service was not sufficient or flexible enough to encourage tourists to stop off at different places throughout the region. It was envisaged that the best mode of transport for accessing the region was by car, but entrepreneurs voiced concerns over the negative impacts that a new proposed bypass on the N5 might have on their businesses. Currently, the region was predominantly a spot for tourists passing through. However, if they were further removed from the main corridor roads, they feared there would be less 'drop-ins'. An alternative to land transportation would be to cruise the Shannon and schedule day trips off the waterway in the surrounding towns and hills given the availability of services and information points.

Entrepreneurs in longer established enterprises cited the natural resource base as the underpinning factor in expanding tourism in the North Midlands region. Creating local festivals to attract visitors was one way that entrepreneurs envisaged further developing, utilising and promoting resources more effectively. A minority felt that human resources were underdeveloped and/or underutilised; some suggested the provision of training locally would be beneficial since most entrepreneurs (92.1 per cent of those surveyed nationally) had not worked in the tourism industry prior to establishing a tourism business. A final ingredient in the resource mix was to maximise the potential of non-indigenous entrepreneurs present within a region. Evidence from the North Midlands showed the indigenous could learn from the non-indigenous because the latter could see more potential in the use of local resources, for example, the Shannon-Erne waterway that went unused for years and now attracts domestic as well as international tourists.

Conclusion

The farm, the countryside and tourism are tightly interwoven under a rural development framework. Rural development encompasses a wide array of practices such as landscape management, agri-tourism, innovative forms of cost reduction, high quality and region-specific produce, direct marketing and new activities (Darnhofer 2005). This study shows that agri-tourism or rural tourism has played a role in strengthening local economies, maintaining open space and local food sources and providing a venue for education.

Yet barriers such as zoning and additional local regulations (e.g. signage) constrain direct marketing of farm products and hamper the growth of rural tourism and agri-tourism. In both Ireland and the United States, liability concerns are an impediment to tourism development. In Ireland, the notable lack of open farms in the nationwide Irish survey has been attributed to 'colossal insurance costs' associated with public liability. When activities such as petting corrals and corn mazes are added on US farms, the businesses are viewed as high-risk, agri-entertainment enterprises, not just farms. Some US states including Michigan, Kansas, Louisiana, North Carolina and Virginia have enacted statues offering agri-tourism businesses an affirmative defense for accidents resulting from the inherent risks of agri-tourism activities in the hopes of shielding them from some liability lawsuits. However, such legislation requiring signage provisions warning of inherent risk may be confusing to providers and not necessarily match public expectations for agri-tourism operations. Centner (2010) thus suggests in lieu of such affirmative defense laws that the agri-tourism industry support a legislative provision that precludes negligence releases and accept a slight increase in activity costs due to providers insuring inherent risk accidents. This approach could generate a more favourable view of agri-tourism resulting in greater participation.

The future development of agri-tourism or rural tourism may also be encouraged in the following ways. First, improved planning regulations are necessary since some obscure examples of where planning permission was granted and refused were recounted. Second, infrastructural improvements including remodelling facilities to support more indoor attractions; provision of more cash points, shower or toilet facilities to encourage longer stays off roads and waterways; and increased transportation alternatives such as public buses, trains and private taxis might also spur growth. Third, a greater local awareness of the resource value was crucial to sustaining the rural landscape. Fourth, emphasising regional clusters can foster rural enterprises. Evidence from the North Midlands case, in particular, highlighted the advantages of regional clusters that provide face-to-face and other spatially proximate marketing strategies. Fifth, the importance of building social capital should be emphasised given the rurality and early development status of these regions. The need for government to support human capacity building leads to the final recommendation. Better access to funding is vital to developing tourism components and making the businesses more competitive. Entrepreneurs in this study are the 'growing kind' who need to be nurtured. Policymakers need to support existing entrepreneurs as well as develop new talent.

In conclusion, rural tourism represents a somewhat difficult but necessary change from farmers' traditional production to a services orientation. While challenges to tourism development exist in both rural United States and Ireland, a comparative case analysis outlines how interactive behaviours in local clusters and with natural, physical and human resources can strengthen rural enterprises forced to diversify.

Acknowledgements

The authors wish to acknowledge the key supporters of this research including Michigan Department of Agriculture, LEADER and SPRITE. Thanks also to Margaret Pearce for cartographic assistance.

References

Bagi, F.S. and Reeder, R. (2012) *Farm Activities Associated with Rural Development Initiatives*, ERR-134, U.S. Department of Agriculture, Economic Research Service.
Black, R.J. and Nickerson, N.P. (1997) *The Business of Agritourism-Recreation in Montana*, Missoula, MT: Institute for Tourism and Recreation Research, School of Forestry, the University of Montana.
Bryden, J. and Bollman, R. (2000) 'Rural employment in industrialised countries', *Agricultural Economics*, 22: 185–197.
Carter, S. and Rosa, P. (1998) 'Indigenous rural firms: farm enterprises in the UK', *International Small Business Journal*, 16(4): 15–27.
Centner, T.J. (2010) 'New state liability exceptions for agritourism activities and the use of liability releases', *Agriculture and Human Values*, 27: 189–198.

Che, D., Veeck, A. and Veeck, G. (2005) 'Sustaining production and strengthening the agritourism product: linkages among Michigan agritourism destinations', *Agriculture and Human Values*, 22(2): 225–234.

Darnhofer, I. (2005) 'Organic farming and rural development: some evidence from Austria', *Sociologia Ruralis*, 45(4): 308–323.

Daugstad, K., Rønningen, K. and Skar, B. (2006) 'Agriculture as an upholder of cultural heritage? Conceptualizations and value judgements – A Norwegian perspective in international context', *Journal of Rural Studies*, 22: 67–81.

Department of Agriculture, Food and Rural Development (1994) *Operational Programme for the Implementation of the EU LEADER II Initiative in Ireland 1994–1999*, Dublin: Stationary Office.

Department of Agriculture and Rural Development for Northern Ireland (2000) *LEADER II in Northern Ireland – A Measure of Success: Rural Development Programme in Northern Ireland*, Belfast: DARD.

European Commission (2003) *Green Paper Entrepreneurship in Europe COM (2003) 27 Final*, Brussels: European Commission.

Faber, B. (1976) *The Social Structure of Eastern Europe: Transition and Process in Czechoslovakia, Hungary, Poland, Romania and Yugoslavia*, New York: Praeger Publishers.

Fitzpatrick Associates Economic Consultants (2000) *Operational Programme for Tourism Report No. 23: The Tourism and Environment Initiative, Final Evaluation Report*, Dublin: Fitzpatrick Associates Economic Consultants.

Gosnell, H. and Abrams, J. (2011) 'Amenity migration: diverse conceptualizations of drivers, socioeconomic dimensions, and emerging challenges', *GeoJournal*, 76(4), 303–322.

Government Information Services (1999) *An Action Programme for the Millennium. The Fianna Fáil — Progressive Democrats Partnership Government. Progress Report at the End of Year Two*, Dublin: Stationary Office.

Hegarty, C. and McDonagh, P. (2003) 'Journeying towards becoming a destination', *Tourism*, 50(3): 301–317.

Hennessy, T., Moran, B., Kinsella, A. and Quinlan, G. (2011) *National Farm Survey 2010*, Dublin: Teagasc.

Holmlund, M. and Fulton, M. (1999) *Networking for Success: Strategic Alliances in the New Agriculture*, Saskatoon, SK: Centre for the Study of Co-operatives, University of Saskatchewan.

Hurst, J.L. and Niehm, L.S. (2012) 'Tourism shopping in rural markets: a case study in rural Iowa', *International Journal of Culture, Tourism and Hospitality Research*, 6(3): 194–208.

Hurst, J.L., Niehm, L.S. and Littrell, M.A. (2009) 'Retail service dynamics in a rural tourism community', *Managing Service Quality*, 19(5): 511–540.

Hynes, S., Morrissey, K. and O'Donoghue, C. (2005) *Building a Static Farm Level Spatial Microsimulation Model: Statistically Matching the Irish National Farm Survey to the Irish Census of Agriculture*, The Rural Economy Research Centre Working Paper Series Working Paper 05-WP-RE-06, Dublin: Teagasc.

Irish Times (2010) 'Isolation and suicide, serious problems in farming report', *Women and Agriculture Conference*, Kilkenny, 9 October 2010.

Jackson, V.P. and Stoel, L. (2011) 'A qualitative examination of decoupling, recoupling and organizational survival of rural retailers', *Qualitative Market Research*, 14(4): 410–428.

Keeble, D. and Tyler, P. (1995) 'Enterprising behaviour and the urban-rural shift', *Urban Studies*, 32(6): 975–997.

Knowd, I. (2006) 'Tourism as a mechanism for farm survival', *Journal of Sustainable Tourism*, 14(1): 24–42.

McCarthy, B.L. (2014) 'Sustainable food systems in northern Queensland', *Journal of Economic and Social Policy*, 16(1): 1–18.

McFerson, J. (2014) 'The climate of weather and politics', *American/Western Fruit Grower*, 134(4): 60–61.

Meyer, Z. (2011) *Homegrown Groceries Get a Boost; Snyder Looking to Build Agribusiness*. Available online: <http://www.freep.com/article/20110124/BUSINESS 06/101240334/1322/Homegrown-groceries-get-a-boost> (accessed 24 January 2011).

Nelson, P., Oberg, A. and Nelson, L. (2010) 'Rural gentrification and linked migration in the United States', *Journal of Rural Studies*, 26: 343–352.

Ó Cinnéide, M. and Walsh, J. (1990) 'Tourism and regional development in Ireland', *Geographical Viewpoint*, 19: 47.

Parker, R. (2009) Springtime for small family farms; Michigan agriculture blooms with lifestyle farming, specialization, 1 March. Available online: <http://www.mlive.com/news/kzgazette/index.ssf?/base/news-32/1235884831195890.xml&coll=7> (accessed 4 March 2009).

Selfa, T. and Qazi, J. (2005) 'Place, taste, or face-to-face? Understanding producer-consumer networks in "local" food systems in Washington State', *Agriculture and Human Values*, 22(4): 451–464.

Stockdale, A. (2006) 'Migration: pre-requisite for rural economic regeneration?' *Journal of Rural Studies*, 22: 354–366.

Storey, D., Keasey, K., Watson, R. and Wynarczyk, A. (1987) *The Performance of Small Firms*, London: Croom-Helm.

Stræte, E.P. (2008) 'Modes of qualities in development of specialty food', *British Food Journal*, 110(1): 62–75.

Teagasc (2001) Presentation to *Tyrone Quality Livestock Group by Gerry Scully*, Teagasc, at Silverbirch Hotel, 12 February 2001, Dublin: Teagasc.

The Economist (2011) 'The adoption of genetically modified crops', *The Economist*. Available online: <http://www.economist.com/blogs/dailychart/2011/02/adoption_ genetically_modified_crops> (accessed 27 October 2011).

The Fruit Growers News (2004) 'Group: census data supports farmland preservation', *The Fruit Growers News*, 43(3): 14.

The University of California Small Farm Program (2011) *What Is Agritourism?*. Available online: <http://sfp.ucdavis.edu/agritourism≥ (accessed 20 January 2015).

US Department of Agriculture (2012) *2012 Census of Agriculture: Michigan – Historical Highlights: 2012 and Earlier Census Year*. Available online: <http://www.agcensus.usda.gov/Publications/2012/Full_Report/Volume_1,_Chapter_1_State_Level/ Michigan/st26_1_001_001.pdf> (accessed 30 June 2015).

Weaver, D. and Fennell, D. (1997) 'The vacation farm sector in Saskatchewan: a profile of operations', *Tourism Management*, 18(6): 357–365.

Youssef, J. (2009) *Small Farms Thrive on Diversity; Local Operations Increase Business by Focusing on Retail, Crop Variety*. Available online: <http://www.detnews.com/ article/20090623/BIZ/906230324/1001/Small-farms-thrive-on-diversity> (accessed 23 June 2009).

Part III
The cultural economy of food and tourism

7 Regional development and Japanese obsession with noodles

The udon noodle tourism phenomenon in Japan

Sangkyun Kim

Introduction

The significance of food in tourism and the relationship between food and tourism has been a major growth sector for recent tourism research. This tourism phenomenon has been known in the relevant literature by numerous terms, including "food tourism" (Hall et al. 2003; McKercher, Okumus & Okumus 2008; Everett 2009, 2012; Getz & Robinson 2014; Kim & Ellis 2015), "gastronomic tourism" (Hjalager & Richards 2002; Correia et al. 2008), "culinary tourism" (Karim & Chi 2010; Horng & Tsai 2012a, 2012b), "tasting tourism" (Boniface 2003) and "gourmet tourism" (Mitchell & Hall 2003; Tussyadiah 2005). Previous studies on food tourism were primarily approached by the management and marketing perspective and include (1) the role of (regional) food in destination marketing and promotion, including destination image (Hall & Mitchell 2000; Hjalager & Corigliano 2000); (2) motivations, market segmentations and travel preferences of food-related tourists (Robinson & Clifford 2007; Karim & Chi 2010; Kim, Suh & Eves 2010; Getz & Robinson 2014); and (3) the significant role of food in tourist experiences (Quan & Wang 2004; Kivela & Crotts 2009).

More recent literature of food tourism has experienced a shift from the management to the cultural and/or sociological perspective that has its intrinsic emphasis on cultural exploration and learning through food production and consumption (see, e.g., Gyimóthy & Mykletun 2009; Bessière 2013; Daugstad & Kirchengast 2013; Hall, 2013; Staiff & Bushell 2013). However, little research has been conducted into how a regional food heritage as a signifier of regional identity contributes to the regional regeneration and (re)development through food tourism. This field of research in the Asian context seems scarce, with the exception of Avieli's (2012) work on the case of Hoi An in Vietnam as a food lovers' destination (see also Chapter 8, this volume).

This chapter attempts to examine and discuss how a regional food heritage and its foodway have been used for successful regional development in Japan. Food tourism in Japan has not been subject to much academic research, but Japan has a long tradition of food tourism. It has been acclaimed for its unique and authentic food and culinary heritage, with a long tradition of pride in regional specialties known as *Kyodo Ryori* (which literally means country dishes in Japanese language). Many locations in Japan are strongly associated with agriculture or fishery products and foods. Traditional Japanese haute cuisine such as *kaiseki* multi-course dishes also represents another aspect of Japan's culinary and gourmet culture. In response to this Japanese food culture, it is a common practice for tour operators and travel agencies to offer a variety of *gurume tabi* (gourmet trip) packages, including visits to an *onsen* (hot spring) and *ryokan* accommodation (Japanese-style inn) (Tussyadiah 2005).

Furthermore, noodle dishes have long been the centre of Japanese food culture as a staple of Japanese cuisine. Noodles had their heyday during the Edo period (1603–1868) but remain very popular. The total noodles consumption in Japan was US$ 10.9 billion in 2009 and this figure includes chilled, frozen, plain, instant and fresh noodles ranging from soba to ramen to udon (Agriculture and Agri-Food Canada 2010). The research context of this chapter focusses on Japanese udon noodle in particular, leading to the udon tourism phenomenon. Udon noodle is commonly known as one of the three major Japanese noodle dishes (i.e. udon, soba and ramen) and is said to be the oldest noodle and remains popular in Japan. Udon is a thick white noodle made of wheat flour, water and salt. It has a creamy colour and a soft, elastic texture and glossy appearance. The three most nationally recognised udon noodle regions in Japan include Kagawa (Sanuki Udon), Gunma (Mizusawa Udon) and Akita (Inaniwa Udon) (Kim & Ellis 2015).

Kagawa, being considered "the Kingdom of Sanuki udon" noodle, has been proactively using "Sanuki udon" as a symbol of its regional identity to revitalise the regional food industry and to promote regional tourism. Udon tour buses, udon taxis, udon passports, udon mascots and various udon-themed souvenirs are examples of successful tourism promotional and marketing stories of Kagawa (Jones 2011; Kim & Ellis 2015). One udon shop claimed that although it served only 10–20 local customers a day until the 1990s, from 2000 the number of visitors increased up to 2,700 at its peak. As a result, the shop changed its main business from a wholesaler to a restaurant targeting tourists (Kawashima 2011). Among 3,500 participants, a tourism survey conducted in 2011 suggests that the great majority (86.7 per cent) of respondents ate Sanuki udon. Accordingly, Sanuki udon was the most popular motivational factor for their travel, followed by visiting attractions of scenic beauty and historical interest (31.7 per cent) (Kagawa Prefecture 2012).

While each of the above three udon regions in Japan has its unique food heritage associated with different historical and cultural background of udon noodle production and consumption, the geographical focus of this chapter is Gunma prefecture in the centre of the Japanese archipelago, approximately 130 km northwest of Tokyo. Gunma is historically and geographically famous for the unique quality of its wheat flour production, benefitting as it does from suitable weather conditions. Gunma is one of Japan's top producers of wheat, ranked fourth with a production of 20,100 tons in 2010 (Gunma Prefecture 2012). As a consequence, noodle businesses in the region have flourished. In 2009, Gunma had 1,006 enterprises serving udon or soba noodle dishes. The number of udon/soba shops per 10,000 residents in Gunma prefecture is almost double the national average of

2.5 shops (Matsushita 2011). The udon noodle shops are mainly concentrated in the cities of Mizusawa, Kiryu and Tatebayashi. The Bureau of Tourism in the Gunma Prefectural Government (2012) highlights the significance of udon noodle as a regional signature, its place in the region's identity, and its contribution to regional tourism, by suggesting that 'Tasty udon noodle can be enjoyed anywhere in Gunma'. This denotes that Gunma is the place where visitors can experience the best locally produced udon noodle in Japan.

Indeed, each city (i.e. Mizusawa, Kiryu and Tatebayashi) has its own historical and cultural association with udon noodle and has been differently involved in revitalising and promoting local area and its tourism through udon noodle. The following discussion is based on the evaluation of secondary sources such as government reports, academic research papers and online documents. It is supplemented by other data that includes observations and a series of interviews with staff members of city office of Kiryu and Tatebayashi conducted between October and November 2012.

Mizusawa udon as a marker of regional food heritage

Mizusawa udon has its origin in two oldest udon shops (Tamaruya and Shimizuya) in Japan that opened during the Tensho period (1573–1592) to serve pilgrims or religious visitors of the Mizusawa Temple founded more than 1,000 years ago. Tamaruya identifies itself as the 'originator of Mizusawa Udon', whereas Shimizuya calls itself the 'founder of Mizusawa Udon' (Gunma Prefecture 2012). Mizusawa udon is known to be slightly thicker than other regional udon noodles such as Sanuki udon, yet very smooth and firm. In the 1960s, new restaurants serving Mizusawa udon opened in the area. In 2004, the old and new udon shops in Mizusawa region started working together to keep the Mizusawa udon brand as central to the regional tourism development. They organised an association of udon shops, using the registered trademark of Mizusawa udon, which consisted of 13 shops only.

In the same year, they published a tourism leaflet featuring Mizusawa udon as one of the most famous udon noodles in Japan that included a map of the Mizusawa udon shops' locations. This has been used as a tourism marketing tool for the regional tourism campaign. Mizusawa udon has since become a success story of regional branding and identity in Gunma and has been strongly associated with positive developments of regional tourism associated with udon noodle. Especially, the two oldest Mizusawa udon shops, Tamaruya and Shimizuya, have long been recognised as the most authentic of Japan's traditional udon noodle. Observing the traditional process of making udon from dough to fresh udon noodle hanging on very old wooden dryers, tourists encountered old, historical photographs, scripted newspapers articles, and other historic documents attached to the walls of the udon shops. All of these were distinctive historical, cultural and physical testimonials that represented the core values of the regional identity, which has been associated with a strong sense of traditional udon-making for more than 400 years.

While udon noodle is normally boiled and served in a flavourful soup or sea-soning with various toppings, *Zaru udon* – cold udon noodle served on a straw mat with a number of cold dipping sauces (e.g. sesame, soy, mushroom) – can be seen as an expression of an authentic foodways in the Mizusawa udon village. According to Timothy and Ron (2013: 99), foodways is defined as 'the culinary smells, sights, sounds, and eating practices of a people or region, as well as culi-nary routes, sites and landscapes'. Also, cooking methods, ingredients, dining customs, social connotations and family ties are all important parts of foodways. As such, the shops and their modes of producing and serving udon noodles con-tribute to the important physical or tangible and intangible manifestations of the history and culture of the Mizusawa udon village.

As the cultural landscapes and identities of a place are made up of a complex combination of tangible and intangible cultural elements including ideas and val-ues (Shamsuddin & Ujang 2008), the intangible elements of food heritage can be seen as key attributes of the Mizusawa udon village that motivates Japanese tour-ists to visit and experience its udon noodles. This intangible food heritage can be summarised in two ways. The first is the physical and psychological continuity of the traditional ways of making udon noodle from one generation to the next with unchanged recipes, ingredients and foodways of their finest udon noodles, unwrit-ten recipes and oral expressions. The second is the shop proprietors' self-esteem in their udon noodles. Indeed, the obsessive craftsmanship and continuity of tra-ditional ways of making fresh udon noodles in Mizusawa function as main drivers maintaining local traditions as the core of selling points for regional tourism.

The pride felt by the proprietors of udon shops can be seen as an especially important part of sustaining the region's intangible food heritage and identity, as the proprietors were proud that they were one of few purveyors in the nation who still provide fresh udon noodles to the Imperial Household Agency. Also, many members of the Imperial family have visited their shops. In this regard, it is useful to reflect on the work of Timothy and Ron (2013), which suggests that a familial patrimony associated with heritage cuisine should be considered as one of the most important markers of regional and ethnic identity as well as one of the most appealing parts of tourist experiences.

Himogawa udon as a metaphor of textile and food industrial tradition and identity in Kiryu

The city of Kiryu has always been famous for its textile industry since it became an important centre for textile manufacturing in the seventeenth century when fine Kiryu silks were worn by Samurai and court nobles. During the Edo Period (1603–1868), there was a famous phrase, 'In the west, there is Nishijin (Kyoto), and in the east, there is Kiryu as leading weaving centre'. The early udon his-tory of Kiryu traces back to the Heian period (794–1192) in which a man from Kiryu working at the Imperial Palace in Kyoto married Princess Shirataki. Upon returning to Kiryu, Princess Shirataki introduced a type of udon noodle to local people in Kiryu.

The popularity and reputation of udon noodle production and consumption in Kiryu is strongly associated with female weavers who worked at textile factories in the Meiji period (1868–1912). The udon noodle was popularised among these workers because it could be eaten quickly and be ordered for delivery from udon shops and enjoyed by the busy workers as a kind of 'fast food'. In Kiryu region, udon noodles have also been served on ceremonial occasions such as funerals and wedding receptions.

In a similar way to Mizusawa, two business associations involved in revitalising and promoting local area through its specialty cuisine, namely udon noodle, were established in Kiryu: the Kiryu Noodle Cooperative in 1957 and the Kiryu Udon Association in September 1998. The latter was formed by 26 members of Kiryu Noodle Cooperative based on the fact that at that time 130 establishments serving udon noodle were counted in Kiryu, representing the largest in terms of type of food businesses. There are approximately 100 establishments serving udon noodle. As of June 2011, the Kiryu Udon Association had 24 members. The promotion of udon noodle has been done mainly by these trade groups. For the past few years, the Kiryu Noodle Cooperative has also produced the Kiryu Udon Map, sponsored by the Kirin Beer Company. The latest map features about 49 restaurants serving udon dishes with special mention of curry udon, udon noodle cooked with curry sauce, and Himogawa udon, wide-flat noodles with a slippery texture (interview with a government officer of Kiryu City Office).

Unlike the Mizusawa udon village, many of the udon shops in Kiryu are relatively small with a home delivery service and provide service for local repeat customers. However, newly invented Himokawa udon has become a regional signature udon noodle dish that attracts tourists from other regions. There are only a few udon shops serving Himogawa udon, and Momotaro and Furukawa are two of the famous ones. The unique shape of the Himogawa udon noodle, often 10 cm in width and 30 cm in length, looks like chopped textiles and is appealing enough to regional tourists in its own right. In particular, Furukawa has become very famous because of its unique recipe using special Himokawa udon noodles. The owner of Furukawa has modified the recipe, making the noodle's width much wider and created almost an original dish. The recipe has often been mentioned in the news as something unique and a new dish and has become one of popular udon noodle dishes in Kiryu, especially as a result of media coverage, including TV shows and travel magazines featuring the shop.

The cleverly invented Himogawa udon denotes the historical symbiotic relationship between the textile and udon-making industries. This metaphor of the textile industrial heritage and identity in Kiryu has been transformed into a consumable and edible food item that has a strong association with another industrial heritage in the form of udon noodle production. Indeed, the invention of Himogawa udon in Kiryu has been considered among locals as a reinvention of its local food heritage, history and identity in the face of global threats to the survival of indigenous culture and identity (Mak, Lumbers & Eves 2012; Cheung 2013).

Udon Heartland Tatebayashi and the Tatebayashi Noodle Grand Prix

The history of udon noodle in Tatebayashi dates back to the Edo period (1603–1868) in which udon was presented to the Shogunate as a regional specialty of the Tatebayashi Clan. It has been since then customary for udon to be hand-made at home on the first and fifteenth of each month when a sakaki twig would be offered to the family Shinto altar. It has thus served as part of ritual ceremonies in Tatebayashi for hundreds of years (Gunma Prefecture 2012). The Shoda Shoyu Company (a Japanese soy sauce manufacturer) and Nisshin Seifun (Nisshin Flour Milling Inc.), established in 1873 and 1900 respectively, are also regarded as having helped the further development of the food heritage and culture of Tatebayashi that has a strong association with udon noodle and is at the heart of the region's identity.

Tatebayashi has promoted community-based regional development through its unique food production heritage and culture for more than a decade, since its motto of "Udon Heartland Tatebayashi" was established in May 1994. Hanging banners of the "city of Men" (meaning noodle in Japanese) are found in the train station and city hall. Membership of the Tatebayashi udon society initially consisted of 47 businesses including udon shops and flour milling factories. However, the city has undergone a severe economic downturn due to a significant decline in the regional agriculture and food production industries. Membership of the udon society had fallen to 23 businesses (16 udon restaurants, 5 flour milling factories, and 2 other businesses) as of November 2012 (Gunma Prefecture 2012).

Unlike Mizusawa and Kiryu, the city of Tatebayashi launched a new regional food festival called "The Noodle Grand Prix" on 25 September 2011 in order to revitalise and redevelop the region. This annual food festival aimed to promote the region's food and tourism industries in particular and was supported by regional and local governments and local communities, including food production associations and local residents. A government officer of Tatebayashi City Office interviewed for the study commented that the Noodle Grand Prix has three main mid- to long-term goals: (1) to (re)capitalise on the city's udon noodle heritage as a potential tourism attraction and enhance the image of Tatebayashi as "Udon Heartland"; (2) to (re)develop new regional signature noodle dishes (e.g. *Bunbuku Chagama*) through active collaboration between agriculture, commerce, food and tourism industries; and (3) to retain and sustain the cultural identity of the region that has a strong historical and geographical association with udon noodle production. Along with these goals, the officer also pointed out the importance of the immediate economic benefit through the food festival that locals hope will overcome the ongoing and uncertain economic downturn in the region.

As such, the food festival in Tatebayashi is not only seen as (re)confirming and reinforcing the identity and heritage of the region, but is also a significant tool for regional community economic development, both through promoting tourism in the wider region and attracting visitors to the festival itself. The Noodle Grand Prix has already become the most important regional event in the

Tatebayashi tourism calendar as it attracts an increasing number of tourists every year, up to 66,000 tourists in 2013 compared to the estimated 55,000 visitors in its initial year in 2011.

Two key features of the Noodle Grand Prix in Tatebayashi include: (1) national award-winning noodle makers and representatives of regional noodle makers from Tatebayashi and its neighbouring regions who are invited to take part in a competition to win the grand prix; and (2) the winner is selected by the tourists' personal tasting experiences of the noodles consumed at the festival (they cast their votes with the chopsticks with which they eat their noodle dishes). It is interesting to note that the top three competitors in the 2012 competition were all from the city of Tatebayashi and two of them were regional signature udon dishes that beat the national award-winning noodles. These regional dishes include *Bunbuku Chagama*, which is served in a raccoon-shaped container. Similar to the Himogawa udon in Kiryu, this udon dish is newly invented and named after *Bunbuku Chagama*, a famous regional fairy tale of a raccoon and a monk in Morinji Temple in Tatebayashi, further suggesting that the distinctive udon noodle heritage and culture of Tatebayashi is appreciated by tourists from outside the region.

Conclusion

The chapter aimed to discuss how traditional Japanese udon noodle and its food-ways and preservation and/or reinvention in Gunma prefecture played a crucial role in developing its regional tourism by creating a udon tourism phenomenon. Three cities in Gunma, namely Mizusawa, Kiryu and Tatebayashi, were chosen due to the high concentration of udon shops and the significance of their his-torical and cultural contexts of udon production and consumption. Despite the different and distinct historical, social and cultural backgrounds of the association between udon noodle and the above three cities, the common denominator is the fact that the quality, uniqueness and authenticity of their udon noodles was rooted in the historical and geographical contexts of udon noodle production heritage associated with the agriculture and food industries. To a greater or lesser extent, this is consistent with what previous studies suggest, that unique and distinctive cultural identities of regions of food production are often rooted in agriculture (Everett & Aitchison 2008; Ma & Lew 2012). The stories of Mizusawa, Kiryu and Tatebayashi also reinforce Bertella's (2011) observation that the success of food tourism and food festivals lies in the distinctiveness, peculiarity and uniqueness of the region.

The social and cultural significance and meaning of udon noodle as a cultural artefact in the region of Gunma prefecture is also a significant contributor to the regional development and identity formation and has potential economic, social and cultural benefits for regional and local communities. As distinctive local food and gastronomy is increasingly becoming a valuable source of new tourism prod-ucts with a high potential for promoting regional development and its identity

(Richards 2002; Everett & Aitchison 2008), the three cities in Gunma capitalised on their regional udon noodles, their histories and traditions as selling points for regional tourism in ways distinctly and differently. This is similar to a recent work of Kim and Ellis (2015) on the historical, social and cultural significance of udon noodle production and consumption in Kagawa prefecture located in the island of Shikoku, the homeland of Sanuki udon.

In Mizusawa, the ways in which traditional udon noodle production and its preservation and continuity have been demonstrated are incomparable with the other two cities in Gunma. They function as an important ingredient in developing and promoting regional tourism through the creation of udon tourism as one of the main tourist attractions. It also confirms that the maintenance and continuity of producing such traditional fresh udon noodles, their foodways and craftsmanship provide an impetus for enhancing and sustaining the regional identity. This is consistent with Edson's (2004) view that the physical and psychological continuity that occurs through the maintenance of traditional local food and foodways functions as an important dimension of identity and a primary ingredient in the notion of heritage. In Kiryu, the (re)invention of Himogawa udon as a metaphor of the two key industrial heritages of the city, namely textile and udon production, not only functions as the main driver of maintaining local tradition, history and heritage but also contributes to the regional (re)development, as it attracts domestic tourists of food tourism.

In Tatebayashi, since the culture and heritage of regional and local food and foodways can be transformed into marketable tourism attraction and food festivals are one of key tourism sources that help enhance the identity of local community (Quan & Wang 2004), the noodles produced, served and consumed in loco at the Tatebayashi Noodle Grand Prix festival were considered an important tangible manifestation of the intangible regional identity, food heritage and culture attached to the city's noodle history. As such, the noodle festival played a crucial role in informing and sustaining regional and cultural identities that have a strong association with, and pride in, the agricultural and industrial food production heritage. It was also an important part of the region's tourism and brought direct and indirect economic benefits to the region.

Kim and Ellis (2015: 164) call the udon noodle 'one of the simplest, cheapest and humblest ordinary dishes in Japan'. Ironically, this mundane and ordinary noodle dish has now become the main tourism attraction for tourists to the udon production regions such as Gunma. Although food cultures and traditions keep changing in the era of modernisation and globalisation, the Japanese public's fascination with, or obsession towards, noodle culture and identity remain, and subsequent travel to udon tourism destinations has been a new tourism phenomenon in Japan.

References

Agriculture and Agri-Food Canada (2010) *Consumer Trends: Noodles in Japan*, Ottawa: Agriculture and Agri-Food Canada.

Avieli, N. (2012) *Rice Talks: Food and Community in a Vietnamese Town*, Bloomington: Indiana University Press.

Bertella, G. (2011) 'Knowledge in food tourism: the case of Lofoten and Maremma Toscana', *Current Issues in Tourism*, 14(4): 355–371.

Bessière, J. (2013) '"Heritagisation", a challenge for tourism promotion and regional development: an example of food heritage', *Journal of Heritage Tourism*, 8(2–3): 1–18.

Boniface, P. (2003) *Tasting Tourism: Travelling for Food and Drink*, Aldershot: Ashgate.

Bureau of Tourism, Gunma Prefectural Government (2012) "Mizusawa udon", *Gunma Prefectural Government*. Available online: <http://www.visitgunma.jp/en/sightseeing/detail.php?sightseeing_id=63> (accessed 3 November 2012).

Cheung, S.C.H. (2013) 'From foodways to intangible heritage: a case study of Chinese culinary resource, retail and recipe in Hong Kong', *International Journal of Heritage Studies*, 19(4): 353–364.

Correia, A., Moital, M., Ferreira Da Costa, C. and Peres, R. (2008) 'The determinants of gastronomic tourists' satisfaction: a second-order factor analysis', *Journal of Foodservice*, 19(3): 164–176.

Daugstad, K. and Kirchengast, C. (2013) 'Authenticity and the pseudo-backstage of agri-tourism', *Annals of Tourism Research*, 43: 170–191.

Edson, G. (2004) 'Heritage: pride or passion, product or service?' *International Journal of Heritage Studies*, 10(4): 333–348.

Everett, S. (2009) 'Beyond the visual gaze? The pursuit of an embodied experience through food tourism', *Tourist Studies*, 8(3): 337–358.

Everett, S. (2012) 'Production places or consumption spaces? The place-making agency of food tourism in Ireland and Scotland', *Tourism Geographies*, 14(4): 535–554.

Everett, S. and Aitchison, C. (2008) 'The role of food tourism in sustaining regional identity: a case study of Cornwall, South West England', *Journal of Sustainable Tourism*, 16(2): 150–167.

Getz, D. and Robinson, R.N.S. (2014) 'Foodies and their travel preferences', *Tourism Analysis*, 19(6): 659–672.

Gunma Prefecture (2012) 'Gunma agrinet, heisei 24nenndo Gunma no nogyo', *Gunma Prefectural Government*. Available online: <http://www.aic.pref.gunma.jp/agricultural/policy/statistics/agriculture> (accessed 17 January 2013).

Gyimóthy, S. and Mykletun J. (2009) 'Scary food: commodifying culinary heritage as meal adventures in tourism', *Journal of Vacation Marketing*, 15(3): 259–273.

Hall, C.M. (2013) 'Why forage when you don't have to? Personal and cultural meaning in recreational foraging: a New Zealand study', *Journal of Heritage Tourism*, 8(2/3): 224–233.

Hall, C.M. and Mitchell, R. (2000) 'We are what we eat: food, tourism and globalisation', *Tourism Culture and Communication*, 2: 29–37.

Hall, C.M., Sharples, L., Mitchell, R., Macionis, N. and Cambourne, B. (eds) (2003) *Food Tourism around the World: Development, Management and Markets*, Oxford: Butterworth Heinemann.

Hjalager, A. and Corigliano, A. (2000) 'Food for tourists: determinants of an image', *International Journal of Tourism Research*, 2: 281–293.

Hjalager, A. and Richards, G. (eds) (2002) *Tourism and Gastronomy*, London: Routledge.

Horng, J. and Tsai, C. (2012a) 'Constructing indicators of culinary tourism strategy: an application of resource-based theory', *Journal of Travel & Tourism Marketing*, 29(8): 796–816.

Horng, J. and Tsai, C. (2012b) 'Exploring marketing strategies for culinary tourism in Hong Kong and Singapore', *Asia Pacific Journal of Tourism Research*, 17(3): 277–299.

Jones, T. (2011) 'The udon economy: food and tourism in Kagawa Prefecture', *International Christian University (ICU) Comparative Culture*, 43: 29–72.

Kagawa Prefecture (2012) 'Heisei 23-nen Kagawa-ken kankokyaku dotai chosa hokoku gaiyo', *Kagawa Prefectural Government*. Available online: <http://www.pref.kagawa.lg.jp/kgwpub/pub/cms/upfiles> (accessed 14 November 2012).

Karim, S. and Chi, C. (2010) 'Culinary tourism as a destination attraction: an empirical examination of destinations' food image', *Journal of Hospitality Marketing and Management*, 19(6): 531–555.

Kawashima, R. (2011) *Soba Udon*, Tokyo: Shibatashoten.

Kim, S. and Ellis, A. (2015) 'Noodle production and consumption: from agriculture to food tourism in Japan', *Tourism Geographies*, 17(1): 151–167.

Kim, Y.G., Suh, B.W. and Eves, A. (2010) 'The relationships between food-related personality traits, satisfaction, and loyalty among visitors attending food events and festivals', *International Journal of Hospitality Management*, 29(2): 216–226.

Kivela, J. and Crotts, J. (2009) 'Understanding travelers' experiences of gastronomy through etymology and narration', *Journal of Hospitality & Tourism Research*, 33(2): 161–192.

Ma, L. and Lew, A.A. (2012) 'Historical and geographical context in festival tourism development', *Journal of Heritage Tourism*, 7(1): 13–31.

Mak, A., Lumbers, M. and Eves, A. (2012) 'Globalisation and food consumption in tourism', *Annals of Tourism Research*, 39(1): 171–196.

Matsushita, H. (2011) 'Anketonimiru Kennai Udon Soba Ten no Genjo to Kongo (The present and future of udon and soba restaurants in Japanese prefectures: from the questionnaire)', *Gunma Economy*, 336: 16–25.

McKercher, B., Okumus, F. and Okumus, B. (2008) 'Food tourism as a viable market segment: it's all how you cook the numbers', *Journal of Travel and Tourism Marketing*, 25(2): 137–148.

Mitchell, R. and Hall, C.M. (2003) 'Consuming tourists: food tourism consumer behaviour', in C.M. Hall, L. Sharples, R. Mitchell, N. Macionis, and B. Cambourne (eds) *Food Tourism around the World: Development, Management and Markets*, Oxford: Butterworth-Heinemann, pp. 60–80.

Quan, S. and Wang, N. (2004) 'Towards a structural model of the tourist experience: an illusion from food experiences in tourism', *Tourism Management*, 25(3): 297–305.

Richards, G. (2002) 'Gastronomy: an essential ingredient in tourism production and consumption?' in A.M. Hjalager and G. Richards (eds) *Tourism and Gastronomy*, London: Routledge, pp. 2–20.

Robinson, R. and Clifford, C. (2007) 'Prime, secondi, salata: augmenting authenticity at special events via foodservice experiences', *International Journal of Event Management Research*, 3(2): 1–11.

Shamsuddin, S. and Ujang, N. (2008) 'Making places: the role of attachment in creating the sense of place for traditional streets in Malaysia', *Habitat International*, 32: 399–409.

Staiff, R. and Bushell, R. (2013) 'The rhetoric of Lao/French fusion: beyond the representation of the Western tourist experience of cuisine in the world heritage city of Luang Prabang, Laos', *Journal of Heritage Tourism*, 8(2–3): 133–144.

Timothy, D.J. and Ron, A.S. (2013) 'Understanding heritage cuisines and tourism: identity, image, authenticity, and change', *Journal of Heritage Tourism*, 8(2–3): 99–104.

Tussyadiah, I.P. (2005) 'A gourmet trip: one direction of domestic tourism in Japan', *Tourism Review International*, 9(3): 281–292.

8 "Modernology", food heritage and neighbourhood tourism

The example of Sheung Wan, Hong Kong

Sidney C.H. Cheung and Jiting Luo

Introduction

The Japanese humanities discipline of "modernology", known as *kogengaku*, is somewhat alien to Western academia. It originated in Japan in the 1920s, but to date, little has been recorded about its emergence and development there during the ensuing century. Although not a specialist on the subject, Cheung (one of the authors) became acquainted with the ideas and backgrounds of modernology during his decade of study of ethnology and cultural anthropology in Japan. From that, he believed modernology would provide a suitable as well as interesting way to explore the historical development of local culture in Hong Kong.

Put simply, modernology studies modern society by interpreting the practices of customs from different perspectives, based on collecting and analysing detailed data. Space and time are the indicators for data collection. In other words, modernology focusses on the study of details about built monuments and their social and cultural contexts at a specific historical moment. That might sound similar to the sociology or phenomenology of Western academics, but modernology differs by its pinpointing of accurate observations in real settings as well as by its mode of data organisation, rather than pursuing and analyzing high-level theories. In this, it follows Japanese humanities research practice, which values the meticulous collection of data over delving into theory in order to construct yet more theory. As a result, in a setting of urban modernisation, modernology is a way for both academics and the general public to understand and reflect on changes in their neighbourhoods.

Kon Wajiro (1888–1973), one important founder of modernology, was a student of Yanagita Kunio (1875–1962), known as the father of Japanese folklore. Kon specialised in the study of traditional folk dwellings (*minka* in Japanese) in Japan. However, the relationship between Kon and Yanagita broke up in 1927 because Kon advocated modernology, and his research had thus shifted significantly from villages to modern city (Kon 2013). Regarding Kon's backgrounds and earlier career, he studied graphic design at Tokyo Fine Arts University and taught architecture at Waseda University; since 1927, he became very much involved in investigating how the 1923 Tokyo earthquake had changed the urban landscape as well as living environment in the downtown area (*shitamachi* in

Japanese) of Tokyo city. Therefore, his approaches and studies became the foundation of modernology.

There are intricate relationships between modernology and archaeology, but also subtle differences, as can be detected from their names. They are alike in that both observe, deduce, hypothesise or even reconstruct a past living style from scattered and incomplete old bits of evidence. For instance, the study of "street observation", derived later, attracted many architectural historians. However, the two fields are different because archaeology is the study of the past, whereas modernology focusses on modern urban development, including the changing lives of ordinary citizens and the rise and fall of recent customs.

This chapter borrows the ideas of modernology with its strength based on the comprehensive and detailed use of various sources, including observation, oral history, historical archives, local records and comparative analysis to understand a complex urban history in a fast-changing neighbourhood in Hong Kong society. The "modernological eye" is focussed on understanding Sheung Wan, a local Chinese business neighbourhood since the colonial period in nineteenth century. This is done for two reasons. The first is to rediscover the local Hong Kong culture that depends intimately on knowledge of a wide range of imported commodities as well as the dried marine and herbal products created in this trading hub. The second is to propose a methodological approach that would enable tourists or other visitors on their own to discover and experience some local tastes and flavours.

Backgrounds of the project

To better understand the history and trade system of Sheung Wan as a coastal hub, interviews were conducted with traders (importers, wholesalers and retailers) as well as shoppers in the local community. This tapped into their knowledge and stories about their trades and heritage preservation strategies. Information gathered from these interviews, surveys and archival materials forms the basis of an interactive website that contains walking maps and academic articles and books for reference. It enables visitors to explore the history and culture of Nam Pak Hong (a south–north trading company), the Chinese herbal medicine street and the salted fish alleys in Sheung Wan.

The overall purpose of this project is to assist in the diversification and enhancement of the management of local cultural resources for Hong Kong's inbound tourists. Most visitors to Hong Kong are encouraged to shop and sample a variety of cuisines in the Central, Tsimshatsui, Causeway Bay, Mongkok districts and elsewhere. In this way, international visitors enjoy the unique atmosphere in Hong Kong as an Asian metropolis. However, this dominant image of Hong Kong as a destination based on consumerism fails to give tourists a comprehensive sense of local culture and the associated, deeply interesting and rewarding experience of tradition and heritage. Hong Kong is unique, so it does not do it justice if we feature only its business-oriented and materialistic aspects. Thus, we undertook this knowledge transfer project in the Sheung Wan neighbourhood.

The immediate objectives of the project were:

1   to examine the roles of a local community such as Sheung Wan in terms of its cultural and heritage aspects and tap into its collective knowledge;
2   to ascertain the needs of the tourists regarding cultural tourism; and
3   to develop a cultural tour prototype of the local community in the Sheung Wan neighbourhood that would systematically feature the culinary heritages of Hong Kong as exemplified by its ethnic and cultural diversity, economic and political interests in food trades as well as urban development and heritage conservation. Also, by using an Internet information base, tourists will be able to learn about local and national history, traditional trade relations, impacts of globalization, Chinese culinary culture, local development and heritage preservation strategies.

This project employs cross-cultural, interdisciplinary and critical approaches to understand the historical background and culinary heritages of Hong Kong society, as a social and cultural basis for the development of sustainable tourism. In the long term, the prototype developed in Sheung Wan can serve as model so that more local neighbourhoods would be included in the overall cultural tourism project. This way, communities' awareness of being promoters for Hong Kong tourism can be enhanced, and both inbound and domestic tourists can enjoy and benefit from learning – from the perspective of everyday life – how Hong Kong developed into a city renowned worldwide. Most importantly, the collective knowledge of a community can be preserved and passed on to future generations. A variety of unique areas have a similar potential to be developed for cultural tourism and walking tours. These include the seafood market in Lau Fau Shan, the organic food market in Tai Po, the freshwater fish wholesale market in Yuen Long, the fruit wholesale market in Yaumatei, the garment wholesale market in Shamshuipo and the migrant neighbourhood in North Point, to name but a few possibilities.

Food heritage and tourism

Food is one of the most important cultural markers of identity in many globalising Asian societies, and analysis of different aspects of food can provide insight to social relations, class structure, gender roles and cultural symbolism. Apart from studying regular daily food which many scholars have contributed their efforts, it is no doubt that food promoted to and eaten by tourists should not be overlooked in the twenty-first century since it reflects people's conceptualisation of culture through real contacts in tourism (Hall et al. 2003). Considering the food items which used to be local but have now became nationwide commercial items, Noguchi (1994: 328) described the development of *ekiben* (train station lunch boxes) in Japan and emphasised that its increased popularity was related to the fact that *ekiben* 'are powerful symbols in Japan because they mediate the new age of speed in travel and the venerated past'. Nevertheless, we can find *ekiben* shops in many train stations, and we assume it is related to the fact that people want to consume the food after being in the relevant place, enjoying the food with the good memories while travelling.

In Asia nowadays, many tourists are willing to try local indigenous food for an authentic cultural experience during their travels. For example, people might go to Japan for a sushi meal or to Beijing for dining in a local private kitchen reserved two months in advance. However, we should also know that:

> Food is also one of the important aspects of the "environmental bubble" that surrounds most tourists on their travels. Many tourists eat the same food on holidays as they would do at home. Mass tourist resorts can often be divided spatially on the basis of cuisine – English tourists in English pubs, German tourists in the *Bierkeller*. Some tourists still engage in the habit of taking their own food with them on holidays.
>
> (Richards 2002: 4–5)

Therefore, food is in fact a barrier upon cultural interaction. Not too long ago, some Asian tourists brought their familiar food when travelling abroad; for example, Japanese tourists brought soya sauce, Korean tourists brought spicy sauce, in order to make foreign food taste familiar and acceptable, while some Hong Kong tourists even brought instant noodles, assuming that they might not have appropriate or sufficient food during their trip. In fact, the choice of food among tourists can really vary. There are also as many tourists who are willing to try local indigenous food in order to have an authentic cultural experience during their travels. As a cosmopolitan city, the people of Hong Kong are not only exposed to food from various parts of the world on their own home ground, but rising affluence has also given ample opportunity for many to travel for food. For example, some Hong Kong nationals have gone to Japan for a sushi meal, or to Cuba for a box of Havana cigars if they can afford the travel expenses; and this might not be limited to Hong Kong people but people from many Asian countries as well.

When do anthropologists pay attention to gastronomic tourism? Traditionally, research on the anthropology of food has in the past centred largely on taboos, feasts, diets, communion and offerings, employing cultural symbolism for a better understanding of social relations among people and their interactions with others and/or the supernatural world (Messer 1984; Mintz & Du Bois 2002). More recent research is multidisciplinary, including issues of cultural identity, gender, ethnicity, social change, cultural nationalism, globalisation/localisation and memory with food, sharing the interests not only of anthropologists but also of historians, feminists and political scientists (Cheung 2009). In recent Asian research, it is not difficult to realise that food and eating have been viewed as important markers of cultural identity, hence their changing meanings have been studied to discern various kinds of social and political issues within a local context (Cheung 2009). Consequently, as tourism has become a major activity for both visitors and local host societies in many Asian countries, it is important to pay attention to the significance of food in tourism for the understanding of relevant social values and cultural meanings beyond economic and political development in the fast globalising world (Hjalager & Richards 2002; Cohen & Avieli 2004).

Again, when talking about gastronomic tourism, people tend to think of destinations in which the original version of a particular kind of gourmet food or drink is produced, for example, Italian pasta, Swiss chocolate, Australian seafood, French wine and Chinese tea. With the support of tourist agents and local government in place making through gastronomic attractions, some tourist attractions are eager to promote local food for tourists to enjoy, which can be, for example, Japanese sake, Korean Imperial cuisine, Singaporean street food and Cantonese seafood. Unheard of in the past, gastronomic tours are now popular (Hall et al. 2003). According to Hjalager (2002), there are four levels of gastronomic tourism, with the emphasis upon four different orders of attitude towards gastronomy varying from how tourists enjoy the food, understand the food, experience the food and exchange knowledge about the food. Even though Hjalager (2002) did not provide many cases for clarification of the above four-order model, it is beyond doubt that there exists many different kinds of gastronomic tours in various countries.

This case study seeks to investigate the meanings of different kinds of food as well as ingredients sold in a specific neighborhood which we consider an unique tourism resource both for domestic and international tourists not only for shopping but also channels for cultural understanding in our society, with particular reference to the relations between one's gastronomic experiences and domestic tourism. As Sheung Wan becomes more and more popular, we would like to rethink its meanings for Hong Kong visitors and unveil what this representative old Chinese trade hub as well as neighbourhood implies for heritage tourism.

Sheung Wan neighbourhood – the oldest Chinese trading hub in Hong Kong

Hong Kong, part of the previous Hsin-an county in Canton (Guangdong in Mandarin) province, was taken by the British in the middle of nineteenth century. The southern part of the Kowloon Peninsula, and Hong Kong Island with all its surrounding islands, was ceded to Britain by the Treaty of Nanking in 1842. However, a large part of the peninsula, called the New Territories, was leased to the British government in 1898 for 99 years. Under the colonial administration, the Hong Kong British government had the highest authority in policy making for the society. Being the major ethnic group, Chinese residents were given enough religious, academic, press and economic freedoms, so that there was not much hostility towards the British, at least compared to other colonies.

Many neighbourhoods in Hong Kong are rich in historical and cultural features that are worthwhile for citizens and tourists to explore. Over the last century, the neighbourhood of Sheung Wan helped make Hong Kong a successful and important trading hub, and traditional trade characteristics remain visible there today. Since the mid-nineteenth century, through the network of overseas Chinese in Thailand, the Nam Pak Hong was established to facilitate the import of various dried products into Hong Kong, for the purposes of trading with Chinese societies throughout Asia. Dating back to when Hong Kong was just a fishing village, the geographical location of Sheung Wan made it a very active trading centre, and its traditional business practices have somehow been preserved and remained this way ever since.

Nowadays, Sheung Wan is still seen as the place with clusters of streets full of dried marine products importers, wholesalers, retailers and modern mini-supermarkets selling dried seafood. This creates an exotic and unique image and leaves a lasting impression for anyone visiting there for the first time. Sheung Wan's traders handle dried food commodities from all over the world, including abalones from Japan, sea cucumbers from Indonesia, salted fish from Bangladesh, herbal medicines from mainland China, paste made from locally harvested and fermented planktonic shrimp, aged tangerine peels, fish maws, ginseng, and birds' nests, among many others. They also bear witness to the evolution of this locality and so have stories to share as part of the oral history of the community.

Because these food items are part of the Chinese culture, we consider this a unique experience for inbound tourists and excursionists looking for the culture and history of Hong Kong. Besides having been a trading hub as well as a commercial centre of Hong Kong for over a century, this kind of Sheung Wan neighbourhood visit contributes to local awareness through the interactions between tourists and local communities.

In 2012, a knowledge transfer project entitled "Learning from neighbourhood tourism in Sheung Wan, Hong Kong" was undertaken (a website was also developed to promote knowledge transfer through the project at http://www.cuhk.edu.hk/ant/sheungwan/) (Cheung & Luo 2013), which prioritised data collection over theoretical analyses. By delving into Nam Pak Hong, we flashed back to the trade development relationships of dried seafood, traditional Chinese medicines and groceries such as salted fish over the past century. By doing so, we hoped to transform the knowledge gained from our community into a tourism resource and hence an opportunity for local people and overseas visitors to learn and explore. We believe the curiosity required in street observation in modernology can be a cornerstone that fosters a mutual interaction between communities and tourism.

Salted fish – Yuen Shing Hong

Yuen Shing Hong is one of the largest salted fish distributors in Hong Kong. 'Fifty per cent of salted fish in Hong Kong is transacted here', estimated the owner, Mr. Wong. An auction is held every few days because the supply is plentiful. Prior to each auction, Mr. Wong sends an invitation letter to all retailers. They gather at Yuen Shing Hong on the auction day for fierce bargaining, which lasts one to one-and-a-half hours, depending on the amount of goods. The process is extremely quick and effective. Boxes of salted fish are taken out of the shop just after being dragged out from the back room.

Salted fish, which come in all sizes and species, and are now seen in shops around Hong Kong, are usually packed in plastic bags with their heads wrapped in paper. Mr. Wong explained:

How do we pick the right fish? Normally, salted fish are categorized as being either "firm" or "tangy", regardless of species. Fermentation makes the difference. When fish are caught in the fair weather months of autumn and winter, they are put into ice right away to keep them fresh and prevent any fermentation. Then they are buried in salt for two to three days, before drying in the sun. The flesh of these salted fish is "firm" and has a strong salty flavour … the fish could not be fermented if any part of it touched the ice.

In contrast, "tangy" salted fish is not chilled, but pickled directly by salting so the fish can be fully fermented and is nicely piquant. Some fish may have touched the ice accidentally during catching. If such fish are treated in the "tangy" way, they could have both flavours of salted fish – the iced part being "firm" and the rest being "tangy". A staff member in the salted fish shop pointed at two rows of identical threadfins: 'Can you tell which is which?' he asked. I shook my head. 'Actually', he continued, 'the secret lies in your fingertip. Pinch the fish softly – "firm" is firm while "tangy" feels squishy'.

Steaming is the best way to perfect the aroma and tenderness of salted fish to its fullest. According to Mr. Wong, salted fish and minced pork patty always make the best match – you may steam them together with some shredded ginger and scallion, so that the flavours of salted fish and meat mingle. Done in this way, the patty is sweet but not greasy. The ratio of fat and thin minced pork should be about 1:5, and it is better to hand-chop it to preserve a bit of the meat fibre and a chewy texture. Adding egg white would make the patty even smoother and taste better. 'Last but not the least', he added, 'don't forget the meaty juice that is left behind after steaming – it is the essence of the dish'. Boiling and pan-frying salted fish are also common household cooking methods. Red snapper head is a common ingredient for simmered soup. Pan-fried salted fish gives a pungent aroma. Mr. Wong has a tip for pan-frying salted fish: 'steam it first, and get rid of the excessive juice so that the fish will be tender and less salty'. Pan-fried white herring is a noble dish in a hotel banquet. The priciest white herrings are sold at US$ 220 per kg, while a normal-grade threadfin or croakers cost only US$ 25–40. Croakers are good for pan-frying because they have more fat. 'Another tip', Mr Wong continued, 'is that minced garlic can bring out its taste better than shredded ginger'.

The two remaining salted fish shops on Des Voeux Road West also sell locally produced shrimp paste, either in jars or as solid blocks. Sautéed Chinese broccoli with shrimp paste has a deliciousness that can fill your nostrils. Also, it is a good source of calcium.

In terms of salted fish production, the fishermen's "unblemished fish" is the most exquisite. An iron hook is inserted into the fish belly, via the gill, to pull out the guts and intestines without cutting open the belly. The belly is then filled with salt, and salt is also spread all over the fish skin. After the fish has been salt-treated for a full day, it is scaled and washed thoroughly, and its head is wrapped in paper before the fish is placed under direct sunlight. Boat people sun-dry their salted fish on the boat to keep flies away as well as to make full use of the more constant temperature on the sea, as well as the sea breeze. Such fish have an amazing "oceanic" flavour and better meat texture. It is a pity that boatmen have opted increasingly for more promising jobs ashore and are leaving the old industry. The sea breeze remains unchanged, but the salty smell of "unblemished fish" has weakened!

Economic changes have altered the entire salted fish industry, especially the source of supply and production, and local production is minimal nowadays. Today, most salted fish found in Hong Kong are from Bangladesh, Vietnam and Thailand. Therefore, the species used are not the same. According to Mr. Wong:

> Croakers were rare a few decades ago. The economic reforms in China in the early 1980s gradually boosted domestic demand so less salted fish were supplied to Hong Kong. That forced Hong Kong to look for new production bases in South Asia. Salted fish makers found that Bangladesh was teeming with quality croakers, so they began to import them massively from there. At the same time, the supply of threadfins remained stable. However, the range of salted fish species has decreased. Now we have mainly threadfins, croakers, white pomfrets, silver moonies and Malabar red snappers. You could buy many more types of salted fish a long time ago – any fish could be salted – but not now. Salted red snappers and pomfrets are not found anymore.

The heyday of the salted fish industry was from 1950 to the 1970s. From Mui Fong Street, Eastern Street to Des Voeux Road West, there were salted fish shops on both sides of the streets. As Mr. Wong remembers, 'salted fish was the only smell on the street'. This area became known locally as "Salted Fish Hood". Veteran staff members at the Hop Lee salted fish shop are immensely proud to recall that best of times. 'The sea was right in front of the shop', one of them pointed outside. 'Fishermen brought the fish right there, once they were pulled out of the water'. Of course, the old buildings in Sai Ying Pun have a special layout for salted fish shops, with a processing workshop and a rooftop for curing and drying fish. Town planning today obviously does not cater for such uses.

Combined with a declining local catch and lack of "new blood", the salted fish industry is dwindling fast. Today on Des Voeux Road West, there are only a couple of wholesalers and a few scattered retailers. 'The rent is too high. When one shop opens, another shuts down', a retailer grieved. Nowadays, the thriving dried seafood trade plays a leading role on Des Voeux Road West. Initiated by the Hong Kong Chinese Medicine Merchants Association and supported by the Hong Kong Tourism Board, in 2000 Des Voeux Road West was officially crowned "Dried Seafood Street". From then on the folk name "Salted Fish Hood" gradually disappeared.

The supplies to and sales in markets in both Mainland China and Hong Kong are actually shrinking. National income has increased since the economic reform that began in the 1980s, and the fish harvested along China's coastline now goes for domestic consumption. A higher living standard leads to a growing demand for fresh seafood, and less salted fish are wanted. Mr. Wong knew the situation very well, 'In the past we ordered the salted fish from China', he said. 'Ng Fung Hong was our agent to import salted fish, which were then auctioned to us. After the 1980s, our trade with the mainland gradually died out'. In Hong Kong, decreasing catches, wealthier lifestyles, urban space design and a changing diet are killing the industry. Ironically, the price of salted fish has not come down but has rather increased 40–50 per cent over the past two years. During the Chinese New Year of 2011, for example, white pomfret was sold at over USD 50 per kilogram, mainly because of a rise in production costs. Mr. Wong told what it is like in Bangladesh: 'Fish is pricier because of a worsened catch, and more expensive items in the production chain, such as salt and paper boxes. With revision of Bangladesh's labour laws and labour competition among investors, Hong Kong salted fish makers have to pay more for manpower'. Yet the biggest crisis faced by the Hong Kong salted fish industry is discontinuity. Experienced salted fish makers have to train workers in Bangladesh and Vietnam to make salted fish instead.

The glorious days are gone and trade is diminishing, but those left in the trade have stood fast against the storm and are upbeat. Loyal old patrons still contribute to part of their sales, and the traditional mode of fish auctioning persists. A distributor would auction the food products to the retailers, who then sell them throughout the community. Taking charge of the whole auction, the distributor holds an abacus with a covered bottom awaiting the highest bid. One by one, the buyers come over and enter their bid price into the abacus, with its covered bottom facing the crowd so that only the distributor knows all the bids. The price is disclosed only when he announces the successful deal. As opposed to computerised buying and selling, fish auctions have a style all their own in this high-tech society, upholding a practice that has lasted for half a century.

Chinese herbal medicine – Pak Cheong Tong

Shark fins, fish maws, natural agarwood, cinnamon sticks and other dried goods may exist beyond the realm of our normal sense and imagination. Each commodity in the Nam Pak Hong area of Sheung Wan can be an interesting topic in modernology. Next we examine a Chinese herbal drugstore, one among many century-old shops in Sheung Wan.

On Bonham Strand West there is an impressive three-storey building with a gracefully embellished shop sign and huge wooden couplets on both sides of the front door – "Pak Cheong Tong". The couplets mean "Pak Cheong Tong Pearl Powder and Camphor" and "Pak Cheong Tong Ginseng, Deer Antler and Cinnamon", respectively, which indicate the main products sold at the shop. 'The couplets were from Guangzhou and relocated to Hong Kong', said shop owner, Mr. Tsang.

Pak Cheong Tong is more than a century old. As recalled by Mr. Tsang, the shop started in Guangzhou and moved to Hong Kong in the 1920s. The shop has been at the same address since 1920 and still sells a similar range of medicinal products as it did then.

Upon entering the shop you first see small boxes of bottled and reasonably priced Macaque Calculus Powder placed in front of all the pricey medicines. Before coming to Hong Kong, Mr. Tsang's grandparents had been making the powder in Guangzhou. At first it was used only within the household to soothe

the children after they had nightmares. Later, people in the neighbourhood often asked for the powder, and so it was bottled and sold at a reasonable price.

Mr. Tsang's shop is certainly a living witness of the Chinese medicine trade in Nam Pak Hong. Anyone stepping into the shop would be immediately intrigued by a strong aroma, yet find it hard to identify. Camphor, also called "Plum Flakes" or "Dragon's Brain", is one of the featured medicinal products of Pak Cheong Tong. Camphor is a colourless solidified gum secreted from wounds on camphor trees. It is often used as an insect repellent. From the Chinese medical classics *Compendium of Materia Medica* in the sixteenth century and *Revised Materia Medica* of the Tang Dynasty in the seventh century, it can be seen that camphor has been long and widely used to ease strokes and locked jaws. Camphor trees are native to Southeast Asia, and camphor has been much sought after by Europeans since the seventeenth and eighteenth centuries.

'Except for camphor, Chinese medicines in Pak Cheong Tong are mostly wholesaled or dispensed', said Mr. Tsang. Imported raw materials are sorted and processed in the shop before being sold to pharmaceutical manufacturers. Only a small amount of medicines are retailed. Among wholesalers, Pak Cheong Tong seems to have the most outstanding selection of medicines, such as the resuscitative drugs of ambergris, amber, musk and camphor that help in directing curative effects to the unwell parts of the body, whereas pearl, "Horse's Gem" and "Macaque Stone" relieve nervousness. The names of some priceless medicines of olden times are handwritten clearly on four antique delivery orders hanging high on the wall. There are, of course, medicines from all over the world, including Tibetan saffron, Yunnan amber and Tianzhou notoginseng, deer products such as pilose antler from eastern Japan, "three-family" elk horn and deer tail from northern China, as well as the six kinds of ginseng, including wood-grown ginseng, North Korean ginseng, Jilin sand ginseng, Shizhu ginseng, Siberian ginseng and American ginseng. In Sheung Wan, traditional Chinese medicine stores other than Pak Cheong Tong are worth a good look into because any such store here is a living classroom for Chinese culture and liberal studies.

Last but not least is the rhyming couplet in the store. Opposite the glass counter with all kinds of precious medicines, there is another couplet on the wall that means "nostrum for guests as noble as azure dragons" and "fine medicine for immortals as elegant as white deer". It was written by Wu Daorong in August 1932 exclusively for Pak Cheong Tong. Wu was a renowned late-nineteenth-century scholar. Having his compliments implies that Pak Cheong Tong is superior among its competitors. In between the couplet is a Chinese calligraphic painting. The rosewood furniture below the couplet makes the décor of the store even more artistic.

Remarks

To conclude with the demonstration of the above example, modernology does not provide comprehensive reflection and analysis of the history, but a glimpse of the fragmentary information and stories of Pak Cheong Tong here and there gives us hints regarding a fuller picture of the years that it has been through. Another episode in the 1920s will illustrate what we mean. Pak Cheong Tong used to hand out medicine to the poor. This practice is an earlier version of today's corporate social responsibility and a historical testimony of the geopolitical relationship between Hong Kong, Guangdong and Macau. The disappearance of some precious medicinal materials in drug production also has a story to tell. Ambergris, for instance, is a medicine as well as an essential ingredient in perfumery. Because natural ambergris is difficult to acquire, and because a synthetic fixative is becoming more common, it is now a rarity in traditional drug stores.

Acknowledgements

Research for this article was made possible by the CUHK Knowledge Transfer project entitled "Learning from neighbourhood tourism in Sheung Wan, Hong Kong" (#3230031). Parts of the chapter were available online in the *SPC Traditional Marine Resource Management and Knowledge Information Bulletin* (Cheung & Luo 2013) as part of the knowledge transfer project.

References

Cheung, S.C.H. (2009) 'Gastronomy and tourism: a case study of gourmet country-style cuisine in Hong Kong', in T. Winter, P. Teo, and T.C. Chang (eds) *Asia on Tour: Exploring the Rise of Asian Tourism*, London and New York: Routledge.

Cheung, S.C.H. and Luo, J. (2013) '"Modernology", cultural heritage and neighbourhood tourism: the example of Sheung Wan, Hong Kong', *SPC Traditional Marine Resource Management and Knowledge Information Bulletin*, 31: 12–20.

Cohen, E. and Avieli, N. (2004) 'Food in tourism: attraction and impediment', *Annals of Tourism Research*, 31(4): 755–778.

Hall, C.M., Cambourne, B., Sharples, L., Macionis, N. and Mitchell, R. (2003) *Food Tourism around the World: Development, Management, and Markets*, Oxford: Butterworth-Heinemann.

Hjalager, A.-M. (2002) 'A typology of gastronomy tourism', in A. Hjalager and G. Richards (eds) *Tourism and Gastronomy*, London: Routledge, pp. 21–36.

Hjalager, A.-M. and Richards, G. (eds) (2002) *Tourism and Gastronomy*, London: Routledge.

Kon, W. (2013) *Kon Wajiro and Modernology*, Tokyo: Kawade Shobo Shinsha Press.

Messer, E. (1984) 'Anthropological perspectives on diet', *Annual Review of Anthropology*, 13: 205–249.

Mintz, S. and Du Bois, C. (2002) 'The anthropology of food and eating', *Annual Review of Anthropology*, 30: 99–119.

Noguchi, P. (1994) 'Savor slowly: Ekiben: the fast food of the high-speed Japan', *Ethnology*, 33(4): 317–340.

Richards, G. (2002) 'Gastronomy: an essential ingredient in tourism production and consumption', in A. Hjalager and G. Richards (eds) *Tourism and Gastronomy*, London: Routledge, pp. 2–20.

9 Regional economic development through food tourism

The case of AsiO Gusto in Namyangju City, South Korea

Timothy J. Lee and Jang-Hyun Nam

Introduction

Food is at the core of cultural content, helping to form a national brand image and provide an opportunity for visitors to experience various cultures based on food preparation and presentation. Each country's food culture is formed and developed based on its particular geographical position (i.e. climate, land, soil, amount of rainfall, landscape, wind), as well as social, religious, and cultural environments. In addition, food plays a particularly important role in traditional Asian cultures and remains a cuisine attracting ever-increasing interest in countries such as the United States. Within this latter trend however, Jang, Ha and Silkes (2009) found that among Asian cuisines, Korean food is perceived differently in terms of both taste and uniqueness, with customers in the United States considering Korean food uniquely hot and spicy. These consumers also tend to perceive Korean food as healthy and nutritionally balanced.

By definition, Korean food can be understood as food cooked using traditional Korean methods, and with food ingredients which have been traditionally used over time. Korean food is also used to mean food cooked using recipes derived from the past (Min 2009). Korean food is cooked using rice and various other grains and a range of seasonal vegetables. In addition, Korean cuisine uses many seafood products. The key characteristics of Korean food are:

- All foods are served at one time for every diner; this distinguishes it from both Chinese and Western cuisines, which generally serve dishes following each other in order.
- Many foods using grains have been developed, with staple foods including rice, beans and barley.
- Korean food is normally divided into staple foods and subsidiary foods. While steamed rice is the core staple food at each meal, many different types of side dishes can be served as subsidiary foods, with over 100 different kinds available. In addition it can include a range of soups and stews.
- There are various recipes for the same food, including soups, stews and *Kimchi* (fermented spicy vegetable, the most common Korean side dish).
- Korean cuisine includes fermented foods and stored foods such as soybean paste and sauces and salted fish.

- Each region in Korea has a different authentic local food.
- Korean food has a range of flavours using many different spices (Na 2008; Lee & Chung 2009; Min 2009).

In many markets Korean food is not well understood (Jang et al. 2009; Ha & Jang 2010). Nevertheless, Korean food tourism is emerging as a new growth, accounting for a significant amount of tourism spending as well as high levels of interest from visitors from China, Japan and Taiwan. With this in mind, the South Korean government and community associations are paying keen attention to food tourism in order to encourage the connections between tourism, commercialisation and regional growth. One part of this strategy is the development of food events. This chapter discusses the International Slow Food Festival held in Namyangju City, a satellite city of Seoul, the capital of South Korea, in October 2013 in order to showcase the Asian Slow Food movement and Korean food in particular. Forty-three Asia Pacific countries and 530,000 visitors, including 20,000 foreign tourists, participated in the 2013 Festival. The event saw 37 billion Korean Won (US$ 37 million) added to the local economy and 100 billion Korean Won (US$ 100 million) in terms of national economic impact. However, before discussing the event the chapter will first discuss the significance of the Slow Food movement.

Slow Food

The Slow Food movement started in the small town of Bra, Italy, where its founder Carlo Petrini was born and raised. The movement attracted global attention with its protest in response to the opening of a McDonald's restaurant in the Piazza di Spagna in Rome in 1986. On December 1989, the Slow Food movement was formally founded as the International Slow Food Movement for the Defense of and the Right to Pleasure at the Opera Comique in Paris (Laudan 2004). The initial Founding Protocol Manisfesto was signed by representatives from 15 countries (Petrini 2007).

Given that Slow Food members have a high interest in food, it might be that they transmit this specific interest and associated values into their daily life when they select a vacation destination. There are few studies, however, that specifically target this special interest group in a tourism context (Hall 2012). Slow Food clearly defines itself as an organisation devoted to cultural politics. While the name of the movement explicitly refers to food, implicit within this name is the notion that memory is entangled in the senses and that through the sensory experience of rediscovering taste memories one recuperates and holds onto the past (Leitch 2003). Slowness, in other words, is linked to pleasure, conviviality and corporeal memory. Slow Food is more than slowness; the Slow Food movement's philosophy gave rise to the new concept of eco-gastronomy, which is based on the belief that every person has a fundamental right to pleasure and that the plate and the planet are interconnected (Tam 2008).

The philosophy of Slow Food is that food should be "good", "clean" and "fair" (Petrini 2007). Good food is regarded as being tasty and diverse and produced in such a way as to maximise its flavour and connections to a geographic and cultural region. Such food should also be sustainable and fair, being produced in socially sustainable ways, with an emphasis on social justice and fair wages (Petrini 2007; Schneider 2008). Slow Food also emphasises as notion of "local" where small is beautiful, suggesting local autarchy, local preservation and local storage (Naess & Rothenberg 1989).

Pietrykowski (2004) explains that through the dual process of pleasure-seeking and politicisation of Slow Food, it is able to transform cultural capital, a taste for food and wine usually associated with class, status and conspicuous consumption, into social capital (see also Paxson 2005). While the United States is one of the fastest growing countries in terms of membership of Slow Food, ironically it is where fast-food was invented. For Belanger (2001), the solution to fast food is Slow Food, where the family sits down together and be connected with their food and its origins. Thus, from this perspective, the Slow Food movement brings back the joy of eating to the family and better eating habits (de Graaf & Kok 2010).

Common observations are that Slow Food members come mainly from middle to high classes of society and the cost of participating in Slow Food activities is quite high (Gaytán 2004; Laudan 2004). In Gaytán's (2004) study of members of nine Slow Food convivia in North California, it was observed that members situate European culture and tradition as benchmarks of superior lifestyle and consumption practice. Similarly, in the Barossa, Australia, "tradition' and "heritage" focused on European culture are intrinsic to Barossa Slow Food (Peace 2006). Nevertheless, Miele and Murdoch (2002) used the case of the Bagnoli restaurant, a family-owned local restaurant in Tuscany, Italy, to explain aesthetics in gastronomy and especially "slow" aesthetics, when food culture, environmental sustainability and local economy converge in an interconnected set of linkages across the gastronomic landscape. Indeed, the usage of "slow" has become popular and the term Slow Tourism has emerged, in contrast to modern society's fast life; that is, stay in one place longer, get to know the area much more thoroughly and deliberately seek to buy local. This may become an extremely attractive idea for fast-paced people (Hall 2006). However, perhaps ironically, it may also suggest commodification (Hall 2012). As Pratt (2007) suggests, by buying Barolo wine, cheeses or Tuscan pigs, the concept of *terroir* or *territorio* was also borrowed; the landscape is also bought.

Product certification and events related to the Slow Food

Coop Italia (The National Association of Consumers Cooperatives), a retailing company for food and grocery distribution, works closely with the Slow Food Ark of Taste's Presidia; they have signed an agreement aimed at the protection of typical products and food tradition (Fonte 2006). However, the certification and/ or selection process of Slow Food products is not very well defined as yet by the Slow Food organisation (Lotti 2010).

The main Slow Food events are the Terra Madre and Salone del Gusto events organised in parallel biannually in October in Turin, Italy. The 2010 Terra Madre brought together over 5,000 worldwide representatives according to the official website of Terra Madre. Slow Food members' regional meetings were organised. The five-day program including earth workshops, taste education and food biodiversity were interpreted simultaneously into different languages to accommodate Slow Food members from, for example, Italy, France, Portugal, Spain, Germany, Russia and Japan. Salone del Gusto has a different emphasis – a food festival that allows direct interaction between artisans and consumers. The five-day event attracted over 200,000 visitors according to Salone del Gusto's official website. Other Slow Food international events on a smaller scale are Slow Fish and Slow Cheese, both of which are also biannual events, while local Slow Food groups also organise events (see also Chapter 5, this volume).

For Pollan (2003), Slow Food has initiated a handful of decidedly eccentric institutions and ideas through the Ark of Taste, the presidia, "eco-gastronomy" and 'virtuous-globalisation'. As Pollan (2003) points out, sometimes the best way to rescue the most idiosyncratic local products and practices is to find a global market for them. Nevertheless, perhaps almost paradoxically, even though it positions itself as an alternative sustainable food network (Heinzelmann 2005; McIlvaine-Newsad et al. 2008) that contrasts with the global "unnatural economic order" (Peace 2008), its international profile provides a significant basis for the promotion of artisanal and regional food products (Hall 2012). Indeed, many researchers have written about the Slow Food movement as a "new" social movement emerging alongside post-industrial capitalism and globalisation (Schneider 2008). The essence of the movement and the usage of "slow" has also spread to other areas, notably "Slow City", "Slow Living", "Slow Tourism" and "Slow Travel" (Chadwick 2002; Leitch 2003; Labelle 2004; Pietrykowski 2004; Hall 2006, 2012; Parkins & Craig 2006; Schneider 2008; Dickinson & Lumsdon 2010; Fullagar, Markwell & Wilson 2012; Gössling & Hall 2013).

Although the Slow Food movement has been criticised with respect to the practicalities of its project (Pollan 2003; Hall 2012), it has nevertheless accumulated over 100,000 members in 150 countries worldwide. Furthermore, its profile means that it remains influential in the media and in culinary networks, which means that its endorsement or involvement is actively sought by some public and private bodies. This chapter introduces an example of how Slow Food can be associated with the tourism industry and contribute to the development of the local economy.

The Slow Food festival: AsiO Gusto in Namyangju City, South Korea

The AsiO Gusto is a biannual international festival which is officially approved by Slow Food International. It was held in the Asia Pacific for the first time in 2013 in South Korea Table 9.1 provides an overview of the festival. AsiO Gusto is one of the world's three major Slow Food international festivals where producers and customers get together. The aims of hosting the festival are

- to offer an unique food festival where producers and customers participate from all over the world;
- to host the biggest biannual Slow Food international festival in the Asia Pacific region;
- to organise a sustainable festival for the taste, culture and food of the Asia Pacific;
- to ensure food's industrial value in agriculture, the environment, education and health;
- to enhance and spread a healthy diet; and
- to develop agriculture and environment-friendly organic farming in the Asia Pacific.

Its overall theme is organic farming for production and Slow Food for the dining table.

Namyangju City, which is located in the north-east part of Seoul and the central part of Gyeonggi Province, has a population of 650,000. The city, which positions itself as a city of "well-being" and a balance between rural and urban life, already had a number of elements that enabled it to act as a host location. For example, it supported the annual national Slow Food festival from 2009 to 2012 and successfully hosted an organic farming festival in 2011, while it has also established the world's first organic farming museum (Namyangju Organic Theme Park). In 2011 it was appointed as the first slow city in the Seoul Metropolitan Area. The notion of slow has, therefore, been integral to its positioning in place marketing terms. Nevertheless, by hosting AsiO Gusto Namyangju sought to enhance its image both nationally and internationally, and as an outcome of the event, the city attracted 630 press reports and 33 foreign reports in 32 countries as a direct consequence of the food Expo.

The festival showcased Korean food, including foods registered in "the ark of taste". The event's Slow Food restaurants accommodated 4,500 persons at lunchtime and 500 persons for dinner, totaling 5,000 persons per day on average.

Table 9.1 Overview of the 2013 Asia and Oceania Slow Food Festival in Namyangju (2013 AsiO Gusto)

Period	1 October (Tuesday) to 6 October (Sunday) 2013
Location	Namyangju Sports and Culture Center, Namyangju City, South Korea
Theme	Organic farming for production, Slow Food for the dining table
Slogan	"Slow food, the world that changes with taste"
Organisers	The Slow Food Culture Center, Slow Food International Headquarters, Namyangju City
Sponsors	The Ministry of Agriculture, Food and Rural Affairs, Gyeonggi Province, Korea Tourism Organisation, Gyeonggi Tourism Organisation
Participants	533,015 participants (including 20,000 foreigners) from 44 countries; 2,018 volunteers; 191,053 tickets sold
Expenditure	A total expenditure of visitors during the six-day festival was approximately 13 billion Korean Won (US$ 13 million)

The festival operated a domestic showroom and displayed local Slow Food and attracted the participation of businesses related to organic, environment-friendly processed goods and Slow Food and provided cultural guidance about the local characteristics. It also provided free samples and stands where participants could buy ingredients and foods produced by domestic small business owners. It introduced the attendees to local food that was pesticide- and MSG-free, as well environment-friendly processed food and traditional food obtained from local primary producers. The number of attendees for the Korean showroom was approximately 190,000 persons and the total gross sales were approximately 503 million Korean Won (US$ 503,000).

A number of other initiatives were also developed to encourage greater connectivity between local agricultural producers and consumers. These included a Slow Food cooking competition in which one of the important judging criteria was whether there was use of traditional recipes and ingredients based on the philosophy of Slow Food. A farmer's market, which is a place for selling local primary agricultural products and local food, was also held. This aimed to create the atmosphere of a traditional Korean market day, and an estimated 66 businesses participated. The total gross sale of the farmer's market was 582 million Won (US$ 582,000) and the operating revenue of the market was approximately 24,162,000 Korean Won (US$ 24,162).

The festival attracted the participation of the locals by operating a slow program in which they could experience various crafts and make a unique souvenir with family and friends if they wished. Other parts of the programme designed to enhance local participation included a Korean traditional wrestling (*ssirum*) event; a quiz for teenagers to help them to understand the concept and idea of Slow Food, improve their diet and food culture, and promote the idea of a slow life; and a sound festival, walking meditation and empty dish experience program.

Participant evaluation survey

A survey of attendees was conducted at the request of the festival organisers. The questionnaire was divided into two main parts: visitor satisfaction and questions regarding the further development of the Namyangju Slow Food international festival. The responses of 64 foreigners who participated in Namyangju Slow Food international festival were analysed.

Just over two-thirds (68.75 per cent) of the foreign participants were visiting Korea for the first time and the remainder for a second time. Those who visited Korea for the first time faced difficult situations beyond their purpose of visit more than once during the festival. For example, they brought samples to introduce their own country's Slow Food ingredients or for business purposes, but Korean visitors in the festival considered the samples as sale items. Also, in some cases, international participants could not attract the Korean visitors' attention. Therefore, in the future, a better system is needed for integrating foreign participants into the festival. This is important as foreign participants were wanting to not only sell and promote their own products but also learn about Korean Slow Food. Furthermore, the evaluation also suggested a need to separate cooking booths and other booths in the international pavilion as the heat and smell of the food was described as unpleasant. Nevertheless, despite these issues, 95 per cent of the respondents showed satisfaction with the festival.

Contribution to the regional economy

During the six-day festival, the city welcomed more than half a million visitors from 43 countries who directly spent more than US$15 million. The festival also contributed to the city solidifying its position as a destination that has a clearly distinctive and differentiated destination image of healthy, fresh and enjoyable products. It also enabled the organic and Slow Food farmers to securing buyers in the metropolitan area that has more than 20 million people within a two-hour driving distance. Out of the more than 10 satellite cities of the capital city of Seoul, Namyangju has now established a strong destination image with the slow brand which is regarded as being helpful to regional economic development and investment attraction.

The festival also helped fulfill wider social goals of encouraging younger generations living in the metropolitan area that experience high daily stress, a heavily competitive environment, fast-food dietary habits and an impatient and aggressive attitude to learn about slow and natural agricultural philosophy. The festival also provides a successful example of how many stakeholders can cooperate and share the benefits of the organic and seasonal agricultural crops. This included not only the farmers but also those working in the municipal government, markets, transportation, storage and fertilisers. In addition, it is believed that the festival has enabled the formation of a worldwide Slow Food network of foreign visitors to promote Korean food culture and traditional dishes.

Conclusion

This chapter discussed the hosting of the Asia and Oceania Slow Food Festival in Namyangju, South Korea, in 2013. The festival provided a number of positive economic returns for the festival organisers as well as attracting over half a million visitors. Although the vast majority of these were from the domestic market, a significant number of foreign visitors were also attracted. In addition, in the longer term the festival was regarded as contributing to the region's destination image and positioning, particularly with respect to creating value-added industry items, boosting local retail sales and sustainable agricultural development. However, also of significance is that regional development was not only conceived of in purely economic terms but that a major aim of the festival was to encourage more general health and well-being and greater understanding of Korean culture while at the same time being able to embrace the benefits of Slow Food.

References

Belanger, J.D. (2001) 'Slow Food – a celebration of life', *Countryside and Small Stock Journal*, 85(2): 54–57.

Chadwick, B. (2002) 'Easy does it: the Slow Food movement takes on the fast food culture', *E: The Environmental Magazine*, 13(5): 42–43.

de Graaf, C. and Kok, F.J. (2010) 'Slow Food, fast food and the control of food intake', *Nature Reviews Endocrinology*, 6(5): 290–293.

Dickinson, J. and Lumsdon, L. (2010) *Slow Travel and Tourism*, London: Earthscan.

Fonte, M. (2006) 'Slow Food's presidia: what do small producers do with big retailers?' *Research in Rural Sociology and Development*, 12: 203–240.

Fullagar, S., Markwell, K. and Wilson, E. (eds) (2012) *Slow Tourism: Experiences and Mobilities*, Bristol: Channel View.

Gaytán, M.S. (2004) 'Globalizing resistance: Slow food and new local imaginaries', *Food, Culture and Society*, 7(2): 97–116.

Gössling, S. and Hall, C.M. (2013) 'Sustainable culinary systems: an introduction', in C.M. Hall and S. Gössling (eds) *Sustainable Culinary Systems: Local Foods, Innovation, Tourism and Hospitality*, Abingdon: Routledge, pp. 3–44.

Ha, J. and Jang, S. (2010) 'Perceived values, satisfaction, and behavioral intentions: the role of familiarity in Korean restaurants', *International Journal of Hospitality Management*, 29: 2–13.

Hall, C.M. (2006) 'Introduction: culinary tourism and regional development: from Slow Food to slow tourism?' *Tourism Review International*, 9(4): 303–305.

Hall, C.M. (2012) 'The contradictions and paradoxes of Slow Food: environmental change, sustainability and the conservation of taste', in S. Fullagar, K. Markwell, and E. Wilson (eds) *Slow Tourism: Experiences and Mobilities*, Bristol: Channel View, pp. 53–68.

Heinzelmann, U. (2005) 'Salone del Gusto and Terra Madre 2004', *Gastronomica*, 5: 1–2.

Jang, S., Ha, A. and Silkes, C. (2009) 'Perceived attributes of Asian foods: from the perspective of the American customer', *International Journal of Hospitality Management*, 28(1): 63–70.

Labelle, J. (2004) 'A Recipe for connectedness bridging production and consumption with Slow Food', *Food, Culture and Society*, 7(2): 81–96.

Laudan, R. (2004) 'Slow Food: the French terroir strategy, and culinary modernism an essay review', *Food, Culture and Society*, 7(2): 133–144.

Lee, S.M. and Chung, H.Y. (2009) 'A study on revisiting, satisfaction and Korean restaurant selection of foreigners living in the Korea', *Journal of Foodservice Management Society of Korea*, 12(1): 293–313.

Leitch, A. (2003) 'Slow Food and the politics of pork fat: Italian food and European identity', *Ethnos*, 68(4): 437–462.

Lotti, A. (2010) 'The commoditization of products and taste: Slow Food and the conservation of agrobiodiversity', *Agriculture and Human Values*, 27(1): 71–83.

McIlvaine-Newsad, H., Merrett, C., Maakestad, W. and McLaughlin, P. (2008) 'Slow Food lessons in the fast food midwest', *Southern Rural Sociology*, 23(1): 72–93.

Miele, M. and Murdoch, J. (2002) 'The practical aesthetics of traditional cuisines: Slow Food in Tuscany', *Sociologia Ruralis*, 42(4): 312–328.

Min, K.H. (2009) 'A study on cultivating Korean chefs for the globalization of Korean food', *Korean Journal of Food Cookery*, 25(4): 506–512.

Na, J.K. (2008) 'A study on the localization models development for the Korean restaurant', *Journal of Foodservice Management Society of Korea*, 11(1): 307–336.

Naess, A. and Rothenberg, D. (1989) *Ecology, Community and Lifestyle: Outline of an Ecosophy*, Cambridge: Cambridge University Press.

Parkins, W. and Craig, G. (2006) *Slow Living*, Sydney: University of New South Wales Press.

Paxson, H. (2005) 'Slow Food in a fat society: satisfying ethical appetites', *Gastronomica*, 5(1): 14–18.

Peace, A. (2006) 'Barossa slow: the representation and rhetoric of Slow Food's regional cooking', *Gastronomica*, 6(1): 51–59.

Peace, A. (2008) 'Terra Madre 2006: political theater and ritual rhetoric in the Slow Food Movement', *Gastronomica*, 8(2): 31–39.

Petrini, C. (2007) *Slow Food Nation: Why Our Food Should Be Good, Clean and Fair*, New York: Rizzoli Ex Libris.

Pietrykowski, B. (2004) 'You are what you eat: the social economy of the Slow Food movement', *Review of Social Economy*, 62(3): 307–321.

Pollan, M. (2003) 'Cruising on the ark of taste', *Mother Jones*, 28(3): 74–77.

Pratt, J. (2007) 'Food values', *The Local and the Authentic*, 27(3): 285–300.

Schneider, S. (2008) 'Good, clean, fair: the rhetoric of the Slow Food movement', *College English*, 70(4): 384–402.

Tam, D. (2008) 'Slow journeys: what does it mean to go slow? (Slow Food movement)', *Food, Culture and Society*, 11(2): 207–212.

10 Consuming the rural and regional

The evolving relationship between food and tourism

Paul Cleave

Introduction

The aim of this chapter is to show how the qualitative social and environmental dimensions are important aspects in food tourism and that interests in food within the context of food tourism evolve, contributing to regional development. The south-west of England will be used as a geographical focus demonstrating how tourism, farming and fishing contribute to economic development in the peninsula. It is a region that has an established contemporary food culture that was born out of a long association between food production, consumption and place. Drawing on contemporary and historical materials, the chapter shows how the past inspires and has a place in the present.

The attraction of food in the framework of tourism has appealed to tourists for generations. This is significant in the development of a regional economy, but is more than that; it is a story of heritage, association, differentiation and the evolving significance and attraction of locally sourced foods. This chapter shows how the past is part of an evolutionary process and that elements of it are enduring. However, it presents more than a retrospective review and draws on the economic and gastronomic heritage of a region, identifying the need for change, adaptation and innovation. Food and culinary heritage and the relationships between food and place are important aspects of a food-producing and tourism area. A case study of Devon, a county in the south-west of the United Kingdom, provides an example of a region closely associated with food production and tourism. It will show how a fortuitous combination of the history and legacy of an industry, community and place provides not only a tangible link with the past but also of the present and is important in future prosperity. Food and food tourism can enhance local identity (Bessiere 1998) and are frequently identified as significant factors in regional development (Hall, Johnson & Mitchell 2000; Gössling & Hall 2013). It is also important to consider changes in consumer tastes and aspirations in the context of food (Mennell 1985; Spencer 2002; Burnett 2004) and eating out for pleasure. These are documented but tend not to emphasise differentiation by place, product and association.

Background to the region

The south-west of England, stretching from Cornwall to Gloucester, is an official region defined by government. It embraces the somewhat informally defined West

Country and peninsula counties of Devon, Cornwall, an area with a sustained tradition of food production and tourism. The agricultural and maritime heritage of the West Country is reflected in the appeal of food in an area with rich farmland, pastures, orchards and contrasting coastlines set against a lush, undulating landscape. Tourists have long been attracted by its climate and geography. Stone (1923) suggests that Cornwall is 'England's Riviera' alluding to the mild climate and verdant landscape, and similarly, *Eyre's Guide* (Anonymous 1878: 73) describes Torquay, in Devonshire, as the 'Montpellier' of England. One of the best sheltered and formed of English bays, Torbay, was often compared to Monte Carlo and the south of France, while in contrast the steep cliffs, wooded valleys and vegetation of the north coast of Devon drew imaginative comparisons with the Rhine and Switzerland.

Knight and Dutton (1910: 4) describe Devon in terms of its scenery as so striking that it is 'generally considered the most beautiful county in England' with a genial and equable health-giving climate, important attributes in its appeal to tourists. Conjointly, these have attracted travellers and tourists from the seventeenth and eighteenth centuries when the region was drawing attention as a fashionable destination. It was considered a place to visit for its antiquities, romantic landscapes and for health. The mild climate and provision of numerous watering places and seaside resorts were in contrast to more urbanised and industrial regions. In the twenty-first century, contemporary food tourism reflects another stage in the evolution of consumers and producers specialised interests in smaller scale, sustainable food production and traditions in a quest for the local, sustainable and authentic.

The attraction of regional food in Devonshire

A county sometimes regarded as rural, rustic and remote, the attraction of food and landscape was often recorded in the accounts and journals of early traveller. The appeal of the different in terms of landscape and a culinary differentiation became a feature of many publications about the region. Travellers and tourists observed the differences in food they encountered together with the distinctive landscape and topography, identifying regional products and practices. Devon received the attention of travelling scholars and clerics, and regional food attracted their interest as a curiosity or speciality. Skinner's (1985) evocative description of his West Country tour in 1797 includes descriptions of the women seine (net) fishing on the shore at Shaldon in South Devon and a Squab Pie (lamb and apples) he enjoyed at a nearby farmhouse. Numerous authors noted the region's foods they tasted on their travels in the seventeenth and eighteenth centuries and provide early examples of the attraction of foods linked to place and regarded as out-of-the-ordinary (e.g. Shaw 1789; Fanshawe 1829; Defoe 1962; Fiennes 1984). For example, Defoe (1962) praised the high quality of shellfish, and Lady Fanshawe while visiting Barnstaple enjoyed a tart made of mazzards (Gee 2004), a type of small black cherry grown in North Devon and served with rich clotted cream.

The attraction of local food and differentiation sometimes becomes blurred between counties in the region, but Jaine (1998) suggests that, in the West Country, chefs are concerned with the present, though not dismissive of the past, and keen to emphasise a sense of place and regional cooking. Much is associated with relatively simple dishes, but the high quality of ingredients gives prominence to the provenance of the local and seasonal (Mason & Brown 1999). However, the influence of the past is important and food heritage was already recorded, for example, in the work of Florence White (1932) and Dorothy Hartley (1954). In the first half of the twentieth century, they travelled throughout Britain searching out regional dishes and foods considered to be disappearing. Through their influential work they pioneered an interest in preserving and reviving food heritage. White (1935) bought many dishes to the attention of visitors in the form of the *Good Food Register* which provided details of establishments serving local dishes and specialities. This acknowledged a quest for culinary differentiation and is indicative of an interest in regional and local food and associated dishes.

Aspects of Devon's food heritage were identified by Trewin (2010) and these are described as contributing to an edible landscape, one with a history, food culture and traditions. A food landscape, foodscape or sensory landscape is important in contributing to the image and food branding of a region or destination (Berg & Sevon 2014). Culinary variations are described by Mabey (1980) in a review of regional foods in England, drawing attention to factors which may have contributed to their success and in some cases demise, for example, large-scale mass production. Foods associated with a region represent a culinary connection, one linked with consumption. Fine, Heasman and Wright (1996) suggest that in the context of food, tourism brings about a system of provision where foods are provided specifically for the visiting public.

The example of a geographical location shows how the tradition of food and food tourism has contributed to the economy of the region and are perpetuated. Minchinton (1969) asserts that a distinctive feature of Devon's industry, whether manufacturing or extractive, was that it was largely based on local resources and is also a maritime county, with two contrasting coastlines (moorland and rich agricultural regions). The maritime trade reached a peak in the nineteenth century, but the herring, pilchard and mackerel fishery went into a later decline. The county has a long and evolving history of food production – from clotted cream to caviar. The significance of local foods, ingredients and dishes in the context of tourism and regional development has contributed to the diverse range of food currently produced in the region. Some foods, for example, fish, fruit, livestock and dairy produce, give scope for regional differentiation and uniqueness associated with place. These have long been connected to tourism, but typically were the unusual specialities not familiar in other parts of the country.

The visitors who stayed in the county from the eighteenth century were advised of the quality of local food markets in Feltham's (1815) *Guide to the Watering, and Sea Bathing Places*; subsequently hotels and restaurants provided food, frequently mentioning its provenance and excellence. This may be contrasted and compared with today's tourists who search for local foods, for example, through farm shops, farmers' markets and food festivals. In July 1850 the chef Alexis Soyer visited the West Country as part of an agricultural promotion celebrating its food. A lavish annual dinner for the Royal Agricultural Society was prepared and served in Exeter using much local produce. This included a whole roasted ox and an *Exeter pudding* (an extravagant baked mixture containing eggs, sugar, bread-crumbs, rum, jam and clotted cream) (Morris 1938; Mennell 1985). The event provided an early regional form of celebrity endorsement, and there are parallels with the current celebrity status of food activities encouraged by extensive media coverage of food trends and interests. These include local food, smaller scale production, artisan producers, heritage, lifestyle, Slow Food, and in Devon, Guy Watson's work in the production of organic food at Riverford Farm close to the "transition town" of Totnes. The economic significance of food production was described by Lloyd, Richards and Cock (c. 1938) as expanding, with an increase in orchard acreage and market gardening in addition to livestock and traditional clotted cream, together with the county becoming 'a national holiday ground'.

Drawing on the 2004 *Strategy for food and drink industry in the south west of England, 2005–2015* (South West Food & Drink 2004), the south-west is described as the most rural of the English regions, many of its businesses emerg-ing from the land. The region is portrayed as a jigsaw of local distinctions and strong food brand identities, for example, Cornish Clotted Cream and Devon Toffee. The strategy considers food in terms of its regional identity and contribu-tion to the economy. Food is currently promoted in the south-west by regional food groups including *Taste of the West*, the first to be formed in 1991, and *Food and Drink Devon*. Ilberry and Kneafsey (2000) suggest that these are important in establishing connections between food quality and place, geographically or his-torically, with a tradition or culture. Food production and consumption contribute significantly to the economy of the region, for example, the export of food, the food component of tourism and in generating and sustaining employment.

Food was of interest to the tourists who visited the West Country in the early twentieth century. Whereas there was a sense of otherness topographically, in a culinary context the food too was perceived as different, regional and of high quality. This was to prove significant in the growth of the food tourism era and interests in the benefits of locally sourced products (Hall et al. 2003; Sims 2009; Croce & Perri 2009). Consumer concerns such as ethics, the environment and sustainability, food scares, and health issues are also noted in the context of food tourism (see also Chapter 1, this volume).

Food and place

The appeal of foods associated with Devon is enduring and indicates an interest in regional specialities and differentiation. An early example is Laver, a form of sea-weed rich in iron and iodine and associated with North Devon, well known for its healthy qualities. Feltham (1815: 17) advised visitors to the area that on the sea-shore near Appledore 'that marine production called *Laver* is found in great plenty, and is esteemed a fine antiscorbutic'. The farms not only produced the food which may have been consumed by tourists but also provided them with an attraction and food interest. This is observed by Morton (1927) who encouraged his readers with tempting descriptions of baskets of strawberries, butter and clotted cream, to discover farmhouse food at the farm or local market. Conversely, he is also describing an economic practice often the domain of the farmer's wife in producing and providing hospitality in the form of accommodation (Oliver 1938).

Harris (1907: 65) enthused about the county's food with bucolic descriptions of the landscape: 'this is fine apple country and the orchards are really worth looking at twice a year, in the spring when in bloom and in the autumn when the fruit is bending the boughs'. Harris's (1907) narratives evoke the livelihood of communities producing the food and dishes considered specialities, identifying nostalgia for food associated with place. The West Country has long been associated with the quality of its dairy products. For example, Fortnum and Mason, London, has sold Devonshire butter since the eighteenth century. Devonshire Clotted Cream, with a minimum butterfat content of 55 per cent, was regarded as a luxury and speciality. Harris (1907: 35) suggested it had 'spread the fame of the county all the world over', certainly it could be conveniently posted home as a gift and souvenir, while Clunie-Harvey and Hill (1937) stated that clotted cream was a healthy food and especially beneficial to children.

Regional differentiation is identified in the production of one of the most popular confectionery souvenirs, fudge. Confectionery, with the addition of Devon's dairy products, became distinguished by association with locally produced ingredients. This conferred uniqueness to the ubiquitous. With its origins in America (Cleave 2013), fudge became popular in the 1950s as the market for softer textured confectionery emerged. In the south-west of England, numerous small-scale confectioners had flourished since the abolition of the Sugar Tax in 1874; colourful sticks of seaside rock and boiled sweets provided an affordable souvenir for the visitors to take home. However, fudge, a confection of boiled sugar, milk and butter, provided West Country confectioners with the opportunity of adding local dairy produce, clotted cream and butter, thereby adding evocative and emotive eating qualities. It enabled consumers to share a product linked to place by the addition of elements of its famous dairy heritage. More than half a century after its introduction as a regional souvenir, the product now embraces principled and environmental issues. Devon Cottage organic fudge, marketed as pure ethical enjoyment from Devon (see devoncottageorganicfudge. co.uk), may be contrasted with mass-produced versions which emphasise location rather than the provenance of ingredients and place.

Changing patterns of consumption provide numerous opportunities for tourists to taste and purchase local foods, for example, farm visits, vineyards, cookery schools and retail outlets. Food is often purchased as an edible souvenir or a gift and is therefore a means of extending or sharing the place and food experience of the holiday. Many become touchstones of memory (Morgan & Pritchard 2005), where a taste or aroma evokes memories and associations or forms them.

Food and place in the context of tourism

Foods associated with Devon by the tourist in the context of holidays and leisure were traditionally associated with summer holidays, but this is changing as the season is extended for many to what were considered off-peak periods in early spring and autumn. The associations between food and place are also regularly linked to the production and processing of food (Hall et al. 2003; Croce & Perri 2009). Schemes to protect geographical indications and traditional specialities were introduced by the EU in 1993 to encourage diverse agricultural production and to protect product names and provenance. For many consumers they are signifiers of quality, heritage and associations with place, for example, Cornish sardines received a Protected Geographical Indication in 2009, which means that they have to be caught within six miles of the Cornish Coast and landed and processed in Cornwall to be named Cornish sardines.

Differentiation in food and its heritage is demonstrated on the platform of burgeoning food festivals and events in the south-west. *Bristol Food Connections* observes the history and food culture of the city, the largest in the region, and in Devon, Tavistock's *Real Cheese Fair* presents one product, cheese, providing an opportunity for consumers to meet the producers of West Country cheese. These are typical of the many food events held through the year which utilise locality in the context of food, bringing producers and consumers together, an interface of production, consumption and differentiation. Hall and Sharples (2008) suggest that festivals do often become tourist attractions serving the interests of the host community and the visitor. Contemporary development of novel and original foods, for example, chillies, tea, and caviar, shows how the new in addition to the traditional and revived are important in the evolution and advance of the regional food and tourism industries.

Clovelly Herrings

Clovelly, a remote village on the North Devon coast, provides a case study of regional food and tourism development. Clinging to the densely wooded cliffs, the village is a well-known tourist attraction, romantic, picturesque and proud of its fishing legacy. It is unique in that it is privately owned and its location prohibits access by car to the steep, cobbled, stepped street and quay.

Clovelly Herrings and the associated fishery are embedded in the history of the village and were, of course, of great importance to its livelihood. Hoskins (1954) describes its emergence as a tourist attraction in the nineteenth century, its popularity attributed to improved accessibility, and appealing depictions in the writing of Charles Kingsley, Charles Dickens and the poetry of Edward Capern.

> A village like a waterfall,
> Or torrent rushing to the tide,
> Where brawny fishers, stout and tall,
> Trip laughing, down its craggy side.
>
> ('The Hobby, Clovelly', from *Wayside Warbles*,
> 1865, in Everett [1884: 120])

Herrings (*Clupea harengus*), known colloquially as "silver darlings", are described by Beeching (1931: 223) as the commonest and most important class of fish 'that visits our shores. The sea for miles around shines with a silvery lustre from their glittering scales, each spring the shoals come afresh, plump and fat, although the season may occasionally vary'. Fish stocks are subject to change; Coombs and Halliday (2011) indicates that pelagic stocks of pilchards, herrings and sardines are cyclical. Southward, Boalch and Maddock (1988) suggest that European fisheries for herrings have fluctuated for hundreds of years and may be linked to changes in climate and fishing practices. In terms of tourism, the interest in herring and other fisheries is constant and strongly associated with place.

Guidebooks and journals constitute an important archival resource and identify the enduring attraction of the village over time. Chope (1967) records early travellers' accounts and itineraries dating from the sixteenth century; for example, Maton's 1794–1796 observations on the western counties of England describe Clovelly as being noted for its herring fishery, but is dismissive of the surrounding landscape. The densely wooded cliffs and whitewashed cottages clad with fuchsia and honeysuckle and the quay are recurring images. Although more recent guidebooks tend to refer to the decline of Clovelly's former herring fishery (Seymour 1974), the association with fishing is emphasised. Typically, descriptions of the village, its history and picturesque situation have been romantically couched. For example, *Murrays Handbook* (Anonymous 1859: 148) suggests that the visitor to the village hung as it were in a woody nook, and the most romantic in Devonshire, if not the kingdom, should, 'rest a day at the little inn, which will entertain him with great hospitality'. Similarly, White (1850: 598) describes 'a singular and picturesque situation', and *Eyre* (Anonymous 1878: 205) described its long street winding up a wooded hill that 'resembles a staircase, each house representing a step, and probably the most precipitous in England'.

The early-twentieth-century descriptions indicate a village meeting the needs of a growing tourist market, but one that looks to its heritage. The harbourside village clinging to the rugged North Devon coast is expressed by Morton (1927: 93) as 'an English Amalfi rising sheer from the bay'. The significance of place was also identified by Clinton-Baddeley (1928: 218–219) who, already aware of the impacts of tourism, described the village as not 'degraded to the state of exhibits in a world museum, but are leading a purposeful life'. Nevertheless, Winbolt (1929) observed that almost every cottage sells picture postcards, cheap antiques and teas. However, most accounts perpetuate a romantic image. For example, Betjeman (1936: 21) commented, 'every bit as picturesque as the guides say, not at all disappointing'.

At this time Clovelly was also evocatively photographed as a fishing village, rather than a tourist attraction by Hoppe (1926) for an illustrated contemporary record of 'picturesque' Great Britain. Rutheven (1938: 16) also writes nostalgically, and prophetically, of the village in the autumn in the herring fishing time, 'when the strings of tourists, and voices of strangers are forgotten'. And goes on to suggest this as a time 'amidst the soft autumn foliage and damp mist, when, there is no better thing than to watch the trawlers bringing in the glistening silver harvest of the sea'. These are not only important as historical references but also continue to contribute to the popular image and legacy of the village.

It is important to consider the enduring appeal of fishing and farming in tourism. They are identified as working communities transcending romantic landscapes. Herring fishing represents community and continuity, generations of fishermen and their families, and periods of growth and decline followed by a resurgence. In the early twentieth century it was estimated that approximately 200,000 tons of herring were brought into English ports (Knight Dutton 1910) were promoted by the Herring Industry Board (1938a, 1938b, 1972) as an inexpensive and nutritious foodstuff. A fall in herring consumption, partly as a result of changing fashions, was noted by Crawford (1938) as being offset by an increase in the sale of white-fish. Clovelly still attracts many visitors and has seen a revival of its former fishing activities. Renewed interest in the healthy qualities of herring (and other oily fish) as a rich source of Omega 3 (Kris-Etherton, Harris & Appel 2003) is encouraging consumption.

Clovelly in the twenty-first century has entered the era of food festivals and diversifying interests in food, providing visitors with a unique combination of food, place and heritage and its harvest from the sea. Food is used to attract visitors throughout the year and encourages repeat business. Herring, lobster and crab, and in 2015 the first seaweed festival have joined the burgeoning list of food events in the county, drawing attention to the significance of place, food and its production. Festivals and celebrations are a means of attracting visitors to the village and its community, throughout the year enhancing and extending the tourist season (Everett & Aitchison 2008; Hall & Sharples 2008). McKercher, Mei and Tse (2006) also propose that festivals may also showcase the intangible heritage, cultural landscape and local traditions of a community. Festivals as tourist attractions become a feature of the location, adding value to the visit, and a seasonal event, and in the example of herrings linked to sustainable fishing and food production.

The Herring festival was established in 2007 to promote sustainable fishing and the underrated and highly nutritious herring. It provides an example of relocalising a food and rebuilding the link between producers and consumers, which Fonte (2008) describes as a reconnection perspective. Although the herring festival is inspired by the past, and the Clovelly donkeys no longer haul the baskets (called mawns) of silver harvest herrings up the cobbles, it is forward-looking and contemporary, not staged as an historical reenactment. The herring festival includes cookery demonstrations, the opportunity to learn about the processing of herrings, flax and a curragh (a fishing boat); it is a one-day event attracting approximately 1,000 visitors. The village has to find ways to finance its survival and to support local charities. Innovative food-based events with a wide appeal bring visitors into contact with the working community and the legacy of the village.

Conclusion

Devon's associations with food past and present recognise food trends and influences. Whether ingredients or dishes, differentiation through relationship with place contributes ideas for future sustainable food tourism and regional developments. Examples of food and place in the context of tourism reinforce the significance of differentiation and the identity of a region or location. Current interests in food are shaped and influenced by the past, and tastes are shown to change, reflecting wider consumer interests. It may be possible to compare what is happening in the south-west with other regions, learning from others in an era of specialised food landscape or foodscape, which Mikkelsen (2011) suggests is important in understanding how and where consumers encounter food and, as shown in the case study, engage with a sensory land-scape in terms of food and experience. Consumers appear to search for the authentic, but also the different and new in terms of food experience. Quan and Wang (2004) propose that tourism is involved in our aesthetic or sensual existence, elements of which have emerged from the longitudinal discussion of food and tourism in Devon.

This chapter has identified an increasingly specialised market for food, whether eating out, on holiday or in the domestic domain. The examples of fish and dairy products show how a glimpse of the past serves as inspiration and influence for the present and the future, but is more than a nostalgic veneer. The future indicates growing interests in food, its production and consumption. Regional differen-tiation and local identity in food is frequently celebrated through festivals and celebrations, many of these becoming fixtures in the calendar. It is an embryonic relationship between food and place, the contemporary and the traditional that reflects the evolving tastes and interests of consumers and their interests in food whether as motivation, function or activity. The opportunities for diversification and differentiation are seen in the example of Clovelly, where food, fishing, climate, geography, tradition, elements of the past, and culture, are interwoven with the human story of a rural community.

References

Anonymous (1859) *Murray's Handbook for Devon and Cornwall*, London: John Murray.
Anonymous (1878) *Eyre's Guide to the Seaside and Visiting Resorts of Devon and Cornwall*, London: Eyre Bros'.
Beeching, C.L.T. (1931) *Law's Grocer's Manual*, 3rd edn, London: William Clowes and Sons.
Berg, P.O. and Sevon, G. (2014) 'Food-branding places – a sensory perspective', *Place Branding and Public Diplomacy*, 10: 289–304.
Bessiere, J. (1998) 'Local development and heritage: traditional food and cuisine as tourist attractions in rural areas', *Sociologica Ruralis*, 38: 21–34.
Betjeman, J. (1936) *Devon: A Shell Guide*, London: The Architectural Press.
Burnett, J. (2004) *England Eats Out: 1830-Present*, London: Pearson/Longman.
Chope, R.P. (1967) *Early Tours in Devon and Cornwall*, Newton Abbot: David and Charles.
Cleave, P. (2013) 'Sugar in tourism: "Wrapped in Devonshire sunshine"', in L. Jollife (ed.) *Sugar Heritage and Tourism in Transition*, Bristol: Channel View, pp. 159–174.
Clinton-Baddeley, V.C. (1928) *Devon*, London: A&C Black Ltd.

Clunie-Harvey, W. and Hill, H. (1937) *Milk products*, London: H.R. Lewis & Co. Ltd.

Coombs, S. and Halliday, N. (2011) *The Russell Cycle. An Update and Review of Trends in Zooplankton and Fish Larvae Off Plymouth 1924–2009*, Occasional Publication. Marine Biological Association of the United Kingdom, 24, p. 27.

Crawford, W. (1938) *The People's Food*, London: William Heinemann.

Croce, E. and Perri, G. (2009) *Food and Wine Tourism*, Wallingford: CABI.

Defoe, D. (1962) *Tour Through the Whole Island of Great Britain (1724–1727)*, London: Dent.

Everett, S. and Aitchison, C. (2008) 'The role of food tourism in sustaining regional identity: a case study of Cornwall, South West England', *Journal of Sustainable Tourism*, 16(2): 150–167.

Everett, W. (1884) *Devonshire Scenery*, Exeter: Pollard.

Fanshawe, A. (1829) *Memoirs of Lady Fanshawe*, London: Henry Colburn.

Feltham, J. (1815) *A Guide to the Watering and Sea Bathing Places for 1813*, London: Longman, Hurst, Rees, Orme and Brown.

Fiennes, C. (1984) *The Illustrated Journeys of Celia Fiennes, 1685–1712*, Exeter: Webb and Bower.

Fine, B., Heasman, M. and Wright, J. (1996) *Consumption in the Age of Affluence: The World of Food*, London: Routledge.

Fonte, M. (2008) 'Knowledge, food and place. A way of producing, a way of knowing', *Sociologica Ruralis*, 38(3): 200–222.

Gee, M. (2004) *Mazzards: The Revival of the Curious North Devon Cherry*, Exeter: The Mint Press.

Gössling, S. and Hall, C.M. (2013) 'Sustainable culinary systems: an introduction', in C.M. Hall and S. Gössling (eds) *Sustainable Culinary Systems: Local Foods, Innovation, Tourism and Hospitality*, Abingdon: Routledge, pp. 3–44.

Hall, C.M., Johnson, G. and Mitchell, R. (2000) 'Wine tourism and regional development', in C.M. Hall, L. Sharples, N. Macionis, and B. Cambourne (eds) *Wine Tourism around the World*, Oxford: Butterworth Heinemann, pp. 196–225.

Hall, C.M. and Sharples, E. (eds) (2008) *Food and Wine Festivals and Events around the World: Development, Management and Markets*, Oxford: Butterworth Heinemann.

Hall, C.M., Sharples, L., Mitchell, R., Macionis, N. and Cambourne, B. (eds) (2003) *Food Tourism around the World*, Oxford: Butterworth-Heinemann.

Harris, J.H. (1907) *My Devonshire Book: In the Land of Junket and Cream*, Plymouth: Western Morning News.

Hartley, D. (1954) *Food in England*, London: Macdonald and Jane's.

Herring Industry Board (1938a) *In Search of Silver Treasure*, London: Herring Industry Board.

Herring Industry Board (1938b) *Lecture Notes on the Herring*, London: Herring Industry Board.

Herring Industry Board (1972) *The Story of the Herring*, Edinburgh: Herring Industry Board.

Hoppe, E.O. (1926) *Picturesque Great Britain, the Architecture and the Landscape*, Berlin: Ernst Wasmuth A.G.

Hoskins, W.G. (1954) *Devon*, London: Collins.

Ilberry, B. and Kneafsey, M. (2000) 'Producer constructions of quality in regional speciality food production: case study from South West England', *Journal of Rural Studies*, 16: 217–230.

Jaine, T. (1998) *1998 Guide to Good Food in the West Country*, Tiverton: Halsgrove.

Knight, F.A. and Dutton, L.M. (1910) *Cambridge County Geographies, Devonshire*, Cambridge: Cambridge University Press.

Kris-Etherton, P.M., Harris, W.S. and Appel, L.J. (2003) 'Omega-3 fatty acids and cardiovascular disease: new recommendations from the American Heart Association', *Arteriosclerosis, Thrombosis and Vascular Biology*, 23: 151–152.

Lloyd, M.W., Richards, L. and Cock, R.F.E. (ca 1938) *Devonshire, for Holidays, Industry and Sport: An Illustrated Review of the Holiday, Industrial and Sporting Amenities in the County*, Cheltenham: Burrow and Co.

Mabey, D. (1980) *In Search of Food: The Traditional Eating and Drinking of Britain*, London: Macdonald and James.

Mason, L. and Brown, C. (1999) *Traditional Foods of Britain: An Inventory*, Totnes: Prospect Books.

Mckercher, B., Mei, W.S. and Tse, T.S.M. (2006) 'Are short duration cultural festivals tourist attractions?' *Journal of Sustainable Tourism*, 14(1): 55–66.

Mennell, S. (1985) *All Manners of Food*, Oxford: Blackwell.

Mikkelsen, B.E. (2011) 'Images of foodscapes: introduction to foodscape studies and their application in the study of healthy eating out-of-home environments', *Perspectives in Public Health*, 131(5): 209–216.

Minchinton, W. (1969) *Exeter and its Region*, F. Barlow (ed.), Exeter: Exeter University Press.

Morgan, N. and Pritchard A. (2005) 'On souvenirs and metonymy, narratives of memory, metaphor and materiality', *Tourist Studies*, 5: 29–53.

Morris, H. (1938) *Portrait of a Chef: The Life of Alexis Soyer*, Cambridge: University Press.

Morton, H.V. (1927) *In Search of England*, London: Methuen.

Oliver, B.W. (1938) *The Book of Devon*, Plymouth: Executive Committee of the Plymouth Division of the British Medical Association.

Quan, S. and Wang, N. (2004) 'Towards a structural model of tourist experience: an illustration from food experiences in tourism', *Tourism Management*, 25: 297–305.

Rutheven, A. (1938) *Clovelly and its Story*, Bideford: Gazette Printing Service.

Seymour, J. (1974) *The Companion Guide to the Coast of South West England*, London: Collins.

Shaw, S. (1789) *A Tour to the West of England in 1788*, London: Robson and Clarke & J. Walker.

Sims, R. (2009) 'Food, place and authenticity: local food and the sustainable tourism experience', *Journal of Sustainable Tourism*, 17(3): 321–336.

Skinner, J. (1985) *West Country Tour: Diary of an Excursion through Somerset, Devon and Cornwall in 1797*, R. Jones (ed.), Bradford-on-Avon: Ex Libris Press.

Southward, A.J., Boalch, G.T. and Maddock, L. (1988) 'Fluctuations in the herring and pilchard fisheries of Devon and Cornwall linked to change in climate since the 16th century', *Journal of Marine Biological Association of the UK*, 68(3): 423–445.

South West Food & Drink (2004) *A Strategy for the Food and Drink Industry in the South West of England, 2005–2015*, Exeter: South West Food & Drink.

Spencer, C. (2002) *British Food: An Extraordinary thousand Years of History*, London: Grub Street with Fortnum and Mason.

Stone, J.H. (1923) *England's Riviera: A Topographical and Archaeological Description of Land's End Cornwall and Adjacent Spots of Beauty and Interest*, London: Kegan Paul, Trench, Trubner & Co.

Trewin, C. (2010) *The Devon Food Book: Linking the Landscape to the Food on Your Plate*, Chard: Flagon Press.

White, F. (1932) *Good Things in England*, London: Jonathon Cape.

White, F. (1935) *The EFCA Good Food Register, or the New Travellers' Guide*, London: English Folk Cookery Association.

White, W. (1850) *History, Gazetteer and Directory of Devonshire*, Sheffield: Leader.

Winbolt, S.E. (1929) *Devon*, London: G. Bell & Sons.

11 Food tourism and place identity in the development of Jamaica's rural culture economy

Ernest Taylor and Moya Kneafsey

Introduction

The Caribbean is the most tourism-dependent region in the world (World Travel and Tourism Council 2014). The area received an estimated 22 million visitors in 2014 contributing 14.6 per cent or US$ 51.9 billion of total GDP. As the main foreign currency earner in most of the 28 island states and provider of employment for an estimated three million people, tourism is often held up as a panacea for all forms of regional development (Cummins 2013). This has been exacerbated by the demise of agriculture in a region where, for decades, export crops such as banana and sugar enjoyed preferential access to protected EU markets (Mlachila, Cashin & Haines 2010). However, EU reforms and international trade liberalisation have eroded this advantage. Caribbean farmers have struggled to compete with large-scale producers from South America, in particular, and so exports have dropped. Not only that, but domestic food markets have been flooded by heavily subsidised imports, especially from the United States (Weis 2004; *Oxford Economics* 2012). With these pressures on export and domestic food markets, regional agricultural economies have been devastated, facing huge debts, rising incidence of poverty and loss of livelihoods (Mlachila, Cashin & Haines 2010). In this context, tourism is centre stage in the development strategies for the region, but this too faces a number of challenges. For example, the 'warming relationship' between Cuba and the United States (*Jamaica Observer* 2015a) means that the socialist state has enjoyed a 36 per cent increase in tourists from the United States and a 14 per cent rise worldwide between January and May 2015. Other islands now fear that the surge in visitors to Cuba will have a deleterious knock-on effect on their tourist numbers (*The Guardian* 2015). As a result, some states are attempting to diversify their tourism product to appeal to new markets.

The Caribbean archipelago is an eclectic mix of cultures, traditions, foods, lifestyles and history, drawing from the heritage of settlers and indentured labourers from Europe, Asia, the Middle East, the Americas and slaves from Africa (Caribbean Tourism Organization 2013). Moreover, the region has some of the world's most spectacular environmental conditions, landscapes, scenery, fauna and flora. The Caribbean is also rich in cultural forms, which accounts for 40 per cent of global tourism revenue and often provide the unique selling point and competitive advantage for tourism destinations (United Nations Educational, Scientific and

Cultural Organization (UNESCO) 2013; Organisation for Economic Cooperation and Development (OECD) 2009). Food, a dimension of these, is increasingly been deployed as an income-generation strategy for communities. While this has been in motion globally for some time (Kneafsey 2001), it is a phenomenon that is becoming more apparent in the Caribbean. The Barbados Food and Wine and Rum Festival, for example, is now seen as a major event in the island's tourism calendar. It is branded around the island's famous flying fish cuisine and an assortment of local liquors. Meanwhile, St Lucia has raised its food tourism profile by appointing their first culinary ambassador. The island's gastronomy offer is centred on Creole, French and African influences. In a revitalised emphasis on food tourism, Trinidad and Tobago too draw on Creole, French and African cuisines along with Spanish, East Indian, Chinese, the Middle East and Portuguese inspirations. With cassava from the native Arawaks, pickled meats and fish from the Europeans, yams and bananas from Africa, curry from the East Indians and kosher from Israel, Jamaica also relies on its global linkages to appeal to food tourists. The island now boasts a host of food tourism events all year round.

Food has thus become a major 'pull factor' for tourism destinations with an 'explosion' of marketing activity promoting new restaurants, food-related attractions, food-centred holidays, cookery schools and gourmet festivals (Everett 2009). Sixty per cent of American tourists say they plan to travel in the next 12 months to engage in culinary activities (Harvey 2012). Food is a powerful means of building a destination brand identity (Lin, Pearson & Cai 2011), and the differentiation and rejuvenation of an area can benefit from a clearly defined gastronomic identity by helping to convey a unique sense of place (Henderson 2009). Food is a critical tourism resource in that it provides physical sustenance, offers pleasure and entertainment and serves a social purpose. It is a primary motivator for many travellers; it engenders new tastes and can present insights into other cultures. The cost of food and drink is a major part of the tourist budget and can account for as much as a third in overall expenditure (Henderson 2009). Tourist demand for food can trigger investment in agriculture and encourage the development of cluster strategies where synergies with other products, services and businesses can be exploited (Gössling & Hall 2013). The globalisation of food consumption habits, changing attitudes towards serving local cuisine in hotels, maturity in regional tourism markets and increased government subsidies to produce locally grown foods are all fuelling the food tourism trend (Rhiney 2009).

Food tourism, argues Harvey (2012), is rooted in agriculture and the rural sector. The activity can help to increase rural revenue and improve income levels and employment of local labour, particularly women (Harvey 2012). Yet there are also many challenges in materialising these benefits to local communities. This chapter illustrates how, in two of Jamaica's most distinctive cultural enclaves, locals are reconstructing their tourism products to incorporate food and drink, as part of a culture economy approach to their community's development. The Maroons, who invented the world-renowned jerk cooking technique, now serve a blend of freshly squeezed passion fruit and plum juice with 'coconut rundown' and young boiled green bananas to tourists. At the other end of the island, visitors to the Seaford Town German community are offered suckling pig stuffed with locally seasoned rice and cooked in an outdoor clay oven. Drawing on ethnographic research, this chapter illustrates the central role of food in generating local place identities and explores its potential as a tool for local economic development. The chapter suggests that, through tourism, local communities are able to reclaim and revalue the significance of local agro-food culture, but they also face serious structural barriers, which hinder their ability to fully exploit these fragile local resources.

Food tourism development in rural Jamaica

In announcing an additional 1600 new apartments to the existing 30,000 hotel rooms in Jamaica, Tourism Minister Dr Wykeham McNeill threw down the challenge to farmers to meet the expected increase in demand for food (*Jamaica Observer* 2015b). 'Someone has to feed these people? We can either bring in the food or grow the food', McNeill told a meeting aimed at sensitising farmers and suppliers to the 'anticipated boom in tourism'. The government wants to ensure 'nearly everything consumed in local hotels is produced in Jamaica' and hopes this will be achieved by offering 'premium products' and using concepts such as 'farm to fork' (*Jamaica Observer* 2015b). The Tourism Linkages Hub, a national initiative, set up to strengthen the relationship between agriculture and tourism, should also help in this regard, argued the minister (*Jamaica Observer* 2015b). With more than 168,000 registered small farmers across Jamaica, synergies with food are promising (FAO 2013). Tourist demand for local foods such as tropical fruits and vegetables is seen as holding great potential for creating and intensifying linkages between agriculture and tourism (IICA 2010). However, this may prove challenging. Jamaica's agricultural infrastructure has been starved of investment coupled with the fact that the best lands are still controlled by plantations (Weis 2004).

An estimated 80 per cent of land in Jamaica is hilly or mountainous and more than half have slopes greater than 20 degrees and are therefore prone to watershed degradation (FAO 2013). The small size of plots diminishes economies of scale, and local hoteliers have complained that it is not economically viable to buy supplies in piecemeal, and with many local farmers refusing to form cooperatives they turn to overseas businesses that can supply in bulk and also offer assurances (Eitzinger et al. 2011). At the same time, 'the neglect of development and innovation in the agricultural sector coupled with the enclave resort development maxim, characterized by its inclusiveness, meant that linkages to the local economy have not formed' (Meyer 2006: 2). It means that while tourism continues its upward trajectory in Jamaica, the downward spiral of agriculture is unabated. In the island's farming-dependent rural communities, 67 per cent of people earn an income from agriculture (Jamaica Social Investment Fund 2009). However, reductions in local tariff charges have made it difficult for home-grown Jamaican foods to compete with imports. Even a once staple product such as sugar is now on the island's buy-in list (*Jamaica Gleaner* 2011). Furthermore, uncontrollable external shocks such as tropical storms, hurricanes and droughts have rendered agriculture an 'unreliable and inconsistent source of revenue' in Jamaica (*Oxford Economics* 2012: 32). With few alternative income-generation strategies, rural inhabitants face severe hardships. Eighty per cent of the 445,000 people living in poverty in Jamaica are in rural areas (Luton 2010; Policy Institute of Jamaica 2009). This is aggravated by a 42.8 per cent fall in mining and quarrying jobs and an 11.9 per cent reduction in construction work (Government of Jamaica 2009). It means new diversification strategies and job-creation initiatives have become matters of urgency in the restructuring and development of rural communities across the island.

The idea of localising the tourism experience and spreading the benefits to ordinary Jamaicans is particularly pertinent for rural inhabitants (Commonwealth Secretariat 2002). A plethora of cultural products, services and activities are now positioned as income-generation and development strategies. These include performances, arts, crafts, spirituality, folklore, languages and dialects, historical sites and trails, food and drink, cooking methods, music and dance, landscape and fauna and flora. Many of these are geared at generating income, which goes directly to locals. It is an operation that is termed the 'cultural economy', a mode of development which involves putting a value on place in terms of its 'cultural identity' (Ray 2001: 16). 'A culture economy both makes use of locality, as an asset and frees local communities from territorial limitations in a market economy' (Jenkins 2000: 310). The rural culture economy approach to development thus functions to recalibrate the growing influence of consumerism and the embeddedness of local production methods. Moreover, the operation of the culture economy incorporates dimensions of local culture commoditisation, creation and promotion of territorial identity and the development of a repertoire of cultural products and services.

Daye, Chambers and Roberts (2008: 115) have argued that the consumption of 'local foods' is bound up with local culture and appeals to tourists seeking authentic travel encounters in Jamaica. Furthermore, Dunn and Dunn (2002) believe that agricultural communities across the island indirectly benefit from tourism, as local guesthouses are more likely to use home-grown produce, as opposed to imported foodstuffs. Tourists' demands for specific local foods could actually lead to conservation of indigenous cuisines (Daye, Chambers & Roberts 2008). Moreover, the increasing "cultural positioning of food" such as coffee with Jamaica's Blue Mountain region can boost jobs, the destination's image, tourist numbers and inhabitants' social values in relation to a local sense of a people, their history and relationship to their area (Giovannucci, Barham & Pirog 2009). Increased visitors add to the multiplier effect of a region; encourage diversification, promotion and branding; and can lead to greater sales of associated food products (Hall, Kirkpatrick & Mitchell 2005).

Food tourism in Charles Town and Seaford Town

This research is based on an ethnographic study which focussed on two distinctive Jamaican groups, the Charles Town Maroon and the Seaford Town German descendants, and their attempts to fashion new livelihoods by exploiting aspects of their culture by means of tourism. The aim of the research was to investigate the role of culture and tourism in the development of rural communities in Jamaica. Charles Town and Seaford Town were selected for detailed data production because of their greater reliance on cultural traditions, including food, as community development strategies. Traditional cuisine, cooking methods and tastes have been accumulated over a significant period of time, and in attempting to tap into new sources of livelihood, members of both communities are seeking to exploit these assets. The topic of this chapter is based on relevant findings from the full data set, which comprised participant observation, 69 face-to-face semi- and unstructured interviews, more than 3,000 digital images, 70 video clips and 3 focus group interviews.

Charles Town is a Maroon enclave at the foothills of the Blue Mountain range in the eastern parish of Portland with a population of 740 people (SDC 2010b). Charles Town is one of nine communities in the Buff Bay Development Area and one of four recognised existing settlements of Maroon descendants in Jamaica. The Maroons are descendants of runaway slaves and the town is steeped in history, as the site of the famous Quao victory over the British Redcoats in 1739. The defeat led to the signing of a peace treaty between the British and the Windward Maroons some 272 years ago. As well as their fighting skills, Maroons are renowned for their resourcefulness in living off their natural environment. However, faced with high rates of unemployment, the Charles Town Maroon Council initiated a range of programmes aimed at exploiting their intangible and tangible cultural traditions by way of tourism and agriculture. Initiatives include beekeeping, nature and cultural heritage trails, storytelling, rituals, music, drumming and dancing, spirituality, cuisine and a museum tour featuring artefacts from surrounding Maroon villages.

Nearly half the population in Charles Town is under 34 with the majority (88.2 per cent) educated up to secondary school level. More than half the people of working age are unemployed, 80 per cent of whom are aged 14–29. Waste disposal is the main environmental issue in the community with 52 per cent of householders burning their rubbish. The area is particularly prone to flooding and landslides. Some 70 per cent of land in Charles Town is used for subsistence farming, primarily crops such as plantains, bananas, cocoa, breadfruit, coffee, etc.

Seaford Town is located in north-east Westmoreland, about 54 km from Montego Bay, the island's main tourism hub, and has a population of 666 people (SDC 2010a). Landowner Lord Seaford, after whom the town is named, donated the 500-acre plot in the early 1830s. Seaford Town is principally known for its German inhabitants, who first settled there in 1835. The town's tourism enterprise is based on a museum housing various artefacts that depicts the history of the German descendants and their cultural heritage. There are an estimated 50 people of full German descent still living in the town. However, at different times of the year, relatives and former inhabitants, who return from abroad on holidays or for special occasions, boost their numbers. Many of those of full German descent are the fifth and sixth generations of the estimated 250 who arrived from

Bremen in northern Germany in 1835. They left Europe to seek their fortune in Jamaica only to encounter hardship and toil. The German descendants are known locally as "Germaicans". Original German architecture and cuisine are very much features of the town.

Half the 404 people available for work in Seaford Town are unemployed. Of these, women account for 59.7 per cent, men 40.3 per cent and 41 per cent youths aged 14–24 (SDC 2010a). The majority of unemployed men have been out of work for more than five years, and 31.4 per cent have never worked in their adult lives. Farming is the main economic activity. Environmental concerns in the community include illegal dumping of rubbish, landslides, rock falls and water pollution.

Development of food tourism in Charles Town

The Maroon descendants maintain a close relationship with nature in all they do. Skilful use of the environment had served their ancestors well during their guerrilla wars with the British colonial forces in terms of hideouts, ambushes, disguise, weapons, herbal remedies, sustenance and shelter. For today's Maroons such strategies are deployed to earn a livelihood, showcase their culture and maintain their links with nature rather than for conflict. During interviews, the Maroon descendants spoke longingly of tales of hunting wild hogs and living off the surrounding Blue and John Crow Mountains, two of the most transcendent terrains in the Caribbean and home to a mass of endemic plants and animal species. Wild pig is still a favourite source of meat for the Maroon descendants and is served on special occasions such as festivals or when entertaining large numbers of tourists. Preparation of the meat dates back to their predecessors' time in the Kromanti region of Ghana, West Africa, where the "jerk" style of cooking using traditional spices originated. The technique has become known across the world, as a Jamaican practice with no acknowledgement of the Maroons, as its originators. Bilby (2005) highlights this as an example of symbols and knowledge of Maroon cultural heritage being "appropriated" and passed off as national culture, which deny them of the exclusivity of their history and traditions. However, Maroon interviewees argue that exploiting aspects of their culture such as the jerk style of cooking could do more to preserve it and attract visitors from whom they can generate an income to develop their community. With half the population in Charles Town out of work, creating jobs is the most pressing concern and the Maroon descendants believe if they cannot exploit their cultural heritage to help build their community then culture is not worthwhile.

Maroon food tradition is valued not just for its economic potential but also for its spiritual significance and cultural connectedness to their ancestors. How it is offered up for consumption is differentiated in terms of the meanings food holds and the way they use and preserve it. Tourists may enjoy their cuisine, because it satisfies their desire for new tastes, the "authentic", the "real", the "other" or provide a basis for interaction, but for the Maroon descendants food has other significance (Hall 2007). During a Sunday evening meal with a Maroon family in Charles Town, we were joined by a community elder who, before eating, placed a spoonful of potato salad, a small piece of chicken and some rice and peas (gungo peas) on a leaf plucked from a nearby yam vine and positioned it on an adjoining chair and summoned the ancestors to join in. It was a symbolic gesture of acknowledgement and reverence to their predecessors and an indication of their ritualistic actions to remain culturally connected to their past. Cultural connectedness applies to 'culturally shared ways of knowing'; it offers 'a shared sense of socially constructed meanings' and fulfils a desire to connect to others and, therefore, to be accepted (Hill 2006: 212). The Maroon descendants' exploitation of their cultural linkages to develop their community ties in with notions of a culture economy (Ray 2001). It centres on endogenous development, to 'raise a community spirit' among local people, boost 'social solidarity' and psychological well-being (Ray 1999: 263). The Maroon descendants believe the income from tourism can help to secure cultural identity, make them stronger, promote greater pride among youths and sustain their existence (McFadden 2012). 'The world is turning into one large village, so it makes no sense for Maroon villages to keep out tourists. Tourists and the money they bring stimulate people in the Maroon communities to produce the products that represent their culture' (McFadden 2012).

Visitors to Charles Town are usually offered a light starter-type meal sourced entirely from locally grown vegetables. A typical dish includes steamed young green bananas, pumpkin, callaloo (a leaf vegetable of West African origin), carrots and plantain in a coconut 'run down' stew served in locally produced utensils made from paki gourd. Meals are washed down by a local mixed fruit drink of June plums, ginger and passion fruit served in cups carved out of coconut shells. Figures supplied by the Maroon descendants show each tourist pays US$ 10 for the visit to Charles Town, five dollars for food and the other five dollars to visit the museum. Food is usually preordered, and when none is required, there is a thinning of the income. The Maroons normally welcome tourists three times a week. On some days there can be three coaches each with approximately a dozen people from Europe or other parts of North America, and on others, only a single vehicle. The community also welcomes overnight visitors with accommodation and breakfast from US$ 50 per night. Even though the Maroons cannot be said to be earning huge profits, in a community with high unemployment and where the average weekly wage is less than US$ 25, the income generated by food tourism cannot be discounted. Not all the tourists visiting Charles Town include food as part of the tour package and it is not known whether tour operators influence such decisions.

Providing food for tourists presents the Maroon descendants with the opportunity to reproduce and reaffirm their cultural heritage and attachment to place and nature. Doing so, the Maroon descendants argue, is the best way of sustaining their culture '*more so than merely preserving it*'. However, some members of the wider community have accused those involved of profitting from the exploitation of their cultural heritage and of not spreading the benefits more broadly.

> (Seeing the tourists) stop, they feel that there is a lot of money making from this. There is not a lot of money making from it. They (the tourists) will pay for the tour of the museum and, yes, they eat food. The greater

portion (of the payment) would be for the food that is prepared, So, that is where they keep saying that money is making down there and nobody know where it is going or what has been done with it. I have been there from day one working and am still not making any money there, but it is something that we dedicate ourselves to and it's something that we want to see go on.

(Elder Maroon descendant 2011)

It is clear that in a deprived community like Charles Town, issues around development are contested and the approaches used can provoke resentment. The intention is for everyone to benefit, and with skilled locals and investment, greater value could be added through the production, packaging and processing of local produce, arts, crafts and souvenirs. The community could also be marketed for its distinctiveness and food specialties, but with no real marketing strategy in place, inhabitants remain dependent on the whim of tourism operators, as to the length of time guest stay in Charles Town and how their money is spent. While food tourism offers great opportunities and possible spin-off benefits, there is clearly a lack of expertise, investment in Charles Town to exploit its full potential.

The development of food tourism in Seaford Town

The German descendants of Seaford Town have lost their language, most of their cultural heritage and have no real connections with Germany. The only significant tradition that remains is related to food, particularly pork. Across the island, the community is known for its roasted pig cuisine; however, in their attempts to develop their community by way of tourism, some interviewees argue that not enough emphasis is being placed on this dimension of their culture. Roasted pork – suckling pig stuffed with rice, local herbs and spices – is only offered for sale in a neighbouring community on Saturday evenings. With people travelling from miles around, within an hour a whole hog is sold. Many interviewees insist food is an important cultural dimension of their German heritage and should be used to attract tourists to help develop Seaford Town. With the increasing growth of food tourism, they argue, pork delicacies could be a unique selling point for the community. Gibson and Connell (2003) contend that products and their uses are not only shaped by how they are represented and the meanings they hold, but also in the location they are produced. Seaford Town's roasted pork is an indelible part of the community's identity and its association with the German descendants. However, some interviewees feel the community is too small and has limited resources to focus on only one particular dimension. They believe they need to adopt a range of strategies to achieve their community development objectives.

It appears that the challenge faced by the people of Seaford Town is how to manage agricultural linkages inherent in their culture economy. For generations, farming has been the mainstay for local inhabitants. Even though some eke out a living from jobs such as carpentry and driving, tilling the soil or rearing animals, particularly pigs, has been preeminent. The relative acreage of land in their possession means only few do so on a grand scale. Irrespective of size, however, the majority of locals rely on farming as their main source of income. Moreover, with the average weekly wage in Seaford Town around US$ 25, even people who have other jobs do some kind of farming to supplement meagre earnings. There are various agricultural diversification initiatives being planted across the community. These include micro-industries such as beekeeping and greenhouses where cash crops can be cultivated. (Some 101 people from Seaford Town and the surrounding area were trained in bee-keeping and given two colonies of the insects after a $J8.4 million grant was obtained from the Japanese embassy. The money was also used to purchase a vehicle, a saw and an extractor.) Furthermore, funding is being sought to establish turmeric powder and breadfruit flour processing units in the community. Even so, focus group participants reveal that the only farming that draws a reasonable regular income around Seaford Town is the cultivation of '*ganga*' (marijuana). They say some locals can only send their children to school or settle arrears when the crop is harvested. Despite the importance of these varying farming initiatives in helping to boost local liveli-hood streams, it is clear they are not enough to fill the huge gap left by the decline in traditional forms of agriculture.

A major blow to Seaford Town has been the demise of its annual garden party, which is a much-debated topic in the community. For years the event had been a traditional local family Boxing Day event, but its popularity grew, attracting people from as far as Kingston, the island capital, which is a four-hour drive away. It meant the local NGO, which took over its organisation from the Roman Catholic Church, could not cope or finance policing of such large crowds. The event was cancelled in 2011, and even though locals organised a similar event on a different site and on a more commercial footing, reports were not as favourable as for the original party. The event had been a significant feature of the town's culture economy. Stalls were packed with local produce, roasted pork dishes and homemade pastries such as gizzadas (grated coconut and pastry cakes), pones (puddings), drops (chopped coconut cakes) and a variety of teas. Despite the con-cerns surrounding the event, interviewees believe it could prove a success if a fully committed person could be found to manage the operation.

As in Charles Town, food is more than an economic development strategy for the people of Seaford Town. The German settlers were mostly artisans and lacked the farming skills needed for life in a predominantly agricultural environment. With inadequate provisions made for their settlement, they became desperate for food. Some turned to the newly freed African slaves that they had been recruited to guard to learn farming skills, while others raided their fields for food. Over time, these interactions, born out of adversity and necessity, developed into bind-ing social relationships between the African and German descendants. It illustrates how food is not only a catalyst for interrelation between tourists and locals but also among inhabitants themselves. Interviewees in Seaford Town contend that farming laid the foundation for the close bonds that exist between German and African descendants in the town today in terms of engendering 'cooperation, con-tinuity, respect, reliability and trust' (Thiele & Marsden 2002: 4) between locals, thus providing a basis for community development.

One participant argued that micro-industries such as turmeric and breadfruit processing, making of jams, jellies and honey and market days could complement a thriving tourism product. German folk dancers, reenactments, storytelling and displays of artefacts could buttress the contribution. Another way forward is health heritage therapy events like the one on a local community farm. The function centred on a visit to the Seaford Town German Heritage Museum and a spectacular lunch at the farm featuring roasted suckling pig cooked in an outdoor clay oven and served with locally sourced vegetables and homemade refreshments. The event also hosted a farmers' style market with a range of local produce and rare exotic plants on sale. The guests were from urban centres such as Kingston and Manchester and their proximity suggests it is an activity that could be sustained. However, Seaford Town is imbued with poor infrastructure, high rates of illiteracy, underinvestment and there are conflicts between locals about their role in development of the community. While the German descendants refute claims that they were not doing enough to help the community, some admit they needed to reclaim and revalue aspects of their cultural heritage that have been lost to help develop the town.

> The Germans that came here met up on so much hardships they forget the language, they had to adopt the language of the slaves to communicate and survive. They forgot everything that they left Germany with. They never even taught their children to make sausages and they are gifted for sausages. Germans are gifted for sausages and they never taught them.
>
> (German descendant 2011)

Such complexities compound local development, which appears to be at a standstill in Seaford Town. While locals are able to recognise the significance of agro-food culture, they face serious social and structural challenges in their attempts to exploit them. 'We need somebody with the money to come forward and the rest will fall into place', said one focus group participant optimistically. 'We have something here that is very rich, but it just needs to be put into motion'.

Discussion and conclusion

The demise of agriculture in regions such as the Caribbean has magnified the role of tourism in local development strategies. Food, with its various synergies with cultural traditions and agriculture, is becoming an increasing dimension in generating new income streams. This is particularly the case for rural communities in Jamaica such as Charles Town and Seaford Town where locals are refashioning cultural traditions to create new products and services for tourists' consumption. While food is an important feature of this, the study found that communities such as Charles Town and Seaford Town are too small to rely solely on one aspect of their culture. Instead, food is among a repertoire of activities and products aimed at attracting tourists. These include farm holidays, local food and drink, spices and sauces, spirituality, language, music, ordinary ways of life, religious worship, therapeutic health activities, natural landscapes, and arts and crafts. The process encompasses differentiated dimensions of the culture economy approach, which articulates the reinvigoration of indigenous culture as the basis for territorial development and social and economic well-being.

Although products have been fashioned out of agriculture for generations, the continued demise of the sector places a greater emphasis on exploiting linkages to inhabitants' identity, cultural connectedness and attachment to place. Agriculture will still play a significant role in this process, as it shares various inherent linkages with tourism, which in turn relies heavily on cultural traditions such as food and drink. A differentiated picture thus emerges of the transition in communities such as Charles Town and Seaford Town from a rural economy based primarily on agriculture to one that is more culturally oriented. It is argued that traditional agricultural communities such as Charles Town and Seaford Town with their distinctive cultural characteristics, identity and sense of place are emblematic of Ray's (2001) notion of a culture economy. Both sets of inhabitants are pursuing endogenous development strategies based on their identity, attachment to place, environmental features, local resources and way of life. In Charles Town there is focus on landscape and how products come into being, in particular, from linkages such as ancestral and locally sourced produce, products and services. In Seaford Town, there is emphasis on local interactions, shared experiences and use of the story of their ancestors' uprooting from Germany and subsequent resettlement in Jamaica. These development activities correlate with ideas of continuity and social networking in terms of the promotion of local cultural resources for economic benefit and access to development support. While a culture economy clearly adds to understanding of the role of food tourism in the development of rural communities in Jamaica, the study finds that greater awareness, skills and investment could help locals in both districts to capitalise on their intangible and tangible cultural heritage.

It is clear that rural communities are able to reclaim and revalue the significance of local agro-food culture, but they also face serious structural barriers, which hinder their ability to fully exploit these fragile resources. In this context, we argue, in line with IICA (2010), that agriculture will continue to be a central feature in Jamaica's national growth and development processes and that the sector cannot be left solely to market forces, but needs government policies and strategies that support private initiatives. Like IICA and the Ministry of Agriculture and Fisheries, we support a new development model, which recognises the importance of a multidimensional agricultural strategy that contributes to the rural economy and to important factors such as food security, energy security, water supply, employment, environmental conservation, social stability and freedom from social unrest (IICA 2010). Moreover, we believe in the mobilisation of the creative use of more local foods in cuisine. Our chapter shows that local communities recognise this potential, but need support to make it a reality.

References

Bilby, K.M. (2005) *True-Born Maroons*, Gainesville: University of Florida.
Caribbean Tourism Organization (2013) *Food Tourism in the Caribbean: Unlocking the Potential*, CWA Agrotourism Seminar, Guyana, 10 October 2013.

Commonwealth Secretariat (2002) *Master Plan for Sustainable Tourism Development*, London: Special Advisory Services Division, Commonwealth Secretariat.

Cummins, K. (2013) 'CTO: tourism must not fail', *Barbados Today*, 21 March.

Daye, M., Chambers, D. and Roberts, S. (eds) (2008) *New Perspectives in Caribbean Tourism*, New York: Routledge.

Dunn, H.S. and Dunn, L.L. (2002) *People and Tourism: Issues and Attitudes in the Jamaican Hospitality Industry*, Kingston: Arawak Publications.

Eitzinger, A., Laderach, P., Benedikter, A., Gordon, J., Quiroga, A., Pantoja, A. and Bunn, C. (2011) *Impact of Climate Change on Jamaican Hotel Industry Supply Chains and on Farmer's Livelihoods*, Cali, Colombia: International Centre for Tropical Agriculture (CIAT) – Oxfam.

Everett, S. (2009) 'Beyond the visual gaze? The pursuit of an embodied experience through food tourism', *Tourist Studies*, 8(3): 337–358.

Food and Agriculture Organization of the United Nations (FAO) (2013) *Climate Change and Agriculture in Jamaica: Agriculture Sector Support Analysis*, Environment and natural resources management series (FAO) [climate change] no. 21, Rome: FAO.

Gibson, C. and Connell, J. (2003) '"Bongo Fury": tourism, music and cultural economy at Byron Bay, Australia', *Tijdschrift voor economische en sociale geografie*, 94(2): 164–187.

Giovannucci, D., Barham, E. and Pirog, R. (2009) 'Defining and marketing "local" foods: geographical indications for US products', *The Journal of World Intellectual Property*, 13(2): 94–120.

Gössling, S. and Hall, C.M. (2013) 'Sustainable culinary systems: an introduction', in C.M. Hall and S. Gössling (eds) *Sustainable Culinary Systems: Local Foods, Innovation, Tourism and Hospitality*, Abingdon: Routledge, pp. 3–44.

Government of Jamaica (2009) *The Jamaica Survey of Living Conditions for the Years 2008 and 2009*, Kingston: Government of Jamaica.

Hall, C.M. (2007) 'Response to Yeoman et al: the fakery of "the authentic tourist"', *Tourism Management*, 28(2007): 1139–1140.

Hall, D.R., Kirkpatrick, I. and Mitchell, M. (eds) (2005) *Rural Tourism and Sustainable Business*, Clevedon: Channel View Publications.

Harvey, E. (2012) *Agro and Culinary Tourism Getting to the Next Level*, San José, Costa Rica: Inter-American Institute for Cooperation on Agriculture.

Henderson, J.C. (2009) 'Food tourism reviewed', *British Food Journal*, 111(4): 317–326.

Hill, D.L. (2006) 'Sense of belonging as connectedness, American Indian worldview, and mental health', *Archives of Psychiatric Nursing*, 20(5): 210–216.

Inter-American Institute for Cooperation on Agriculture (IICA) (2010) *The Contribution of Agriculture to Sustainable Development in Jamaica*, San José, Costa Rica: IICA.

Jamaica Gleaner (2011) 'Sugar imports to offset shortage – Montague', *Jamaica Gleaner*, 21 July.

Jamaica Observer (2015a) 'Cuba-US détente is a great opportunity for Jamaica – Mahood', *Jamaica Observer*, 5 June.

Jamaica Observer (2015b) 'Plan to benefit from tourism boom, McNeill urges farmers', *Jamaica Observer*, 8 July.

Jamaica Social Investment Fund (2009) *Rural Enterprise Development Initiative – Tourism Sector*, Kingston: Jamaica Social Investment Fund.

Jenkins, T.N. (2000) 'Putting postmodernity into practice: endogenous development and the role of traditional cultures in the rural development of marginal regions', *Ecological Economics*, 34(2000): 301–314.

Kneafsey, M. (2001) 'Rural cultural economy: tourism and social relations', *Annals of Tourism Research*, 28(3): 762–783.

Lin, Y., Pearson, T.E. and Cai, L.A. (2011) 'Food as a form of destination identity: a tourism destination brand perspective', *Tourism and Hospitality Research*, 11(1): 30–48.

Luton, D. (2010) 'Poverty crisis In Jamaica', *The Jamaica Gleaner*, 14 October.

McFadden, D. (2012) 'Caribbean maroons hope tourism can save culture', *Associated Press*, 9 July.

Meyer, D. (2006) *Caribbean Tourism, Local Sourcing and Enterprise Development: Review of the Literature*, Pro-poor tourism partnership, Working Paper No. 18, London: The Travel Foundation and Pro-Poor Tourism Partnership.

Mlachila, M., Cashin, P. and Haines, C. (2010) *Caribbean Bananas: The Macroeconomic Impact of Trade Preference Erosion WP/10/59*, Washington, DC: International Monetary Fund.

Organisation for Economic Co-operation and Development (2009) *The Impact of Culture on Tourism*, Paris: OECD.

Oxford Economics (2012) *Travel and Tourism as a Driver of Economic Development in Jamaica*, Oxford: *Oxford Economics*.

Policy Institute of Jamaica (2009) *Vision 2030 Jamaica: National Development Plan*, Kingston: Policy Institute of Jamaica.

Ray, C. (1999) 'Endogenous development in the era of reflexive modernity', *Journal of Rural Studies*, 15(3): 257–267.

Ray, C. (2001) *Culture Economies: A Perspective on Local Rural Development in Europe*, Newcastle: Newcastle University.

Rhiney, K. (2009) '(Re) defining the link? Globalisation, tourism and the Jamaican food supply network', in D. McGregor, D. Dodman, and D. Barker (eds) *Global Change and Caribbean Vulnerability: Environment, Economy and Society at Risk*, Kingston: University of the West Indies, pp. 237–258.

Social Development Commission (SDC) (2010a) *Community Profile of Westmoreland: Seaford Town*, Kingston: SDC, Government of Jamaica.

SDC (2010b) *Community Profile of Charles Town*, Kingston: SDC, Government of Jamaica.

The Guardian (2015) 'US travel to Cuba surges 36% following thaw in diplomatic relations', *The Guardian*, 26 May.

Thiele, M. and Marsden, S. (2002) 'P(ART)icipation and social change', Paper presented at *Cultural Sites, Cultural Theory, Cultural Policy: The Second International Conference on Cultural Policy Research*, 23–26 January 2002, Wellington, New Zealand.

United Nations Educational, Scientific and Cultural Organization (2013) *The Power of Culture for Development*, Paris: UNESCO.

Weis, T. (2004) 'Restructuring and redundancy: the impacts and illogic of neoliberal agricultural reforms in Jamaica', *Journal of Agrarian Change*, 4(4): 461–491.

World Travel and Tourism Council (2014) *Travel and Tourism Impact 2014: Jamaica*, London: WTTC.

12 Gastronomy does not recognise political borders

Marisa Isabel Ramos Abascal

Among all living creatures, only humans have objected to the diet nature has imposed on them, so that, even before the invention of fire, they found a way to season and improve the flavours of food, thus differentiating themselves from the rest of the animals that eat only in order to survive. The act of cooking helped to set civilisation on its evolutionary path. It is through gastronomy – understood as the culinary interpretation of edible resources available in the environment and the way they are used – that scattered humanity simultaneously gave way to a complex biocultural interaction (Cordón 2009). From the dawn of humankind, and spurred to find more and better food, nomadic groups travelled, returning in cycles according to yearly seasons, to places where they had previously satisfied not only their appetite but also their hedonist desire. Subject to environmental and territorial constraints, agriculture made it possible to grow what people preferred, and soon humanity began to differ not just by language but also with respect to the food they had and how they ate it.

The gastronomic landscape that hosts a social group also defines gustatory preferences. The catalogue of flavours is the personal reference which, as omnivores, determines our culinary predilections. Philias and phobias regarding flavours and textures are fixed at a very young age: just after weaning – around the age of six months – to two years infants will receive food from their family group. These flavours become the reference for reliable food and create philias towards these gustatory references, possible food from the gastronomic landscape of the territory where the group lives and which generally changes throughout the year's four seasons, including non-endemic food available there. After the age of two years, introducing new flavours gets more complicated (Pollan 2006), as the child's omnivorous nature leads to a mistrust of unknown flavours and textures.

What some people consider food may not necessarily even be considered as such by another social group, although the human preservation instinct establishes almost universal preferences. There are philic or survival flavours which are usually interpreted as a necessary food to face times of shortage; or those which, even if naturally scarce, due to their great acceptance seem omnipresent in industrialised food today: the sweet and salty, as well as fatty textures. On the other hand, a phobic flavour may be derived from a sour taste when related to fermented or spoilt food, or bitterness as related to toxic food, and some mushy textures, usually associated with rotten food. As omnivores, humans base food philias and phobias not only on cultural aspects but also on biological ones (Fox 1931). Genetics will determine certain affinities and intolerances to spicy food, alcohol or dairy products, among many others (Nabhan 2006).

We can thus say that when a traveller arrives to a destination and is invited to share a host's table, tastes can be found that make her feel welcome, identified as an individual and comforted, but she will also find aggressive tastes that will make her suspicious, such as very spicy food or edibles that may be taboo in her own culture. In such a case the table then becomes a strategic place to establish links between host and guest, where gastronomy, consisting of the dishes, utensils and manners, communicates messages which may encourage or hinder commensality. In other words, there are flavours which link and flavours which exclude.

For thousands of years, due to the impossibility of massive and frequent travel, people dedicated themselves to the dishes they could prepare within their gastronomic landscape. That is why the humblest typical stews are often so admirable. They are the result of many attempts to improve them, and the wisdom of generations poured into a single dish. However, the relatively newer travel modes of human beings have aroused a curiosity for foreign tables, to taste otherness and, even if their omnivorous nature discourages them from trying new tastes, there are more and more travellers who, interested in understanding exotic cultures, find in food one of the most effective ways to actively involve themselves in their host's culture.

The way travellers satisfy their recurring need to eat, and their relationship with food during their stay, is arguably limited by two extremes: on the one hand, the extent to which gastronomy is a main purpose of the trip and, in opposition, the tourist supplying his own food and beverage, remaining impervious to the culinary culture of the visited site and building a culinary bubble to protect himself (Urry 1990). Between the two extremes is a wide range of eating preferences, each becoming a valuable opportunity to establish and strengthen links between visitors and hosts.

Among all the activities the tourist performs, eating is the most social and frequent. If compared to moving about and sleeping, eating implies remarkable and sometimes unforgettable sensory characteristics. Such experiences correspond to the interest of many current tourists who are no longer satisfied with travelling in hordes by bus and eating preestablished menus, pejoratively called "tourist food" in the past, known for their cheap quality. Nowadays, many travellers seek unique and transforming experiences that may enhance their lifestyle and involve themselves in a more personal way with the hosts and their culture (Sánchez-Cañizares & López-Guzmán 2012). Thereby, perhaps finding contrasts that help them to identify characteristics of their own identity.

Gastronomy

As a biocultural process, gastronomy is arguably one of the few things that even now cannot travel successfully, since it is not about the mere culinary reproduction of a dish (which is possible outside its native surroundings), but rather the gastro-nomic experience consists mainly of culinary interpretation, which also involves other tangible and intangible elements that allow it to be perceived as a complex and legitimate cultural manifestation.

Gastronomy exhibits all the elements which the traveller interested in food appreciates: the production, preparation, traditions, meanings, tableware, man-ners, even superstitions and magical thoughts and, of course, food. If the proposed cuisine is akin to the tastes and preferences in the traveller's catalogue of flavours, the local gastronomy can potentially position itself as a powerful tourist attraction.

Commensality is a deeply human act and it depends on geographical and anthropological conditions, and biocultural conditions can prevail over political restrictions or economic advantages. The freedom to choose what and how to eat frequently ignores the rules established for that. Examples throughout history show that social groups would even rather change their religion than renounce their cuisine and their culinary traditions, such as the case of the Roman Empire's conversion to Catholicism almost two thousand years ago. The winter solstice festivity became Christmas when – due to the impossibility of eradicating the *Sol Invictus* commemoration, known as *Saturnalia* – it was substituted by the Christian Christmas (Beard, North & Price 1998). The Roman Empire festivity held in honour of Saturn, god of agriculture, was transformed by the imposed celebration of the birth of Jesus, whose birth date was unknown, although it was necessary to find an excuse that, despite the change of religious belief, would preserve the gastronomic tradition of banquets and the exchange of gifts charac-teristic of that celebration, which also included decorating houses with plants and lighting candles.

During *Saturnalia* people were given loaves of bread in public squares; hidden in one of those loaves was a broad bean, and the person who found it would be "king for one day". Nowadays, that tradition has been transformed into the French *galette du roi* or the Hispanic American *rosca de reyes* which Roman Catholics enjoy at the start of the year and whose original broad bean was turned first into a ceramic child, and because of a growing non-Catholic population, in some coun-tries it has undergone more transformations, to become today even a Mario Bros figurine, an Eiffel Tower or any other character, but the bread and the festivity prevail after 20 centuries.

It is natural then to admit that social groups are so reluctant to modify their eating habits that political divisions become invisible as far as gastronomy is con-cerned. The most frequent cases of this are found in diasporas, expatriates and multicultural cuisines.

Diasporas and groups whose social identity is strongly linked to food

The Jewish community around the world is the best example of how a people's identity can prevail, even after having lost their territory. They have been able to maintain their gastronomy, their language and their religion despite the many years when they did not have a specific physical place to shelter them and were thus dispersed in small groups around the world. Their strict precepts demand careful selection, production and eating processes that have forced them to recreate their cookery, adapting it to the gastronomic landscape of the area where they have settled. These subtle adaptations have guaranteed the survival of Jewish kosher gastronomy, which strengthens the identity of this social group by means of its festivities and their corresponding foodways (Niewiadomska-Flis 2013). In a typical supermarket in the United States during 2011, it was possible to find more products labelled kosher than organic, natural or premium, and generating annually more than US$12 billion in the retail market (Lytton 2014).

Similar cases may be found in nomadic or semi-nomadic groups, such as the Romany, Yörük and Tuareg people, among others. In contrast is the case of the more than 365 kinds of typical French cheeses whose particular characteristics clearly define gastronomic limits between people who are geographically close. There are subtle differences in the taste of milk, due to the kind of pasture where cows graze or ways of curdling it – and in the landscapes, which, although similar, are different and slowly define cultural borders, which may or may not coincide with political borders, but which undoubtedly demarcate the vital space inhabited by the social group, making it its territory.

Colonies of expatriates who reinterpret their cuisine

A different case is that of expatriate colonies, communities that for various reasons must relocate in a place beyond their political borders and which successfully adapt their gastronomy to the new gastronomic landscape. Specific groups stand out, such as the Italians who arrived in New York at the beginning of the twentieth century and settled in what is now known as Little Italy in Manhattan, who far from abandoning their gastronomic habits spread their democratising food all over a nation (Levenstein 1985). Pasta and the typical pizza from southern Italy have been reinvented in the United States. Ingredients such as mozzarella and buffalo milk cheese have been reinvented with a version similar in production technique, but made from cow's milk and called *fior di latte*. The same happened with espresso coffee and *cannoli*. This occurs because food as a cultural expression reflects the pride of belonging; it is a symbol whose faithful reproduction reasserts identity and is therefore protected from the natural evolution to which every cuisine is exposed (Shortridge & Shortridge 1999).

In contrast are examples of multicultural communities that are formed by the need to relocate, but which manage to integrate into the new location so strongly that they can create their own gastronomic identity based on their original cuisines, but with results that distinguish them from the original. A very good example of this kind of identity is Tex-Mex gastronomy, found in the border zone between the United States and Mexico. In this region, Mexicans co-exist with descendants of convert Jews; native people such as the Kickapoos; Chichimecas; descendants of Spaniards who settled in this arid border area; as well as French, English and African people who moved to this area due to the American Civil War (1861). However, these groups identify themselves as Mexican or Texan, forgetting about their ethnic roots and creating new dishes such as *chili con carne, burritos* and *nachos* (Pilcher 2001).

Clear samples of the fusion of ingredients and techniques which distinguish Tex-Mex cuisine from nearby gastronomies are bread, usually made of wheat in the United States, which in this region can be found made of corn, and tortillas, a Mesoamerican heritage generally made of corn dough, reinterpreted in Tex-Mex cuisine with wheat flour. Frequently, this cuisine is misjudged as failed Mexican gastronomy but Tex-Mex cookery has its own identity. It is the genuine expression of the region's culture and nature; it uses local products and is tightly linked to the history and social processes of the multiethnic group from which it was born and that inhabits a region on both sides of the political border (Pilcher 2001, 2014).

However, there are dishes which are naturalised and successfully integrated into the host country's culinary offer, such as the hamburger of German origin in the United States (Pilcher 2014) that erased forever its Teutonic origin. But there are other dishes that remain identifiable as ethnic food. An example of such cultural resistance is the *kimchi* produced and consumed by Korean communities around the world and considered an element of nationalist construction for Koreans (Cho 2006). Between these two extremes is the possibility of creating a new cuisine.

Multicultural gastronomy, inclusive and expansive

One of the most representative cases of a cuisine born and consolidated as a tourist attraction can be seen in the region of California, where two states belonging to economically and socially different countries, yet sharing a common geography, meet: the state of California in the United States, and Baja California in Mexico. Californian cuisine serves as an element of identity in both states. It was born out of the cultural evolution of a region marked by successive waves of migrant integration. The arrival of missionaries like Junípero Serra in 1767 brought European agricultural techniques and species which enabled the growth of alien vegetal species in the region such as wheat and *Vitis Vinifera*, which were used to produce the hosts and wine essential for the celebration of the Catholic mass and evangelisation.

Further migration as a result of the gold rush from 1848 to 1855, during which 300,000 people, mainly men, arrived in California from all over the United States and the rest of the world, further changed the demographic and culinary landscape. The number of native people fell from 150,000 to 30,000 in 25 years, mainly due to the spread of exotic illnesses. For the European settlers, financial prosperity provided families with luxuries that were reflected on the tables of the whole region. During the gold rush period, San Francisco was reputed to have had more luxury restaurants than Paris (Fairfax et al. 2012) and the import of exotic foods increased remarkably. However, at the same time there was also the development of local cheese factories, bakeries and other workshops of high-quality culinary production demanded by society.

Books on California from the late nineteenth and early twentieth centuries show the fusion of various non-endemic culinary techniques and the incorporation of ingredients. Among them, *How to Keep a Husband or Culinary Tactics* (Anonymous 1872) stands out. It contains recipes adapted to ingredients available in the region that were gradually introduced, and a Cal-Mex style can be recognised (Pilcher 2012). The term "Cal-Mex" appears intermittently since the nineteenth century, gaining presence throughout the twentieth century. We can even find gastronomic businesses whose names include the word such as the one established in the 1960s and managed by Joe and Emma Todd, "El Cal-Mex", or at present the chain of restaurants called "Aquí Cal-Mex".

The name immediately evokes the Tex-Mex gastronomic movement, but the evolution of these trends, although derived from a similar origin, had a different destiny. In the Californian region more and more cultures were integrated into the original Mexican-American culinary culture, surpassing the limits of gastronomic capital that the term Cal-Mex could contain. On the contrary, to the east of the map, on the Texan border, Tex-Mex cuisine became stronger and even international. Which term appeared first is unknown and, although there are few historical records, it is accepted that the origin of the term Tex-Mex is derived from the railway under construction in that region at the end of the 1800s. As to the term Cal-Mex, its origin may have as background the combination of the names of the border cities founded during the first five years of the twentieth century, such as Mexicali, the capital of the Mexican State of Baja California (word composed by linking the words Mexico and California), and the town of Calexico (derived from the fusion of the words California and Mexico) in the United States.

Although at a domestic level this particular gastronomy, tightly linked to historical processes of the California region, was gaining definition and strength, it was not until 1945 that the gastronomic editor of the *Los Angeles Times*, under the pen name Marian Manners, mentioned this particular culinary style as "Californian cuisine". Later, in 1966, New York's renowned Hotel Waldorf Astoria presented a culinary event at its Peacock Alley restaurant under the name of "California Festival" (Thompson 2012). Both events provided evidence of this region's gastronomy and aroused the curiosity of gourmets (Shortridge & Shortridge 1995). In 1976 Californian wine fame was consolidated during the legendary blind tasting in France known as the "Judgment of Paris", where Steven Spurrier gathered several international renowned judges to taste and grade French and Californian wines. American wines easily won the competition and, thanks to media coverage, positioned Californian gastronomy as a culinary expression of high quality (Taber 2006).

The wine-making industry began a collaboration movement among farmers, creating a synergy that has strengthened vineyards, wineries and cellars in the border area, on the US side mainly in the Napa Valley, and on the Mexican side in Valle de Guadalupe. Wine makers share, despite paperwork and processes at customs and consulates, technology, knowhow, machinery, experts and workforce, which result in wines of similar quality on both sides of the border, although different due to the nature of each *terroir*. The economic impact of wine production and its function as a tourist attraction are better documented in the United States than in Mexico, but numbers show how important this activity has become on both sides. Statistics published by the Wine Institute of California (2013) show that the Californian wine-making industry had a national economic impact of US$ 121.8 billion, generating 820,000 jobs nationwide. They also show that wine-making areas in California received 20.7 million tourists. One of this institute's functions is to deal with migratory barriers to allow Mexican vineyard workers to harvest grapes in the United States. More than 600,000 professional vineyard workers labour in the California border area. Their specialisation allows them to harvest by hand 907 kg of grapes per worker daily, surpassing by far the international harvest average. Due to the migration laws, many of these workers are obliged to cross the border illegally in close collaboration with vineyard owners (vineyards are mostly family businesses), with workers often travelling four months a year in order to harvest grapes (Yelvington, Simms & Murray 2012).

Governance and artisanal processes strengthen the region's sustainable development with the benefits this entails (Hall 2013). The harvest of fruits and other vegetables occurs in a similar way in farm areas, such as at Imperial Valley, where picking strawberries, carrots, tomatoes and asparagus attracts many temporary workers, some of them with legal visas, others with temporary permits, but most of them with no legal document to identify them as workers in a foreign country.

On the other side of the border, wine production in Baja California represents 90 per cent of total wine production in Mexico. In 2009 Valle de Guadalupe received 100,000 visitors, of whom 35 per cent were Americans supporting the role of the Wine Route as a tourist product (Valderrama Martínez et al. 2012), a model that links producer and consumer and incorporates wine cellars and vineyards into the tourist system as well as encouraging regional economic development (Hall, Johnson & Mitchell 2000).

With the growth of *Vitis Vinifera* and the production of wine, Californian cuisine developed full of multicultural features and innovations that soothed the nostalgia for tastes of the region's settlers. At the domestic culinary level, a well-defined Californian gastronomic style was already perceived in the middle of the twentieth century, with fresh ingredients, a combination of spices brought from remote eastern and western places, the use of various techniques and cookeries with multinational paraphernalia. Housewives would have a Mexican *molcajete,* a Chinese *wok* and a European rolling pin to prepare daily food. However, family gastronomic capital is characterised by its secrecy, being part of the family's cultural heritage, recipes which form the identity of a group of people connected by genealogical or filial bonds, often having a weak and almost invisible social impact.

Instead, we can consider restaurants and other institutional catering venues as a society's spaces for culinary transformation. Professional cooking presents new proposals, and the customer either accepts or rejects them, incorporating approved ones to her personal gastronomic culture. By observation, customers at a restaurant learn new eating habits, table fashions and complement their own traditions, for example by incorporating wine in their diet, using chopsticks or properly eating a *taco*. All these manners of different cultural and geographical origin are present on the Californian table.

Reinterpreting cuisines from afar under Californian rules – which demand fresh seasonal ingredients, fish and seafood of exceptional quality, sweet fruits grown in the sunny region, and so on – produces dishes whose Californian origin many would question. One example would be "Chinese" fortune cookies, made of wheat (of European origin), sugar (African), vanilla (Mexican) and sesame oil (Oriental). Inspired by the Japanese cookie *tsujiura senbei*, they were a reinterpretation by the bakers of the Benkyodo bakery shop in San Francisco at the beginning of the twentieth century. Another example is *chop suey*: although it comes from Chinese gastronomy (*chow mein*), it is in the United States where fresh endemic ingredients are incorporated (Danforth et al. 1999). Another example is hard-shell *tacos*, an attempt to satisfy the craving of Mexicans from the country's centre and south living in the United States. Due to the impossibility of finding fresh-made corn *tortillas*, they preferred fried *tortillas* to stale ones (Arellano 2012). The catering industry found inspiration in the customers' demands (Flax & Rosenfield 1999), as *kung pao spaghetti* shows: it is Italian pasta seasoned in an Oriental style and sprinkled with American peanuts, a dish successfully sold by the California Pizza Kitchen chain in countries as gastronomically alien as the United Arab Emirates. It can be eaten with fork or Chinese sticks. It is by means of this passport of industrial cooking that we can find pork tacos with green sauce in India or Guam, a dish which easily could be considered Mexican, but which in fact is a Californian creation since it is served not with corn but with wheat *tortillas.*

The consolidation of Californian cuisine took place at the beginning of the new millennium, with the demography of the state showing that less than half the population is white and that there is no single dominant ethnic group (McWilliams & Heller 2003). There is also a growing tendency to form multicultural families. The same phenomenon is seen in Baja California, where most inhabitants were born elsewhere. Multiethnic coexistence at both sides of the border has created an environment of cultural inclusion. This border's peculiar characteristics are therefore reflected on the tables as a zone that generates hybridisation (Walker 2013).

The political border

The political border that divides the region represents an obstacle for gastronomic expression, which is a seal of identity even more powerful than language and that may cause sanctions when people dare to bring forbidden ingredients across either side of this imaginary line that humans impose on nature. For example, much Mexican-style soft cheese illegally crosses the Tijuana–San Diego political borders, with a high percentage of California's inhabitants being Mexican or of Mexican ancestry (Los Angeles has the world's second largest Mexican population, behind Mexico City). As it is not pasteurised, Mexican soft cheese has been declared a health risk by the US Food and Drug Administration. As of 2009, importing pieces of Mexican soft cheese heavier than five pounds is forbidden. However, for some people, giving up eating this cheese is impossible, despite the government's efforts to make people aware of the risks they are exposed to. It is elderly people who most tend to take this cheese across the border from Mexico to the United States. This practice is so frequent that a survey carried out in 2014 with a random sample of 687 people crossing the border showed that 44.5 per cent carried cheese (Nguyen et al. 2014) despite the legal consequences their action might have. They said it was a present for their family and friends, who eagerly expected it, a resistance exercise which favours old artisanal processes above the modern dairy industry and which surprisingly reveals that taste is more important than safety for those people.

The opposite case would be young Americans, 18–21 years old, who being under the permitted legal age cannot drink alcohol at home and travel to Mexico to visit bars. The same situation took place during the prohibition years in the United States (1920–1933), with Tijuana, Rosarito, Ensenada and Mexicali destinations where Americans went to drink. Cocktails currently known worldwide were born in those years, like the *margarita*, made with tequila, a distilled drink with protected Mexican designation of origin.

But it is not only people who travel motivated by food. Companies like artisanal breweries, attracted by tax benefits and lower overheads, have also left the United States to relocate to Mexico. Nowadays, Californian gastronomy has become a common ground for geographically distant cultures: using forks, sticks or fingers are valid ways to enjoy an inclusive cuisine. This food reference surely makes the traveller interested in knowing how regional food has evolved miles away from home, with ideas and images dispersed through another major Californian industry: entertainment, mainly cinema and television.

Understanding the evolution of a cuisine as a biocultural process indifferent to political borders makes us discover on every table the human act of cooking and sharing food. At the same time, it allows us to take advantage of its characteristics in order to create the gastronomic tourist product, determine the territory, activities, paraphernalia and dishes, but especially to provide us with the ways and flavours to create a bond of hospitality between host and guest, and thus strengthen local economy. Since it is impossible for gastronomy to travel, humans must move in order to taste otherness and, after comparing the differences, she will be able to reassert her identity and the place she occupies in a continuously more globalised world.

References

Anonymous (1872) *How to Keep a Husband, or, Culinary Tactics*, San Francisco: Cubery & Co., Book and Ornamental Job Printers.
Arellano, G. (2012) *Taco, USA: How Mexican Food Conquered America*, New York: Simon & Schuster.
Beard, M., North, J. and Price S. (1998) *Religions of Rome, Volume 2 – A Sourcebook*, Cambridge: Cambridge University Press.
Cho, S. (2006) 'Food and nationalism: Kimchi and Korean national identity', *The Korean Journal of International Relations*, 46(5): 207–229.
Cordón, F. (2009) *Cocinar hizo al hombre*, 7th edn, Madrid: Tusquets Editores.
Danforth, R., Feierabend, P., Chassman, G. and Ullmann, H.F. (1999) *Estados Unidos. Un descubrimiento culinario*, Colonia: Könemann.

Fairfax, S.K., Guthey, G.T., Dyble, L.N., Gwin, L., Moore, M. and Sokolove, J. (2012) *California Cuisine and Just Food*, Cambridge, MA: MIT Press.

Flax, L. and Rosenfield, R. (1999) *California Pizza Kitchen: Pasta, Salad, Soups, and Sides*, New York: William Morrow Cookbooks.

Fox, A.L. (1931) 'Taste-blindness', *Science*, 73(14): b1.

Hall, C.M. (2013) 'Framing behavioural approaches to understanding and governing sustainable tourism consumption: beyond neoliberalism, "nudging" and "green growth?"' *Journal of Sustainable Tourism*, 21(7): 1091–1109.

Hall, C.M., Johnson, G. and Mitchell, R. (2000) 'Wine tourism and regional development', in C.M. Hall, L. Sharples, N. Macionis, and B. Cambourne (eds) *Wine Tourism around the World*, Oxford: Butterworth Heinemann, pp. 196–225.

Levenstein, H. (1985) 'The American response to Italian food, 1880–1930', *Food and Foodways*, 1(1–2): 1–23.

Lytton, T.D. (2014) 'Jewish foodways and religious self-governance in America: the failure of communal kashrut regulation and the rise of private kosher certification', *Jewish Quarterly Review*, 104(1): 38–45.

McWilliams, M. and Heller, H. (2003) *Food around the World: A Cultural Perspective*, Englewood Cliffs: Prentice Hall.

Nabhan, G.P. (2006) *Por qué a algunos les gusta el picante. Alimentos, genes y diversidad cultural*, México: Fondo de Cultura Económica.

Nguyen, A., Cohen, N., Gao, H., Fishbein, D., Keir, J., Ocana, J., Senini, C., Flores, A. and Waterman, S. (2014) 'Knowledge, attitudes, and practices among border crossers during temporary enforcement of a formal entry requirement for Mexican-style soft cheeses, 2009', *Journal of Food Protection*, 77(9): 1571–1578.

Niewiadomska-Flis, U. (2013) 'Ethnic diaspora through the kitchen: foodways in the postcolonial feminist discourse of Gurinder Chadha's What's Cooking?' *Moravian Journal of Literature & Film*, 4(2): 35–53.

Pilcher, J.M. (2001) 'Tex-Mex, Cal-Mex, New Mex, or whose Mex? Notes on the historical geography of southwestern cuisine', *Journal of the Southwest*, 43: 659–679.

Pilcher, J.M. (2012) *Planet Taco: A Global History of Mexican Food*, Oxford: Oxford University Press.

Pilcher, J.M. (2014) '"Old stock" tamales and migrant tacos: taste, authenticity, and the naturalization of Mexican food', *Social Research: An International Quarterly*, 81(2): 441–462.

Pollan, M. (2006) *The Omnivore's Dilemma: A Natural History of Four Meals*, New York: Penguin.

Sánchez-Cañizares, S.M. and López-Guzmán, T. (2012) 'Gastronomy as a tourism resource: profile of the culinary tourist', *Current Issues in Tourism*, 15(3): 229–245.

Shortridge, B. and Shortridge, J. (1995) 'Cultural geography of American foodways: an annotated bibliography', *Journal of Cultural Geography*, 15(2): 79–108.

Shortridge, B. and Shortridge, J. (eds) (1999) *The Taste of American Place: A Reader on Regional and Ethnic Foods*, Lanham: Rowan & Littlefield.

Taber, G. (2006) *Judgment of Paris: California vs France and the Historic 1976 Paris Tasting that Revolutionized Wine*, New York: Simon and Schuster.

Thompson, M. (2012) *Vintage California Cuisine: 300 Recipes from the First Cookbooks Published in the Golden State*, Philadelphia: Seasonal Chef Press.

Urry, J. (1990) *The Tourist Gaze: Leisure and Travel in Contemporary Societies*, London: Sage.

Valderrama Martínez, J.A., Trejo, J.C.F., Arredondo, C.I. and Contreras, S.G.S. (2012) 'Desarrollo turístico en el Valle de Guadalupe, Baja California, México. Ruralidad, producción de vinos y hoteles', *Global Conference on Business & Finance Proceedings*, 7(2): 1424–1428.

Walker, M.A. (2013) 'Border food and food on the border: meaning and practice in Mexican haute cuisine', *Social & Cultural Geography*, 14(6): 649–667.

Wine Institute of California (2013) *California Wine Industry Statistical Highlights*. Available online: <http://www.wineinstitute.org/resources/statistics> (accessed 31 May 2015).

Yelvington, K.A., Simms, J.L. and Murray, E. (2012) 'Wine tourism in the Temecula Valley: neoliberal development policies and their contradictions', *Anthropology in Action*, 19(3): 49–65.

Part IV
Products, regions and regionality

13 Understanding disparities in wine tourism development

Evidence from two Old World cases

Elsa Gatelier

Introduction

This chapter deals with wine tourism development. Its aim is to fill gaps in our understanding of disparities that occur between wine regions. Wine tourism is usually defined by the meeting between wine and tourism sectors (Hall et al. 2000). The cooperation between the two sectors is especially recognised as the key for wine tourism (Debos 2008) allowing benefits for both wineries and the whole tourist area to be maximised. In this chapter, we assume that the meeting between wine and tourism activities has different characteristics according to the regions in which this occurs, which thus leads to differences in wine tourism development throughout the world.

The chapter first demonstrates the existence of wine tourism disparities via a review of relevant literature. The review suggests that wine tourism is studied at either the winery level or at the tourist area level. Taking into account the two dimensions simultaneously appears to be difficult. Nevertheless, it is essential to capture the entire reality of the wine tourism phenomenon (Hall 2004). Consequently, this chapter intends to contribute to the understanding of those wine tourism differences by focussing on the relationship between the two dimensions of wine tourism analysis: wine tourism at the winery level and wine tourism at the tourist regional level.

For this purpose, comparisons are made between two Old World wine regions: Champagne (France) and Tuscany (Italy). Using interviews with wine producers and other wine tourism stakeholders in each region, the chapter shows that tourism services provided by wineries and the way wineries interact with the whole tourist area are specific to each region studied. The chapter ends by discussing and proposing some assumptions on the interaction between wine tourism at the winery and at the whole tourist area. In addition, some implications for further research will be drawn.

A review of wine tourism disparities

Wine tourism develops differently between wine regions. However, how can these disparities be described? The behaviour and practices of tourists clearly impact the wine tourism area (Caccomo & Solandrasana 2006), but the objective of this chapter is to focus on the wine tourism offer and its provision and provider's strategies in particular. It is clear that wine tourism differences exist between wine regions, as illustrated by the amount of case studies in wine tourism academic works (e.g. Mitchell & Hall 2006). However, their understanding is relatively neglected. Nevertheless, research can be categorised into those that focus on wine tourism at the whole tourist area level and those that focus on wine tourism at the winery level.

Disparities at the whole tourist area level

The tourist area is consistently considered a space for coordination between heterogeneous stakeholders, often by using an organisational and/or a branding-focussed approach. Some literature dealing with wine tourist areas adopt a performance view to describe their diversity. With regions following notional stages of wine tourism development, areas can thus be ranked according to the stage they have reached. These works emphasise that the more coordination is undertaken in the tourist region, the more wine tourism is developed and the more it benefits the local economic development (Hall, Johnson & Mitchell 2000; Hall & Michael 2007; Carmichael & Senese 2012; Deery, O'Mahony & Moors 2012). However, a development stages approach (especially based on Butler's (1980) tourism area life cycle) is arguably unsuitable for many geographical areas (Suchet 2014; see also Butler 2006).

Some other works incorporate these issues, often explaining diversity in wine tourism by the differences in organisational patterns. They, for instance, describe the different cooperation patterns we can find in wine tourism area (but without highlighting their performance). They evaluate wine tourism coordination according to the number of stakeholders that cooperate (Hall et al. 1998), to the nature of these stakeholders (Telfer 2001; Jones, Singh & Hsiung 2013; Oliveira-Brochado, Silva & Paulino 2014), or to the kind of partnerships they develop (Telfer 2001). For example, Vandecandelaere and Touzard's (2005) study of wine routes suggest that wine routes can be more or less focussed on wine resource. It means that wine routes can be associated with other local resources or just be connected to wine heritage. They also demonstrate that wine routes can be more or less focussed on wine producers and their wineries, thereby emphasising the different nature of wine tourism stakeholders from one wine region to another. In some cases, wineries are predominant in the wine tourism offer, and in other cases, the nature of stakeholders is diverse (hotel, restaurant, wine bars). These issues become a major focus of the case studies used in the present chapter.

Disparities at the winery level

With respect to wine tourism at the winery level, there is substantial effort in assessing the tourism involvement of wineries. At this level, models of winery tourism life cycle development also exist (e.g. Beverland & Lockshin 2000; Dodd & Beverland 2001). But the focus in this chapter is on the diversity of strategic patterns in wineries without necessarily having these contextualised by a notional life cycle. Wine producers do not necessarily think in the same way with respect to the benefits from wine tourism for their wineries (e.g., see Hojman & Hunter-Jones 2012 for Chilean vineyards; Lignon-Darmaillac 2009 for France; and Baird & Hall 2014 for New Zealand), therefore leading them to adopt different wine tourism strategies. These strategies concern the extent to which wineries offer tourist services.

The scope of tourist services that can be provided in wineries is very large and of varied nature (Bruwer 2003; Getz & Brown 2006; Kirkman, Strydom & van Zyl 2013). Wineries can thus be assessed according to the tourist services they provide. The Great Wine Capitals Global Network (GWCGN) undertook a survey on the wine tourism performances of their members (GWCGN 2013), which highlighted that the main sources of profit are different from one region to another (see Figure 13.1). This also suggests that wineries provide different kind of tourist services among regions and that wineries are not equally important in each region in providing each kind of services.

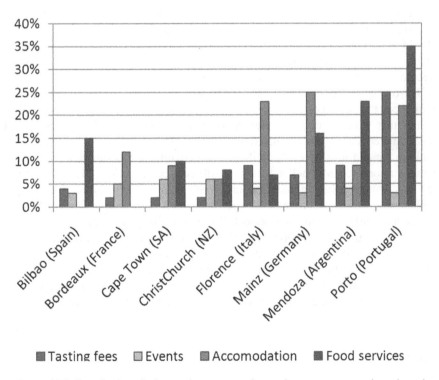

Figure 13.1 Contribution of wine tourism revenues by service category excepting wine sales
Source: Derived from executive summaries of the 2013 GWCGN study.

The GWCGN is also interesting because it allows winery comparisons between and within Old and New World wine cities (see also Garcia-Parpet 2009; Charters & Mitchell 2014; Harvey, White & Frost 2014). However, differences are empirically observed at a narrower dimension. Differences exist between different regions as attested by the amount of food services revenues in Mendoza (Argentina) and their relative lack in Bordeaux (France). In Bilbao (Spain), little benefit is had from accommodations, whereas it is the first source of wine tourism profit in Florence (Italy). In Mendoza (Argentina), 23 per cent of wine tourism revenues come from food services, whereas in Christchurch (New Zealand) or in Cape Town (South Africa), they represent less than 10 per cent of wine tourism revenues. In addition, the ratio of wineries involved in tourism within all wineries inside a region is also different. Some regions are characterised by a high involvement of wineries in tourism and other by a very low involvement (Kreilkamp & Quack 2012).

Encompassing both levels of wine tourism diversity

Wine tourism is often considered at two levels of analysis that are not addressed concomitantly. In interpretations of the relationship between these two levels, the sense of the relationship usually operates from the winery level to the tourist area level. Winery strategies often influence the whole tourist area by forming dominant wine tourism forms at wineries. For instance, wineries are often little involved in tourism in Europe, whereas they tend to be highly involved in New World wine regions (Charters 2009). There is therefore a kind of "proportion effect", this means that the same strategy led by a large amount of wineries within a region affects the wine tourism form of the whole tourist area.

Beyond the proportion of each kind of winery strategies their content also influences the organisation of the tourist destination. Dawson (2013) demonstrates that wineries consider their location in their individual strategies and what impacts the region's (collective) identity. However, her work deals more with image and identity building than with networks and destination building. Other authors (e.g. Mitchell, Charters & Albrecht 2012; Telfer 2001) argue that the way wineries think about their involvement in tourism impacts how they collaborate with respect to their wine tourism offer. For example, Telfer (2001) notes that winery's high involvement in tourism gives more opportunities for collaboration than low involvement. But this argument will be revisited in the findings in the following case studies. The key point is that winery strategies involving cooperation with other wine tourism stakeholders is also a link to the above-mentioned analysis levels as "Cooperation" provides for a linkage between winery strategies and the collective destination-building dimension of analysis.

Case studies: Champagne and Tuscany

The following cases describe winery involvement in tourism by the extent to which they provide tourist services and by the way they cooperate with other

Table 13.1 List of interviewed institutions in Champagne and Tuscany

Champagne	Tuscany
Champagne-Ardenne Regional Council for Tourism (CRT)	Tuscany Regional Institute for economic development (IRPET)
Tourist offices (Rheims, Epernay, Marne, Aube)	Tourist office of Florence district (APT Firenze)
Champagne interprofessional committee (CIVC)	Florence chamber of commerce (Camera di commercio di firenze)
Winegrowers'union (SGV) and Merchants'union (UMC)	Tuscany Regional Council, wine department
Economic, Social and environmental regional committee of Champagne-Ardenne (CESER)	Slow Food Tuscany

providers. With respect to wine tourist area, the chapter follows Vandecandelaere and Touzard's (2005) definition of wine tourism diversity (i.e. according to its more or less high degree of focalisation on wineries and on wine resource). The cases studies examine as to whether some differences in wine tourism development at one level induce differences at the other? Furthermore, we question how the different levels can influence one another. To carry this out, an exploratory comparison is made between Champagne (France) and Tuscany (Italy).

In these regions, winery involvement and the organisational structure of the wine tourism offered at the destination level are different. But the regions also share a number of similarities. In each region a large and predominant wine-producing area is recognised by a Protected Denomination of Origin (PDO) Champagne and Chianti. The Champagne area is almost 34,000 hectares (100 per cent of the PDO wine area in the region), and the Chianti area is more than 16,000 hectares representing 66 per cent of the PDO wine area of the Tuscany region. The recognised quality of each wine production gives them a similar attractive potential, since wine renown is considered the first vector of wine tourists' attraction (Dumont & Lespinasse-Taraba 2010; Kreilkamp & Quack 2012). Furthermore, beyond the wine, each region contains other quality, locally produced goods, with some recognised by PDO or Protected Geographic Indication (PGI). This also gives the regions a highly attraction potential as tourist destinations.

The materials used to compare Champagne and Tuscany are diverse. In addition to literature reviews, interviews were conducted with wine producers, wine and tourism institutions and academics (Table 13.1). In Champagne, a questionnaire survey has also been done to wineries. From all this information, we describe wine tourism at winery level and at the destination level in each region.

Findings

The cases are first compared at the tourist area level and then at the winery level.

The wine tourist area: a collaborative pattern in Champagne and a winery-focussed pattern in Tuscany

Wine tourism requires the discovering of other local resources apart from wine (Croce & Perri 2010); wine tourists are most frequently not only interested in wine and seek an overall experience (Carlsen & Charters 2006). Consequently, wine tourism was investigated at the destination level with a substantial focus on the co-promotion of wine resource with other resources in building the destination as well as relationships with other wine tourism stakeholders.

In Champagne, wine is the main driver of the destination and is the prime motivating factor for tourists to come in the region (Dumont & Lespinasse-Taraba 2010). The Champagne region is provided with many other resources apart from Champagne wine. There are gastronomic resources sometimes protected by PDO or PGI such as the *Chaource* or *Epoisse* cheese or meat as *Boudin de blanc de Rethel*. There is also significant architectural and historical heritage, such as Rheims Cathedral where many French kings have been crowned, or First and Second World War sites. However, Champagne wine is rarely promoted in relationships with all these resources. They are more juxtaposed than coordinated (Delaplace, Gatelier & Pichery 2012). If joint promotion is an objective for the Champagne Regional Council, it is still unrealised. For instance, there is no collaboration between the Champagne committee (CIVC) and cheese committees.

However, wine resources are often used by other local actors to develop tourism activities. If accommodation and catering mainly exist out of wineries, their offer is often not linked to Champagne, apart from some gastronomic and starred restaurants (seven starred restaurants as of May 2015). Nevertheless, there are an increasing number of businesses that develop wine tourism, especially wine bars, wine boutiques and independent wine tour guides. This means that wine resources have been recently appropriated by other and diverse actors to develop their own business. In addition, wine tourism branding and wine routes are used to promote and build collectively the wine tourism offer.

In Tuscany and the Chianti, PDO wine is not the destination leader. It instead constitutes a component among others and together they contribute to the "Tuscany lifestyle". Tuscany is filled with emblematic heritage, especially urban culture and architecture (Florence, Pisa and Siena) as well as a countryside with many medieval villages (Radda in Chianti, Certaldo, Montalcino, Montepulciano). There are also numerous local food products protected by PDO or PGI (honey, truffle, "Pecorino" cheese, cured boar meats). There is no joint promotion of wine with all the resources for tourism development, except for encouraging local consumption of local products via the "Vetrina Toscana" project. Interviewees explain that all local resources contribute together to the reputation of the place; their co-promotion is not organised but occurs in an obvious or "natural" way. They therefore compose with wine a basket of goods that reinforce each other (Mollard & Pecqueur 2007). Yet high-renowned wines could help enhance other production. For instance, there is a PDO olive oil called Chianti Classico which is produced in the area of the Chianti Classico PDO wine. In the Chianti Classico area, there is therefore a diversified agriculture of quality products labelled by

PDO. Olive oil could benefit from the renown of the "Chianti Classico" wine and encourage the co-enhancement of quality products in the area. In the case of Champagne, its reputation could help enhance other quality products, but this was not observed in the case study.

Agritourism providers, that is to say wineries developing tourist services, are the main wine tourism actors in Tuscany. Sometimes they open wine bars and boutique in nearby cities. But apart from tour operators, very few private stake-holders are involved in wine tourism.

The winery level: a small scope of services in Champagne wineries and a wide scope of services in Tuscany wineries

The tourism involvement of wineries is not only defined by the service they pro-vide in-house but also by the way they interact with tourist area stakeholders. This implies the need to investigate the existence of partnerships between wineries and other wine tourism businesses.

Moreover, wineries can focus on wine resource tourist enhancement as well as enhance other local resource.

In the Champagne region, wineries are divided into two kinds (Gatelier, Delaplace & Barrére 2012). The Champagne industry is built on the relationship between the two. The first kind of wineries is the vinegrowers that could also be winegrowers. They own the land designated by PDO, and they can sell what they produce (at different stages of wine production) to the second type of winery (the merchant), or they can hold their production in order to promote it and sell it under they own trademark. The merchants buy the wine at a more or less finished stage and then sell it under their own trademark. Usually wineries that are only vinegrowers are not interested by tourism because they do not have bottles to sell. In contrast, winegrowers who are interested in cellar door sales can benefit from tourism. In most cases, this is their main motivation to be involved in tourism. Some merchants also open their doors to tourists, but it is less a way to sell wine than a way to promote their brand and convey a positive image of it.

The amount of wineries with tourism service is very low. As of mid-2015, of the 15,800 wineries in Champagne, only 403 open their doors to tourists. Moreover, the services they provide are essentially visitation and wine tasting; accommodation in the wineries is rare. Only 88 wineries provide farm holidays and are identified by the specialised organisation *Gîtes de France*. Nevertheless, recently some wineries have developed novel and pioneering services, such as the opportunity to participate in the harvest, oenology courses, and horse and buggy rides in the vineyard. But these efforts remain unusual.

In addition, winery production is mostly wine labelled with Champagne PDO. Two other PDO wines can be produced in the Champagne area (*Coteaux champe-nois* and *Rosé des Riceys*), but they are not widespread. As noted previously, other local products with a PDO label exist in the region. However, they are not promoted in wineries. This means that wineries do not promote wine and other local resources together, except for resources directly linked to wine such as wine landscape (e.g. applying for the inscription of "Champagne Landscapes" on the World Heritage list) or wine history of the area (e.g. the story of the Benedictine monk Dom Perignon).

With respect to partnerships, wine tourism stakeholders deplore that cooperation arrangements are difficult to develop in the region. Nevertheless, some partnerships exist between the wineries and between wineries and other wine tourism providers. As the Champagne PDO area is very large, wineries form small associations and try to differentiate according to the diversity of terroir. We thus find several associations whose purpose is to promote their small area of production in the wider Champagne PDO area. Wineries involved in wine tourism also collaborate with tourism service providers. Among wineries interviewed, 38 per cent collaborate most frequently with local accommodation and catering businesses but also with tour operators. But their partnerships remain most often informal (68 per cent); commercial partnerships are less widespread (24 per cent). The majority are thus non-market partnerships.

In the case of Tuscany the structure of Chianti wineries appears more homogenous (Regione Toscana 2012), especially if we consider the Siena and Florence districts which are leaders in PDO wine production with 55 per cent of Tuscany PDO wine production being concentrated there (ISMEA 2008). In these districts, wineries are twice as large as the rest of Tuscany. Moreover, their tourism involvement is also more homogenous with a strong agritourism emphasis. Agritourism in this case can be defined as holidays on a farm, where the farm provides tourists with services allowing tourist to rest (accommodation, catering and others) and discover local products (tasting, visitation). The Siena and Florence districts have the highest average number of beds, which support the observation that local wineries are highly involved in wine tourism. Like their Champagne counterparts, they provide tasting and visitation but they are much more numerous in providing other tourist services such as accommodation or catering. Moreover, they generally add tourist infrastructures to their winery such as swimming pool, tennis court, camping site, entertainment and spa.

Wineries play a key role in the joint promotion of wine and other local resources. In Tuscany, several wineries are not only focussed on wine production, even if it is their main activity, but many of them also produce olive oil. Tourists can thus discover several local products during their visits to wineries.

As noted above, the main wine tourism actors in Tuscany are agritourism businesses. For instance, the tourist office of Siena district identifies about 3,000 accommodation providers of which more than 1,200 are agritourism businesses. Moreover, interviewees note that except for some commercial partnerships with tour operators, wineries do not collaborate with other wine tourism stakeholders. They do cooperate for wine routes but these are mainly a way to help tourists to travel in the countryside rather than a real relationship between providers.

In summary, in the Champagne region, tourism is highly focussed on wine resource, but the joint promotion of wine and local heritages is not usual or is even difficult. Champagne producers have low involvement in wine tourism. They do not provide a significant scope of tourist services. This lack is balanced by the involvement of other private actors. The latter offer basic tourist services (accommodation, catering, transport), and they also provide activities directly linked to Champagne wine. Thus wine tourism stakeholders are diverse in Champagne region, but tourist activities remain focussed on wine.

In Tuscany, wine is a component among others concerning tourism. Tourists in the region are also motivated by cultural amenities and particularly by city visitation. Wine is well integrated in regional tourism and the joint promotion of diverse cultural and natural heritage seems to occur easily. As wine producers are highly involved in tourist services provision, the set of services provided is substantially wide. Moreover, they offer the discovering of another local product (olive oil). Hence, other wine tourism actors are not numerous apart from tour operators. The latter often being asked to sell agritourism beds. That is why when wineries collaborate, it mostly concerns market partnerships.

How do the winery level and the tourist area level relate?

These two cases lead us to assume that the interaction between wine tourism at the winery and wine tourism in the whole tourist area works in both directions. First, we assume that wine tourism at wineries (and especially the scope of their service provision) allows (or not) other local stakeholders to join the wine tourism sector. For instance, in Tuscan vineyards, accommodation is essentially offered by wineries. In Champagne, relatively few wineries propose this kind of service, and tourists thus need to use accommodation offered by other tourism stakeholders. The more wine producers integrate tourist services in their wineries, the less other kinds of providers develop their wine tourism activity. In other words, there appears the existence of a division of the labor to provide the overall wine tourism experience. This assumption gives an interpretation of the relationship between wineries' strategies and the tourist area: it actually could explain why the wine tourism is focussed on wineries or is open to other actors. Nevertheless, this interpretation arises from the study of two cases and needs further research to be tested.

Second, the characteristics of the tourist area (natural and cultural heritage, existing tourist infrastructure) may also influence service provision in the wineries. In particular, other local heritage and their identity could (or not) facilitate their joint promotion with wine. Thus, it is more or less easy for wineries to integrate activities linked to other local heritage into their scope of services. Although olive oil is "naturally" linked to wine in Tuscany and inside wineries, this is not the case in Champagne. Tourist enhancement of Champagne wine is not done in relationship with other resources. The promotion of Champagne is undertaken individually both inside and outside wineries. Moreover, as Delaplace et al. (2012) explain, Champagne identity is not in line with the identity of other local resources, hence there are difficulties in promoting them together. At the tourist area level, local resources can thus be easily co-promoted or not, depending on the identity of each. In other words, there is a need to specify the context within which wine tourism develops (Charters 2009; Mitchell et al. 2012; Dawson 2013;

Hall & Baird 2014; Randelli, Romei & Tortora 2014). Each local wine resource has peculiarities that influence its tourist enhancement and co-enhancement with other resources.

Conclusion

This chapter contributes to the understanding of wine tourism diversity between regions. From a review of existing literature, it pointed out the characterisation of the diversity at each level: the winery and the whole tourist area. Therefore, it proposes an assumption based on case studies that there is a kind of division of labor between wineries and other local wine tourism providers to provide the overall wine tourism experience. Two examples were presented: sometimes wine and tourism activities meet at the winery level and sometimes at the tourist area level as a result of the collaboration between different kinds of actors. Moreover, the joint promotion of wine and other resources seems to be territory-specific, which calls for context specification in studies of wine tourism and regional development.

Future research needs to examine the impact of different organisational patterns of wine tourism service provision on local economic development. In other words, is there a shape that provides more benefits to local development? Which organisational structure generates the more benefits? Given that academic literature often argues for a more collaborative structure (Debos 2008), we can wonder if the integration of tourist services at the winery could also generate jobs. For instance, agritourism in Tuscany is well structured and developed. Tuscany is thus the Italian region in which agritourism generates most permanent contract and uses less family labour (Conti 2011). Further studies need to be done in this field to compare benefits for local economic development of each pattern of wine tourism.

References

Baird, T. and Hall, C.M. (2014) 'Between the vines: wine tourism in New Zealand', in P. Howland (ed.) *Social, Cultural and Economic Impacts of Wine in New Zealand*, Abingdon: Routledge, pp. 191–207.

Beverland, M. and Lockshin, L. (2000) 'Organisational life cycles in small NZ wineries', *Australian & New Zealand Wine Industry Journal*, 15(4): 50–58.

Bruwer, J. (2003) 'South African wine routes: some perspectives on the wine tourism industry's structural dimensions and wine tourism product', *Tourism Management*, 24(4): 423–435.

Butler, R.W. (1980) 'The concept of a tourist area cycle of evolution: implications for management of resources', *The Canadian Geographer/Le Géographe canadien*, 24(1): 5–12.

Butler, R.W. (ed.) (2006) *The Tourism Life Cycle*, 2 vols, Clevedon: Channelview.

Caccomo, J.-L. and Solandrasana, B. (2006) *L'innovation dans l'industrie touristique. Enjeux et stratégies*, Paris: L'harmattan.

Carlsen, J. and Charters, S. (2006) *Global Wine Tourism: Research, Management and Marketing*, Wallingford: CAB International.

Carmichael, B.A. and Senese, D. (2012) 'Competitiveness and sustainability in wine tourism regions: the application of a stage model of destination development to two Canadian wine regions', in P.H. Dougherty (ed.) *The Geography of Wine*, Dortrecht: Springer, pp. 159–178.

Charters, S. (2009) 'New world and Mediterranean wine tourism a comparative analysis', *Tourism*, 57(4): 369–379.

Charters, S. and Mitchell R. (2014) 'Food and wine events in Europe and the new world: a comparison', in A. Cavicchi and C. Santini (eds) *Food and Wine Events in Europe: A Stakeholder Approach*, New York: Routledge, pp. 15–27.

Conti, E. (2011) *L'agriturismo in cifre: Punto di forza per lo sviluppo regionale*, IRPET.

Croce, E. and Perri, G. (2010) *Food and Wine Tourism*, London: CABI.

Dawson, D.B. (2013) 'Winery entrepreneurs rooted in "Their Place": how lifestyle decisions, business motivations and perceptions of place influence business practices and regional initiatives in the wine and tourism industries', Unpublished PhD thesis, Lincoln University, New Zealand.

Debos, F. (2008) 'Le partenariat "viticulteurs-institutionnels du tourisme": Clé de voûte d'un oenotourisme performant', *Marketing et Communication*, 1(2): 62–73.

Deery, M., O'Mahony, G. and Moors, R. (2012) 'Employing a lifecycle typology to generate a unified and strategic approach to regional wine tourism development', *Tourism Planning & Development*, 9(3): 291–307.

Delaplace, M., Gatelier, E. and Pichery, M.-C. (2012) 'Patrimonialisation de la vitiviniculture et développement du tourisme dans les régions viticoles : une comparaison Bourgogne/Champagne', in 49ème colloque de l'ASRDLF, Industrie, villes et régions dans une économie mondialisée, Belfort.

Dodd, T.H. and Beverland, M. (2001) 'Winery tourism life-cycle development: a proposed model', *Tourism Recreation Research*, 26(2): 11–21.

Dumont, M. and Lespinasse-Taraba, C. (2010) *Tourisme et Vin. Les clientèles françaises et internationales, les concurrents de la France. Comment rester compétitif?* Paris: ATOUT France.

Garcia-Parpet, M.F. (2009) *Le marché de l'excellence. Les grands crus à l'épreuve de la mondialisation*, Paris: Seuil.

Gatelier, E., Delaplace, M. and Barrère, C. (2012) L'oenotourisme en Champagne: Entre valorisation d'un produit de luxe et développement territorial de la Champagne in Colloque AsTRES 2012, Nice.

Getz, D. and Brown, G. (2006) 'Benchmarking wine tourism development: the case of the Okanagan Valley, British Columbia, Canada', *International Journal of Wine Marketing*, 18(2): 78–97.

Great Wine Capitals Global Network (GWCGN) (2013) *Etude de Marché Great Wine Capitals 2013 – Les piliers de la performance oenotourisme*. Available online: <http://greatwinecapitals.com/resources/reports/1694> (Accessed 1 April 2015).

Hall, C.M. (2004) 'Small firms and wine and food tourism in New Zealand: issues of collaboration, clusters and lifestyles', in R. Thomas (ed.) *Small Firms in Tourism: International Perspectives*, Oxford: Elsevier, pp. 167–181.

Hall, C.M. and Baird, T. (2014) 'Innovation in New Zealand wine tourism businesses', in G.A. Alsos, D. Eide, and E.L. Madsen (eds) *Handbook of Research on Innovation in Tourism Industries*, Cheltenham: Edward Elgar, pp. 249–274.

Hall, C.M., Cambourne, B., Macionis, N. and Johnson G. (1998) 'Wine tourism and network development in Australia and New Zealand: review, establishment and prospects', *International Journal of Wine Marketing*, 9(2): 5–31.

Hall, C.M., Johnson, G. and Mitchell, R. (2000) 'Wine tourism and regional development', in C.M. Hall, L. Sharples, B. Cambourne, and N. Macionis (eds) *Wine Tourism around the World: Development, Management, and Markets*, Oxford: Elsevier, pp. 196–225.

Hall, C.M. and Michael, E.J. (2007) 'Issues in regional development', in E. Michael (ed.) *Micro-Clusters and Networks: The Growth of Tourism*, Amsterdam: Elsevier, pp. 7–20.

Hall, C.M., Sharples, L., Cambourne, B. and Macionis, N. (2000) 'Wine tourism: an introduction', in C.M. Hall, L. Sharples, B. Cambourne, and N. Macionis (eds) *Wine Tourism around the World: Development, Management, and Markets*, Oxford: Elsevier.

Harvey, M., White, L. and Frost, W. (eds) (2014) *Wine and Identity. Branding, Heritage, Terroir*, New York: Routledge.

Hojman, D.E. and Hunter-Jones, P. (2012) 'Wine tourism: Chilean wine regions and routes', *Journal of Business Research*, 65(1): 13–21.

Istituto de Servizi Per Il Mercato Agricolo Alimentare (ISMEA) (2008) *Aspetti strutturali e di mercato nel comparto dei vini DOC-DOCG*, Rome: ISMEA.

Jones, M.F., Singh, N. and Hsiung, Y. (2013) 'Determining the critical success factors of the wine tourism region of Napa from a supply perspective', *International Journal of Tourism Research*, 17(3): 261–271.

Kirkman, A., Strydom, J.W. and van Zyl, C. (2013) 'Stellenbosch wine route wineries: management's perspective on the advantages and key success factors of wine tourism', *Southern African Business Review*, 17(2): 93–112.

Kreilkamp, E. and Quack, H.-D. (2012) *Inventaire et évaluation de l'offre oenotouristique dans les régions européennes viticoles*, Europäisches Tourismus Institut pour l'Association des Régions Européennes Viticoles.

Lignon-Darmaillac, S. (2009) *L'oenotourisme en France. Nouvelle valorisation des vignobles. Analyse et Bilan*, Bordeaux: Féret.

Mitchell, R., Charters, S. and Albrecht, J. (2012) 'Cultural systems and the wine tourism product', *Annals of Tourism Research*, 39(1): 311–335.

Mitchell, R. and Hall, C.M. (2006) 'Wine tourism research: the state of play', *Tourism Review International*, 9(4): 307–332.

Mollard, A. and Pecqueur, B. (2007) 'De l'hypothèse au modèle du panier de biens et de services', *Économie rurale*, 300: 110–114.

Oliveira-Brochado, A., Silva, R. and Paulino, C. (2014) 'The world of great wines: the Douro Valley experience', *International Journal of Social, Human Science and Engineering*, 8(4): 1016–1023.

Randelli, F., Romei, P. and Tortora, M. (2014) 'An evolutionary approach to the study of rural tourism: the case of Tuscany', *Land Use Policy*, 38: 276–281.

Regione Toscana (2012) *La vite et il vino in Toscana. Campagna vendemmiale 2011/2012*, Regione Toscana.

Suchet, A. (2014) 'Pour en finir avec Butler (1980) et son modèle d'évolution des destinations touristiques. Le cycle de vie comme concept inadapté à l'étude d'une aire géographique', *Loisir et Société/Society and Leisure*, 38(1): 7–19.

Telfer, D.J. (2001) 'Strategic alliances along the Niagara wine route', *Tourism Management*, 22: 21–30.

Vandecandelaere, E. and Touzard, J.-M. (2005) 'Création de ressources territoriales et construction de la qualité. Les routes des vins', in *Proximités et changements socio-économiques dans les mondes ruraux*. Paris: INRA Editions, pp. 59–72.

14 Does regionality matter?

The experience in Ireland

John Mulcahy

Introduction

Historically Ireland has had a difficult relationship with food driven by its history of colonisation, the painful famine and stoic Catholicism, and is only just on the cusp of realising its own food culture and identity, which is still evolving and emerging. However, Irish food culture has undergone a significant and exciting transformation in the last decade and particularly in the last five years, with the advent of an emerging, ingredient-driven Irish cuisine. Interestingly, Ireland's current recession since 2008 has focussed the population on the importance of supporting Irish products and producers, resulting in changing food purchasing habits and generating a new appreciation of how good Irish food can be. Understandably, consumers believe it is now more important than ever to buy guaranteed Irish goods and services and that it is important to them that restaurants serve local ingredients. The growing interest in food on the part of the Irish consumer is reflected in many aspects of Irish life and behaviour. This is clearly reflected in the increased presence of food features in the media, the expansion in the number of artisanal food producers and farmers' markets, the growth in demonstrations and cooking schools, and the range of restaurants and pubs now proudly and confidently sourcing, serving and shouting about using Irish ingredients. Despite the recent growth in food-related experiences and activities, and the championing of local ingredients and produce by a cohort of chefs and restaurateurs, there is still a disconnect between produce and cuisine, and the relationship between these and the visitor experience. Much has been achieved in a short space of time, but developing a food tourism culture in Ireland, from both a domestic market and an industry practitioner perspective, is an ongoing process.

In 2010, food tourism was becoming a growing market segment internationally, and many destinations, including those in Ireland's competitive set, were beginning to develop this sector as a means to gaining competitive advantage. A seismic shift occurred, where Fáilte Ireland, the national tourism development authority, moved from a traditionally very action-orientated role in food tourism to that of a more enabling and facilitative role in their capacity of supporting the industry (Mossberg et al. 2014).

It has been recognised that the linkages between food and tourism can provide a platform for local economic development (Richards 2002), and food experiences help to brand and market destinations (Sims 2009) while also contributing towards the competitiveness of a destination (du Rand & Heath 2006). From a regional development perspective, the critical question becomes how does food and tourism fit into the bigger picture and the overall tourism development strategies of a region or country – in this case, specifically Ireland? This chapter examines how perceptions can affect policy and strategy, vary the notion of regionality, and recalibrate food tourism's role in regional development. In doing so, it will contextualise the genesis of Ireland's approach to food tourism and subsequent strategic journey on the road towards developing potential as a food tourism destination. Within the wider tourism industry in Ireland, food tourism may not yet be a mainstream product in itself, but food *in* tourism is something that is integral across all sectors, markets and populations.

'Regional' – through whose lens?

The island of Ireland is situated on the north-western edge of Europe, in the North Atlantic Ocean at a similar latitude to Alaska in the United States and Hamburg in Germany. There are two national jurisdictions on the island, one of which, the Republic of Ireland, comprises five-sixths of the island of Ireland. The other, in the north-eastern part of the island, is Northern Ireland, and this is part of the United Kingdom. As an independent country, Ireland has a population of 4.6 million (0.9 per cent of the total EU population) and covers just under 70,000 km². For the purposes of this discussion, it is important to appreciate this, as, by comparison, Ireland's key source markets of tourists (UK, US, France, Germany) (over 50 per cent; see Fáilte Ireland 2015c) are considerably larger in order of importance to tourism in terms of population and geographical size (European Union 2015).

Ireland, therefore, in terms of the perspective of a majority of its visitors, is comparatively quite a small place, accessible largely by air (but also by sea), relatively sparsely populated for a West European country or even a city, and of a scale that is unlikely to provide cultural, touristic or entertaining diversity. This is both a blessing and a curse, of course, in common with many regions or destinations. A blessing, as the reality can prove to be very different from the perception, leading to serendipitous experiences in a variety of landscapes, environments and contexts, the outcome of which arguably converts visitors into passionate advocates for what they have discovered when they return home or when they engage with their friends, followers and colleagues on social media. A curse, as the potential tourists in these key markets are unlikely to make a purchasing decision to visit Ireland in the absence of either standout destination propositions in the marketplace, or in the face of an information deficit about Ireland or any of the possible or potential experiences within it. Instead, they are likely to actively consider a plethora of specifically regional choices both within their own country along with a wide menu of proven, established destinations elsewhere.

In the eyes of the indigenous population, of course, the emphasis is rather different. Each river valley, parish, coastal area, townland, suburb, county, city, province – or whatever form a community takes – believes that it can differentiate itself sufficiently to entice the international tourist (primarily) and then also the domestic tourist and their locality (see Bell & Valentine 1997 for a deeper examination of this). Understandably, this can lead to difficulties, such as competition for exchequer funding both at local and national levels, duplication of effort and resources (such as market research, promotion and labour), reduced opportunities for economies of scale and a likely lack of focus in a national tourist proposition due to the existing fragmentation. For the international visitor to Ireland, their lack of local knowledge is compounded when faced with marketing messages and various calls to action for their business from, for example, places called "Shannonside", "The Lakelands" or "Ireland East". Despite the parochialism that can take place on the ground, there is evidence that Ireland is considered to be too small to present itself to visitors as a destination with multiple regions offering broadly similar packages. Ireland recognised this problem in the first years of the twenty-first century when the eight regional tourism organisations or authorities in place in Ireland (Dublin, Ireland East, South East, South West, Shannonside, West, North West, Midlands) since the 1980s were merged with the National Tourism Development Authority after its establishment in 2003 as part of a wider restructuring of the tourism framework by the government (Fáilte Ireland 2015b).

Despite the local competition for international and domestic visitors, it is worth noting that indigenous consumer understanding of the links between regions and purchase of quality products, such as food, appears to be good. This awareness of local products, driven perhaps by local loyalties, can be important to establish a reputation, and, if this translates into exposure in bigger markets, then the benefits may not just be limited to the product and the local economy, but could also bring other benefits in terms of establishing, or improving, cultural identity (Parrott, Wilson & Murdoch 2002). In addition, good food is strongly associated with spaces that are sites of transaction, where food transfers from the producer to the person likely to consume it, creating relations of mutual regard (Sage 2003). Yet there is also evidence that many Irish consumers identify with Ireland as a single region and this signals a low level of awareness and understanding of Irish regional food labels (Henchion & McIntyre 2000). Unlike consumers in France and Spain, but in common with those in the UK and Greece, the understanding of "regional" meant country of origin (Parrott et al. 2002). An obvious implication is that if Irish consumers had difficulty in distinguishing regionality in Ireland, then international visitors would, given the size of Ireland and the visitor's lack of local knowledge, experience similar difficulties, perhaps on a larger scale. Possible exceptions might include areas that are already components of the international Irish image, such as Connemara, the Ring of Kerry, or the Cliffs of Moher, although visitor and consumer research would be required to substantiate this view. The use of Ireland's regional imagery by organisations highlights how image is not just that communicated by a tourism promotion but through a wide variety of other activities such as literature, media, commercial advertising, the sector-specific promotional work of state agencies and personal experience (Henchion & McIntyre 2000). Examples of commercial advertising that impact the Irish image internationally are easily found; Guinness, Jameson whiskey, and Kerrygold butter are obvious candidates. In the United States, American products such as Lucky Charms breakfast cereal and Irish Spring soap have specifically utilised themes of Irishness to sanitise or romanticise their commodities, and the advertisements for Irish tourism are perceived to translate the traditional American consumption of Ireland into a touristic concept (Negra 2001).

This perspective has proven to be important when considering the future development and marketing of tourism in Ireland and food tourism's role in that development.

"Regional" – now mediated as a visitor proposition

In its Review of the National Tourism Policy of Ireland, the Tourism Committee of the Organisation for Economic Cooperation & Development (OECD) noted:

> Tourism has become an important instrument of regional development, notably through the development of a vibrant and largely Irish-owned tourism industry, with enterprises and jobs dispersed throughout the island. Some of the key tourism areas are ones which have little or no industrial employment.
>
> (OECD 2004: 1)

Given the context in the previous section, it is clear that the notion of regional has a range of meanings depending on perspective and desired outcomes and that tourism has an active role in regional development, but what constitutes "regional development"? This, of course, depends on how the phrase is defined. Historically, it has been dominated by economic concerns such as growth, income and employment, but that perspective has widened to include social, ecological, political and cultural concerns (see Pike, Rodríguez-Pose & Tomaney 2007 for a more detailed discussion on this; also Hadjimichalis & Hudson 2013; Tomaney 2010). By 2009, the OECD identified how regional policy had evolved, citing evidence of recent reforms of regional policy in a number of member countries demonstrating a paradigm shift in relation to city and regional development (OECD 2009b). The objective of the new regional approach appears to be to boost national output by encouraging each individual region to achieve its growth potential based on actions in that region, on the principle that opportunities for growth exist across all types of regions (OECD 2009a).

How, then, is a region defined? The question appears to be topical enough to have a Wikipedia entry and, under 'Tourism region', it offers this view:

> regions are often named after a geographical, former, or current administrative region or may have a name created for tourism purposes. The names often evoke certain positive qualities of the area and suggest a coherent tourism experience to visitors. Countries, states, provinces, and other administrative regions are often carved up into tourism regions to facilitate attracting visitors.
>
> (Wikipedia 2015)

However, this appears to be overly simplistic, as contemporary regions cannot be only understood as neatly delimited administrative territories. They are inherently multidimensional, encompassing social relations that range from the parochial to the global. For example, Bell and Valentine include region in their outline of the continuum of places of consumption: body, home, community, city, region, nation, global (Bell & Valentine 1997). Within their consideration of "region", they elaborate on what they describe as "regional rhetorics" and how the notion or concept can be utilised as an imagined, producing or invented region. This means that regions are no longer only geographical or administrative, but conceptual, depending on the indigenous assets, as defined by the actors in the region: 'an essentialised notion of what constitutes the region – its selling point' (Bell & Valentine 1997: 161). This is not a new concept, where something distinctive, other than or perhaps in addition to a location, is the selling point.

There is the example of Bologna, Italy, where a local food product, Mortadella (a large pork sausage, which now has Protected Geographical Indication status under European Union law), became a symbolic catalyst in exporting the image of a destination or region – and this in the sixteenth and seventeenth centuries (Montanari 2012). In this case, Bologna, as a university city, had regular contacts and trade with Germany, France and Eastern Europe. Arguably, it is reasonable to regard this as a very early example of globalisation where a region can have not only geographical characteristics but also economic, social and cultural structures that differentiate it against other regions. Montanari makes the point, however, that the selling point alone does not guarantee success as a region – two other elements are required. First, there must be something distinctive, but that distinctiveness must also communicate an associated sense of quality which adds to its unique nature. Second, some sort of exchange is necessary to communicate the selling point, and in terms of the Bologna example, Montanari makes the point that: 'Identity does not exist without exchange. Identity is defined and constructed *as a function* of an exchange that is simultaneously economic and cultural, the market and the skill, the merchandise and the experience' (Montanari 2012: 163–164).

In the case of Ireland, then, the question has been how to construct a sustainable tourism identity around selling points which deliver economic, social, cultural and environmental benefits at local and national levels, while also attracting valuable business. The solution has emerged out of the challenging economic environment created by the international economic crisis that began in 2007 and 2008. In common with many other countries, Ireland found itself in a testing economic environment from 2008 onwards. This clearly had major negative consequences for the Irish economy in general (Lewis 2011) and for Irish tourism in particular. One positive outcome from the downturn was that it led to a fundamental review of the Irish tourism industry by the state and a redefinition of strategic priorities, target markets and segments.

In particular, the Irish tourism industry was in survival mode due to reduced tourism numbers allied with significantly reduced spending by consumers and visitors alike. This decline was evident in 2009 when overseas visitor numbers fell by 12 per cent and revenue by 19 per cent (Fáilte Ireland 2010: 9). The primary objective of the National Tourism Development Authority in Ireland, a government organisation known as Fáilte Ireland, was to help the Irish tourism industry to cope and respond to the unprecedented challenges presenting themselves. Although Fáilte Ireland had severely constrained resources, in common with all other state agencies in Ireland, its strategy for the period 2010 to 2012 focussed on supporting sustainable tourism enterprises, stimulating demand, and improving the wider tourism experience (Fáilte Ireland 2009), reflecting government policy on tourism (Department of Transport Tourism and Sport 2012). Given the circumstances, it is understandable why food in tourism, or food tourism, was neither a policy nor a strategic feature at this time, notwithstanding a regular commentary by established writers highlighting interest and activity on the ground (Goldstein & Merkle 2005; Andrews 2007; White 2008; Doorley 2009; Campbell 2010).

As economic conditions improve, both domestically and internationally, Fáilte Ireland is now focussing on generating growth and employment. Fáilte Ireland's vision for 2014–2016 is defined as:

> To promote and facilitate sustainable growth in Irish tourism by supporting competitive tourism enterprises to develop, sell and deliver valued, authentically Irish tourism experiences to new and repeat visitors.
>
> (Fáilte Ireland 2014: 27)

Realistically, this vision must be realised against a relatively new resource paradigm of frugality, prudence and considerable restraint by government. Consequently, the approach to development had to change by concentrating on areas where the greatest value could be added, rather than the traditional broad-based remit which public agencies usually adopt. Accordingly, one of the organisational goals for the 2014–2016 plan indicated a move from a "product" model to an "experience" model by implementing an experience development framework driven by market insight.

The first evidence of this as a particular outcome of the strategy was the establishment of the Tourism Recovery Taskforce (TRT). Established in 2011, this was a partnership between the tourism industry and state tourism agencies to address current and future challenges in restoring growth in international tourism to Ireland. The TRT commissioned research which involved a robust sample of 10,000 residents of Great Britain who had taken holidays in Great Britain and the island of Ireland at least once in the past three years. The researchers asked the residents to rate destinations on the basis of 30 motivational statements, and the results showed that they perceive the island of Ireland primarily as a short-break destination that competes mostly against domestic British destinations (TRT 2012). Furthermore, regional destinations such as Scotland, the Lake District, Wales and Devon/ Cornwall were identified as the island of Ireland's primary competitors for short-break holidays. Clearly, Ireland itself is seen as a discrete region by this market, competing with other domestic regions as distinct from other international destinations. Subsequent studies in France and Germany came to similar conclusions. As a result of the extensive research undertaken by the TRT, radical changes were initiated in the development and marketing of Irish tourism. These changes centred on the primary ideas around the brand that is Ireland, that is, its propositions to the target audiences, and these had to be strong, genuine and meaningful if they were to resonate with those target audiences. Consequently, Irish tourism has concentrated on developing and marketing three primary propositions

Ireland's Ancient East. This is supported by four distinct thematic pillars based on the following themes within Irish history: Ancient Ireland, Early Christian Ireland, Medieval Ireland and Anglo Ireland.

The Wild Atlantic Way. Ireland's first long-distance touring route, stretching 2,500 kilometres along the Atlantic coast from Donegal in the north to West Cork in the south.

Dublin. Distinguishing itself and its hinterland as a stand-alone city destination and an aspirational European short-break destination.

to three key demographic segments:

Social Energisers (young, fun-loving urban adventurers)
Culturally Curious (over 45s who want to broaden their minds)
Great Escapers (younger couples who want to get away from it all)

in four key markets (Great Britain, the United States, France and Germany).

This is similar to work done in Denmark, where carefully crafted place brands that respect distinctive cultural legacy can provide a rejuvenation in opposition to the wider global consumer culture in local markets (Askegaard & Kjeldgaard 2007). Effectively, Ireland is leveraging the demand for cultural difference by reconstructing local culture as commercial and cultural brands. Clearly, in this tourism development strategy, regionality is not a factor – with good reason, as has been seen with the insights gained from the research. Rather, propositions are regions. The propositions which have been developed actually constitute a new form of region based not on orthodox parameters such as administrative boundaries or geographic features like a valley or a city but on a concept likely to appeal to a specific demographic in a target market. As such, the propositions can deliver a considerable opportunity for development and growth and all that this entails, that is, maximised return on investment, regional spread, increased agricultural and services employment, and Everett and Aitchison's (2008) triple bottom line of economic, social and environmental sustainability.

Food tourism, or food *in* tourism?

In common with the overall approach to tourism development in Ireland, the genesis of Ireland's approach to food tourism also lies in the wider context of the global and domestic recession from 2008 onwards, described above. During this time, as has already been pointed out, food in tourism, or food tourism, was neither a policy nor a strategic feature in national tourism plans.

This changed in 2010, when Fáilte Ireland led the development and introduction of a *National Food Tourism Implementation Framework 2011–2013* (Fáilte Ireland 2010), a stakeholder-driven and consumer-focussed initiative which was designed to improve the range, value, quality and availability of food tourism products, events and activities. Essentially, this was about food *in* tourism, rather than food tourism. Such changes were intended to impact on how food experiences are enhanced over time and are therefore worth serious consideration. There was also a need to be cognisant of how individuals from other cultures and geographies experience Irish gastronomy, and for Ireland to take care that food was not being presented in a way which signposts exclusivity, as that would be in conflict with the well-known inclusivity of Irish hospitality. A working group of key industry stakeholders was established to assist in the development of the plan and support its execution. This approach was validated in an OECD (2012) study which succinctly captures the contribution that food makes to tourism development and in achieving broader economic objectives. In that study, Ireland was already recognised through its brand as being green and clean, which resonated in its food (OECD 2012). Domestically, however, commentators at the time worried about how realistic the Framework was going to be, given the highly fragmented structure of the tourism and hospitality industry in Ireland (Corr 2011) and the scale of the problem (White & Wynne Jones 2008). Conversely, there was evidence that recession focussed the Irish population on the importance of supporting Irish products and producers, resulting in changing food purchasing habits and generating a new appreciation of how good Irish food can be (Mossberg et al. 2014).

While there was significant 'on the ground' activity with regard to business supports, research, promotional activity, online business tools, and driving food quality and value, there was also a need to establish creative collaboration in communities if the implementation framework was to be relevant and effective. Historically, locals in their community constitute a powerful asset as evangelists of their region, as identified in the late twentieth century (Warde 1997), and appear to continue to do so. Locals are the emissaries of culture, and as Laudan (2012: 210) points out, 'what makes a food or a cuisine local is culture, not geography or agriculture or the "rich bounty" of the region'.

The challenge was how to harness the power of these locals, the people that call their locality their home. Consequently, in 2012, Fáilte Ireland embarked on a journey of discovery and engagement to find and work with those locals. A social media campaign was launched to identify, through peer selection in their communities, local emerging food "ambassadors". The peers were asked to nominate those in their locality who had a resounding passion and belief in Irish food, together with the commitment and drive to actively influence and shape the future of food in tourism and Irish cuisine in their region. Fourteen ambassadors were selected and taken on a benchmarking trip to Ontario, Canada, to see best practice first hand and meet to the individuals involved (for a summary of their approach, see Ontario Culinary Tourism Alliance 2015). This exposed them to new ideas and ways of doing things that they could implement in Ireland. The exercise was repeated in 2013 and the new group visited Norway driving routes, which tied in with Fáilte Ireland's objectives of establishing quality food experiences along the Wild Atlantic Way. Currently, there are now 22 food ambassadors (see Fáilte Ireland 2015a) who act as change agents, actively influencing food experience development in their areas so that it supports the appropriate proposition for their area, while also exchanging information with those operating at national level in Fáilte Ireland.

Given the fundamental competitive changes, the Food Ambassadors' relationship, the greater emphasis being placed on key propositions, and the growing significance of food in tourism, the *National Food Tourism Implementation Framework* required review. An important element of the review was the insights gained from research, particularly in terms of changing perceptions about the role of food in tourism. Heretofore, food tourism was frequently viewed in somewhat narrow terms as applying predominantly to visitors whose main travel motivation was food. In the context of visitors to Ireland, the research showed that 80 per cent of tourists are 'food positive' in that food motivates satisfaction, while only 10 per cent were 'food enthusiasts' in that food motivates travel (Fáilte Ireland 2014: 26). The remaining 10 per cent were identified as 'general tourists', with low levels of interest in food. This insight is important in that it signals that food is an element of a visit to Ireland, but is not yet the primary reason to come. This is not necessarily bad news, but tourists must be on location to consume the food experience, and if it drives overall satisfaction for 80 per cent of tourists to Ireland, then food is important in the wider context. By simply arriving, the tourist initiates a range of other opportunities for tourism providers and the wider economy. Food in tourism, therefore, is not only an instrument of destination development, but also general economic development (Mulcahy 2015).

The outcome of the Framework review was the *Food Tourism Activity Plan 2014–2016*, which proposes a more facilitative, rather than hands on, approach (Fáilte Ireland 2014). Specifically, the objective of the plan is the continued development of a ground-up approach to developing Irish food tourism credentials based on robust insights and a strong belief that most innovation comes from local community-driven networks and collaboration. Thus, as a starting point, food in tourism is being integrated as a part of the overall proposition of coming to Ireland, leading to gains in social, cultural and economic capital. There is already evidence that a significant contribution by food in tourism is realistic, viable and sustainable (Mulcahy 2014). Currently, food in tourism offers a scalable, cost-effective means of local and regional development, with the potential to strengthen identity, enhance appreciation of the environment and encourage the regeneration of local heritage and the local economy. In such a scenario, as the provision of food in tourism matures, the plan provides for the prospect that Ireland could become a food tourism destination. This can be achieved through thought leadership, enhancing and championing food experiences, and capacity building, thereby driving incremental development opportunities in every county of Ireland (Fáilte Ireland 2014).

In conclusion, it appears that the notion of regional development is being redefined and contextualised in a world where promotion is global and experience consumption is local, but remaining critical to local and national economies, nonetheless. For an island destination like Ireland, whose primary markets are external, regionality can only be sustainably utilised as a commercial brand to attract visitors. However, the benefits in terms of development remain considerable, particularly in the role that food can play as a factor of satisfaction for the tourist; as a generator of employment, revenue and growth for the economy; and as a sustainable means of preserving and maintaining cultural, social and environmental assets in the community. The key, however, is a thorough understanding of the difference between food in tourism and food tourism, how to capitalise on each one and how the tourist perceives both.

References

Andrews, C. (2007) 'Ireland from farm to fork', *Saveur*, USA, 12 March. Available online: <http://www.saveur.com/article/Travels/Ireland-from-Farm-to-Fork> (accessed 7 December 2015).

Askegaard, S. and Kjeldgaard, D. (2007) 'Here, there, and everywhere: place branding and gastronomical globalization in a macromarketing perspective', *Journal of Macromarketing*, 27: 138–147.

Bell, D. and Valentine, G. (1997) *Consuming Geographies: We Are Where We Eat*, London: Routledge.

Campbell, G. (2010) *Ireland for Food Lovers: Everything the Food Lover in Ireland Needs to Know*, Dublin: Georgina Campbell Guides.

Corr, F. (2011) Is food tourism 'for real'? *Hospitalityenews*, 14 March. Available online: <http://hospitalityenews.ie/index.php/tourism/5338-is-food-tourism-for-real-> (accessed 7 April 2015).

Department of Transport Tourism and Sport (2012) *Statement of Strategy 2011–2014*, Dublin: Irish Government.

Doorley, T. (2009) 'Tom Doorley's selection: restaurant list 2009', *The Irish Times*, 26 September.

du Rand, G.E. and Heath, E. (2006) 'Towards a framework for food tourism as an element of destination marketing', *Current Issues in Tourism*, 9: 206–234.

European Union (EU) (2015) *Ireland*, Brussels: EU. Available online: <http://europa.eu/about-eu/countries/member-countries/ireland/index_en.htm> (accessed 8 April 2015).

Everett, S. and Aitchison, C. (2008) 'The role of food tourism in sustaining regional identity: a case study of Cornwall, South West England', *Journal of Sustainable Tourism*, 16: 150–167.

Fáilte Ireland (2009) *Strategy Statement 2010–2012*, Dublin: Fáilte Ireland.

Fáilte Ireland (2010) *National Food Tourism Implementation Framework 2011–2013*, Dublin: Fáilte Ireland.

Fáilte Ireland (2014) *Enhancing Irish Food Experiences – The Way Forward. Food Tourism Activity Plan 2014–2016*, Dublin: Fáilte Ireland.

Fáilte Ireland (2015a) *Food Champions*, Dublin: Fáilte Ireland. Available online: <http://www.failteireland.ie/Supports/Food-Tourism-in-Ireland/Food-Champions.aspx> (accessed 10 July 2015).

Fáilte Ireland (2015b) *Our History*, Dublin: Fáilte Ireland. Available online: <http://www.failteireland.ie/Footer/What-We-Do/Our-History.aspx> (accessed 15 June 2015).

Fáilte Ireland (2015c) *Tourism Facts 2014: Preliminary*, Dublin: Fáilte Ireland.

Goldstein, D. and Merkle, K. (eds) (2005) *Culinary Cultures of Europe: Identity, Diversity and Dialogue*, Strasbourg: Council of Europe Publishing.

Hadjimichalis, C. and Hudson, R. (2013) 'Contemporary crisis across Europe and the crisis of regional development theories', *Regional Studies*, 48: 208–218.

Henchion, M. and McIntyre, B. (2000) 'Regional imagery and quality products: the Irish experience', *British Food Journal*, 102: 630–644.

Laudan, R. (2012) 'Afterword', in B.N. Lawrance and C.T. de la Peña (eds) *Local Foods Meet Global Foodways: Tasting History*, London: Routledge, pp. 203–210.

Lewis, M. (2011) 'When Irish eyes are crying', *Vanity Fair*, March.

Montanari, M. (2012) *Let the Meatballs Rest, and Other Stories about Food and Culture*, New York: Columbia University Press.

Mossberg, L., Mulcahy, J., Shah, N.M. and Svensson, I. (2014) 'Best practices in destination food tourism branding', in E. Wolf, J. Bussell, C. Campbell, K. McAree, and W. Lange-Faria (eds) *Have Fork Will Travel: A Practical Handbook for Food and Drink Tourism Professionals*, Portland, Oregon: World Food Travel Association, pp. 337–352.

Mulcahy, J.D. (2014) 'Transforming Ireland through gastronomic nationalism promoted and practiced by government, business, and civil society', in M. Mac Con Iomaire and E. Maher (eds) *Tickling the Palate: Gastronomy in Irish Literature and Culture*, Oxford: Peter Lang, pp. 159–173.

Mulcahy, J.D. (2015) 'Future consumption: gastronomy and public policy', in I. Yeoman, U. Mcmahon-Beattie, K. Fields, J. Albrecht, and K. Meethan (eds) *The Future of Food Tourism: Foodies, Experiences, Exclusivity, Visions and Political Capital*, Bristol: Channel View Publications, pp. 75–86.

Negra, D. (2001) 'Consuming Ireland: lucky charms cereal, Irish spring soap and 1-800-Shamrock', *Cultural Studies*, 15: 76–97.

Ontario Culinary Tourism Alliance (2015) 'The rise of food tourism', *Skift Trends Reports*. Available online: <http://products.skift.com/trend/free-report-the-rise-of-food-tourism/> (accessed 6 April 2015).

Organization for Economic Cooperation and Development (OECD) (2004) *National Tourism Policy Review of Ireland*, Paris: OECD.

OECD (2009a) *Policy Brief: How Regions Grow*, Paris: OECD.

OECD (2009b) *Regions Matter: Economic Recovery, Innovation and Sustainable Growth*, Paris: OECD.

OECD (2012) *Food and the Tourism Experience: The OECD-Korea Workshop, OECD Studies on Tourism*, Paris: OECD.

Parrott, N., Wilson, N. and Murdoch, J. (2002) 'Spatializing quality: regional protection and the alternative geography of food', *European Urban and Regional Studies*, 9: 241–261.

Pike, A., Rodríguez-Pose, A. and Tomaney, J. (2007) 'What kind of local and regional development and for whom?' *Regional Studies*, 41: 1253–1269.

Richards, G. (2002) 'Gastronomy: an essential ingredient in tourism production and consumption?' in A.-M. Hjalager and G. Richards (eds) *Tourism and Gastronomy*, London: Routledge, pp. 2–20.

Sage, C. (2003) 'Social embeddedness and relations of regard: alternative "good food" networks in south-west Ireland', *Journal of Rural Studies*, 19: 47–60.

Sims, R. (2009) 'Food, place and authenticity: local food and the sustainable tourism experience', *Journal of Sustainable Tourism*, 17: 321–336.

Tomaney, J. (2010) *Place-Based Approaches to Regional Development: Global Trends and Australian Implications*, Sydney: Australian Business Foundation.

Tourism Recovery Taskforce (TRT) (2012) *GB Path to Growth*, Dublin: Fáilte Ireland, North Ireland Tourist Board and Tourism Ireland.

Warde, A. (1997) *Consumption Food and Taste*, London: Sage.

White, T. (ed.) (2008) *100 Best Restaurants 2009*, Dublin: Dubliner Media.

White, T. and Wynne Jones, S. (2008) 'Food fight; the gloves are off. Why Dublin's restaurant heavyweights are suddenly in a fight to the death', *The Dubliner*, Dublin: Dublin Media.

Wikipedia (2015) *Tourism Region*. Available online: <https://en.wikipedia.org/wiki/Tourism_region> (accessed 7 December 2015).

15 Craft beer, tourism and local development in South Africa

Christian M. Rogerson

Introduction

Among others, Hall et al. (2003) and Hall and Gössling (2013) stress that the relationships between cuisine, place and experience are critical matters for tourism development. Bell and Valentine (1997: 149) go so far to assert that as localities and regions 'seek to market themselves while simultaneously protecting themselves from the homogenising force of globalization, regional identity becomes enshrined in bottles of wine and hunks of cheese'. Local food and beverages thus assume a vital role not only in regional cultures but are acknowledged also as essential motivations for tourists to travel to certain destinations and offering opportunities for diversifying local economic bases (Everett & Aitchison 2008; Foley 2009). For rural areas and small towns in particular, local food and beverages represent a potential basis for the making of "post-productivist" spaces and thereby to function as vehicles for local and regional growth or revival (Hall & Sharples 2008). Local governments in several countries now recognise the capacity of food and beverage tourism to enhance the sustainability of tourism development and correspondingly have launched a policy-oriented agenda to reinforce the nexus of tourism and food (Everett & Slocum 2014).

In deepening our understanding around the productive relationships between tourism, food and different kinds of beverages, researchers in tourism studies confirm that food and beverages 'can be a useful instrument of destination and general development' (Henderson 2009: 317). Currently, most scholarship around beverages is devoted to issues about wine tourism which has been recognised widely as a catalyst for local and regional development in many parts of the world (Hall et al. 2000, 2003). Among several examples, Portugal, Spain, France and South Africa illustrate the leveraging of wine, wine routes and festivals as anchors for local and regional economic development (Bruwer 2003; Correia, Ascencao & Charters 2004; Hall & Sharples 2008; Lopez-Guzman, Canizares & Garcia 2010). This said, apart from wine, the productive relationships of several other forms of beverages with linkages to tourism are highlighted. The agenda of beverages tourism has broadened in scope such that scholarship exists on opportunities related to products as diverse as coffee, tea, tequila, sake, whisky or bourbon.

Most recently, there has emerged and consolidated the growth of academic interest in beer and about the opportunities surrounding beer tourism as a lever

for locality development (Plummer et al. 2005). Against the backcloth of burgeoning international interest on beer and beer tourism this chapter interrogates
one facet of its emergence in South Africa, namely the appearance of a network
of craft beer breweries. In the international context of academic enquiry around
beverage tourism this focus is of interest for three reasons. First, South Africa
is a well-established culinary tourism destination albeit usually associated with
the activity of wine tourism. The latter topic has garnered considerable attention
especially concerning the wine farms and wineries, wine routes and food and
wine pairings which are iconic attractions for many of the country's international
tourists visiting the Western Cape (Preston-Whyte 2000; Nowers, de Villiers &
Myburgh 2002; Bruwer 2003; Ferreira & Muller 2013). Second, there is growing policy interest in South Africa in tourism's potential as a driver for local
and regional development and for addressing spatial inequalities in national patterns of economic development (Rogerson 2002, 2014, 2015). In particular, for
South African local governments charged with the mandate of promoting local
economic development (LED), tourism is now the most common basis for local
development programmes. In a recent national survey of LED strategies 87 per
cent of all South African local governments identified tourism as a driver for local
development planning; in the country's cohort of the most economically marginal (mainly) rural and small town districts 85 per cent were focussed on tourism
promotion. The popularity of tourism-led local development extends across the
urban hierarchy of South African settlements encompassing all the country's
leading cities, secondary centres, and especially its small towns (Nel & Rogerson
2007; Rogerson & Visser 2007; Hoogendoorn & Visser 2011; Rogerson 2013;
Rogerson & Rogerson 2014a, 2014b). Finally, as is documented below, South
Africa represents an example of the phenomenon of beer tourism in the Global
South thus adding a new element to the mainstream literature on beer tourism
which mainly is dominated by writings concerning tourism development in the
Global North (Bujdoso & Szucs 2012b; Rogerson & Collins 2015).

The growth of beer tourism and beer tourism scholarship

In several parts of the world, beer has become a tourism asset and a foundation
for destination development. European examples are those of brewery tourism in
Germany and the Munich Oktoberfest, Belgium with its range of vintage beers,
Ireland and the popularity of Guinness Stonehouse, the Netherlands with its
mix of lager producers and new craft beer products, the surge of beer tourism
in the Czech Republic, Slovakia and the Baltic states (especially Estonia); the
strength of real ale tourism in the United Kingdom; and, the recent renaissance
of micro-brewing in Italy (Niester 2008; Foley 2009; Pechlaner, Raich & Fischer
2009; Savastano 2011; Maye 2012; Jablonska, Pobis & Timcak 2013; Spracklen,
Laurencic & Kenyon 2013; Strydom 2014). Another dimension of beer tourism is
observed in Spain by Munar (2012) in terms of the drinking rituals and extreme
alcohol consumption which is accompanied by 'outrageous tourist behaviour'
exhibited in the 'tourist bubbles' of Majorca. In North America, both Canada and

the United States have witnessed the burgeoning of craft beers as a base for tourism destination development especially when accompanied by the establishment of beer festivals and of organised ale trails (Plummer et al. 2005; Baginski & Bell 2011; Howlett 2013; National University System Institute for Policy Research 2013; Eberts 2014; Reid, McLaughlin & Moore 2014; Shears 2014). Outside of Europe and North America the significance of beer tourism has been acknowledged in brewery tours and beer festivals in parts of China (especially Qingdao), Australia (particularly Victoria) and New Zealand (Rogerson & Collins 2015).

For certain observers the activity of beer tourism is considered as 'a young form of special interest tourism' (Howlett 2013: 32). Jablonska, Pobis and Timcak (2013: 67) delineate it as a genre of tourism in which 'participants are motivated by gastronomic experience of drinking different types of beer and typical atmosphere of brewing restaurants or knowing history and current technology of beer manufacture'. In common with other beverages its opportunities for energising economic and social development are under scrutiny across both city and rural environments most especially in North America and Western Europe (Niester 2008; Alonso 2011; Savastano 2011; Dillivan 2012; National University System Institute for Policy Research 2013; Dunn & Kregor 2014; Eberts 2014; Koziol 2015).

Notwithstanding the international growth of beer tourism, academic research on this topic is described as immature (Niester 2008). As has been documented, beer-specific tourism scholarship lags far behind the volume of research that is, for example, devoted to wine tourism (Rogerson & Collins 2015). Howlett (2013: 23) observes brewery-based tourism is 'a small and relatively unknown form of tourism' and Niester (2008: 1) bemoans 'a significant lack of previous research and associated theory' concerning beer tourism. Plummer et al.'s (2005, 2006) work on the Waterloo-Wellington Ale Trail in Canada was the pioneer study. More recent investigations examine an array of issues pertaining to the impacts of beer tourism for destinations; the characteristics of beer tourists; the organisation of beer tourism through visits to breweries, beer museums, exhibits, special events and festivals; and, a burst of works around the "spaces" of beer tourism (e.g. Niester 2008; Pechlaner et al. 2009; Alonso 2011; Baginski & Bell 2011; Bujdoso & Szucs 2012a, 2012b; Dillivan 2012; Howlett 2013; Jablonska, Pobis & Timcak 2013; Spracklen et al. 2013; Dunn & Kregor 2014; Eberts 2014; McLaughlin, Reid & Moore 2014; Minihan 2014; Reid et al. 2014; Koziol 2015).

Overall, it is evidenced beer production and consumption can be a means to revitalise or foster the economic development of tourism areas (Pechlaner, Raich & Fischer, 2009; Munar 2012; Eberts 2014). Henderson (2009), Dillivan (2012) and Spracklen et al. (2013) point out beer tourism is an integral part of tourists 'consuming' local heritage and of experiencing local history and cultures as reflected in food and drink. It is argued tourists perceive craft beer culture 'as being unique and authentic in opposition to commercialized mass-produced beer' (Munar 2012: 7). Indeed, craft breweries often emerge as culinary tourism attractions and can exemplify one of many ways that communities reaffirm local identities in the wake of the impacts of globalisation on homogenising tastes and products (Flack 1997; Schnell & Reese 2003; Hede & Watne 2013; Schnell & Reese 2014). Moreover, by branding beers with local themes a unique beverage culture can be fostered to enhance the distinctiveness of localities for tourism development (Schnell & Reese 2014). Eberts (2014: 196) asserts that tourism has surfaced as 'an important component of the craft breweries business model and increases their connection to local communities'. For Schnell and Reese (2014: 175) brewery tours 'have now taken their place alongside winery tours' and are 'a means of experiencing the "authentic" nature of a place'. So far only limited work has explored the nature of beer tourists (Francioni 2012; Kraftchick et al. 2014). The existing research findings point to the popularity of craft beers especially among Millennials – individuals born after 1980 – an age group who are 'seeking a taste revolution' (Kleban & Nickerson 2011: 34) and 'enjoy the enhanced flavors that craft beer provides' (Reid et al. 2014: 119). In addition, they typically also 'enjoy the sense of community that comes with a brewpub or (craft) brewery' and the exclusivity of directly supporting the "local" (Pendleton 2015). As a whole it is disclosed that beer tourists prefer visiting regions or localities where they can tour multiple breweries and taste multiple products, which gives further impetus to the establishment of beer trails (Howlett 2013; Murray & Kline 2015).

The international expansion of the craft beer industry

Since the 1980s the production of craft beers has been surging in several parts of the world (Patterson & Hoalst-Pullen 2014). In many markets the sector of craft beer outperforms the 'conventional' or mainstream beer industry segment on indices of margins and growth because of its unique product characteristics, organisational structure and marketing (Shears 2014; Koziol 2015). For example, in the United States, trajectories of a decline in beer consumption per capita and a "hollowing out" in the numbers of mainstream breweries have been countered by a concomitant burst in the growth and market share enjoyed by craft breweries (McLaughlin et al. 2014; Reid et al. 2014). In terms of their key characteristics craft breweries are small in production volume, independent enterprises, and focus on differentiation with their value proposition anchored upon 'utilizing both traditional styles, using malted barley, combined with their own unique formulas by adding non-traditional ingredients, hence developing new styles that have no precedent' (Kleban & Nickerson 2011: 34). Craft brewers are viewed as 'highly experimental, innovative, and opportunistic' with experimentation in different flavours and kinds of beer that they produce (Reid et al. 2014: 120). Competition within the craft beer segment essentially is rooted on product quality, freshness, product taste, strength and consistency (Kleban & Nickerson 2011). As this cohort of small producers is unable to compete with the marketing budgets of the macro-brewers 'craft brewers have been successful in the market place by providing consumers with a truly differentiated product' (McLaughlin et al. 2014: 135). Craft beers thus are horizontally differentiated with a limited number of substitutes. The central differentiating factor between them and the mainstream beer market is the uniqueness of the brewing style and the flavour characteristics of the product (Kleban & Nickerson 2011). Another distinguishing set of characteristics about the craft beer industry is that these purposefully local market-oriented producers exhibit close connections with the communities that they serve with, for example, involvement in corporate social responsibility programmes, local event sponsorships and a range of philanthropic endeavours (Reid et al. 2014). The global image and reality of the craft beer segment is thus described as a 'counter-culture business' (Koziol 2015: 8).

In international debates around the rise of craft beer two sets of explanations are proffered to account for its growth. First, is resource partitioning theory with its roots in organisational ecology, which holds that increasing concentration enhances the life chances of specialist organisations (Vermeulen & Bruggeman 2001). According to the logic of several organisational theories, the dominance of large firms in an industry should constrain the emergence and operation of small specialist enterprises. Resource partitioning theory challenges this notion by high-lighting the existence of a variety of industries in modern economies that exhibit simultaneous trends of increased concentration and specialist proliferation, viewing these two trends as interdependent (Carroll, Dobrev & Swaminathan 2002). When industries become highly centralised and controlled in monopolistic or duopolistic arrangements the large players are regarded as "generalists" and opening up opportunities for small firms to enter the market as "specialists".

Patterson and Hoalst-Pullen (2014: 5) attribute the worldwide burst of craft beer production to the fact that by the 1980s 'globalization was firmly entrenched in the beer industry, and few styles were readily available to consumers'. The consolidation of the global beer industry in the hands of a small number of global players thus 'left a vacuum for the modern craft beer movement' and allowed craft micro-breweries and brew-pubs to step into this vacant market space (Patterson & Hoalst-Pullen 2014: 5). Likewise, both Baginski and Bell (2011) and Reid et al. (2014) argue craft brewery expansion in the United States can be understood within resource partitioning theory whereby firms that address small niche markets challenge the monopolistic competition of the large enterprises that dominate the industry. Using resource partitioning theory Watne, Kautonen and Hakala (2012) suggest craft beers service a segment of the overall beer market that "generalists" cannot serve which underscores that being a specialist can be a highly viable and sustainable business strategy.

Carroll and Swaminathan (2000) present a rich analysis of the rise of the US micro-brewery industry and demonstrate craft beer's popularity arose alongside a shift in beer culture which was a reaction to the "blandness" of the pale lagers which were produced by the dominant large enterprises (see McLaughlin et al. 2014; Reid et al. 2014; Dighe 2015). New craft brewers capitalised on a market niche that macrobrewers were not seeking to address (Patterson & Hoalst-Pullen 2014). Koziol (2015: 4) maintains craft beer is positioned 'as an alternative to macrobreweries; not just in terms of flavour profiles, but in regard to business practices and culture as well'. Commonly, the niche of craft brewing is driven by entrepreneurs who emerge out of the home brew movement (Murray & O'Neill 2012) and initiate 'business from passion'. Watne, Kautonen and Hakala (2012) build upon the foundations of a typology of entrepreneurial role identities established by Cardon et al. (2009). In an examination of Victoria, Australia they assert that the craft beer industry is populated by entrepreneurs who experience 'passion' which unleashes energy, enhances commitment and facilitates efforts by entrepreneurs to adapt and deal with challenges in a dynamic business environment (Watne, Kautonen & Hakala 2012; Watne & Hakala 2013).

Neolocalism represents a second conceptual base invoked to account for the international growth of the craft beer industry. The initial term is often attributed to Shortridge (1996: 10) who describes it as 'the deliberate seeking out of regional lore and local attachment by residents within a community'. Increasingly neolocalism is viewed as a countermovement to the homogenising force of globalisation. For Flack (1997) it refers to the movement whereby people search to rejuvenate or preserve the local, unique qualities and personal aspects related to their community. Schnell and Reese (2003: 46) consider craft breweries signify a partial response to the 'smothering homogeneity of popular national culture' and a corresponding desire to 're-establish connections with local communities, settings and economies'. This reconnection occurs through processes whereby craft breweries concentrate efforts upon "the local" often utilizing the naming and labelling of their beers to create a sense of place and strengthen ties with local communities (McLaughlin et al. 2014: 137). Among others Patterson and Hoalst-Pullen (2014: 4) observe imageries of 'clear mountain streams, urban landmarks and other regional iconography have been used to foster loyalty to local beers'.

Hede and Watne (2013) stress craft breweries are reacting to the concerns of beer consumers that their space is being invaded by global brewers and instead driving a trend by nurturing a unique local "sense of place" for consumers, forging a set of narratives that humanise brands. Schnell and Reese (2003, 2014) state that neolocalism is refracted in the active, conscious and maintenance of attachment to place. Furthermore, through innovative naming and imagery craft brewers foster a psychological attachment and 'rootedness to place' which functions as a powerful marketing tool for their products. Strong emphasis is put upon local identity and distinctiveness with craft breweries 'important purveyors and promoters of place attachment in local communities' (Schnell & Reese 2014: 168). Overall, as Eberts (2014: 176) points out, because brewers usually must draw their key raw ingredients, such as barley and especially hops, from a variety of non-local sources necessarily they rely on evoking localness primarily through 'the art of brewing itself and the narratives of place they employ in their marketing'.

The rise of craft beer and the beginnings of craft beer tourism in South Africa

In common with trends in North America, Europe and Australia, there has appeared a craft beer sector of micro-breweries in South Africa (Collins 2013; Corne & Reyneke 2013). Until the mid-1950s the mainstream national beer industry was served essentially by three regional brewers – Ohlsson's Cape Breweries Ltd, South African Breweries (SAB) Ltd and Chandlers Union Breweries. In 1956 these three enterprises merged to create SAB (Mager 2010). During the apartheid era Mager (2008) documents the country's brewing industry experienced considerable growth in particular after the lifting of a prohibition on the sale of "European liquor" to blacks (Africans). Although several international brewing companies sought to enter the market they were unable to withstand the competition from SAB the dominant player such that its 'status as "sole supplier to the industry" remained virtually unchallenged until the demise of apartheid and the end of South Africa's international isolation' (Mager 2008: 272). Post-1994 there is renewed competition in the South African beer industry, albeit SAB's dominance in clear beer was little impacted. From its South Africa base the company began a phase of energetic international expansion which culminated with the merger and creation of SABMiller.

It is argued that following global trends and triggered by the enormous consolidation of SABMiller with its production of increasingly standardised lager and light beers, there emerged a countermovement in South Africa's beer industry resembling trends in other countries. This reaction against consolidation and lack of variety offered to local consumers essentially resulted in a revitalised interest in 'older' beer styles, such as pale ales, porter, brown cask ales, stout and bitters (Corne & Reyneke 2013). In this respect the development and growth of the South African craft beer industry can be explained in relation to resource partitioning theory and is not dissimilar to experiences of the UK and the United States during the 1980s. This said, certain noticeable differences are that the craft beer movement in South Africa occurred later and on a much smaller scale than in either the United States or the UK with the rate of enterprise formation gradual until recently (Corne & Reyneke 2013).

The beginnings of micro-brewing in South Africa are in 1983 during the apartheid years with the establishment of Mitchell's Brewery in the small coastal town of Knysna. This craft brewery was an isolated development, however. Only after democratic change in 1994 which accompanied a number of structural changes in the beer industry did there occur a larger movement of local beer consumers towards the artisanal crafted beers in preference to the conventional mass-produced beer products offered to the South African market by SABMiller and Brandhouse (Mager 2010). The craft beer market in South Africa is estimated currently to be growing at an annual rate of 30 percent as the consequence of 'increased demand driven by trends around authenticity and originality in the food and beverage space' (Standard Bank 2015). In one recent market analysis it was reflected that consumers 'want locally-made products with a story behind them rather than a mainstream produced product' (Standard Bank 2015).

Figure 15.1 reveals the emergence and growth of this industry over a 30 year period. Of note is how micro-brewery numbers increased steadily between 1983 and 2003. It is apparent that growth in micro-breweries stagnated during the 1980s as no new breweries launched. This is attributed by Strydom (2014) to political unrest, violence and the general uncertainty surrounding the transition to democracy. With the close of apartheid and peaceful democratic elections in 1994, however, an upturn in the rate of establishment of craft breweries is observable.

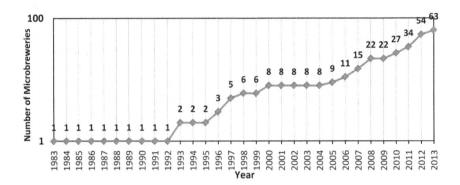

Figure 15.1 Development and growth of micro-breweries in South Africa 1983–2013
Source: Collins (2013).

From the 1990s an increasingly influential role in the expansion of the craft beer industry is played by the local home brewing community and of the activities of a small number of home brewing clubs mostly situated in the country's major cities. The most notable of these clubs are Wort Hog Brewers in Gauteng, South Yeasters in Cape Town and East Coast Brewers in Durban. The activities of these home brewing clubs are viewed as the foundation for the incubation by 'passionate entrepreneurs' of several craft micro-breweries (Collins 2013).

Based upon a national audit conducted in 2013 a national total of 63 licensed craft breweries is recorded. Throughout the 1990s and 2000s a small trickle of craft breweries begin to be launched across the country; by 2000 there were eight craft breweries in total. New craft industry developments mainly occurred in and around Cape Town and in the province of KwaZulu-Natal around Durban and 'the Midlands' as opposed to Gauteng, the major national market for beer consumption. It is suggested that the concentrated early growth of craft breweries in Cape Town and its surrounds represented a "natural" development which followed on the appearance and proliferation of boutique wineries in the area from the 1990s. Since 2003, however, there has been a surge of new micro-breweries spread across much of the country, including several craft breweries in Gauteng, South Africa's economic heartland. By 2008 the number of breweries had almost tripled to 22 in total. The most rapid pace of expansion is recorded in the following five year period from 2008 to 2013. An additional 41 licensed breweries came into operation resulting in near doubling in the number of breweries. The burst of new brewery openings in this period 2008 to 2013 accounts for 65 percent of the existing (2013) population of micro-breweries in the country. Strydom's (2014) investigation of the craft beer industry in South Africa confirms this remarkable surge of craft brewery establishment births during the period 2008–2013.

An uneven geography of craft breweries is recorded. The spatial distribution of micro-breweries at provincial scale is mapped on Figure 15.2 revealing the largest

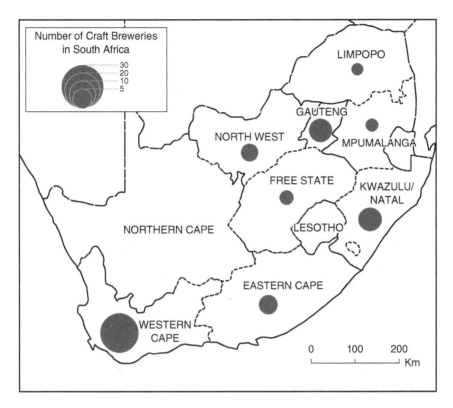

Figure 15.2 The location of craft breweries in South Africa 2013: provincial scale

clusters of breweries occur in the country's most economically most prosperous provinces. Of the national total of 63 licensed micro-breweries in 2013 the largest share are in Western Cape (27) followed by Gauteng (9) and KwaZulu-Natal (9), which collectively account for 71 percent of all licensed craft beer breweries. Smaller numbers of micro-breweries are situated in Limpopo, Free State, North West and Mpumalanga provinces; the Northern Cape is unrepresented in terms of craft micro-breweries. The dominance of the Western Cape is explained in terms of its first mover status as the location of many of the earliest breweries built in the 1990s and early 2000s, its local heritage of boutique craft wineries and its importance as a leisure tourism destination.

Figure 15.3 shows at the urban scale the location of all micro-breweries in South Africa for 2013. It is evident the greatest number of craft breweries are in the metropolitan areas of Cape Town, Johannesburg, Pretoria and Durban. Within Johannesburg and Cape Town a trend at the micro-scale of location is for establishing micro-breweries in inner-city areas undergoing economic regeneration and renewal. Examples are the Maboneng precinct of inner-city Johannesburg and Woodstock in Cape Town, both spaces of economic renewal linked to creative

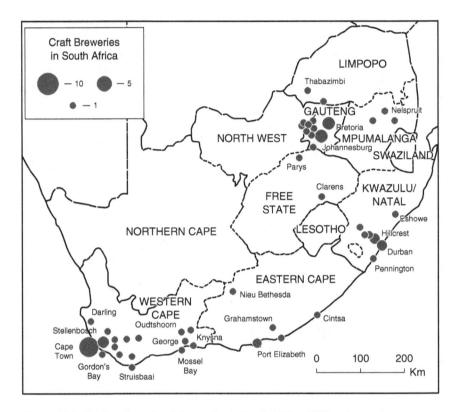

Figure 15.3 The location of craft breweries in South Africa, 2013: urban scale

industries. Outside of the major markets offered by the cities, micro-breweries are located in several other tourism localities such as Stellenbosch, Knysna, Mossel Bay, Cullinan, Clarens, Nieu Bethesda and the Natal Midlands.

This network of craft breweries provides the anchor for a new form of beer tourism in South Africa around craft beer. Mager (2010) shows that a small volume of 'heritage beer tourism' was generated by tourist visits to beer museums in Johannesburg and Cape Town which were created by the monopoly brewer SAB. The rise of craft beer opened a new chapter in beer tourism with the launch of brewery visits, brew pubs and restaurants centred on craft beer. In addition, several craft beer festivals, beer tours and routes have been initiated as further supports for the expansion and new directions of beer tourism in the country. In KwaZulu-Natal beer tourists are encouraged to traverse "the brewtiful country" (Corne 2010) across a beer route which is marketed as offering a highly specialised taste experience to parallel that of wine tasting with visits to five craft micro-breweries as well as two larger commercial breweries. Other ale trails and beer routes with accompanying tours to craft breweries have been initiated in Johannesburg and especially around Cape Town and its surrounds where such beer offerings often intersect with the area's established wine tourism. The target market for these brewery tours and tastings extends beyond domestic visitors; in Cape Town it would incorporate a segment of international tourists. Craft beer festivals are a further element of the growth of beer tourism. Currently, the largest of these festivals occur in Cape Town and Johannesburg and mainly are attended by local day visitors, mostly Millennials. In small town South Africa, however, a number of festivals are becoming tourism attractions with the majority of festival participants being non-locals.

Overall, at present, the major local development impacts of the emerging craft beer industry in South Africa are concentrated in Johannesburg, Cape Town and Stellenbosch, all established existing tourism destinations. This said, there is evidence of craft breweries in small towns functioning as local tourist attractions. Neolocalism is observed as these breweries invoke a strong place attachment through the naming of local beers, storytelling and brand imageries. Three of many examples of neolocalism are at Nieu Bethesda where the Sneeuberg brewery is named after the nearby mountain range; at Oudtshoorn the Karusa craft brewery derives from the local Khoi San language for Karoo meaning "thirstland"; and, at Dirk's Bru brewery at De Rust, where its local beer features a set of paintings produced by the entrepreneur's daughter, a well-established local artist (Collins 2013). Beyond neo-localism, with the hosting of local craft beer festivals and the geographical extension of beer trails into small towns, further opportunities arise for craft beer to become a tourism asset for local economic development in South Africa.

Conclusion

This chapter extends the mainstream agenda of research on local food and beverage tourism to include the commodity of beer. From a range of international examples it is evident beer can function as a foundation for the emergence and strengthening of tourism destinations. In many parts of the Global North, it is the shift to small batch craft beer, a reaction against the homogeneity of global beer brands, that is the driver for new forms of beer tourism. In South Africa, a destination well established for wine tourism, beer tourism is of rising significance. In recent decades the dominance of the country's beer market by a monopoly brewer has been eroded at the margins by the appearance of a thriving craft beer segment under the leadership of "passionate entrepreneurs". The current axis of the craft beer industry and of craft beer tourism is concentrated around the country's major cities which also are the leading tourism destinations of South Africa (Rogerson & Rogerson 2014b). In this respect craft beer and its associated tourism is reinforcing these destinations' dominance of the tourism space economy. Nevertheless, there is another strand in the craft beer sector, increasingly nurtured by neolocalism, which shows the possibilities for craft beer to contribute towards local economic diversification and the revival of many economically marginal South African small towns. In terms of the broader picture of local economic development in South Africa these are "little victories", albeit worthy of acknowledgement.

References

Alonso, A.D. (2011) 'Opportunities and challenges in the development of micro-brewing and beer tourism: a preliminary study from Alabama', *Tourism Planning and Development*, 8(4): 415–431.

Baginski, J. and Bell, T.L. (2011) 'Under-tapped? An analysis of craft brewing in the Southern United States', *Southeastern Geographer*, 51(1): 165–185.

Bell, D. and Valentine, G. (1997) *Consuming Geographies: We Are Where We Eat*, London: Routledge.

Bruwer, J. (2003) 'South African wine routes: some perspectives on the wine tourism industry's structural dimensions and wine tourism product', *Tourism Management*, 24: 423–435.

Bujdoso, Z. and Szucs, C. (2012a) 'Beer tourism from theory to practice', *Academica Turistica*, 5(1): 103–111.

Bujdoso, Z. and Szucs, C. (2012b) 'A new way of gastronomic tourism: beer tourism', *Acta Turistica Nova*, 6(1): 5–20.

Cardon, M.S., Wincent, J., Singh, J. and Drnovsek, M. (2009) 'The nature and experience of entrepreneurial passion', *Academy of Management Review*, 34(3): 511–532.

Carroll, G.R., Dobrev, S.D. and Swaminathan, A. (2002) 'Organizational processes of resource partitioning', *Research in Organizational Behaviour*, 24: 1–40.

Carroll, G.R. and Swaminathan, A. (2000) 'Why the microbrewery movement? Organizational dynamics of resource partitioning in the U.S. brewing industry', *American Journal of Sociology*, 106(3): 715–762.

Collins, K.J.E. (2013) 'South Africa's craft beer industry. In search of neo-localism?' Unpublished BA Hons Research Report, Department of Geography, Environmental Management & Energy Studies, University of Johannesburg, South Africa.

Corne, L. (2010) 'Along the ale trail', *TNT Magazine*, 26 April–2 May, Issue 1391.

Corne, L. and Reyneke, R. (2013) *African Brew: Exploring the Craft of South African Beer*, Cape Town: Struik.

Correia, L., Ascencao, M.J.P. and Charters, S. (2004) 'Wine routes in Portugal: a case study of the Bairrada wine route', *Journal of Wine Research*, 15(1): 15–25.

Dighe, R.S. (2015) 'A taste for temperance: how American beer got to be so bland', *Business History*, doi:10.1080/00076791.2015.1027691

Dillivan, M.K. (2012) 'Finding community at the bottom of a pint glass: an assessment of microbreweries' impacts on local communities', Unpublished Masters thesis, Urban and Regional Planning, Ball State University, Muncie, Indiana.

Dunn, A.M. and Kregor, G.M. (2014) 'Making love in a canoe no longer? Tourism and the emergence of the craft beer movement in California', in CAUTHE, *Proceedings Tourism and Hospitality in the Contemporary World: Trends, Changes and Complexity*, Brisbane, 10–13 February, pp. 190–198.

Eberts, D. (2014) 'Neolocalism and the branding and marketing of place by Canadian microbreweries', in M. Patterson and N. Hoalst-Pullen (eds) *The Geography of Beer*, Dordrecht: Springer, pp. 189–199.

Everett, S. and Aitchison, C. (2008) 'The role of food tourism in sustaining regional identity: a case study of Cornwall, South-West England', *Journal of Sustainable Tourism*, 16(2): 150–167.

Everett, S. and Slocum, S.L. (2014) 'Collaboration in food tourism: developing cross-industry partnerships', in C.M. Hall and S. Gossling (eds) *Sustainable Culinary Systems: Local Foods, Innovation, Tourism and Hospitality*, London: Routledge, pp. 205–222.

Ferreira, S.L.A. and Muller, R. (2013) 'Innovating the wine tourism product: food-and-wine pairing in Stellenbosch wine routes', *African Journal for Physical, Health Education, Recreation and Dance*, 19(Suppl. 2): 72–85.

Flack, W. (1997) 'American microbreweries and neolocalism: "Ale-ing" for a sense of place', *Journal of Cultural Geography*, 16(2): 37–53.

Foley, A. (2009) *The Contribution of the Drinks Industry to Irish Tourism*, Dublin: Dublin City University Business School.

Francioni, J.L. (2012) 'Beer tourism: a visitor and motivational profile for North Carolina Breweries', Unpublished MSc thesis, University of North Carolina, Greensboro.

Hall, C.M. and Gössling, S. (eds) (2013) *Sustainable Culinary Systems: Local Foods, Innovation, Tourism and Hospitality*, London: Routledge.

Hall, C.M. and Sharples, L. (eds) (2008) *Food and Wine Festivals and Events around the World*, Oxford: Butterworth-Heinemann.

Hall, C.M., Sharples, L., Cambourne, B., Macionis, N., Mitchell, R. and Johnson, G. (2000) *Wine Tourism around the World: Development, Management and Markets*, Oxford: Butterworth-Heinemann.

Hall, C.M., Sharples, L., Mitchell, R., Macionis, N. and Cambourne, B. (2003) *Food Tourism around the World: Development, Management and Markets*, Oxford: Butterworth-Heinemann.

Hede, A.-M. and Watne, T. (2013) 'Leveraging the human side of the brand using a sense of place: case studies of craft breweries', *Journal of Marketing Management*, 29(1–2): 207–224.

Henderson, J. (2009) 'Food tourism reviewed', *British Food Journal*, 111(4): 317–326.

Hoogendoorn, G. and Visser, G. (2011) 'Economic development through second home development: evidence from South Africa', *Tijdschrift voor Economische en Sociale Geografie*, 102(3): 275–289.

Howlett, S. (2013) 'Bureaus and beer: promoting brewery tourism in Colorado', Unpublished Master of Science in Hotel Administration/Business Administration Management Dissertation, University of Nevada, Las Vegas.

Jablonska, J., Pobis, T. and Timcak, G.M. (2013) 'Beer tourism in Slovakia', in KGHM Cuprum Ltd Research and Development Centre, Technical University of Kosice, University of Miskolc, *Geotour and Irse 2013 Conference Proceedings 25–27 September: Strategies of Building Geotourist and Geoheritage Attractions*, Wroclaw and Zloty Stok: KGHM Cuprum Ltd Research and Development Centre, Technical University of Kosice, University of Miskolc.

Kleban, J. and Nickerson, I. (2011) 'The U.S. craft brew industry', in *Proceedings International Academy for Case Studies: Allied Academies International Conference Orlando*, Florida, 5–9 April, Arden, NC: DreamCatchers Group.

Koziol, A. (2015) 'Crafting beer, crafting community: an exploration into the portrayal of craft beer', Unpublished thesis, Swarthmore College, Swarthmore.

Kraftchick, J.F., Byrd, E.T., Canziani, B. and Gladwell, N.J. (2014) 'Understanding beer tourist motivation', *Tourism Management Perspectives*, 21: 41–47.

Lopez-Guzman, T., Canizares, S.M.S. and Garcia, R. (2010) 'Wine routes in Spain: a case study', *Tourism: An Interdisciplinary Journal*, 57(4): 421–434.

Mager, A.K. (2008) 'Apartheid and business: competition, monopoly and the growth of the malted beer industry in South Africa', *Business History*, 50(3): 272–290.

Mager, A.K. (2010) *Beer, Sociability and Masculinity in South Africa*, Cape Town: University of Cape Town Press.

Maye, D. (2012) 'Real ale microbrewing and relations of trust: a commodity chain perspective', *Tijdschrift voor Economische en Sociale Geografie*, 103: 473–486.

McLaughlin, R.B., Reid, N. and Moore, M.S. (2014) 'The ubiquity of good taste: a spatial analysis of the craft brewing industry in the United States', in M. Patterson and N. Hoalst-Pullen (eds) *The Geography of Beer*, Dordrecht: Springer, pp. 131–154.

Minihan, C. (2014) 'Exploring the culinary tourism experience: an investigation of the supply sector for brewery and restaurant owners', Unpublished PhD dissertation, Colorado State University, Fort Collins, Colorado.

Munar, A.M. (2012) *Revealing the Attractiveness of Outrageous Beer Tourism*, Copenhagen: Copenhagen Business School Centre for Leisure and Culture Services Working Paper.

Murray, A. and Kline, C. (2015) 'Rural tourism and the craft beer experience: factors influencing brand loyalty in rural North Carolina, USA', *Journal of Sustainable Tourism*, 23(8–9): 1198–1216.

Murray, D.W. and O'Neill, M.A. (2012) 'Craft beer: penetrating a niche market', *British Food Journal*, 114(7): 899–909.

National University System Institute for Policy Research (2013) *The Economic Impact of Craft Breweries in San Diego*, San Diego: NUSIPR.

Nel, E. and Rogerson, C.M. (2007) 'Evolving local economic development policy and practice in South Africa with specific reference to smaller urban centres', *Urban Forum*, 18(2): 1–11.

Niester, J.G.A. (2008) 'Beer, tourism and regional identity: relationships between beer and tourism in Yorkshire, England', Unpublished Masters of Applied Environmental Sciences thesis, University of Waterloo, Canada.

Nowers, R., de Villiers E. and Myburgh, A. (2002) 'Agricultural theme routes as a diversification strategy: the Western Cape wine routes case study', *Agrekon*, 41: 195–209.

Patterson, M.W. and Hoalst-Pullen, N. (2014) 'Geographies of beer', in M. Patterson and N. Hoalst-Pullen (eds) *The Geography of Beer*, Dordrecht: Springer, pp. 1–5.

Pechlaner, H., Raich, F. and Fischer, E. (2009) 'The role of tourism organizations in location management: the case of beer tourism in Bavaria', *Tourism Review*, 64(2): 28–40.

Pendleton, J.L. (2015) 'Craft beer: manufacturing muscle meets local tastes', Unpublished Honours thesis, University of Tennessee Thesis Project, Knoxville.

Plummer, R., Telfer, D. and Hashimoto, A. (2006) 'The rise and fall of the Waterloo-Wellington ale trail: a study of collaboration within the tourism industry', *Current Issues in Tourism*, 9(3): 191–205.

Plummer, R., Telfer, D., Hashimoto, A. and Summers, R. (2005) 'Beer tourism in Canada along the Waterloo-Wellington ale trail', *Tourism Management*, 26(3): 447–458.

Preston-Whyte, R. (2000) 'Wine routes in South Africa', in C.M. Hall, L. Sharples, B. Cambourne, and N. Macionis (eds) *Wine Tourism around the World: Development, Management and Markets*, Oxford: Butterworth Heinemann, pp. 102–114.

Reid, N., McLaughlin, R.B. and Moore, M.S. (2014) 'From yellow fizz to big biz: American craft beer comes of age', *Focus on Geography*, 57(3): 114–125.

Rogerson, C.M. (2002) 'Tourism-led local economic development: the South African experience', *Urban Forum*, 13: 95–119.

Rogerson, C.M. (2013) 'Urban tourism, economic regeneration and inclusion: evidence from South Africa', *Local Economy*, 28(2): 186–200.

Rogerson, C.M. (2014) 'Reframing place-based economic development in South Africa: the example of local economic development', *Bulletin of Geography: Socio-Economic Series*, 24: 203–218.

Rogerson, C.M. (2015) 'Tourism and regional development: the case of South Africa's "distressed areas"', *Development Southern Africa*, 32: 277–291.

Rogerson, C.M. and Collins, K.J.E. (2015) 'Developing beer tourism in South Africa: international perspectives', *African Journal of Hospitality, Tourism and Leisure*, 4(1): 1–15.

Rogerson C.M. and Rogerson, J.M. (2014a) 'Agritourism and local economic development in South Africa', *Bulletin of Geography: Socio-Economic Series*, 26: 93–106.

Rogerson C.M. and Rogerson, J.M. (2014b) 'Urban tourism destinations in South Africa: divergent trajectories 2001–2012', *Urbani izziv*, 25(Suppl.): S189–S203.

Rogerson, C.M. and Visser, G. (eds) (2007) *Urban Tourism in the Developing World: The South African Experience*, New Brunswick, NJ and London: Transaction Press.

Savastano, S. (2011) 'Microbrewing – a renaissance in Italian beer production?' Paper presented at symposium '*Beeronomics: The Economics of Beer and Brewing*', Davis, California, 3 November.

Schnell, S.M. and Reese, J.F. (2003) 'Microbreweries as tools of local identity', *Journal of Cultural Geography*, 21(1): 45–69.

Schnell, S.M. and Reese, J.F. (2014) 'Microbreweries, place and identity in the United States', in M. Patterson and N. Hoalst-Pullen (eds) *The Geography of Beer*, Dordrecht: Springer, pp. 167–187.

Shears, A. (2014) 'Local to national and back again: beer, Wisconsin and scale', in M. Patterson and N. Hoalst-Pullen (eds) *The Geography of Beer*, Dordrecht: Springer, pp. 45–56.

Shortridge, J.R. (1996) 'Keeping tabs on Kansas: reflections on regionally based field study', *Journal of Cultural Geography*, 16: 5–16.

Spracklen, K., Laurencic, J. and Kenyon, A. (2013) 'Mine's a pint of bitter: performativity, gender, class and representations of authenticity in real ale tourism', *Tourist Studies*, 13(3): 304–321.

Standard Bank (2015) *SA Craft Beer Market Set for Fabulous Growth Trajectory*. Available online: <www.drinkstuff-sa.co.za/sa-drinks-stuff/683> (accessed 27 July 2015).

Strydom, N.T. (2014) 'The origins and development of the South African and Dutch craft beer industries', Unpublished paper, University of Johannesburg, South Africa.

Vermeulen, I. and Bruggeman, J. (2001) 'The logic of organizational markets: thinking through resource partitioning', *Computational and Mathematical Organizational Theory*, 7(2): 87–111.

Watne, T. and Hakala, H. (2013) 'Inventor, founder or developer? An enquiry into the passion that drives craft breweries in Victoria, Australia', *Journal of Marketing Development and Competitiveness*, 7(3): 54–67.

Watne, T., Kautonen, T. and Hakala, H (2012) 'Business from passion? An enquiry into the business models of craft breweries in Victoria, Australia', in *Proceedings International Council for Small Business World conference (ICSB)*, Wellington, New Zealand, 10–13 June.

16 Cheese tourism

Local produce with Protected Designation of Origin in the region of Galicia, Spain

Francesc Fusté Forné

Introduction

Food tourism has become an area of substantial interest for both academics and tourism industry in recent years. While food is an inherent part of any trip, and it is essential in the lives of both residents and visitors, travelling to experience culinary preparations or the food consumption patterns of a culture are at the core of the practice of food tourism. This chapter deals with the case of cheese produced in areas with an official Designation of Origin in Spain and is particularly focussed on cheese production in the region of Galicia, a rural destination where food plays an essential role as part of the identity of a society and in the shaping of a unique landscape.

Landscape, territory and definitely the sense of place are the signs of identity which give regions an authenticity factor that is turned into a tourist attraction and a destination's icons. At the same time, the landscape and the involvement of the community within the territory also becomes part of the framework for the holistic development of the linkages between agriculture and tourism – hosts and guests – that work together to promote regional development. In the context of gastronomy, cheese is a product strongly rooted in the territory; it is made from milk obtained from the animals which are grazing and feeding on the land itself. Visits to workshops, culinary tours, festivals or local markets are therefore platforms for the promotion and distribution of a product that has gradually become the focus of a specific form of food tourism type – cheese tourism.

Food tourism and regional development

When examining the relationships between tourism and agriculture, it is not sufficient to only consider the figures in terms of visitors or their expenditure, because if employment opportunities and incomes do not reach local people, communities lose more than they gain from tourism development (Telfer & Wall 1996). There are a number of authors who recognise the benefits of food tourism as a tool for the local and regional development (e.g. Telfer & Wall 1996, 2000; Bessière 1998; Hall, Johnson & Mitchell 2000; Hjalager & Richards 2002; Torres 2002; Hall et al. 2003; Sims 2009; Cebrián 2010; Valdés, Menéndez & Torres 2010; Díez 2012; Gössling & Hall 2013; Berno, Laurin & Maltezakis 2014; López-Guzmán,

Di-Clemente & Hernández-Mogollón 2014; Millán, Morales & Pérez 2014; Fusté Forné 2015a; Sidali, Kastenholz & Bianchi 2015). Food tourism is a key actor in regional development because of the close connection between food, land and community; and because, as well as including food specialties and food establishments, it also incorporates products and experiences that encapsulate both cultural and natural factors of a place (Richards 2002; Hashimoto & Telfer 2008; Sims 2009; Fusté Forné 2015a; Kim & Ellis 2015).

However, tourism development can provide for infrastructure improvement and potentially benefit the agricultural sector; it is not unusual to find that many farmers fail when they seek to change their traditional ways of working to respond to the special needs of tourism demand. Indeed, adjusting schedules and activities to the needs of visitors may be what makes them lose the essence of traditional agricultural activities (Fusté Forné 2015a). In rural and peripheral destinations, tourism businesses are often family-owned, and a limited number of people manage all aspects of the business, bookings, customer service, cooking, housekeeping, in addition to continuing to run farms (Hall 2004; Hall & Rusher 2004). Nevertheless, agriculture is the starting point of food tourism, because 'agriculture provides the product; culture provides the authenticity; and tourism provides the infrastructure and services' (Berno, Laurin & Maltezakis 2014: 113). In addition, there is a growth of niche markets that have revalued local food artisan producers, especially in Europe and Australasia (Barrera 1999; Henderson 2009; Hall 2016).

From the food producers' point of view, quality and quality assurance are understood as a strong marketing tool which also helps to increase sales (Hughes 1995). At the same time, increasing number of consumers are showing a growing interest in food tourism for various reasons: an increasing concern about safety in relation to food products, a growing interest in the environment and animal welfare implications in relation to methods of production, and, at the same time, a growing demand for quality food products and their perceived value in terms of appearance and freshness, taste and texture (Hughes 1995). In addition, Fusté Forné (2014) argues that production, processing and quality controls of the products, and the ways to maintain traditional values and allow development without damaging the underlying resources, are also crucial. One way to distinguish local and regional food is, therefore, their quality attributes, and especially food produced under certified quality standards linked to regional environmental and cultural characteristics (Barrera 1999). The added value which is created in the framework of products with a Designation of Origin is potentially also an important factor for regional development (Bigné 2011), which means quality production is set on a specific *terroir* (Tresserras & Medina 2008). In this context, the key to success is to integrate what is natural, what is local and what is traditional (MacDonald 2013), in relation to consumers who associate food consumption with the identity of a landscape and its authenticity.

Cheese tourism

Food is a heritage resource which takes on a much greater importance as a visitor's main motivation to visit a destination or a specific location (Hall 2016). The authenticity of heritage food is transferred to the tourism industry in products transformed into souvenirs, museums, routes or visits to farms and workshops (Timothy 2016), and also using local produce in the hospitality industry (see Chapter 17, this volume). Therefore, cheese has a high tourism potential and several uses as an appealing factor for destinations (Fusté Forné 2015c). Cheese tourism reflects the previously mentioned relationship between food, land and community through locally handcrafted production. Food tourism, and cheese tourism in particular, can contribute as well to the diversification of offers and reductions in seasonality of demand, based on a tourist use of a local product, while maintaining the natural and cultural essence of its culinary heritage tradition.

Cheese tourism involves visits to the areas of cheese making and milk production. Although cheese tourism as a specific type of tourism is little studied (Fusté Forné 2015b, 2015c), there are many references to cheese as a tourist attraction, for example, visits to the *Société des caves Roquefort*, the Wisconsin Cheese Factories (United States) or cheese producers' facilities in Canterbury Trails (New Zealand), as well as events or markets (Hall & Sharples 2008). There are also examples of researches that show the conversion of cheese as an agricultural product into a tourist product in some regions of Belgium (De Myttenaere 2011), Brazil (França 2012), Canada (Dumas et al. 2006), Costa Rica (Blanco & Riveros 2004; Blanco & Gómez 2010; Boukris 2013), France (Lizet 1998), Italy (Cantarelli 2001), Mexico (Thomé, Vizcarra & Espinoza 2015), Nepal (Yonzon & Hunter 1991) and Spain (Fusté Forné 2015d). The origin of cheese tourism is founded on the interest in the development of a product that is closely linked to the territory, from the pastures and herds which are the milk suppliers, until the retail selling point, both in their own facilities and in local and international markets. However, in the current context of globalisation, the existence of many small rural businesses is threatened because they do not reach high enough levels of productivity (Blanco & Riveros 2004). These local produce settlements could have an extra outcome if they were able to articulate themselves through rural tourism activities, where the provision of experiences would help to meet tourist demand.

Food products like cheese are able to provide a wide range of synergies that enable production areas not only to gain consumer and regulatory recognition (Ortiz 2003; Fusté Forné 2014) but also in consolidating the product as a pull factor for the destination. In this sense, the production of cheese has always been a symbol of regional distinction, at least in much of Europe, and over recent years, this product, and their ways of processing, has also become part of tourist circuits. Arguably, cheese tourism comes from the concern with the development of a product strongly rooted in the land, and it is now a type of tourism that includes not only the visit to the craft workshop but also complementary food consumption and leisure (Fusté Forné 2015c), which is significant for holistically oriented regional development. Nevertheless, although gastronomy is highly related to territory, culture and seasonality, food artisans may also have to become generators of experiences for tourists in their search of authenticity. An example of pseudo-backstage is found in the cheese cellars and dairies in the Alps, in the

Bregenzerwald – places where tourists are officially not permitted to enter due to hygiene regulations (Daugstad & Kirchengast 2013); however,

> cheese production on alpen is regarded a rare and even an endangered practice. Alpine dairies and the cheese cellars are places of production for the most valuable and prestigious products of agricultural activities; cheese that is wholly produced on alpen is said to be the best. Hence, cheese cellars and dairies on alpen are special places, which the farmers are usually eminently proud of and which many tourists are eager to view.
>
> (Daugstad & Kirchengast 2013: 185)

Growing demands for locally produced foods (Coren & Clamp 2014) can also benefit the creation of cooperatives of smaller farms and ventures within tourism sector, such as alliances between food producers, distributors, hotels and restaurants that promote the use of local products in the tourism industry (Telfer 2000). Cheese tourism can, therefore, potentially enhance the regional development benefits from the linkages between agriculture and tourism. The case of cheese and quality labels in the Spanish region of Galicia is described in the next section.

Cheese and quality labels in Spain

The process of cheese making was born from the need to preserve milk, through its transformation into cheese. The manufacture of cheese was initially the best way to use surplus milk at the same time as allowing its use throughout the whole year, as well as transportation and trade. In Spain, with a long tradition in milk production and the consequent cheese making, local producers of cheese are abundant, as well as the events which surround this product (Fusté Forné 2015c, 2015d). One of the most important features of this product in the Spanish context is the recognition at European level of 25 milk and cheese production areas as Protected Designation of Origin (PDO), and another one as Protected Geographical Indication (IGP). Almost two-thirds of the areas are on Northern Spain, and four of them are located in Galicia (Figure 16.1). The quality label of PDO gives to the production area a high visibility that benefits not only selling the product but also its conversion into a tourist resource with respect to cheese as a product and the region as a destination.

The label distinction is utilised to describe and brand a product whose production and processing are performed in a particular area and whose quality and characteristics are based on the various influences in the local landscape. The characteristics of each place, its sense of place, that is, its topography, soil, climate, hydrography and flora, are conveyed in the final product. Each region has its own regional characteristics, closely linked to territory and seasonality, giving as a result different smells and flavours and creating an authentic taste. This contributes to regional development through the various synergies between the cheese as local product and tourism and in Spain are reflected in examples like well-known cheeses as Cabrales, Idiazábal or Manchego, and also events as the Arzúa Cheese

Figure 16.1 Location of cheese produce with PDO and IGP in Spain

Source: Developed from Ministerio de Agricultura, Alimentación y Medio Ambiente (2015).

Festival (Galicia), the *afuega'l pitu* cheese contest in Morcín (Asturias), Trujillo Cheese National Fair (Extremadura), the cheese festival in Santa María de Guías (Canary Islands) or Artisan Cheese Fairs and tastings located in Catalonia.

Impact of the cheese industry in Galicia

The case of Galicia is particularly of interest because it has four PDO cheeses: Arzúa-Ulloa, Cebreiro, Queixo Tetilla and San Simon da Costa. It is a largely rural region, located in north-west Spain, just above Portugal. Galicia has an area of almost 30,000 km² and 2,731,406 inhabitants. It is divided into four provinces of A Coruña, Lugo, Ourense and Pontevedra and its capital city is Santiago de Compostela. The production of its PDO cheeses involves more than 3,000 agricultural units and a total turnover that, in 2014, amounted to over 30 million euros. Galicia is structured with small villages and farms scattered throughout its rural territory; its undulating terrain and temperate climate makes it an ideal area for cattle. For example, Galicia is the Spanish region with the greatest production of cow's milk (Xunta de Galicia, Consellería do Medio Rural e do Mar 2015a). Livestock has always been very important, especially in the central regions of Galicia, thanks to the optimum climatic and soil conditions. As a result of the high productivity of the agricultural sector, an agro-industrial sector has been also developing, especially in terms of production of feed, meat and dairy products, including cheeses as an outstanding product.

The four PDO cheeses are all made from cow's milk, from the breeds *rubia gallega*, *frisona*, *pardo-alpina* and their respective crossings. The Designation of Origin of Arzúa-Ulloa was achieved in 1995, and its production area covers over three provinces in the centre of Galicia, in the pathways of the Camino de Santiago (the province of A Coruña, Lugo and Pontevedra). According to Xunta de Galicia (2015b), the sensory characteristics of the cheeses *Arzúa-Ulloa* and *Arzúa-Ulloa de Granja* are a fresh milk and yogurt flavour and an aroma of butter which appears as the maturing time increases, with hints of vanilla, cream and nuts. The producers also solved the shortage and poorer quality of milk in summer, by making the *Arzúa-Ulloa Curado* cheese, with a longer maturation process (over six months).

Cebreiro earned the Designation of Origin in 1999. The production area is in the province of Lugo. The origin of these cheeses is attributed to the first monks who brought the recipe from France in the late ninth century and settled in the village of Cebreiro, which is the entry point of the French Camino de Santiago into Galicia and the main route of pilgrimage to Santiago. They came with the aim of helping in the hospital that was built to meet the needs of pilgrims. Throughout the centuries, pilgrims tasted this cheese, made in a form similar to a mushroom or a chef's hat, in the mountains of Cebreiro and making it popular throughout Spain and Europe (Xunta de Galicia 2015c).

Tetilla's Designation of Origin received its distinction in 1992, and milk production area includes all the Autonomous Community of Galicia. Tetilla cheese is characterised by its conical or tapered-convex forma, a straw yellow rind and a mild aroma but slightly acid flavour, reminiscent of the raw milk. Xunta de Galicia (2015d) states that it is the most traditional Galician cheese. Historical references regarding this cheese date back to the eighteenth and nineteenth centuries, when it was sold in markets and fairs, such as the one held in the field of A Illana, in the parish of Fisteus (Curtis) the fifth of each month. These markets were as important as Tetilla's cheese even used to be called *A Illana*.

Finally, cheeses belonging to the Designation of Origin of San Simón da Costa gained recognition in 1999. The production area is located in the province of Lugo, in the region of A Terra Chá. According to Xunta de Galicia (2015e), this cheese is characterised by two features in the process of production that give this cheese its special flavour and aroma: the basic raw material, the cow's milk, but especially the smoking process, which uses birch wood from the region.

Table 16.1 illustrates the overall importance that cheese production has in terms of regional development in the whole Autonomous Community of Galicia. A total of 3,518 dairy farmers and 72 cheesemakers are involved in the production of milk and cheese in Galicia, generating an output of more than 5 million kilograms of cheese per year with an economic value of €31,106,359 in 2014. Livestock, in relation to the production of both meat and milk, has been gaining importance in the economy, becoming the main activity of farms (Xunta de Galicia 2015a). In addition, milk production is based on family farms where feeding is done primarily on the basis of fodder produced by the farm and the purchase of cattle feed produced off the farm is scarce.

Table 16.1 Features of cheeses with PDO in Galicia, Spain

Designation of origin	Dairy farmers	Cheese makers	Production (2014) kg	Economic value (2014) Euro	Provinces	Municipalities
Arzúa-Ulloa	1 222	21	3 209 794	19 452 639 €	3	32
Cebreiro	7	4	41 256	408 104 €	1	13
Tetilla	2 188	36	1 392 169	8 687 135 €	4	314
San Simón da Costa	101	11	363 985	2 558 481 €	1	9

Source: Derived from Xunta de Galicia, Consellería do Medio Rural e do Mar (2015b, 2015c, 2015d, 2015e).

With respect to the role of cheese as a tourism product, there are several synergies that link agriculture and livestock with tourism. These product linkages, which include factory visits, festivals and markets, tours, souvenirs and quality labels, need to be exploited to expand economic impact. There are several examples of transformation of cheese from an agricultural product to becoming a tourism resource, product and attraction in Galicia. Quality labels are one of the main factors that create a platform for attracting tourists. Furthermore, the large number of local producers increases the chances of visits to the facilities, both farms and workshops where cheese is made. Another example is the presence of this product in the local and regional markets and fairs, such as *Fiesta del Queso de Arzúa, Feria del Queso de Cebreiro* and *Feria del Queso San Simón da Costa*, in Vilalba. These examples of promotion of this product create a basis for the development of cheese tourism, and they have an impact on the regional development, thanks to markets, fairs and also food souvenirs, as well as in the offering of local cuisine in restaurants. In addition, the relationships between cheese and other products that are also produced locally, as in the case of *Feria del Requesón y la Miel* (cheese and honey) celebrated in As Nieves, or *Feria del Queso de Friol y del Pan de Ousá* (cheese and bread), where cheese tastings are combined with honey or handmade bread, are also significant in Galician tourism. These synergies, which occur on food routes, are also a pathway for the economic impact of food tourism throughout the region.

Conclusion

Cheese is a traditional product in many countries, but especially in rural Spanish areas, as in the case of Galicia. This is a region with a long tradition in artisanal cheese making, and where the dairy sector is a very important part of the economy. There are a number of different ways in which cheese tourism benefits regional development, where cheese as a tourism resource can take on many guises: a tasting, a traditional craft or an ice cream. There is, therefore, a huge heterogeneity in the use of cheese as an attraction, for example, in a fair, a workshop or a plate. This chapter highlights the importance of cheese tourism for regional development as a result of the interrelationships between agriculture and tourism. Cheese tourism contributes not only to the economic development of a small settlement but also to wider regional economic development, especially because producers are spread throughout the entire region. Nevertheless, future research could identify the quantitative impact of cheese tourism as well as analysing how cheese tourism can enhance the sense of pride of local people and the motivations and perceptions of visitors.

Cheese tourism is able to create a link with the local culture and its culinary history that encourages visitors not only enjoy but also remember and to recommend. In addition, the tourist encounter occurs within a specific landscape in which, even when returning to the same place again and again, every visit is to some degree unique. Specific gastronomic products such as cheese can become a new type of tourism and contribute to regional development with a consequent economic impact through sales on local markets, use in restaurants, or events and festivals. Consumers are often seeking environmental and landscape values, history, culture and traditions, and these values are transmitted through food. Food tourism not only provides the taste and smell of a place in situ, but also can reinforce these when tourists go home (i.e. edible souvenirs). All of this occurring in a current reality of high competition among destinations that is challenging in terms of differentiation and specialisation, as well as the development of a sustainable but profitable relationship between the primary and tertiary sectors.

References

Barrera, E. (1999) 'Las rutas gastronómicas: Una estrategia de desarrollo rural integrado', *IV Seminario Internacional de Turismo Rural del Cono Sur*, Santiago de Chile, 1–3 September 1999.

Berno, T., Laurin, U. and Maltezakis, G. (2014) 'The special role of agriculture in food tourism', in E. Wolf and W. Lange-Faria (eds) *Have Fork Will Travel: Handbook for Food Tourism*, Portland: World Food Travel Association, pp. 105–114.

Bessière, J. (1998) 'Local development and heritage: traditional food and cuisine as tourist attractions in rural areas', *Sociologia Ruralis*, 38(1): 21–34.

Bigné, E. (2011) 'Las respuestas del turista ante la imagen del lugar de origen del producto', in C. Flavian and C. Fandos (coords.) *Turismo gastronómico: Estrategias de marketing y experiencias de éxito*, Saragossa: Prensas Universitarias.

Blanco, M. and Gómez C. (2010) 'La ruta agroturística del queso Turrialba', in H. Hernando Riveros, A. Lucio-Paredes, and M. Blanco (eds) *Una mirada a experiencias exitosas de agroturismo en América Latina*, San José (Costa Rica): Instituto Interamericano de Cooperación para la Agricultura.

Blanco, M. and Riveros, H. (2004) 'Las rutas alimentarias, una herramienta para valorizar productos de las agroindustrias rurales. El caso de la ruta del queso Turrialba (Costa Rica)', *Congreso Agroindustria Rural y Territorio – ARTE*, Toluca, Mexico, 1–4 December 2004.

Boukris, L. (2013) 'Du produit touristique à la figure territoriale patrimonialisée: La route du fromage Turrialba, Costa Rica', *Food Geography*, 2: 31–41.

Cantarelli, F. (2001) 'Formaggi tipici e turismo', *Economia Agro-alimentare*, 2001/1: 44–71.

Cebrián, F. (2010) 'Turismo rural, elementos definidores, estrategias públicas de apoyo y problemas estructuras. La perspectiva de Castilla-la-Mancha', *Revista de Análisis Turístico*, 9: 63–73.

Coren, C. and Clamp, C. (2014) 'The experience of Wisconsin's wine distribution co-operatives', *Journal of Co-operative Organization and Management*, 2: 6–13.

Daugstad, K. and Kirchengast, C. (2013) 'Authenticity and the pseudo-backstage of agri-tourism', *Annals of Tourism Research*, 43: 170–191.

De Myttenaere, B. (2011) 'Tourisme rural et valorisation des ressources alimentaires locales: Le cas de l'AOP fromage de Herve', *Bulletin-Société géographique de Liège*, 57: 37–51.

Díez, D. (2012) 'Los turismos de interior: Un enfoque desde la dimensión de las modali-dades turístico-recreativas', *Documents d'Anàlisi Geogràfica*, 58(3): 373–396.

Dumas, L., Menvielle, W., Perreault, D. and Pettigrew, D. (2006) 'Terroirs, agrotourisme et marketing: Le cas des fromages québécois', *Téoros*, 25(1): 34–41.

França, O.E. (2012) *O caso Queijo do Serro como Sistema Agroalimentar Local – SIAL: Complementaridade entre produção agroalimentar e turismo.* Brasília: Programa de Pós Graduação em Agronegócios, FAV, Universidade de Brasília.

Fusté Forné, F. (2014) 'L'autenticitat en el patrimoni gastronòmic: La Vall de Boí com a destinació turística gastronòmica', *3rd International Congress UNITWIN Network UNESCO Chair "Culture, Tourism, Development" on "Tourism and Gastronomy Heritage – Foodscapes, Gastroregions and Gastronomy Tourism"*, Barcelona, 16–20 June 2014.

Fusté Forné, F. (2015a) 'El turisme gastronòmic: Autenticitat i desenvolupament local en zones rurals', *Documents d'Anàlisi Geogràfica*, 61(2): 289–304.

Fusté Forné, F. (2015b) 'Cheese tourism: exploratory comparison between local cheese producers in Vall de Boí (Catalonia, Spain) and Banks Peninsula (Canterbury, New Zealand)', *13th Asia Pacific Council on Hotel, Restaurant, and Institutional Education (APacCHRIE) Conference, Hospitality and Tourism in a Greening World: Challenges and Opportunities*, Auckland, New Zealand, 10–12 June 2015.

Fusté Forné, F. (2015c) 'Cheese tourism in a World Heritage site: Vall de Boí (Catalan Pyrenees)', *European Journal of Tourism Research*, 11: 87–101.

Fusté Forné, F. (2015d) 'Las queserías en los espacios naturales: una comparativa de patri-monio y paisaje', *International Congress on Cultural Tourist Routes in a Creative and Innovative Society*, Jaca, Spain, 26–29 November 2015.

Gössling, S. and Hall, C.M. (2013) 'Sustainable culinary systems: an introduction', in C.M. Hall and S. Gössling (eds) *Sustainable Culinary Systems: Local Foods, Innovation, Tourism and Hospitality*, Abingdon: Routledge, pp. 3–44.

Hall, C.M. (2004) 'Small firms and wine and food tourism in New Zealand: issues of collaboration, clusters and lifestyles', in R. Thomas (ed.) *Small Firms in Tourism: International Perspectives*, Amsterdam: Elsevier, pp. 167–182.

Hall, C.M. (2016) 'Heirloom products in heritage places: farmers markets, local food, and food diversity', in D. Timothy (ed.) *Heritage Cuisines: Traditions, Identities and Tourism*, Abingdon: Routledge, pp. 88–103.

Hall, C.M., Johnson, G. and Mitchell, R. (2000) 'Wine tourism and regional development', in C.M. Hall, L. Sharples, B. Cambourne, and N. Macionis (eds) *Wine Tourism around the World: Development, Management, and Markets*, Oxford: Elsevier, pp. 196–225.

Hall, C.M. and Rusher, K. (2004) 'Risky lifestyles? Entrepreneurial characteristics of the New Zealand bed and breakfast sector', in R. Thomas (ed.) *Small Firms in Tourism: International Perspectives*, Amsterdam: Elsevier, pp. 83–97.

Hall, C.M. and Sharples, L. (eds) (2008) *Food and Wine Festivals and Events around the World: Development, Management and Markets*, Oxford: Butterworth-Heinemann.

Hall, C.M., Sharples, L., Mitchell, R., Macionis, N. and Cambourne, B. (eds) (2003) *Food Tourism around the World: Development, Management, and Markets*, Oxford: Elsevier.

Hashimoto, A. and Telfer, D.J. (2008) 'From sake to sea urchin: Food and drink festivals and regional identity in Japan', in C.M. Hall and L. Sharples (eds) *Food and Wine Festivals and Events around the World: Development, Management and Markets*, Oxford: Butterworth-Heinemann, pp. 249–278.

Henderson, J.C. (2009) 'Food tourism reviewed', *British Food Journal*, 111(4): 317–326.

Hjalager, A. and Richards, G. (2002) *Tourism and Gastronomy*, New York: Routledge.

Hughes, G. (1995) 'Authenticity in tourism', *Annals of Tourism Research*, 22(4): 781–803.

Kim, S. and Ellis, A. (2015) 'Noodle production and consumption: from agriculture to food tourism in Japan', *Tourism Geographies*, 17(1): 151–167.

Lizet, B. (1998) 'Le génie des alpages. Paysage, vache, fromage en Abondance', *Revue de Géographie Alpine*, 86(4): 35–50.

López-Guzmán, T., Di-Clemente, E. and Hernández-Mogollón, J.M. (2014) 'Culinary tourists in the Spanish region of Extremadura, Spain', *Wine Economics and Policy*, 3(1): 10–18.

MacDonald, K.I. (2013) 'The morality of cheese: a paradox of defensive localism in a transnational cultural economy', *Geoforum*, 44: 93–102.

Millán, G., Morales, E. and Pérez, L.M. (2014) 'Turismo gastronómico, denominaciones de origen y desarrollo rural en Andalucía: Situación actual', *Boletín de la Asociación de Geógrafos Españoles*, 65: 113–137.

Ministerio de Agricultura, Alimentación y Medio Ambiente (2015) *Turismo agroalimentario. Calidad diferenciada.* Available online: <http://www.alimentacion.es/es/turismo_agroalimetario/mapas_de_alimentos_con_calidad_diferenciada> (accessed 18 August 2015).

Ortiz, C. (2003) 'Gastronomy, tourism and the revitalization of festivals in Spain', in C. Sánchez-Carretero and J. Santino (eds) *Holidays, Ritual, Festival, Celebration, and Public Display*, Alcalá de Henares: Universidad de Alcalá, pp. 67–89.

Richards, G. (2002) 'Gastronomy: an essential ingredient in tourism production and consumption?' in A.M. Hjalager and G. Richards (eds) *Tourism and Gastronomy*, London: Routledge, pp. 3–20.

Sidali, K.L., Kastenholz, E. and Bianchi, R. (2015) 'Food tourism, niche markets and products in rural tourism: Combining the intimacy model and the experience economy as a rural development strategy', *Journal of Sustainable Tourism*, 23: 1179–1197.

Sims, R. (2009) 'Food, place and authenticity: local food and the sustainable tourism experience', *Journal of Sustainable Tourism*, 17(3): 321–336.

Telfer, D.J. (2000) 'Tastes of Niagara: building strategic alliances between tourism and agriculture', *International Journal of Hospitality & Tourism Administration*, 1(1): 71–88.

Telfer, D.J. and Wall, G. (1996) 'Linkages between tourism and food production', *Annals of Tourism Research*, 23(3): 635–653.

Telfer, D.J. and Wall, G. (2000) 'Strengthening backward economic linkages: local food purchasing by three Indonesian hotels', *Tourism Geographies*, 2(4): 421–447.

Thomé, H., Vizcarra, I. and Espinoza, A. (2015) 'Performancia y fractalización como herramientas de metabolización de los espacios rurales. El caso de la Ruta del Queso y el Vino de Querétaro', *Spanish Journal of Rural Development*, 6(1): 29–44.

Timothy, D. (ed.) (2016) *Heritage Cuisines: Traditions, Identities and Tourism*, Abingdon: Routledge.

Torres, R. (2002) 'Toward a better understanding of tourism and agriculture linkages in the Yucatan: tourist food consumption and preferences', *Tourism Geographies*, 4(3): 282–306.

Tresserras, J. and Medina, F.X. (2008) *Patrimonio gastronómico y turismo cultural en el Mediterráneo*, Barcelona: Ibertur.

Valdés, L., Menéndez, J.M. and Torres, E. (2010) 'El turismo gastronómico en Asturias: Análisis del gasto en alimentación según el tipo de turista', *Revista de Análisis Turístico*, 9: 55–62.

Xunta de Galicia, Consellería do Medio Rural e do Mar (2015a) *O Medio Rural. Alimentación. Productos de Calidad. Quesos.* Available online: <http://www.medioruralemar.xunta.es/es/areas/alimentacion/productos_de_calidad/quesos/> (accessed 15 August 2015).

Xunta de Galicia, Consellería do Medio Rural e do Mar (2015b) *C.R.D.O.P. Arzúa-Ulloa.* Available online: <http://www.medioruralemar.xunta.es/es/areas/alimentacion/produtos_de_calidade/queixos/arzua_ulloa/> (accessed 10 August 2015).

Xunta de Galicia, Consellería do Medio Rural e do Mar (2015c) *C.R.D.O.P. Cebreiro.* Available online: <http://www.medioruralemar.xunta.es/es/areas/alimentacion/produtos_de_calidade/queixos/cebreiro/> (accessed 10 August 2015).

Xunta de Galicia, Consellería do Medio Rural e do Mar (2015d) *C.R.D.O.P. Queixo Tetilla.* Available online: <http://www.medioruralemar.xunta.es/es/areas/alimentacion/produtos_de_calidade/queixos/queixo_tetilla/> (accessed 18 August 2015).

Xunta de Galicia, Consellería do Medio Rural e do Mar (2015e) *C.R.D.O.P. San Simón da Costa.* Available online: <http://www.medioruralemar.xunta.es/es/areas/alimentacion/produtos_de_calidade/queixos/san_simon_da_costa/> (accessed 18 August 2015).

Yonzon, P.B. and Hunter Jr, M.L. (1991) 'Cheese, tourists, and red pandas in the Nepal Himalayas', *Conservation Biology*, 5(2): 196–202.

Part V

Barriers and constraints

17 Barriers and constraints in the use of local foods in the hospitality sector

Hiran Roy, C. Michael Hall
and Paul Ballantine

Introduction

Over the past decade, interest in local foods has grown among the public as well as policy makers and researchers. This current "buzz" over local food has also captured the attention of chefs, journalists, politicians, farmers and food retailers (Mount 2012). In recent years consumer demand for local food has appeared to have grown substantially. Locally based food movements have emerged in North America and Europe in response to the perceived failings and injustices of the global industrial food system on economic, environmental, health and social indicators of equity (Blouin, Chopra & van der Hoeven 2009; Martinez et al. 2010; Gössling & Hall 2013). In North America the driving force behind the local food movement is consumer demand (Wormsbecker 2007; Central Oregon Intergovernmental Council 2012). Reasons for consumer support for local food systems include: wanting access to fresh food, wanting to support local farmers, wanting to support the local community and wanting to engage in social interactions (Feagan, Morris & Krug 2004; Brown & Miller 2008; Seyfang 2008; Vecchio 2010: Hall 2013; Hall & Gössling 2013a). Consumer concerns have also been associated with concepts such as trust, locality and transparency, animal welfare and food safety (Renting, Marsden & Banks 2003; Sonnino & Marsden 2006; Feagan & Morris 2009; Onozaka, Nurse & McFadden 2010). As a result, farmers' markets, food box delivery programs, community-supported agriculture and other forms of farm direct sales have grown in popularity since the late 1990s throughout much of the developed world (Hinrichs 2000; Zepeda & Li 2007; Hall & Gössling 2013a).

Canadian municipalities and their counterparts in the United States and other countries have begun to put relocalising the food system on the municipal agenda by forming food policy councils, drafting food charters and adopting mandates to develop 'just and sustainable food systems' for cities (Mendes 2008). Key components of such initiatives include the (re)development of urban and regional agriculture and the encouragement of shorter local supply chains, the most visible of which is farmers' markets (Hall & Sharples 2008). Farmers' markets have become significant for urban regeneration projects as a result of both their capacity to enliven public space and make a positive contribution to local economies (Hall 2016). In Canada, for example, Farmers Markets Canada (2009) report over a billion dollars of sales annually with an overall impact over three billion dollars. However, this growing interest in local foods has primarily been explored from the consumer's perspective (Martinez et al. 2010) and the role of farmer's markets (Hall 2013), with much less attention being given to other actors in the local food system such as restaurants, famers and food wholesalers and the interrelationships between the different actors.

While there is no consensus on defining "local" and what constitutes a local food system (Pearson et al. 2011), most definitions are based on a general idea of where local food is coming from (Dunne et al. 2011; Hall 2013). Local food systems are variously described as face-to-face agricultural markets (Hinrichs 2000), local food networks (Jarosz 2008), politically constructed boundaries (Selfa & Qazi 2005), and as an alternative to conventional food systems (Mount 2012). They are also closely related to ideas of sustainable culinary systems which, as the name suggests, focus on the social, environmental and economic dimensions of food systems including the role of restaurants, catering and food services (Hall & Gössling 2013b).

Local food is, of course, not new. Prior to the development of industrialised food systems, food, generally, has to be sourced locally, as evidenced by the existence of different regional culinary cultures in Europe (Askegaard & Madsen 1998). What is new about the current interest in local foods is that it is a reaction to the industrialisation of food supplies and the globalisation of taste whereby many attributes of local and artisanal foodways and production are either in danger of being lost or are already lost. Importantly, such concerns have also become entwined with growing awareness of the potential impacts of food insecurity and the need for more sustainable supply chains (Hall & Gössling 2013a).

Because of their capacities to purchase, promote and provide local foods, restaurants are an extremely significant stakeholder in local food systems. The US National Restaurant Association's (NRA) *What's Hot* publication has consistently claimed that locally grown products are the number one trend for restaurants over multiple years from 2009 to 2015 (NRA 2009, 2013, 2015). In Canada, according to the Canadian Restaurant and Food Service Association's (CRFA) Canadian Chef Survey conducted in early 2012, local foods were the hottest menu trend for the third straight year. The 2013 survey conducted by the CRFA had locally sourced foods topping the trend list again. Some of the perceived benefits of local food purchasing by restaurants include good public relations, supporting local producers, better quality, fresher and safer food, superior taste, supporting the local economy, ability to purchase small quantities and improved customer satisfaction (Thilmany & Watson 2004; Green & Dougherty 2008; Inwood et al. 2009; Schmit & Hadcock 2012). Nevertheless, there are also a number of perceived barriers to purchasing local food by restaurants, which include payment procedure conflicts, lack of knowledge about local sources, inconvenient ordering and delivery times, limited availability and amounts, variable costs, packaging and handling, lack of authority to choose suppliers, inadequate distribution systems, poor communication skills and additional time to process the food in the operation (Feenstra et al. 2003; Green & Dougherty 2008; Curtis & Cowee 2009; Inwood et al. 2009).

Despite these known barriers, local food sourcing has been linked to enhanced economic development in local communities and providing opportunities for both farmers and restaurants to promote environmental sustainability and create positive perceptions with customers (Jensen 2010). As Bachmann (2004: 1) suggests, 'selling to local chefs is among the alternatives that will help to build a diverse, stable regional food economy and a more sustainable agriculture'.

However, producer and farm perspectives on the benefits and barriers to marketing their products directly to local restaurants are less clear in empirical research. Furthermore, in contrast to the image portrayed in the food media with respect to the chef regularly purchasing supplies from the farmers' markets, little is known about the role of restaurants and chefs as purchasers and users of local food from farmers' markets. This chapter, therefore, presents the findings of a restaurant and chef survey conducted on restaurants in Vancouver, Canada. The survey was conducted to examine restaurant and chef perceptions, motivations and the barriers and constraints of buying local food and promoting local food ingredients on their menu from local suppliers. The researchers believe these data could help to identify strategies for more successful sustained local purchasing by hospitality sector buyers.

Methods

In order to collect primary data on the interrelationships between food service establishments and local food, a survey was conducted with the food service establishments in Vancouver, Canada, in 2014. The database was compiled from all businesses listed according to the type of cuisine served under the restaurant and catering establishment category in the city telephone book, while additional establishments were identified from multi-online website sources. This resulted in a database consisting of 759 food service establishments.

A survey questionnaire was developed that provided questions on demographic and respondent's choice of definition of local food, the respondent's use of and relationship to local food products and questions regarding attitudes and barriers towards use of local food products. All the questions were adopted or adapted from previous research related to the reasons of purchasing local food products by consumers (non-restaurant settings) from farmers' markets and from food service operations that influence their food purchasing decisions (e.g. Wolf, Spittler & Ahern 2005; Curtis & Cowee 2009; Inwood et al. 2009; Murphy 2011). The questionnaire was accompanied by a cover letter that explained the purpose of the survey and was addressed to the manager, owner or the chef of the restaurant establishment. The respondents were asked to answer closed Likert-scale questions. Descriptive statistics were generated in SPSS version 22 for all data analysis.

A total of 759 questionnaires were mailed out with freepost return envelops between second week of July 2014 and end of August 2014 to select foodservice establishments in Vancouver after follow-ups were also conducted to non-respondents. A total 69 establishments returned usable surveys, providing a response rate of 9.09 per cent (69/759), which is a typical response rate in other restaurant surveys (Casselman 2010; Sharma, Moon & Strohbehn 2014) as obtaining responses from industry personnel is difficult in the hospitality industry (Brown 2008). Therefore, the usable response rate of 9.09 per cent reported in this study compares favourably with studies of a similar nature in North America.

Results and discussion

Profile

Of the 69 respondents, 37.68 per cent (26 respondents) identified their establishment as casual/family full-service restaurant, 21.73 per cent (15 respondents) stated their establishment is an upscale full-service restaurant, and 17.39 per cent (12 respondents) described their establishment as a hotel restaurant. While 76.81 per cent (53 respondents) establishments were identified as independently owned and 13.04 per cent (9 respondents) stated their establishments were from the chain/corporate category, the remaining 10.14 per cent (7 respondents) were franchise-owned restaurants. All respondents held a management position in their establishment with 28.98 per cent (20 respondents) being chef owner/operators. The study was dominated by male respondents (89.85 per cent, 62 respondents), reflecting the highly gendered nature of senior management in the sector.

The most common style of cuisine served at the responding establishments was 'Canadian cuisine (included Contemporary Canadian cuisine)', with 31 (44.93 per cent) restaurants in the sample identifying this as their main cuisine type. Sixteen establishments (21.74 per cent) served mainly Asian cuisine that consisted of Indian, Chinese, Korean and Vietnamese restaurants (the result is consistent with Thorsen & Hall 2001; Smith & Hall 2003), while 13 establishments (18.84 per cent) served European cuisine which also included Italian and French restaurants. Different cuisines are also significant for local foods because of the capacity to supply specific ingredients at the local level.

Respondent definition of local food

Respondents were asked to choose from a single choice of definition of "local food" that included both a distance measure (radius spanning between 30 and 120 miles) and a geographic or political boundary (province). The majority of respondents (52.17 per cent) defined local food according to political boundary lines (the province of British Columbia), with 13.04 per cent defining local food as grown and/or produced 'in the metro or greater Vancouver area (lower mainland)'. Of those who responded in terms of distance, 11.59 per cent agreed with local being encompassed by a radius of 100 km (60 miles) of travelling distance from the restaurant and 8.69 per cent a radius of 161 km (100 miles).

Establishment's preferred source for local food products

All participants were asked whether they currently purchase any local food products/ingredients or not. Results from responses showed 92.75 per cent

(64 respondents) currently purchased local food products, while the remaining 7.24 per cent (5 respondents) do not. Respondents who purchase local food products were asked to identify all distribution methods through which they normally purchase for their establishment. Most restaurants and chefs utilise several local channels from which they procure the local farm products for their establishment (Table 17.1). Results indicated that wholesale distributor channels were associated with the largest share of ingredients purchased with 93.65 per cent (59 respondents) of establishments purchasing from local food service distributors. Local food service distributors were used most frequently followed by regional and national distributors (61.90 per cent and 44.44 per cent respectively). These results are similar to those of Reynolds-Allie and Fields (2012). However, it is important to note that the role of wholesalers in local food systems has often not received much attention because of the emphasis on shortening supply chains. In addition, 57.14 per cent (36 respondents) and 50.79 per cent (32 respondents) of responding restaurants have purchased direct from a farmer or from farmers' markets, respectively. The result is also consistent with Casselman's (2010) study where respondents preferred to purchase their local food products direct from farmers either via direct shipments from farm or pick up from the farm or other delivery method. Additional distribution channels included local manufacturer/processor, community supported agriculture and roadside farm stands.

To get a clearer idea of the specific channel utilised by the establishment, respondents were asked whether they currently purchase any local food products/ingredients from farmers' market vendors, farmers/producers and wholesalers/distributors or not. Findings indicated differences in local food adoption between farmers' market vendors, farmers and wholesalers/distributors. The following sections of this chapter evaluate and discuss the results from each of the supply channel used relative to previous studies and their roles within local food systems.

Table 17.1 Utilisation of alternative procurement sources by restaurants

Procurement source	Frequency yes	Percent yes[a]
Local distributors	59	93.65
Regional distributors	39	61.90
National distributors	28	44.44
Farmers' markets	32	50.79
Roadside farm stands	8	12.69
Direct purchase from a farmer/producer (not from farm stands or farmers' markets)	36	57.14
Local manufacturer/processor	35	55.55
Community supported agriculture	17	26.98
Others (please specify)	3	4.76

[a] Percentage is greater than 100, as respondents selected all that applied; thus, multiple responses.

n = 63 (one respondent did not answer this question).

Use of farmers' market

To identify the attraction of farmers' markets, respondents were asked to rate their reason for attending farmers' market according to a variety of attributes using a Likert scale of "1" (strongly disagree) to "7" (strongly agree). Of the 64 respondents, half (32) currently purchase from farmers' market vendors. Most attributes received a mean rating of four or greater, suggesting that respondents perceived them as beneficial to purchasing local food products from farmers' market (Table 17.2). The most highly ranked desirable categories in terms of agreement with respect to purchasing from farmers' market focussed on the freshness and quality aspects of the food as well as the significance of supporting the local food economy. In addition, the capacity to meet suppliers was also rated highly. These results reflect some of those of previous studies (e.g. Strohbehn & Gregoire 2003; Feagan et al. 2004; Inwood et al. 2009; Zepeda & Deal 2009; Duram & Cawley 2012; Hall 2013; Dodds et al. 2014).

The survey results also indicated that respondents recognise their role as promoters of local food products to be important in terms of agreement to provide culinary tourism experiences (see also Nummedal & Hall 2006). However, the results also indicated that about a fifth of respondents did not see themselves as promoters of local foods and visitor culinary tourism experiences.

Analysis indicated that there were statistically significant responses to attributes from different types of restaurants. The European cuisine style restaurants rated 'Food products/ingredients are safer' and 'Food products/ingredients are free from or use less pesticide and/or hormones' attributes as more important than Canadian cuisine restaurants. It was found that European cuisine style of restaurants most commonly chose the farmers' market vendors for their local food procurements. This is also an important finding, as it indicates that European cuisine style of restaurants in Vancouver think local foods are reasonably safe in being sourced from farmers' markets.

Of the 64 respondents, 50 per cent (32) do not currently purchase from farmers' market vendors. Respondents were provided 12 possible barriers and asked to rate their levels of agreement with respect to the statements using a scale of "1" (strongly disagree) to "7" (strongly agree). The four most highly ranked perceived barriers were 'Do not offer delivery' (mean responses of 6.00), 'Lack of time and staff to visit to the market' (5.84), 'Satisfied with current distributors' (5.29), and 'The volume cannot satisfied with the farmers' market vendors' (5.00) (Table 17.3). The identification of barriers in the Vancouver context is generally consistent with those other studies (Food Processing Centre 2003; Duram & Cawley 2012; Curtis & Cowee 2009; Schmit & Hadcock 2012). For example, the results of an Ohio restaurants survey reported that their dissatisfaction with low volumes of available produce and lack of time to visit the market were two of the noticeable barriers for purchasing local food products from farmers' market vendors (Inwood et al. 2009). When these results were evaluated in terms of the cuisine style of restaurants using one-way AVOVA tests, there were no other statistically significant differences found among these four cuisine styles of restaurants.

Table 17.2 Restaurants' attitude towards purchasing local food products/ingredients from farmers' market vendors

Category/Attribute	Entire sample (N = 32)				C (N = 10)		E (N = 8)		A (N = 8)		O (N = 6)		F-test	P-value
	N	M	Neutral	Rank	N	M	N	M	N	M	N	M		
Farmers' market(s) food products/ingredients helps me to meet customer demands	32	5.09	25.00	17	10	5.00	8	5.00	8	5.25	6	5.17	0.05	0.98
Food products/ingredients are able to serve a variety of menu applications to customers	32	5.50	15.62	12	10	5.30	8	6.13	8	5.50	6	5.00	1.20	0.32
Food products/ingredients allow me to charge a premium price	30	3.90	30.00	19	9	4.44	7	3.00	8	4.38	6	3.50	1.27	0.30
Able to get higher quality of food products/ingredients	31	6.26	12.90	2	9	6.56	8	6.50	8	5.75	6	6.17	0.99	0.41
Able to get fresher food products/ingredients	32	6.31	3.12	1	10	6.50	8	6.75	8	5.75	6	6.17	1.49	0.23
Food products/ingredients grown/produced locally	31	6.26	6.45	2	10	6.40	7	6.71	8	5.38	6	6.67	4.20	0.01*
Able to get uniqueness/specialty (including heirloom varieties) of food products/ingredients	30	5.57	20.00	11	9	5.78	8	6.13	8	4.88	5	5.40	1.13	0.35
Food products/ingredients have better taste	32	5.94	12.50	5	10	6.10	8	6.63	8	5.13	6	5.83	2.27	0.10
Food products/ingredients are safer	32	5.09	28.12	17	10	4.40	8	6.00	8	5.50	6	4.50	3.30	0.03*
Food products/ingredients are nutritious and healthy	32	5.69	25.00	9	10	5.40	8	6.25	8	5.88	6	5.17	1.18	0.33
Ability to obtain small volume of products	31	5.84	9.67	7	10	6.30	7	5.71	8	4.88	6	6.50	1.58	0.21
Greater availability of organic products	31	5.45	25.80	13	9	5.00	8	6.13	8	5.50	6	5.17	0.87	0.46

(Continued)

Table 17.2 (Continued)

Category/Attribute	Entire sample (N = 32)				C (N = 10)		E (N = 8)		A (N = 8)		O (N = 6)		F-test	P-value
	N	M	Neutral	Rank	N	M	N	M	N	M	N	M		
Know how products/ingredients were raised or grown	31	5.87	12.90	6	9	6.33	8	6.25	8	5.38	6	5.33	1.49	0.23
Attending farmers' market(s) helps to build working relationship with vendors	30	5.87	16.66	6	9	5.78	8	6.25	8	5.38	5	6.20	0.60	0.61
Attending farmers' market(s) allows to meet vendors and become acquainted with regional foods	30	6.00	10.00	4	9	5.67	7	6.71	8	5.88	6	5.83	1.13	0.35
Value for money	30	5.27	36.66	14	10	4.60	7	5.57	8	5.38	5	6.00	1.55	0.22
Required lower transportation costs	30	4.73	26.66	18	9	4.67	7	4.14	8	4.75	6	5.50	0.79	0.51
Food products/ingredients promote regional food security	32	5.81	15.62	8	10	5.80	8	6.25	8	5.00	6	6.33	2.16	0.11
Utilising local food products from farmers' market(s) is an effective way to promote local foods and support local vendors	31	6.23	3.22	3	9	6.44	8	6.25	8	5.88	6	6.33	0.44	0.72
Purchasing from farmers' market(s) allows to support local economy	31	6.23	6.45	3	10	6.50	8	6.50	7	5.57	6	6.17	0.83	0.48
Food products/ingredients from farmers' market(s) allows the establishment as a promoter to provide culinary tourism experience for domestic visitors	30	5.20	20.00	16	10	5.10	7	5.43	7	5.43	6	4.83	0.17	0.91

Food products/ingredients from farmers' market(s) allows the establishment as a promoter to provide culinary tourism experience for international visitors	30	5.23	23.33	15	9	5.11	8	5.75	7	5.14	6	4.83	0.50	0.68
Food products/ingredients are free from or use less pesticide and/or hormones	30	5.20	20.00	16	9	4.33	8	6.00	7	5.43	6	5.17	2.75	0.06*
Purchasing from farmers' market(s) helps to the environment due to the shorter distance travelled from farm to the market (food miles)	30	5.67	13.33	10	10	5.20	7	6.14	7	5.86	6	5.67	0.74	0.53

Note: Mean based on scale of 1 = "Strongly Disagree", 4 = "Neither Agree nor Disagree", 7 = "Strongly Agree". C refers to "Canadian", E refers to "European", A refers to "Asian", and O refers to "Other".

*F-test significant at the 0.05 level.

Summary of Post Hoc Tests

Food products/ingredients grown/produced locally	A < O < E
Food products/ingredients are safer	C < E
Food products/ingredients are free from or use less pesticide and/or hormones	C < E

The mean difference is significant at the 0.05 level.

Table 17.3 Factors affecting restaurant selection of local food products from farmers' market vendors

Category/Attribute	Entire sample (N = 32)				C (N = 10)		E (N = 8)		A (N = 8)		O (N = 6)		F-test	P-value
	N	M	Neutral	Rank	N	M	N	M	N	M	N	M		
Satisfied with current distributors	31	5.29	19.35	3	17	5.41	5	4.40	7	5.86	2	4.50	1.04	0.39
Prefer to have one supplier	29	4.52	17.24	9	16	4.44	4	4.75	7	5.14	2	2.50	0.89	0.45
Do not have time for several vendors	31	4.77	12.90	5	17	4.65	5	4.40	7	5.71	2	3.50	0.78	0.51
The volume cannot be satisfied with farmers' market vendors	30	5.00	3.33	4	16	5.63	5	3.20	7	5.00	2	4.50	1.82	0.16
Unsure of quality or consistencies of products/ingredients	30	4.70	13.33	6	17	4.65	4	4.50	7	5.43	2	3.00	0.69	0.56
Lack of information of products/ingredients availability	30	4.53	16.66	8	17	4.59	4	3.75	7	5.43	2	2.50	1.55	0.22
Do not offer delivery	30	6.00	0.00	1	16	5.81	5	6.40	7	6.14	2	6.00	0.32	0.80
Lack of refund policies	29	4.45	3.84	10	16	4.31	4	3.75	7	5.71	2	2.50	1.41	0.26
Lack of time and staff to visit the market	31	5.84	6.45	2	17	5.82	5	5.40	7	5.86	2	7.00	0.46	0.70
Products/ingredients are too expensive	31	4.65	19.35	7	17	4.47	5	4.40	7	5.29	2	4.50	0.40	0.75
Parking is a problem	29	3.48	17.24	12	16	3.31	4	2.25	7	4.71	2	3.00	1.60	0.21
Farmers' market(s) are too far away	28	4.39	3.57	11	16	4.31	3	4.67	7	4.71	2	3.50	0.16	0.92

Note: Mean based on scale of 1 = "Strongly Disagree", 4 = "Neither Agree nor Disagree", 7 = "Strongly Agree ". C refers to "Canadian", E refers to "European", A refers to "Asian", and O refers to "Other".

*F-test significant at the 0.05 level.

Use of farmers/producers

Purchasing local food direct from farmers/producers can be a barrier to using local food as opposed to the ordering from wholesalers/distributors. Of the 64 respondents, 35.93 per cent (23 respondents) do not directly purchase or do not directly purchase more from local farmers/producers for their local food procurement, while the remaining 62.50 per cent (40 respondents) of establishments are directly purchasing their local food ingredients/products from the farmers. Respondents were asked to rate the relative barriers of 13 factors that they perceived or experienced when purchasing local food ingredients directly from farmers/producers (Table 17.4). Results revealed that "Satisfied with current distributors" (mean response of 5.86), "Do not have time to contact several farmers, inconvenient" (5.65), "Farms are too far away" (5.57), and "Unsure of consistency of products delivered" (5.36) were the four most highly ranked important barriers in terms of agreement to the establishments. Although the highest ranked barriers have also been identified in other studies (e.g. Sharma, Gregoire & Strohbehn 2009; Casselman 2010; Duram & Cawley 2012; Schmit & Hadcock 2012; Dougherty, Brown & Green 2013; Kang & Rajagopal 2014), the role of barriers such as inconsistency of product delivery, inability to produce products and price appeared less problematic in this survey (Curtis & Cowee 2009).

Use of food service distributors

Findings from the survey showed that all respondents used at least one kind of distributor on a regular basis for a range of locally grown food products. When broken down into different cuisine style of restaurant groups, Canadian cuisine style restaurants utilise a higher number of distributors (up to 11), while Asian, European and 'Other' cuisine style of restaurants have used the lowest number of distributors to source their local food products.

Expected change in local food purchases

Many respondents expect to increase their purchasing different local food products from farms and farmers' market vendors in the future (Table 17.5). The results also indicate that as well as food being local, restaurants are also valuing other more environmentally friendly product attributes in their purchasing. However, the majority of respondents indicate no change in purchasing patterns in the short term. The findings indicate that establishments are currently satisfied with their vendors and farmers they deal with and may not prefer to deal with a larger number of farmers and vendors because of the time, quality and supply issues involved (Smith & Hall 2003; Nummedal & Hall 2006; Schmit & Hadcock 2012).

Is purchasing local food products profitable?

Respondents were asked whether purchasing local food products had a positive impact on their establishment's profits. Of the 57 respondents, 49.10 per cent of

Table 17.4 Factors in restaurant adoption of local food products from farmers

Category/Attribute	Entire sample (N = 32)				C (N = 10)		E (N = 8)		A (N = 8)		O (N = 6)		F-test	P-value
	N	M	Neutral	Rank	N	M	N	M	N	M	N	M		
Satisfied with current distributors	22	5.86	22.72	1	9	6.11	2	4.00	9	6.22	2	5.00	3.30	0.04*
Do not have time to contact several farmers, inconvenient	23	5.65	8.69	2	9	5.33	2	5.00	9	5.78	3	6.67	0.71	0.55
The volume cannot be satisfied with local farmers/producers	22	4.77	13.63	12	8	6.00	2	3.00	9	4.67	3	3.00	2.53	0.08
Unsure of quality of products delivered	22	5.23	9.09	7	9	5.67	1	7.00	9	5.22	3	3.33	1.55	0.23
Unsure of consistency of products delivered	22	5.36	9.09	4	9	5.67	1	7.00	9	5.44	3	3.67	1.16	0.35
Unable to produce needed products	23	5.35	13.04	5	9	5.56	2	4.50	9	5.22	3	5.67	0.46	0.71
Lack of information of products/ingredients availability	22	5.09	13.63	10	9	5.00	1	4.00	9	5.44	3	4.67	0.36	0.78
Do not offer delivery	22	4.91	4.54	11	9	4.56	1	4.00	9	5.22	3	5.33	0.23	0.87
Products are not delivered on the date or time agreed	21	5.14	28.57	9	8	5.75	2	5.50	9	4.56	2	5.00	1.05	0.39
Local health and food safety issues	22	5.32	0.00	6	9	5.89	1	6.00	9	5.44	3	3.00	1.86	0.17
Unable to provide formal receipts	22	5.18	9.09	8	9	5.67	2	6.00	8	4.5	3	5.00	0.77	0.52
Price of the products/ingredients are too high	22	5.32	18.18	6	9	5.67	2	6.00	9	5.00	2	4.50	0.70	0.56
Farms are too far away	21	5.57	4.76	3	8	5.38	2	3.50	8	5.75	3	7.00	1.54	0.23

Note: Mean based on scale of 1 = "Strongly Disagree", 4 = "Neither Agree nor Disagree", 7 = "Strongly Agree". C refers to "Canadian", E refers to "European", A refers to "Asian", and O refers to "Other".

*F-test significant at the 0.05 level.

Summary of Post Hoc Tests

Satisfied with current distributors (1)	E < C < A

The mean difference is significant at the 0.05 level.

Table 17.5 Expectations of future local purchase by restaurants from vendors and farmers

Farmers	Farmers Increasing	Decreasing	Staying same
Conventional	6	6	17
Certified organic	13	3	17
Non-certified organic	17	2	10
Mixed practices	8	2	16
Free range	8	3	13
Other	0	0	0
Total[a]	52	16	73
Vendors	Vendors Increasing	Decreasing	Staying same
Conventional	4	5	13
Certified organic	7	4	16
Non-certified organic	9	0	16
Mixed practices	9	1	10
Free range	10	1	8
Other	0	0	0
Total[a]	39	11	63

[a] Multiple answers accepted.

restaurants agreed or strongly agreed that purchasing locally grown food products improved profitability. A third of respondents were neutral and 17.53 per cent of the establishments either disagreed or strongly disagreed that selling locally grown food products through the menu is "profitable".

Willingness to promote local food to restaurant customers

The respondents were asked if their establishment currently promote the use of local food products/ingredients information on their menu or other promotional material. Results showed 71.87 per cent (46 respondents) promote the use of local food products to their customers while the remaining 26.56 per cent (17) respondents do not. However, of those who do not currently promote local food at their establishments indicated that they were interested in promoting local food products on their menu or on other promotional materials in the future.

Conclusion

The results of this chapter indicate that there is substantial interest in the purchase of local food products by Vancouver restaurants and chefs even though there is no clear definition of what local food means (Conner et al. 2009; Pearson et al. 2011; Hall 2013; Trivette 2015; see also Chapter 18, this volume). There is positive attitude among the restaurants towards increasing the number of farmers' market vendors and farmers to purchase local food products from in the future. Findings indicated that local farm product purchases supply a wide range of products. However, it is significant that there appears to be a growing emphasis on organic and free-range practices as a purchase factor, what perhaps could be described as a "local plus sustainable practices". In other words, local food can also be understood within the broader context of a sustainable culinary system (Gössling & Hall 2013). The reasons for this are undoubtedly complex but likely complement the perception of local good as being fresher, of a high quality, tastier and more sustainable than food that has further to travel (Hall 2013). In addition, many establishments mentioned that selling local food products through the menu is a profitable business practice. This is significant information for producers as they can use this as a selling point themselves in business-to-business sales when contacting potential restaurants or chefs regarding their products.

The extent of direct purchase from farmers' market vendors and farmers by restaurants and chefs varied in this study and the revealed barriers may limit the expansion of this growing market channel. But many of these barriers could be managed by better communication and supply channels between the different actors in the food system. For example, cooperative marketing strategies or a group of farmers can band together to make purchasing arrangements with the restaurants and chefs. However, this study also presented evidence that restaurant satisfaction with current wholesale distributors is an important purchasing factor, often because of time and assurance of quality and supply issues; therefore, this is clearly a potentially important channel for farmers to move their products through if they wish to supply local restaurants. The study therefore suggests that there is potential to further expand the sales of local foods to restaurants, thereby also potentially developing another route through to consumers to embrace local food. Yet it also suggests that there are significant barriers that need to be managed as well as the need for greater awareness of the potential role of wholesalers in encouraging local food purchase, which has not previously been emphasised in local food studies given the desire to shorten supply chains so as to increase returns to producers.

References

Askegaard, S. and Madsen, T.K. (1998) 'The local and the global: exploring traits of homogeneity and heterogeneity in European food cultures', *International Business Review*, 7(6): 549–568.

Bachmann, J. (2004) Selling to Restaurants: Business and marketing, Fayetteville, AR: ATTRA Publication #IP255, August. ATTRA (Appropriate Technology Transfer for Rural Areas) – National Sustainable Agriculture Information Service, National Center for Appropriate Technology (NCAT). Available online: <https://attra.ncat.org/attra-pub/summaries/summary.php?pub=266≥ (accessed 20 May 2015).

Blouin, C., Chopra, M. and van der Hoeven, R. (2009) 'Trade and social determinants of health', *The Lancet*, 373(9662): 502–507.

Brown, C. and Miller, S. (2008) 'The impacts of local markets: a review of research on farmers markets and community supported agriculture (CSA)', *American Journal of Agricultural Economics*, 90(5): 1298–1302.

Brown, E.A. (2008) 'Dimension of transformational leadership and relationship with employee performance in hotel front desk staff', Unpublished PhD thesis, Iowa State University, Ames.

Canadian Restaurant and Food Service Association (CRFA) (2012) *CRFA's 2012 Canadian Chef Survey: Hot Trends.* Available online: <https://www.restaurantscanada.org/Portals/0/Non-Member/2013/Research_ChefSurvey_2012.pdf≥ (accessed 20 May 2015).

Casselman, A.L. (2010) 'Local foods movement in the Iowa catering industry', Unpublished Master thesis, Iowa State University, Ames.

Central Oregon Intergovernmental Council (2012) *Central Oregon Food Hub Feasibility Study.* Available online: <http://www.ngfn.org/resources/ngfn-database/knowledge/central-oregon-food-hub-feasibility-study2.pdf> (accessed 20 May 2015).

Conner, D.S. Montri, A., Montri, D. and Hamm, M. (2009) 'Consumers demand for local produce at extended season farmers' markets: guiding farmers marketing strategies', *Renewable Agriculture and Food Systems*, 24(4): 251–259.

CRFA (2013) *CRFA's 2013 Canadian Chef Survey: Hot Trends.* Available online: <https://www.restaurantscanada.org/Portals/0/Non-Member/2014/chefsurvey_2013_english.pdf≥ (accessed 20 May 2015).

Curtis, K.R. and Cowee, M.W. (2009) 'Direct marketing local food to chefs: chef preferences and perceived obstacles', *Journal of Food Distribution Research*, 40(2): 26–36.

Dodds, R., Holmes, M., Arunsopha, V., Chin, N., Le, T., Maung, S. and Shum, M. (2014) 'Consumer choice and farmers' markets', *Journal of Agricultural and Environmental Ethics*, 27(3): 397–416.

Dougherty, M.L., Brown, L. and Green, G. (2013) 'The social architecture of local food tourism: challenges and opportunities for community economic development', *Journal of Rural Social Sciences*, 28(2): 1–27.

Dunne, J., Chambers, K., Giombolini, K. and Schlegel, S. (2011) 'What does "local" mean in the grocery store? Multiplicity in food retailers' perspectives on sourcing and marketing local foods', *Renewable Agriculture and Food Systems*, 26(1): 46–59.

Duram, L. and Cawley, M. (2012) 'Irish chefs and restaurants in the geography of "local" food value chains', *The Open Geography Journal*, 5: 16–25.

Farmers Markets Canada (2009) *Economic Impact Study 2009.* Available online: <http://www.farmersmarketscanada.ca/Documents/FMC%20FINAL%20Brochure%202009-ENG.pdf≥ (accessed 20 May 2015).

Feagan, R. and Morris, D. (2009) 'Consumer quest for embeddedness: a case study of the Brantford Farmers' Market', *International Journal of Consumer Studies*, 33(3): 235–243.

Feagan, R., Morris, D. and Krug, K. (2004) 'Niagara region farmers' markets: local food systems and sustainability considerations', *Local Environment*, 9(3): 235–254.

Feenstra, G.W., Lewis, C.C., Hinrichs, C.C., Gillespie, G.W. and Hilchey, D. (2003) 'Entrepreneurial outcomes and enterprise size in US retail farmers' markets', *American Journal of Alternative Agriculture*, 18(1): 46–55.

Food Processing Centre (2003) *Approaching Foodservice Establishments with Locally Grown Products*, Lincoln, NE: University of Nebraska, Institute of Agriculture and Natural Resources. Available online: <http://digitalcommons.unl.edu/cgi/viewcontent.cgi?article=1000&context=fpcreports> (accessed 20 May 2015).

Gössling, S. and Hall, C.M. (2013) 'Sustainable culinary systems: an introduction', in C.M. Hall and S. Gössling (eds) *Sustainable Culinary Systems: Local Foods, Innovation, Tourism and Hospitality*, Abingdon: Routledge, pp. 3–44.

Green, G.P. and Dougherty, M.L. (2008) 'Localizing linkages for food and tourism: culinary tourism as a community development strategy', *Community Development*, 39(3): 148–158.

Hall, C.M. (2013) 'The local in farmers markets in New Zealand', in C.M. Hall and S. Gössling (eds) *Sustainable Culinary Systems: Local Foods, Innovation, Tourism and Hospitality*, Abingdon: Routledge, pp. 99–122.

Hall, C.M. (2016) 'Heirloom products in heritage places: farmers markets, local food, and food diversity', in D. Timothy (ed.) *Heritage Cuisines: Traditions, Identities and Tourism*, Abingdon: Routledge, pp. 88–103.

Hall, C.M. and Gössling, S. (eds) (2013a) *Sustainable Culinary Systems: Local Foods, Innovation, Tourism and Hospitality*, Abingdon: Routledge.

Hall, C.M. and Gössling, S. (2013b) 'Reimagining sustainable culinary systems', in C.M. Hall and S. Gossling (eds) *Sustainable Culinary Systems: Local Foods, Innovation, Tourism and Hospitality*, London: Routledge, pp. 293–304.

Hall, C.M. and Sharples, L. (eds) (2008) *Food and Wine Festivals and Events around the World: Development, Management and Markets*, Oxford: Butterworth-Heinemann.

Hinrichs, C.C. (2000) 'Embeddedness and local food systems: notes on two types of direct agricultural market', *Journal of Rural Studies*, 16(3): 295–303.

Inwood, S.M., Sharp, J.S., Moore, R.H. and Stinner, D.H. (2009) 'Restaurants, chefs and local foods: insights drawn from application of a diffusion of innovation framework', *Agriculture and Human Values*, 26(3): 177–191.

Jarosz, L. (2008) 'The city in the country: growing alternative food networks in metropolitan areas', *Journal of Rural Studies*, 24(3): 231–244.

Jensen, J. (2010) *Local and Regional Food Systems for Rural Futures*. RUPRI Rural Futures Lab Foundation Paper no. 1. Available online: <http://www.rupri.org/Forms/RUPRI_Rural-Futures-Lab_2010_Food_Systems_for_Rural_Futures.pdf> (accessed 20 May 2015).

Kang, S. and Rajagopal, L. (2014) 'Perceptions of benefits and challenges of purchasing local foods among hotel industry decision makers', *Journal of Foodservice Business Research*, 17(4): 301–322.

Martinez, S., Hand, M., Da Pra, M., Pollack, S., Ralston, K., Smith, T., Vogel, S., Tauer, L., Lohr, L., Low, S. and Newman, C. (2010) *Local Food Systems: Concepts, Impacts, and Issues*, Washington, DC: Department of Agriculture.

Mendes, W. (2008) 'Implementing social and environmental policies in cities: the case of food policy in Vancouver, Canada', *International Journal of Urban and Regional Research*, 32(4): 942–967.

Mount, P. (2012) 'Growing local food: scale and local food systems governance', *Agriculture and Human Values*, 29(1): 107–121.

Murphy, A.J. (2011) 'Farmers' markets as retail spaces', *International Journal of Retail & Distribution Management*, 39(8): 582–597.

National Restaurant Association (NRA) (2009) 'Food and healthy living: Strategy for winning stomach share', in *Every Move Matters: Strengthening Your Game in 2009*, Washington, DC. Available online: <http://actionsystems.com/downloads/09presentations/NRA_Industry_Forecast_2009.pdf> (accessed 20 May 2015).

NRA (2013) 'Local sourcing and healthful kids' meals top national restaurant association's "what's hot in 2013"', *Culinary Forecast*. Available online: <http://www.restaurant.org/Pressroom/Press-Releases/Whats-Hot-in-2013-Culinary-Forecast> (accessed 20 May 2015).

NRA (2015) 'What's hot in 2013', *Culinary Forecast*. Available online: <http://www.res-taurant.org/Downloads/PDFs/News-Research/WhatsHot2015-Results.pdf≥ (accessed 20 May 2015).

Nummedal, M. and Hall, C.M. (2006) 'Local food in tourism: an investigation of the New Zealand South Island's bed and breakfast sector's use and perception of local food', *Tourism Review International*, 9(4): 365–378.

Onozaka, Y., Nurse, G. and McFadden, D.T. (2010) 'Local food consumers: how motivations and perceptions translate to buying behavior', *Choices*, 25(1): 1–6.

Pearson, D., Henryks, J., Trott, A., Jones, P., Parker, G., Dumaresq, D. and Dyball, R. (2011) 'Local food: understanding consumer motivations in innovative retail formats', *British Food Journal*, 113(7): 886–899.

Renting, H., Marsden, T.K. and Banks, J. (2003) 'Understanding alternative food networks: exploring the role of short food supply chains in rural development', *Environment and Planning A*, 35(3): 393–412.

Reynolds-Allie, K. and Fields, D. (2012) 'A comparative analysis of Alabama restaurants: local vs non-local food purchase', *Journal of Food Distribution Research*, 43(1): 65–74.

Schmit, T.M. and Hadcock, S.E. (2012) 'Assessing barriers to expansion of farm-to-chef sales: a case study from upstate New York', *Journal of Food Research*, 1(1): 117–125.

Selfa, T. and Qazi, J. (2005) 'Place, taste, or face-to-face? Understanding producer–consumer networks in "local" food systems in Washington State', *Agriculture and Human Values*, 22(4): 451–464.

Seyfang, G. (2008) 'Avoiding Asda? Exploring consumer motivations in local organic food networks', *Local Environment*, 13(3): 187–201.

Sharma, A., Gregoire, M.B. and Strohbehn, C. (2009) 'Assessing costs of using local foods in independent restaurants', *Journal of Foodservice Business Research*, 12(1): 55–71.

Sharma, A., Moon, J. and Strohbehn, C. (2014) 'Restaurant's decision to purchase local foods: influence of value chain activities', *International Journal of Hospitality Management*, 39: 130–143.

Smith, A. and Hall, C.M. (2003) 'Restaurants and local food in New Zealand', in C.M. Hall, L. Sharples, R. Mitchell, N. Macionis, and B. Cambourne (eds) *Food Tourism around the World: Development, Management, and Markets*, Oxford: Elsevier, pp. 249–267.

Sonnino, R. and Marsden, T. (2006) 'Beyond the divide: rethinking relationships between alternative and conventional food networks in Europe', *Journal of Economic Geography*, 6(2): 181–199.

Strohbehn, C.H. and Gregoire, M.B. (2003) 'Case studies of local food purchasing by central Iowa restaurants and institutions', *Foodservice Research International*, 14(1): 53–64.

Thilmany, D. and Watson, P. (2004) 'The increasing role of direct marketing and farmers' markets for western US producers', *Western Economics Forum*, 3(2): 19–25.

Thorsen, E.O. and Hall, C.M. (2001) 'What's on the wine list? Wine policies in the New Zealand restaurant industry', *International Journal of Wine Marketing*, 13(3): 94–102.

Trivette, S.A. (2015) 'How local is local? Determining the boundaries of local food in practice', *Agriculture and Human Values*, 32(3): 475–490.

Vecchio, R. (2010) 'Local food at Italian farmers' markets: three case studies', *International Journal of Sociology of Agriculture and Food*, 17(2): 122–139.

Wolf, M.M., Spittler, A. and Ahern, J. (2005) 'A profile of farmers' market consumers and the perceived advantages of produce sold at farmers' markets', *Journal of Food Distribution Research*, 36(1): 192–201.

Wormsbecker, C. (2007) 'Moving towards the local: the barriers and opportunities for localizing food systems in Canada', Unpublished Master thesis, University of Waterloo, Ontario.

Zepeda, L. and Deal, D. (2009) 'Organic and local food consumer behaviour: alphabet theory', *International Journal of Consumer Studies*, 33(6): 697–705.

Zepeda, L. and Li, J. (2007) 'Characteristics of organic food shoppers', *Journal of Agricultural and Applied Economics*, 39: 17–28.

18 Culinary collisions

The vision of local food use collides with daily restaurant practice

*Lotte Wellton, Inger M. Jonsson
and Ute Walter*

Introduction

The enrichment of regional culinary status and the use of local food is a part of developing rural tourist destinations. Bessière (1998) discusses local heritage in the food context as an element of tourist development on a local level. She means that culinary heritage in rural areas can be considered as an identity construction linked to a peasant identity with special features concerning eating habits and food production, such as conserving historical skills and techniques in the making of a food product. The use or meaning of the term "local food" is discussed by many stakeholders including researchers, as Sims (2010) questions: What is local food? What are the distinctions? Is it grown in the nearby vicinity? Regionally? Or is it simply produced in the country? Is it connected to the promotion of local farmers and is it socially beneficial? According to Sims (2010), there is no guarantee, for example, that local food is produced in an environmental friendly way even if it is often implicitly presented as healthier and tastier than other food products. She points out that the production of local food is often connected to cultural, ethical and sustainable issues (see also Hall & Gössling 2013). For example, if a product has an historical and symbolic connection to the region or an impact on local employment or small food business start-ups that use local ingredients. Consumers/guests and restaurant owners/chefs may also have different views on the matter of local food (see also Chapter 17, this volume). Chefs may interpret the term widely and often use it as a marketing instrument via labelling and storytelling and as a way to describe cooking practices. Sims (2010) also notes that a way of attracting customers is to highlight sustainability and ecofriendliness. Guests are often interested in the cultural aspect of local food but are not always willing to travel far or pay higher prices for local products.

Small and medium-sized seasonal restaurants in tourist destinations may evolve creatively concerning culinary heritage and the use of local food and thus contribute to enhance the number of visits and increase revenues in the region. This may be done by ensuring that visitors get quality meal experiences and also by attracting media attention and being flagships for the destinations' particular food products (Getz et al. 2014). Furthermore, promotion and publicity are common strategies at regional agency levels to augment food tourism, as noted by

Hall and Mitchell (2002) in the case of Australian and New Zealand. A similar pattern is discussed by Heldt-Cassel (2003) concerning the project "Culinary heritage network", which aimed to promote and profile "food"-regions in Europe in the beginning of this century.

This chapter examines the daily work practice in small-scale restaurants in rural tourist destinations in relation to the restaurateurs' visions of local food use. The complexity of ensuring quality in guests' meal experiences and seasonal restaurateurs' contribution to regional development is also discussed based on a study, with an ethnographical research approach, of 11 small restaurant owners/chefs in a Swedish tourist destination.

Background

Local food use

The use of local foodstuffs is an important value aspect for small-scale restaurateurs in rural areas (see also Chapter 17, this volume). Local food can attract guests on many levels as, for example, concerning the cultural heritage, serving a well-known regional dish made from local products or even from their own farmed products. The development of new dishes from local products such as special cheese or using particular local herbs or plants in the cooking of a meal can also add value to a restaurant's meal offering. Furthermore, restaurants are potential users of local food products (Alonso & O'Neill 2010) because of their taste and freshness which also influence the appearance of the dishes. In addition, highlighting seasonal variations and food origin are ways to further develop restaurants' menus (Duram & Cawley 2012). To connect small-scale producers with buyers is a relevant local food issue (Nummedal & Hall 2006). Information about products from producers is crucial for the chefs' willingness to order locally, although price is less relevant especially for high-end restaurants (Starr et al. 2003). This was supported by Curtis and Cowee (2009) who also found – when asking chefs about barriers for purchasing local products – that most prohibiting was to not be guaranteed a constant delivery of the right amount and quality of local products.

Cooperation through networking is, by many researchers, seen as optimal for innovatively developing a product or service among small hospitality and restaurant enterprises (Parsa et al. 2005; Markowska 2011; Brouder & Eriksson 2013; Kompula 2013). Restaurant entrepreneurs in Swedish rural regions learn from others in the area to be able to develop their business ideas and their networks (Markowska, Saemundsson & Wiklund 2011). For instance, food networking in rural areas can enhance the use of locally acquired quality food products (Alonso & O'Neill 2010) and overcome obstacles such as irregular supply or logistical problems (Inwood et al. 2009). Inwood et al. (2009) identify a preference among chefs for the "middlemen" (local or regional distributors) to efficiently and consistently deliver locally grown foods instead of a multitude of different local producers; thus their conclusion is to create distributional structures that recognise the time constraints of chefs/buyers (as well as producers).

Restaurant practice

Daily work in restaurants consists of calm, systematic preparation and routine work as well as high tempo, stress and unexpected challenges. The daily work is a combination of knowledge, timing, focus and interaction (Gustafsson et al. 2006; Fine 2008; Jönsson 2012). Fine (2008) concludes that working in restaurant kitchens demands the ability to cope with a fluctuating work pace, make adequate preparations, know the craft of cooking many different courses simultaneously, have an aesthetic feel and know how to cooperate with others in an often hard-working environment. Fine also concludes that successful restaurants use time effectively due to their organisation of time and place. Time is especially important concerning the throughput of guests in relation to how much they spend, considering that it is not possible to "save" an opportunity to sell a restaurant seat from one day to another (Hayes & Miller 2011). The way time is used is therefore crucial for the daily performance of a restaurant meal (Fine 2008). For example, to meet challenges such as generating full revenue during a short time interval in seasonal restaurant businesses while maintaining service and product quality (Baum & Lundtorp 2001), business owners in tourist destinations may have to work for 12–16 hours a day during the peak season (Lundtorp, Rassing & Wanhill 1999). One of the main reasons why small-scale restaurant owners work hard and long hours is the dream fulfilment of having one's own business (Hultman 2013; Parsa et al. 2005). To own and run an enterprise implies social status, and the restaurant business is looked upon as an attractive trade, rendering the owner social prestige regardless of prior education or experience (Skalpe 2003). The majority of the business owners in seasonal tourist destinations are non-entrepreneurs and have little or no formal education (Ioannides & Petersen 2003; Getz & Petersen 2005). As an effect, risk evaluation and work practice seems to be made and organised by heart and gut feeling in the lifestyle-oriented restaurant industry. This is due to the complexity of reasons involved in choosing to be a part of the restaurant business, rather than maximisation of wealth and minimisation of risk (Skalpe 2003; Hall & Rusher 2004). To become successful, restaurateurs in rural areas must not only become skilful in entrepreneurship in their trade but also retrieve a regionally based identity (Markowska 2011). Additionally Fine (2008) points out that operating a restaurant provides an opportunity to make an aesthetic and personal statement. Wellton (2015) shows that running a restaurant is reflected in the short cycles of a day-to-day operation with quick decision making and limited time to produce the food and hospitality established by the restaurateur and that the offering of a restaurant meal is dependent upon the multitude and variation of professional culinary and hospitality competence in the daily practice of restaurant work.

Method

An ethnographic research approach was chosen for this study in order to mirror and comprehend the daily work practice of small-scale restaurant owners in a tourist destination. The background of the researchers in this study contributes to an insider perspective, which is defined by Alvesson and Sköldberg (2008) as being the point of view of a researcher who uses his or her position to do research in her/her own environment. At the same time, they emphasised that reflexivity is crucial for the researcher, who has to analyse his or her own cultural context without letting personal experience get in the way. Ehn (2011) points out that it can be difficult to identify sequences of events unless the researcher has previous knowledge of work organisation and routines in the field. All data collection was conducted by one of the researchers with extensive experience in the restaurant business as well as a familiarisation with the seasonal tourist destination: the island of Öland, Sweden.

Sampling

Eight small-scale restaurants, with 11 owners, some run in combination with accommodations, were chosen to participate in the study. Criteria for inclusion were membership in a restaurant association that outspokenly guarantees the sincerity and reliability of its members (taking into account economic, sustainable and educational issues) or being known for making high-quality products. Six of the restaurants were chosen because of membership in the restaurant association and two because they were well known for their products throughout the region.

Websites

To find out more about the restaurant owners' meal offerings, the restaurants' pricing, opening hours and overall hospitality concepts, the sampling was supported by an exploration of the restaurant websites and their advertising, and articles in local tourist magazines. The restaurant menus containing outspoken ambitions about use of local food and relationship to local culinary heritage were especially noted as well as declarations of the same kind in the magazines.

Interviews – pre-season

Interviews were conducted with all 11 owners. The semi-structured interviews were conducted for one-and-a-half to two hours each. Five owners were interviewed separately at their respective restaurants, while six owners – three married couples at their respective restaurants – were interviewed together. The interviews contained questions about experience, education, visions and business ideas, marketing, business plans and revenue and lifestyle, working conditions, seasonality and networking, as well as local food and sustainability. All interviews were transcribed verbatim.

Fieldwork – high season

Field studies were carried out at six of the restaurants; two declined to be field-studied due to being too busy during high season. The researcher participated in the kitchen practice as well as in dining room work, working together with and talking to restaurateurs and personnel. There were also shorter meetings and spontaneous visits at all the restaurants throughout the season (two to four occasions at each restaurant). All of the fieldwork and visits were continuously documented in notes and diaries.

Analysis

The research group studied the findings both individually and together. The interview topics were arranged in accordance with the most significant answers from the informants, and the answers were then condensed into meaningful units, which in turn were coded and then categorised (Graneheim & Lundman 2004). The notes from the fieldwork, visits and meetings were treated in the same manner (i.e. condensed, coded and categorised). Data analysis was then conducted in two stages. First, the categories from interviews and field notes that were judged to have similarities were identified. Second, those categories were brought together in a categorising framework. In this study, representative quotations from the transcribed texts are shown, and agreement was sought among co-researchers in line with Graneheim and Lundman's (2004) statements on ways to obtain credibility in the analysing process. The validity of the analysis was also enhanced, as the datasets were reviewed and discussed in many rounds by the research group.

Discussion

Visions of local food use

The websites of the restaurants in this study showed different ways of promoting the owners' visions and business ideas. Six out of eight websites declared the use of local food in the menus or/and that the cooking had a base in culinary heritage. But the declarations were somewhat downplayed and of a general nature, as for example:

> The table is set for the classic flavors with a touch of Öland. The restaurant
> [...] focus on local ingredients with a varied menu. The goal is to use as
> much locally grown and locally produced ingredients as possible in the food
> we serve.
>
> (Excerpt from restaurant website)

Mostly meat was labelled as being from the near surroundings. Vegetables were either grown in the region or from the own farm (in one case). Organically grown vegetables were in some cases highlighted as coming from the near vicinity, and at the same time certain organic products were imported from far away, as was the case in one of the restaurants menus:

- KRAV (certified organic) cod from Svalbard, the Arctic Ocean
- Cream and white wine cooked KRAV (certified organic) mussels from the Northeast Atlantic

(Examples from one menu)

The owners of this particular restaurant, cited above, were very much putting forward in the research interview how their ecological vision imbued all parts of their enterprise. This combination of origin labelling mixes local products with organic products, which may risk confusing the message of regional food localization, but on the other hand it can attract consumers/guests as a message of an overall sincerity of the restaurant.

Another restaurant's website pointed to the kitchen's use of "old-fashioned" cooking practices, such as braising, smoking and making confits. Also highlighted was the way the chef was influenced by seasonal local products (described as being from the close vicinity and as well as from throughout Sweden) in menu development.

One of the restaurants conveyed the message that they make a special regional course with peasant origins and handcraft techniques out of potatoes grown at the own farm. This particular restaurant has been a success since it started 20 years ago and can be considered an ideal contributor to tourism development through utilisation of culinary heritage (Bessière 1998): a local farm making a culinary heritage course with local, partly home-grown products, open all year round although with limited opening hours during low season and contributing, in a small scale, to job creation and to revenues earned via income from tourists.

The terms local food or locally produced food items or culinary heritage are used simultaneously by the restaurants in their websites and menus with several different connotations, in the same way as described by Sims (2010) but foremost as implicit messages of quality.

Logistics

In the interviews, all the restaurant owners/chefs stated that they were interested in buying local products but they found them hard to come by. They were also unsure of what producers they could address and what products were available. Two of the restaurant owners/chefs reckoned that local products grown nearby were of lesser quality than organic products from further away, because they thought that their neighbouring farms probably used pesticides. This is in line with Starr et al. (2003) who point out that a major obstacle for chefs to order locally grown food products was lack of information from producers. Getting the quality and right amount delivered was not mentioned as a risk by the restaurateurs in this study, in contrast to what was found by Curtis and Cowee (2009). The most apparent problem of the informants concerning local products was the failure of the delivery system or rather the lack of a delivery system, which according to Inwood et al. (2009) seems to be a recurrent problem for many rural restaurants, as stated by one respondent:

> ... but we had such trouble of getting hold of locally produced. We had to go and get it ourselves. And the time it takes to drive around, we don't have that.

> (Interview with A)

Even if they had an ambition to use local food, the restaurateurs/chefs most of all lacked time in their daily practice to get hold of local products. They had not specifically organised their work according to the seasonal work pressure, which Lundtorp et al. (1999) identified regarding small restaurant owner's extreme working hours, so they ordered from nationwide chains of suppliers because that was the simplest and quickest solution. A "middle-man" as delivery solution, suggested in the study by Inwood et al. (2009), would probably be helpful in the tourist destination of Öland since the distances between producers and restaurants are not especially long. This could also contribute to more job opportunities in the area.

Daily challenges

One way to get around the delivery problems was to order local products, such as locally caught fish, months in advance or if possible once a week. Then the raw materials were frozen or vacuum-packaged by the chef:

> When the delivery of vegetables arrived they were immediately vacuum packed so in a sense they work with "almost" fresh vegetables, rather than using the newly delivered very fresh vegetables, instead they use the ones they vacuum-packed a few days earlier
>
> (Field note at small restaurant with experienced chef/owner)

This practice decreases immediate freshness and taste of the dishes and the aesthetic attractiveness (Alonso & O'Neill 2010) is lowered and also risks a decrease in the quality of the meal offering. Handling of fresh food stuff also requires strict hygiene, which sometimes was overlooked by the restaurant owners as a result of time pressure by, for example, not keeping the contents of refrigerators in good order according to expiration dates. Furthermore, the planning of the throughput of guests (Hayes & Miller 2011), which can, due to the conditions in seasonal tourist destinations, be especially complicated, contributes to difficulties in calculation of food orders and maintaining food quality/freshness. All this is part of the complexity of daily practice in restaurant work (Wellton 2015), which in turn suggests the need of knowledge and experience in everything from food hygiene to composition of courses and menus (Fine 2008). In several of the restaurants studied, the solution of handling of food stuff was to minimise variations by using the same garnish for all the dishes. Simplifying menus and courses is a way to balance consumption of food stuff and also amount of working hours. But creativity and development of menus and courses are, in the long run, presumptions for attracting media and becoming "flag-ships" for a destination's food products (Getz et al. 2014).

Branding and sometimes storytelling is a part of the communication of the origin and seasonality of the local food used in the menus (Duram & Cawley 2012), which both promotes the local producers and adds value for guests. However, this practice was almost always overlooked in the studied restaurants, an oversight probably due to time pressure but also to ignorance of marketing strategies:

The restaurant has a strict ecological approach, but the food wasn't specified as such on the daily menu.

(Field note from small seasonal restaurant)

Networking and independency

Among the restaurateurs in this study, there was a certain willingness and capability to network, but it seldom led to further contacts or collaboration in the long run. The restaurateurs were not taking time to contact and cooperate with others, even when there were opportunities during off-season. Networking with peers and producers, as suggested by Markowska et al. (2011), could have been useful to these rural restaurateurs for creative developments and making it easier for their concepts and meal offering to live up to guests' expectations and to promote entrepreneurial growth. But these kinds of connections, between networking and development, seemed unknown to the restaurateurs in this study. Also the utility of different kinds of networks was not apparent to all of the restaurateurs. Some considered being on Facebook as a time waste, and they all felt that local networks are unsustainable over time. One informant commented:

There are so many compounds, and new are organised all the time, and they are supposed to start a lot of different things, well it is fun in the beginning. And then … it turns to nothing, people have some energy to begin with, then everyone has so much to do. The problem in these kinds of places [seasonal tourist destinations] is that everybody have ambitions but then summer comes and nobody has the time … and after the summer season nobody has the strength.

(Interview with L)

Networks organised regionally by destination development projects seldom live longer than the project money lasts, as was discussed by several of the restaurateurs in the study. In certain cases the values and codes of the compounds and networks were not upheld and therefore did not attract the studied restaurateurs in the destination for any longer periods. The restaurant owner with the culinary heritage dish as a speciality had an extensive experience of regional and national development programs but was no longer interested to take part in them. The reasons mentioned were that the programs seldom lead to any practical utility of the intended purposes, such as promoting local development and that the programs often suggested that the participants on the local level should spend time and effort without being economically compensated. This can result in a situation where the strategies of the regional/national agencies and their promotion program may fade and the strategies have limited impact on, in this case, the restaurateurs' daily practice (Hall & Mitchell 2002; Heldt-Cassel 2003).

The cooperation between food suppliers and restaurateurs in the studied area exists but is not particularly well developed. The local organisation of restaurateurs has an ongoing project to list local suppliers and their products, but the work is not going forward probably due to the suppliers' disappointment of the restaurateurs' unwillingness to buy from them, according to one of the restaurateurs in this study.

When asked about networking by joint advertising with other local firms as a marketing strategy, it was not considered an option for the restaurateurs. It was said to be too expensive and with little or no measurable effect, whereas word of mouth was a preferred strategy. An interesting finding, expressed both in interviews and in conversations during field studies, was that doing things jointly intruded on the restaurateurs'/small business owners' independency:

> But I need to decide about my own company, that's how it is.
>
> (Interview with E)

Knowledge, time-use and benefits

Lifestyle reasons for choosing to become a small-scale restaurateur were predominant among the informants in this study, and lifestyle entrepreneurs often have no or little education and experience in the field that they adopt (Ioannides & Petersen 2003; Getz & Petersen 2005; see Hall & Rusher 2004 as a countering perspective). None of the informants had a higher education in Culinary Arts and Hospitality and only three had long-term experience of the business. It is well known that working as a small-scale entrepreneur is time-demanding, but it seems to be less common knowledge that daily restaurant practice is also very time-consuming. Furthermore, to compensate for lack of knowledge and skills, it is often a solution to put in even more working hours, as was the case for several of the restaurateurs in this study. The time use contributed to the extreme workload of these restaurateurs/chefs (Parsa et al. 2005; Hultman 2013) and consequently there was a collision between their energy and interest to find local suppliers and to use local food products in their cooking and the perceived benefit.

The restaurateurs/chefs' knowledge and ability to do menu planning according to seasonal food products naturally influenced the choice of food products (Duram & Cawley 2012). The securing of the availability of local food and the estimation of consumption are also complicated matters and certainly need to be planned and evaluated from season to season. This was seldom done in a systematic way by the restaurateurs in this study, because when the season was over, other things such as renovating and making up new business ideas were in focus rather than looking back and analysing the product and meal offering (Wellton 2015). Ideas of culinary heritage and networking are often too far away from the daily practice of the work in seasonal restaurants. The restaurateurs in the study thought that they had no or very little time to spend on continuous education or in networking, as the advantage was not especially clear to them. Of course they all understood the value of local food and culinary heritage, especially as a marketing strategy, but as one of restaurateurs expressed: 'I've been working with this [locally produced food] since 2006, and at that time it wasn't trendy. No one talked about it then' (*interview with K*). The other restaurateurs, except for the couple who had organic as an overall business idea, considered that the use of local food was one way of choosing a business strategy as good as any other.

Conclusions

There is a collision between making use of local food products and everyday work in small-scale restaurants in tourist destinations. The visions and business ideas concerning local food includes promotional value and is attractive for the restaurant owners in this study, as it seems natural to include local products in a seasonal restaurant menu. But there are obstacles such as incomplete information about products and producers, delivery problems and storage problems, which are both time-consuming and work-demanding. Unless the restaurateur has good knowledge and experience of planning and organisation of the complex daily restaurant practice, as well as skills in cooking and menu composition, it is difficult to ensure quality of the dishes made from local products. All in all the restaurateurs in this study were highly motivated to put local food items and references to culinary heritage on their menus, but actually only used local food in their cooking when it was easy to come by.

In a sense there is a collision between "being your own" and networking, especially if the networks are supported by authorities that are perceived to impose rules and regulations on the individual entrepreneur. Individualised education, offered during a period of special EU support for the region, was acclaimed by the restaurateurs in this study, but to take part in something that suggests a more general long-term commitment is not of interest to these restaurateurs, mostly due to unwillingness to spend precious time on something that is not immediately beneficial to one's own business.

Based on the results of this study, our suggestion is that if the use of local food products and promotion of culinary heritage is going to be beneficial for regional development of tourist destinations, professionalisation of especially lifestyle entrepreneurs in the restaurant business is much needed. Education in restaurant work can augment professionalisation, but most of all, it will require further reflectivity concerning evaluation, planning and networking in the industry. The possibilities for the small restaurant businesses to grow and contribute to regional development would be reinforced if there could be new ways to make education attractive for different groups of practitioners.

References

Alonso, A.D. and O'Neill, M. (2010) 'Small hospitality enterprises and local produce: a case study', *British Food Journal*, 112(11): 1175–1189.

Alvesson, M. and Sköldberg, K. (2008) *Tolkning och reflektion. Vetenskapsfilosofi och kvalitativ metod [Interpretation and reflection. Philosophy of science and qualitative method]*, Lund: Studentlitteratur.

Baum, T. and Lundtorp, S. (2001) 'Seasonality in tourism: an introduction', in T. Baum and S. Lundtorp (eds) *Seasonality in Tourism*, London: Routledge, pp. 1–4.

Bessière, J. (1998) 'Local development and heritage: traditional food and cuisine as tourist attractions in rural areas', *Sociologia Ruralis*, 38(1): 21–34.

Brouder, P. and Eriksson, R.H. (2013) 'Staying in power: what influences micro-firm survival in tourism?' *Tourism Geographies*, 15(1): 125–144.

Curtis, K. and Cowee, M. (2009) 'Direct marketing local food to chefs: chef preferences and perceived obstacles', *Journal of Food Distribution Research*, 40(2): 27–36.

Duram, L. and Cawley, M. (2012) 'Irish chefs and restaurants in the geography of "local" food value chains', *The Open Geography Journal*, 5: 16–25. doi:10.2174/1874923201205010016

Ehn, B. (2011) 'Doing-it yourself. Auto-ethnography of manual work', *Irregular Ethnographies, Etnologia Europaea, Journal of European Ethnology*, 41(1): 53–63.

Fine, G.A. (2008) *Kitchens: The Culture of Restaurant Work*, Berkeley, CA: University of California Press.

Getz, D. and Petersen, T. (2005) 'Growth and profit-oriented entrepreneurship among family business owners in the tourism and hospitality industry', *International Journal of Hospitality Management*, 24(2): 219–242.

Getz, D., Robinson R.N., Andersson, T.D. and Vujicic, S. (2014) *Foodies and Food Tourism*, Oxford: Goodfellow Publishers.

Graneheim, U.H. and Lundman, B. (2004) 'Qualitative content analysis in nursing research: concepts, procedures and measures to achieve trustworthiness', *Nurse Education Today*, 24(2): 105–112.

Gustafsson, I.B., Östrom, Å., Johansson, J. and Mossberg, L. (2006) 'The five aspects meal model: a tool for developing meal services in restaurants', *Journal of Food Service*, 17: 84–93.

Hall, C.M. and Gössling, S. (eds) (2013) *Sustainable Culinary Systems*, Abingdon: Routledge.

Hall, C.M. and Mitchell, R. (2002) 'The changing nature of the relationship between cuisine and tourism in Australia and New Zealand: from fusion cuisine to food networks', in A.-M. Hjalager and G. Richards (eds) *Tourism and Gastronomy*, London: Routledge, pp. 186–206.

Hall, C.M. and Rusher, K. (2004) 'Risky lifestyles? Entrepreneurial characteristics of the New Zealand bed and breakfast sector', in R. Thomas (ed.) *Small Firms in Tourism: International Perspectives*, Amsterdam: Elsevier, pp. 83–97.

Hayes, D. and Miller, A. (2011) *Revenue Management for the Hospitality Industry*, Hoboken, NJ: Wiley.

Heldt-Cassel, S. (2003) 'Att tillaga region – Den regionala matens representationer och praktik – exemplet Skärgårdssmak [To cook a region – the representation and practice of regional food – the example Archipelago taste]', Unpublished doctoral dissertation in Social and Economy Geography, Uppsala University, Uppsala.

Hultman, H. (2013) *Liv och arbete i pizzabranschen [Life and Work in the pizza-industry]*, Lund: Arkiv Förlag & Tidskrift.

Inwood, S.M., Sharp, J., Moore, R. and Stinner, D. (2009) 'Restaurants, chefs and local foods: insights drawn from application of a diffusion of innovation framework', *Agriculture and Human Values*, 26(3): 177–191.

Ioannides, D. and Petersen, T. (2003) 'Tourism "non-entrepreneurship" in peripheral destinations: a case study of small and medium tourism enterprises on Bornholm, Denmark', *Tourism Geographies*, 5(4): 408–435.

Jönsson, H. (2012) *Den gastronomiska revolutionen [The gastronomic revolution]*, Stockholm: Carlssons.

Kompula, R. (2013) 'The role of individual entrepreneurs in the development of competitiveness for a rural tourism destination – a case study', *Tourism Management*, 40: 361–371.

Lundtorp, S., Rassing, C.R. and Wanhill, S. (1999) 'The off-season is "no season": the case of the Danish Island of Bornholm', *Tourism Economics*, 5(1): 49–68.

Markowska, M. (2011) 'Entrepreneurial competence development – Triggers, processes & consequences', Unpublished JIBS dissertation, Jönköping University, Sweden.

Markowska, M., Saemundsson, R.J. and Wiklund, J. (2011) 'Contextualizing business model development in Nordic rural gourmet restaurants', in G.A. Alsos, S. Carter, E. Ljunggren, and F. Welter (eds) *The Handbook of Research on Entrepreneurship in Agriculture and Rural Development*, Cheltenham: Edward Elgar, pp. 162–179.

Nummedal, M. and Hall, C.M. (2006) 'Local food in tourism: an investigation of the New Zealand South Island's bed and breakfast sector's use and perception of local food', *Tourism Review International*, 9(4), 365–378.

Parsa, H.G., Self, J.T., Njite, D. and King, T. (2005) 'Why restaurants fail', *Cornell Hotel and Restaurant Administration Quarterly*, 46(3): 304–322.

Sims, R. (2010) 'Putting place on the menu: the negotiation of locality in UK food tourism, from production to consumption', *Journal of Rural Studies*, 26(2): 105–115.

Skalpe, O. (2003) 'Hotels and restaurants – are the risks rewarded? Evidence from Norway', *Tourism Management*, 24(6): 623–634.

Starr, A., Card, A., Benepe, C., Auld, G., Lamm, D., Smith, K. and Wilken, K. (2003) 'Sustaining local agriculture: barriers and opportunities to direct marketing between farms and restaurants in Colorado', *Agriculture and Human Values*, 20: 301–321.

Wellton, L. (2015) 'Improved meal offerings in tourist destinations provided by professional practitioners', Unpublished Licentiate thesis, Department of Restaurant and Culinary Arts, Örebro University, Sweden.

Part VI

Conclusions

19 Conclusions

Food tourism and regional development – new localism or globalism?

Stefan Gössling and C. Michael Hall

There is much evidence that perceptions of food are changing in many countries: food quality, production processes and the origin of foodstuffs have all become vastly more important to consumers (Hall & Gössling 2013; Yeoman et al. 2015). As examples from all over the world in this book illustrate, changes along the value chain of food production and consumption are increasingly becoming visible, as manifested in the success of food regions, food events or niche foods (Hall & Mitchell 2001; Hall et al. 2003; Hall & Sharples 2008; Getz et al. 2014), which appear to be co-evolving with the growing awareness of the social and ecological implications of food production, and in particular a growing interest in healthy and "quality food" in significant parts of the population (Martinez et al. 2010; Belasco 2014; Johnston, Fanzo & Cogill 2014). Changes in perceptions of the role of food may be primarily driven by consumers who are increasingly becoming aware of where their food comes from (Roy, Hall & Ballantine, this volume), though actors with influence on consumer perceptions are now as diverse as celebrity chefs, micro-lifestyle producers, farm shop owners, initiators of farmers' markets, food critics, journalists and culinary writers, agricultural organisations, destinations, and politicians seeking to support the development of more regional (and sometimes organic) agricultural production systems with strong economic linkages between producers and consumers (Hall & Gössling 2013). It is evident that food has become the new recipe for rural development, economic diversification, innovation and the strengthening of regional economic networks on a broad basis.

Food and development interrelationships are complex and positive outcomes not self-evident, particularly where food production is part of global agricultural trade (Marsden, Murdoch & Morgan 1999; Everett & Slocum 2013; Norton, Alwang & Masters 2014). Often, the initiation of food networks, events or products will depend on external funding, though this does not necessarily result in growing demand for regional food products. Outcomes may be difficult to measure in economic terms, as they may often make mixed contributions to social and environmental dimensions of sustainability. This book consequently focusses on the complexity of these interrelationships. Economic dimensions include the economic viability of enterprises or food products, diversification (sources of farm income), food events and festivals, as well as destination attractiveness. Economic benefits can also relate to tourist spending, the circulation of money in the regional economy (multiplier effects), employment or the number of actors profitting from food networks. These benefits can accrue in developing and developed country destinations and have considerable value for destination loyalty, as well as marketing and branding effects. Many chapters in this book confirm that food-related values are economic, but also relational, and sometimes social or ecological (cf. Hjalager & Richards 2002).

The chapters in this book also show, however, that food tourism and regional development is not unambiguous, and value creation remains fraught with difficulties. To overcome various barriers consequently remains a key obstacle to the development of economically more sustainable culinary systems. This volume adds insights specifically with regard to institutional and bureaucratic, educational and economic barriers, adding to Thompson and Prideaux (this volume), who identify barriers related to the location of markets, lack of skills or capital, regulatory frameworks, lack of infrastructure, government inefficiencies or disinterest in regional collaboration.

Institutional and bureaucratic barriers

Many of the recommendations to develop food experiences and networks that can be found in the literature may involve considerable complexity in the real world. As outlined in this book, governments in many countries now provide financial incentives for innovation and development of rural networks and farm diversification, but policies including health and hygiene controls, tax rules, environmental and employment-related legislation, insurance needs and specific national legislation, such as alcohol monopolies in Sweden (Malm, Gössling & Hall 2013), can make it difficult for farmers to innovate, as they have to learn about new relevant legislation and liabilities, while often facing time-consuming administrative burdens (Nilsson, this volume; Hegerty & Che, this volume). To simply encourage farmers and local food producers to innovate, even where this is based on financial incentives, is thus often falling short of realities at the local production level.

This is equally true for recommendations to farmers to sell directly to restaurants to build food economies. As revealed in several chapters in this book, chefs and restaurant owners may have reason not to be overly enthusiastic about such networks: Barriers to local purchases include problems associated with purchasing foodstuffs from various sources, food deliveries, storage, as well as volume and quality issues, all of which make it more attractive to buy from one wholesaler, rather than a range of individual local producers (Gössling & Hall, this volume; Roy, Hall & Ballantine, this volume; Wellton, Jönsson & Walter, this volume). Networks of small producers thus create considerably greater complexity for chefs, because they need to call and order from every producer separately, be flexible with regard to the amount and quality of the products delivered, and handle additional administrative tasks, such as multiple invoices. Current politically motivated attempts to increase farm sales or local food production may often ignore such barriers for both supply and demand sides, as is, for instance, evident in Jamaica's "farm to fork" concept, pitched as a challenge to an agricultural sector fighting cheap(er) imports, and with few local economic linkages due to tourism's resort character (Taylor & Kneafsey, this volume). To reconsider institutional and bureaucratic problems faced by farmers and food producers may be highly relevant to facilitate innovation in the food sector: Policy makers need to rethink how specific forms of legislation create barriers for farmers and others seeking to diversify, and whether legislative demands related to taxation, consumer health, safety at the farm or animal welfare are becoming ever more complex for small-scale entrepreneurs, that is, those who are more likely to consider such aspects in the first place.

Stakeholder knowledge and awareness

To create producer–consumer networks requires cooperation between farmers and restaurants. In this context, an important finding is that chefs have a very limited understanding of local food production, environment and ecological sustainability, which limits their interest in regional foodstuffs, including organic produce. Furthermore, perceptions of high costs, perceptions of unreliable deliveries by local farmers – both in terms of quality and volume – are reasons to rely on conventional foods delivered by wholesale suppliers (Gössling & Hall, this volume; Wellton, Jönsson & Walter, this volume). As Mulcahy (this volume) emphasises, to realise the tourism potential of food experiences, it will be crucial to build capacity. This notion is also reflected by Wellton, Jönsson and Walter (this volume), suggesting that the education of chefs and food entrepreneurs has to be made more attractive, and to specifically consider issues of economic evaluation, planning and networking in the context of local food products. Chefs and restaurant owners currently focussing on food purchases with a primary (and often only) interest in cost are thus a major barrier to regional development based on food, and it would seem paramount to find ways to increase the interest of these key stakeholders in the culinary system in regional and organic food production. In this regard, chapters in this book have found that chefs do generally consider local foods valuable, because they can make positive contributions to profits and the restaurants' profile, including opportunities for storytelling. Attitudes towards increasing the share of local products in restaurant purchases are thus generally positive, and highlighting the potential of regional or local foods for marketing and branding purposes is considered a viable strategy to make local foods more attractive for restaurants (Gössling & Hall, this volume; Roy, Hall & Ballantine, this volume).

Economic values

In order to make a contribution to local development, products, events or festivals based on food need to create economic value. The enormous success that food promotion can have for regions has been described by Kim (this volume) on the basis of udon noodle identity in Japan, showing that regional branding on the basis of a single foodstuff can be very successful, for instance, if traditions and heritage are used as selling points. While the success of many foods depends on food enthusiasts not primarily interested in or dependent on their products' profitability, niche products can have rapid uptakes, as shown by Rogerson (this volume) in the context of South Africa, where the craft beer market is estimated to grow at 30 per cent annually. Cheung and Luo (this volume) show how, in the case of Hong Kong, entire city quarters have developed on the basis of exotic foods, also with medical properties. Forné (this volume) discusses the potential of cheese in rural Galicia, highlighting that a single type of food such as cheese can be characterised by considerable heterogeneity, while also contributing to regional exports as an "edible souvenir". Lee and Nam (this volume) report on the success of slow food branding efforts of the city of Namyangju in South Korea that also considers organic and more environmentally friendly production, and the massive interest in its Asia and Oceania Slow Food Festival, with more than half a million visitors. Yet, even smaller events focussing on region, food, climate, geography, heritage and a specific foodstuff can make economically and socially important contributions, as has been shown by Cleave (this volume) in the context of the village of Clovelly in the UK. These are examples of the considerable potential of food to contribute to regional development. Value generated by foods is, in these cases, not only related to direct sales; however, Adeyinka-Ojo and Khoo-Lattimore (this volume) illustrate how food contributes to destination identity, as well as tourist satisfaction and destination loyalty, aspects of economic sustainability less often considered.

In economic value terms, food tourism and specifically agritourism can contribute to cost reductions and higher economic returns as a result of direct marketing (Hegerty & Che, this volume), but interrelationships are complex. For instance, the importance of organisational structures and "territory" is pointed out by Gatelier (this volume), who calls for context-specific studies of wine tourism, as joint promotion efforts show considerable regional difference. Within destinations, demand can be pushed, for instance, by chefs highlighting regional foodstuff choices, as well as farmers and producers offering niche products. With regard to the former, interest barriers have been outlined, but these may also be overcome by tourists' willingness to pay premiums. As the example of Sweden shows, heightened willingness-to-pay would be one of the most convincing arguments to overcome cost perception barriers of chefs (Gössling & Hall, this volume). Further insights with relevance have been provided by Wellton, Jönsson and Walter (this volume) who indicate that consumers may be particularly sensitive with regard to some foods, that is, it may be more important to reveal the origin of meats than other foodstuffs, perhaps also because more food scandals have been related to animals and meat production than vegetables, fruits, carbohydrates, dairy products or seafoods. Chefs and restaurant owners may take this as advice for storytelling.

The future of food, tourism and regional development: an outlook

Tourism, as an important precondition for food demand, is often attracted by the attributes of the countryside, including agricultural (park) landscapes, heritage linkages and the romantic image of the farm. Among Generation Y families, this image continues to have considerable, and perhaps growing, appeal and thus constitutes an important aspect of the success of rural tourism. Food experiences are highly relevant in this context, as they have the potential to contribute to the overall attractiveness of rural holidays, while adding new, yet highly demanded product dimensions. This echoes Quan and Wang's (2004) notion of supporting and peak (food) tourist experiences, and the smell- and tastescapes (Urry 2002) that food products can add as 'sensory attractions' (Getz et al. 2014). Notably, as an experience involving multiple senses, food may have greater memorability than other experiences (Quan & Wang 2004). Yet, emotions related to food tourism experiences appear to have been insufficiently studied, and many important insights of relevance for food experience design, storytelling and marketing may be gained from the psychological and sociological literature (Canetti, Bachar & Berry 2002; Desmet & Schifferstein 2008).

Several other insights have emerged from the research presented in this book. First of all, as outlined by Roy, Hall and Ballantine (this volume), local food development is to a considerable degree driven by consumer demand, with prominent reasons for local and direct food purchases including notions of freshness, as well as a desire to support local farmers and local communities. Roy et al. also suggest that consumers seek to engage in social interactions. This is an important motive linked to individual and social identities increasingly focussed on self and the communication of experiences through social media (Gössling, Cohen & Hibbert 2016). Tourism has an important role in social connectedness, and consumer interest in foodstuff origin, along with growing importance of personal contacts, host encounters, authenticity and individualised hospitality in tourism, food tourism becomes increasingly important, as it offers meetings with farmers/ food producers and tourists and allows for discussions about foodstuffs in farm shops or at farmers markets, which become loci of interaction between consumers and producers. The importance of such social encounters is consequently of great importance and deserves to be studied in greater detail, including the role of social media in creating, maintaining and strengthening linkages between consumers and producers. Where foods become a means of social connectivity, this also has implications for the social capital for both producers and consumers.

Another interesting new field of research has been opened up by Ramos (this volume) who shows that tastes are culturally specific and that some flavours, but also foods that may be uncommon or even taboo in other cultures, communicate meanings that are outside common analyses of food and tourism interrelationships. Tourist food, she points out, is often remarkably standardised, and, it may be added, in most cases this standardisation refers to cheapness. This insight provides a valuable viewpoint, in that it reminds us that the global tourism system is moving away from sustainability: mass markets are supplied with foodstuffs from global markets, bought at the lowest cost, and setting in motion ever less sustainable production cycles based on agro-engineering and large-scale production with little interest in longer-term environmental or social implications (Hall & Gössling 2013). Where local foodstuffs become more relevant, Ramos suggests, there is potential to develop attractions on the basis of geographical differences, reinterpretation of specific cuisines, or multicultural gastronomy. In framing food consumption as a biocultural process, flavours can create bonds between cultures while also strengthening local economies. These processes, but in particular tourist perceptions of food textures, attributes and flavours as exotic, alien, aggressive, "super" or welcoming and comforting, thus offer great potential for further research.

In this context, the environmental and social sustainability of regional development through tourism has perceived comparably little attention in the chapters of this volume. Yet, a number of important linkages have been identified. Rogerson (this volume) observes, for instance, how the growing interest in unique, local or niche products is an antithesis to the globalisation in food production (Hall & Gössling 2013), as the market dominance and omnipresence of the "generalists" has opened up opportunities for "specialists". From an ecological viewpoint, there is now growing evidence that organic production is less relevant to consumers than regional produce. Yet, there is demand for organic produce, which in combination with niche product offers may also prove to create markets large enough for producers to diversify or to economically survive on new products. This is also of importance for restaurants, which are confronted with new demands in a world increasingly characterised by ecosystem limits: This will not only include changes from purchases of globally sourced to local foodstuffs, or from conventional to organic production: given world population growth and changing diets in favour of higher-order foods, it will also be necessary to discuss how vegetarian choices can be increasingly marketed by restaurants as well as retailers (Tjärnemo & Södahl 2015).

Of equal importance are opportunities for direct purchases from farms or farmers' markets, as they create interlinkages between producers and consumers, that is, interrelationships that have been characterised by abstraction for at least half a century in most countries: agricultural upscaling and agro-engineering practices continue to increasingly pertain virtually all domains of food production. This loss of context is much wanted by global corporations engaging in production practices that would repel many consumers, if they were known. The success of documentaries such as *Super Size Me* (2003), *FOOD, INC.* (2008) and dozens of other food-related movies have brought attention to global food market concentration, (un)healthy foodstuffs, obesity, biodiversity decline, overuse of foods, genetic engineering and labour exploitation – all now contributing to consumer awareness and to significant market changes in many countries. Yet, market concentration processes continue, including land grabbing and other issues that have received very scarce attention in the academic literature (Borras et al. 2012; von Braun & Meinzen-Dick 2009). These will also have to be explored in the context of food, tourism and regional development.

Finally, though chapters in this book have provided various important insights, they mirror a lack of quantitative data, specifically with respect to the economic dimensions of policy arguments. Economic issues may also be linked to a greater degree to sustainable culinary systems, and specifically the cost of externalities tied to fresh water use and emissions of greenhouse gases (Gössling et al. 2011; Gössling, Hall & Scott 2015). Both of these broad themes are related to issues of appropriate state interventions for change that shift social practices as these affect consumer behaviour as well as business-to-business relations, which are critical for substantially changing regional development trajectories along with other economic structural changes.

References

Belasco, W.J. (2014) *Appetite for Change: How the Counterculture Took on the Food Industry*, Ithaca: Cornell University Press.

Borras Jr, S.M., Franco, J.C., Gómez, S., Kay, C. and Spoor, M. (2012) 'Land grabbing in Latin America and the Caribbean', *Journal of Peasant Studies*, 39(3–4): 845–872.

Canetti, L., Bachar, E. and Berry, E. (2002) 'Food and emotion', *Behavioural Processes*, 60(2): 157–164.

Desmet, P.M. and Schifferstein, H. (2008) 'Sources of positive and negative emotions in food experience', *Appetite*, 50(2): 290–301.

Everett, S. and Slocum, S.L. (2013) 'Food and tourism: an effective partnership? A UK-based review', *Journal of Sustainable Tourism*, 21(6): 789–809.

Getz, D., Robinson, R., Andersson, T. and Vujicic, S. (2014) *Foodies and Food Tourism*, Oxford: Goodfellow Publishers.

Gössling, S., Cohen, S. and Hibbert, J. (2016) 'Tourism as connectedness', *Current Issues in Tourism*, accepted.

Gössling, S., Garrod, B., Aall, C., Hille, J. and Peeters, P. (2011) 'Food management in tourism. Reducing tourism's carbon "foodprint"', *Tourism Management*, 32: 534–543.

Gössling, S., Hall, C.M. and Scott, D. (2015) *Tourism and Water*, Bristol: Channel View Publications.

Hall, C.M. and Gössling, S. (eds) (2013) *Sustainable Culinary Systems: Local Foods, Innovation, Tourism and Hospitality*, Abingdon: Routledge.

Hall, C.M. and Mitchell, R. (2001) 'Wine and food tourism', in N. Douglas, N. Douglas, and R. Derrett (eds) *Special Interest Tourism: Context and Cases*, Brisbane, Australia: Wiley, pp. 307–329.

Hall, C.M. and Sharples, L. (eds) (2008) *Food and Wine Festivals and Events around the World: Development, Management and Markets*, Oxford: Butterworth-Heinemann.

Hall, C.M., Sharples, L., Mitchell, R., Macionis, N. and Cambourne, B. (eds) (2003) *Food Tourism around the World*, Oxford: Butterworth-Heinemann.

Hjalager, A.-M. and Richards, G. (eds) (2002) *Tourism and Gastronomy*, London: Routledge.

Johnston, J., Fanzo, J. and Cogill, B. (2014) 'Understanding sustainable diets: a descriptive analysis of the determinants and processes that influence diets and their impact on health, food security, and environmental sustainability', *Advances in Nutrition*, 5(4): 418–429.

Malm, K., Gössling, S. and Hall, C.M. (2013) 'Regulatory and institutional barriers to new business development: the case of Swedish wine tourism', in C.M. Hall and S. Gössling (eds) *Sustainable Culinary Systems: Local Foods, Innovation, Tourism and Hospitality*, Abingdon: Routledge, pp. 241–255.

Marsden, T., Murdoch, J. and Morgan, K. (1999) 'Sustainable agriculture, food supply chains and regional development: editorial introduction', *International Planning Studies*, 4(3): 295–301.

Martinez, S., Hand, M., Da Pra, M., Pollack, S., Ralston, K., Smith, T., Vogel, S., Tauer, L., Lohr, L., Low, S. and Newman, C. (2010) *Local Food Systems: Concepts, Impacts, and Issues*, Washington, DC: Department of Agriculture.

Norton, G.W., Alwang, J. and Masters, W. (2014) *Economics of Agricultural Development: World Food Systems and Resource Use*, London: Routledge.

Quan, S. and Wang, N. (2004) 'Towards a structural model of the tourist experience: an illustration from food experiences in tourism', *Tourism Management*, 25(3): 297–305.

Tjärnemo, H. and Södahl, L. (2015) 'Swedish food retailers promoting climate smarter food choices – trapped between visions and reality?', *Journal of Retailing and Consumer Services*, 24: 130–139.

Urry, J. (2002) *The Tourist Gaze: Leisure and Travel in Contemporary Societies*, 2nd edn, London: Sage.

von Braun, J. and Meinzen-Dick, R.S. (2009) *"Land Grabbing" by Foreign Investors in Developing Countries: Risks and Opportunities*, Washington, DC: International Food Policy Research Institute.

Yeoman, I., McMahon-Beattie, U., Fields, K., Albrecht, J. and Meethan, K. (eds) (2015) *The Future of Food Tourism: Foodies, Experiences, Exclusivity, Visions and Political Capital*, Bristol: Channel View Publications.

Index